WILLIAM BLAKE'S
COMMERCIAL
BOOK ILLUSTRATIONS

WILLIAM BLAKE'S COMMERCIAL BOOK ILLUSTRATIONS

A Catalogue and Study of the Plates
Engraved by Blake after Designs by Other Artists

ROBERT N. ESSICK

CLARENDON PRESS · OXFORD

1991

Oxford University Press, Walton Street, Oxford, OX2 6DP
Oxford New York Toronto
Delhi Bombay Calcutta Madras Karachi
Petaling Jaya Singapore Hong Kong Tokyo
Nairobi Dar es Salaam Cape Town
Melbourne Auckland
and associated companies in
Berlin Ibadan

Oxford is a trade mark of Oxford University Press

Published in the United States
by Oxford University Press, New York

British Library Cataloguing in Publication Data
(data available)
ISBN 0–19–817390–3

Library of Congress Cataloging in Publication Data
Essick, Robert N.
William Blake's commercial book illustrations: a catalogue and
study of the plates engraved by Blake after designs by other artists/
Robert N. Essick.
Includes index.
1. Blake, William, 1757–1827—Catalogs. 2. Blake, William,
1757–1827—Criticism and interpretation. 3. Artists' preparatory
studies—England—Catalogs. 4. Illustration of books—18th century-
England—Catalogs. 5. Illustration of books—19th century-
England—Catalogs. I. Blake, William, 1757–1827. II. Title.
NE2047.6.B55A4 1991
769.92—dc20 90–26128
ISBN 0–19–817390–3

Printed in Great Britain by
Butler & Tanner Ltd
Frome and London

Preface

OVER the last dozen years the study of William Blake as an artist has been greatly advanced by the publication of several illustrated catalogues. The most significant is Butlin 1981, a detailed *catalogue raisonné* of the paintings and drawings. The etchings and engravings designed and executed by Blake, as well as contemporary prints of his designs engraved by other craftsmen, are well reproduced and briefly described in Bindman 1978. The so-called 'separate plates', both those designed by Blake and those only engraved by him, are treated in Essick 1983. This generous production of basic scholarly tools, complemented by books devoted to individual works, has neglected only one area of Blake's activities—the commercial book illustrations he engraved after designs by other artists. This volume is intended to meet the need for an illustrated catalogue of these reproductive prints published in books.

The relationship between this catalogue and two others needs mention here. In the early 1970s Roger R. Easson and I began to co-author a projected three-volume survey of all Blake's commercial book illustrations. The first volume, Easson and Essick 1972, is still useful for its detailed bibliographical descriptions (by Easson), catalogue of prints (by Essick), and reproductions of prints both designed and executed by Blake. The second volume, Easson and Essick 1979, covers books with prints either designed or engraved by Blake to 1796. Unfortunately, the reproductions in the second volume are of poor quality and the book was not widely distributed. The planned third volume, treating plates from 1796 to 1828, was never published. The present catalogue is not a revision of Easson and Essick, but it is intended to replace the print catalogue and reproductions in the second volume and treat most of the materials intended for the absent third. There are, however, two important differences in coverage. Plates designed by Blake but executed by others (for which see Bindman 1978) are excluded here, as are detailed bibliographical descriptions of the books. The latter exclusion is prompted by the bibliography of books with Blake's commercial book engravings in Bentley 1977, pp. 509–647. Bentley's standard work, however, is not illustrated, and its focus differs from this catalogue. Although his text includes basic information on the plates, it is principally a bibliography of books. This volume is a catalogue of prints, with an emphasis on what Blake produced and with only minimum bibliographic information on the publications that contain his work. When used as companion volumes, this catalogue, Bentley 1977, and his forthcoming supplement should provide full information on their shared subject.

I have taken as my first responsibility the recording of facts about Blake's reproductive book illustrations—their sizes, inscriptions, progressive states, locations of preliminary drawings, and the quotation or summary of all documents relating to their production. I have supplemented this basic information with discussions of graphic techniques and styles, Blake's revisions of preliminary designs, his borrowings of motifs for his own compositions, the relationships of illustrations with their texts, and the role major commissions played in Blake's life and the shaping of his ideas. This material, along with the introductory survey of Blake's career as a commercial book engraver and of research opportunities in the field, gives this volume a larger interpretive and critical dimension than that offered by most print catalogues. Although mainly directed at the needs of Blake scholars, I hope that this catalogue will prove of use to collectors and dealers of illustrated books.

The format of the catalogue and appendices should be self-explanatory in the main, but a few guidelines to their use may prove helpful.

All plates catalogued here are intaglio line etchings/engravings unless noted otherwise. The term 'engravings' is used generically in reference to these prints.

The location of full-page plates in volumes is indicated by the number of the facing text page.

Print measurements (height followed by width) are of the pictorial image exclusive of frames, borders, and inscriptions unless noted otherwise.

Unless indicated to the contrary, all recorded signatures of designers and engravers are inscribed beneath the images. Titles, and inscribed quotations from the letterpress text that serve as titles, are centred below the images; imprints are centred below all other inscriptions.

Whenever the attribution of plates to Blake is open to question, the reasons for accepting or rejecting the ascription are set forth. See the introductory essay for general comments on problems of attribution.

Pre-publication proof states, even if printed in some quantity and perhaps sold as separate prints, are described separately and are not included in the sequential enumeration of states published in books.

For many books, the change from one edition to the next corresponds to a change in its plates from one state to another. One of the more common exceptions to this rule is the presence of remainder impressions of earlier states of the plates in one or two copies of a second edition containing later states in all other copies examined. I have recorded all such cases I have come upon, but it would not be surprising to find others.

References in the introductory essay to catalogued books, and cross-references among the entries on those books, are made by the roman numeral entry numbers in bold-face type.

All reproductions are of first published states unless noted otherwise. I have tried to select for reproduction clean impressions with all inscriptions present. For a few plates, no such impression was available, but any missing inscriptions are recorded in the catalogue entries.

All quotations of the letterpress texts illustrated by Blake's plates are taken from the first editions containing those plates.

The index includes all references to Blake's contemporaries and the owners, past and present, of drawings and pre-publication proofs. References to scholarly and critical works are not indexed.

For plates probably executed for publication in books but known only through separate impressions, see Essick 1983, pp. 232–53. One such plate has now been found to be a proof of a published book illustration—see **III**, pl. 1.

More book engravings attributable to Blake will probably come to light. I suggest that the discoverers of such plates announce their findings in the journal of record in the field, *Blake: An Illustrated Quarterly*, published in the Department of English, University of Rochester, Rochester, New York.

Robert N. Essick

Altadena, California
April 1990

Acknowledgements

SEVERAL institutions have provided essential financial support for this book. Both the Clarendon Press and I are particularly grateful to the William Blake Trust, Ltd., for a generous publication subvention. Professor Kay Easson, Memphis State University, kindly lent many photographs from the archive of the American Blake Foundation; others were acquired with the assistance of the Research Committee of the Academic Senate, University of California, Riverside. My final year of research and writing was supported by a University of California President's Research Fellowship in the Humanities.

For permission to reproduce works in their collections, I thank the British Library, the Department of Prints and Drawings of the British Museum, the Rosenwald Collection of the Library of Congress, Princeton University Library, the National Gallery of Canada, the Henry E. Huntington Library, the National Library of Medicine, the Mitchell Library of the State Library of New South Wales, the Victoria and Albert Museum, the Beinecke Library of Yale University, the Rosenwald Collection of the National Gallery of Art, Washington, and the Yale Center for British Art. Ownership of each work reproduced is indicated in the Contents.

Writers of catalogues depend heavily on the assistance of librarians, curators, and specialist scholars in several fields. For such help I am grateful to Pauline Adams of the Somerville College Library, Shelley Bennett of the Huntington Art Gallery, Gaye Blake-Roberts and Lynn Miller of the Wedgwood Museum, Sylvia Bull of the Cowper and Newton Museum, Frances Carey of the British Museum, Ruth Fine of the National Gallery of Art, Washington, Kenneth Garlick, D. W. J. Gill, and David Scrase of the Fitzwilliam Museum, Paul Grinke, Martin Phillips of the University of Keele Library, H. D. Lyon, Kathleen Mang of the Rosenwald Collection, Library of Congress, Morton Paley, George Pigman, Robin Reilly, Virginia Renner of the Huntington Library, Nick Savage of the Royal Academy of Arts, and Annette Wengle of the Metropolitan Toronto Reference Library. I am particularly grateful to Frances Whistler of the Clarendon Press, who expertly managed the initial publication plans for this book, and to Anne Ashby, for her skilful direction of my work from typescript to letterpress. Hilary Walford's copy-editing and design suggestions have been major contributions.

Several friends have given me the benefit of their kindness and knowledge. David Bindman's initial enthusiasm for the project was invaluable, as were the art-historical insights of Detlef Dörrbecker. Thomas V. Lange graciously responded to my many enquiries about prints at the Huntington and Princeton University libraries and was a continual source of expert assistance with general matters bibliographical and chalcographical. G. E. Bentley, jun., has done a great deal to shape the nature of this book, both through the example of his dedicated scholarship and through his generosity in sharing information. I am grateful for his many helpful suggestions and willingness to co-ordinate our research on Blake's commercial book illustrations. My greatest debt, as always, is to Jenijoy La Belle.

Contents with List of Figures

CATALOGUE

[The dates recorded below are of the first editions to include Blake's plates.]

Abbreviations and Works Frequently Cited

BL	British Library, London
BMPR	British Museum, Department of Prints and Drawings, London
E (followed by page number)	*The Complete Poetry and Prose of William Blake*, rev. edn., ed. David V. Erdman (Berkeley: Univ. of California Press, 1982). All quotations of Blake's writings are from this edition.
HEH	Henry E. Huntington Library and Art Galleries, San Marino, California
K (followed by page number)	*Blake: Complete Writings with Variant Readings*, ed. Geoffrey Keynes (Oxford: Oxford Univ. Press, 1966; rev. edn. 1979)
LC	Lessing J. Rosenwald Collection, Library of Congress, Washington, DC
RNE	Collection of Robert N. Essick, Altadena, California

The following standard works are referred to by author's name and publication date. Works of reference and criticism pertinent to only a single group of engravings are listed chronologically under *Literature* at the end of the appropriate title entry.

BENTLEY, G. E., jun., 1969: *Blake Records* (Oxford: Clarendon Press).

—— 1977: *Blake Books* (Oxford: Clarendon Press). All plate references to designs in Blake's illuminated books follow their enumeration in this standard bibliography.

—— 1988: *Blake Records Supplement* (Oxford: Clarendon Press).

—— and NURMI, MARTIN K., 1964: *A Blake Bibliography* (Minneapolis: Univ. of Minnesota Press).

BINDMAN, DAVID, assisted by TOOMEY, DEIRDRE, 1978: *The Complete Graphic Works of William Blake* (London: Thames and Hudson).

BUTLIN, MARTIN, 1981: *The Paintings and Drawings of William Blake* (2 vols.; New Haven and London: Yale Univ. Press). The second volume contains reproductions of all of Blake's paintings and drawings noted here, except for the illustrations to Young's *Night Thoughts*.

EASSON, ROGER R., and ESSICK, ROBERT N., 1972, 1979: *William Blake: Book Illustrator*, vol. i (Normal: American Blake Foundation, 1972); vol. ii (Memphis: American Blake Foundation, 1979). The first volume catalogues books with plates both designed and engraved by Blake; the second catalogues books with plates designed or engraved by Blake, 1774–96.

ESSICK, ROBERT N., 1980: *William Blake Printmaker* (Princeton: Princeton Univ. Press).

—— 1983: *The Separate Plates of William Blake: A Catalogue* (Princeton: Princeton Univ. Press).

GILCHRIST, ALEXANDER, 1863, 1880: *Life of William Blake* (2 vols.; London: Macmillan, 1863; 2nd edn., 1880). The list of engravings in vol. ii, frequently referred to here, was probably compiled by William Haines.

KEYNES, GEOFFREY, 1921: *A Bibliography of William Blake* (New York: Grolier Club).

—— 1971: *Blake Studies* (2nd edn., Oxford: Clarendon Press).

RUSSELL, ARCHIBALD G. B., 1912: *The Engravings of William Blake* (London: Grant Richards).

SCHIFF, GERT, 1973: *Johann Heinrich Füssli* (2 vols.; Zurich: Berichthaus).

WILLIAM BLAKE'S COMMERCIAL BOOK ILLUSTRATIONS

Introduction
Blake's Reproductive Book Illustrations

WILLIAM BLAKE's work as a copy engraver of book illustrations is an often ignored part of his career as one of England's finest graphic artists. The modern aesthetic, one that Blake helped to initiate, emphasizes original print-making and devalues reproductive prints. Consequently, Blake's translations on to copperplates of images first executed in other media by other artists are given short shrift and their multifaceted importance to his life is overlooked. It would be foolish to claim for these copy plates artistic equivalence with *Songs of Innocence* or the illustrations to The Book of Job, but an understanding of the economic and graphic matrix in which Blake created these visual and verbal masterpieces requires some attention to the lesser productions of his etching needle and graver. In this essay I trace the main outlines of Blake's endeavours in the genre catalogued here and suggest some ways its relationship to his other pictorial works and his writings can be explored.[1]

Blake's seven-year apprenticeship to James Basire provided him with more than the requisite technical skills of etching and engraving.[2] The profession established Blake's social position for the majority of his contemporaries, placing him in the class of urban artisans—slightly above tradesmen (such as his father and brother James, both hosiers), but below portrait painters and university-trained authors. Many in Blake's class shared a number of cultural attitudes familiar to students of his writings: enthusiastic and dissenting in their Christianity, liberal or radical in their politics. As products of a centuries-old system of apprenticeship, engravers were often slighted by men such as Sir Joshua Reynolds, who wished to elevate the traditional crafts of painting and sculpture into the fine arts, equal to literature as intellectual activities and cultural contributions. The exclusion of engravers from membership in the Royal Academy offers the clearest demonstration of this social hierarchy. The dependency of the reproductive engraver on someone else's inventions, even when the copyist received a higher fee than the original artist, objectified and reinforced these class distinctions within the production process.

Before he could establish an independent presence within the profession, a young engraver's reputation, and hence the types of commissions he was likely to receive, depended on his master's name. Although Basire was capable of producing large and fine separate engravings based on paintings, most of the plates turned out by his shop were book illustrations. In his capacity as official engraver to the Royal Society and the Society of Antiquaries, Basire produced utilitarian images of artefacts and scientific instruments set within the neutral space of blank backgrounds. Such work required the subordination of the engraver's hand and eye

---

[1] For a much broader survey of Blake's graphic works of all types, see Essick 1980. Additional information on Blake's autographic technique of relief etching is provided in Joseph Viscomi, *The Art of William Blake's Illuminated Prints* ([Manchester]: Manchester Etching Workshop, 1983).

[2] See Appendix i for plates Blake may have worked on during his apprentice years, 1772–9. For a description of the basic graphic processes Blake learned from Basire, see Essick 1980, pp. 8–38.

to linear precision, in accord with texts defining objects in terms of their shape, and the rendering of surface textures in direct, unshaded light to represent different materials (stone, metal, cloth, etc.). But this type of graphic production also included some less restrictive activities. The linear patterns typical of Basire's house style were surprisingly bold, even at times crude by late-eighteenth-century standards, and often well above the threshold of pictorial apprehension. This old-fashioned and straightforward system of outline, hatching, and cross-hatching was easier (and cheaper) to produce than more detailed and illusionistic techniques. In addition to these practical advantages, simplicity and directness were encouraged by the nature of the objects reproduced. A sophisticated graphic syntax of dots, flicks, and fine lines densely packed together, developed for the representation of depth, light, and shadow, would serve little purpose for pictures of stone axes or ancient coins and could even obfuscate the very qualities demanded by scientific illustration.

Since Basire, his journeymen, and apprentices were frequently creating pictures of three-dimensional objects, as distinct from images already reduced to the two dimensions of drawings and paintings, the intermediary step had to be supplied by the engraver or someone in his employ. In at least one well-documented case (see Appendix i, F), Blake played this role by making careful pencil or pen-and-wash drawings of sepulchral monuments in Westminster Abbey, thereby adding draughtsmanship to his apprentice training as an engraver. As we shall see, all these characteristics of Basire's shop practices influenced Blake's later career and aesthetic concepts.

By 1779 Blake was ready to launch his own business as an independent craftsman for hire. Before tracing that history, it will be useful to outline the basic systems for the production of intaglio copperplate book illustrations in the late eighteenth and early nineteenth centuries.[3] A bookseller who wished to publish a text accompanied by new illustrations would first acquire the services of an artist to create designs. That choice might be influenced by recommendations from a living author, but, since it was the bookseller/publisher whose purse was at risk at this and other points in the production process, his views were usually decisive. Although some illustrators prepared coloured drawings for reproduction as prints, or even oil paintings if the project included public exhibition (and eventual sale) of the designs, the more common procedure was to execute monochrome wash drawings. If the format of the book had already been determined, the artist would design illustrations with appropriate proportions. More drawings were often prepared than the number eventually published, with the bookseller generally having the major voice in making final selections.[4] He acquired both possession and all rights to the preliminary designs.

The next step was to hire an engraver, for the same artist did not both design and execute the plates in the vast majority of illustrated books. Here again, the bookseller's views were

---

[3] Documentary evidence for these procedures is scanty, and thus the following is pieced together from various bits of circumstantial evidence, including conclusions based on progress proofs of the plates themselves. For the generally similar methods of producing and selling separate engravings, see David Alexander and Richard T. Godfrey, *Painters and Engraving: The Reproductive Print from Hogarth to Wilkie* (New Haven: Yale Center for British Art, 1980), 11–13. For a general history of reproductive graphics, see Susan Lambert, *The Image Mul-*

tiplied: Five Centuries of Printed Reproductions of Paintings and Drawings (London: Trefoil, 1987).

[4] When commissioned by Richard Edwards to illustrate Edward Young's *Night Thoughts* in about 1795, Blake prepared thirty watercolours for the first 'Night', but only ten were selected for publication. In 1805 he drew about twenty designs for R. H. Cromek's edition of Robert Blair's *The Grave*, but only twelve plates were published.

often decisive, although either the designer or the author may have played a key role in some instances. For example, the writer William Hayley and the artist John Flaxman were directly or indirectly responsible for securing a number of Blake's commissions from about 1800 to 1818. The engraver's first task was to transfer, often by some semi-mechanical means, the preliminary designs to the surfaces of the metal plates. If the preliminary was not the proper size, it had to be 'reduced', a process that often included intermediary copy-drawings by the engraver. Once an illustration was on the plate surface, outlined in pencil or chalk or sketched in drypoint, the engraver had to translate the continuous tones of the original wash drawing or painting into the discontinuous syntax of linear patterns and dots. The illusion of tone was created by varying the width and density of these marks, with the pointillist technique of stipple etching/engraving generally reserved for the more delicate passages, such as faces. Almost all so-called 'engravings' of the period were partly etched in their preliminary stages—as, for example, the first proof state of Blake's Hogarth plate (*Fig. 66*). In one documented case (**XXXVII**), several small illustrations were engraved on, and printed from, a single strip of copper. This was a standard practice by the mid-nineteenth century, and may have been common at a much earlier period.

At appropriate points in the production of a plate, an engraver would print impressions to check the progress of his work. Blake owned his own rolling press—rather unusual for a single engraver without a large shop—and would have had no difficulty in pulling such proofs. But a professional engraver probably needed to do this less frequently than one might suppose, since one of his skills was the ability to envision how impressions would look on the basis of the incised copperplate. It seems to have been common practice, however, to pull a proof of a plate at a late stage in its development and submit it for approval to the bookseller, designer, or (less frequently) the author. If changes were recommended, they could be indicated directly on the print and returned to the engraver, who might then add his own notes or redraw parts of the image with pencil or pen and ink. Such inscribed or 'touched' working proofs were usually not preserved; no such print is known for any of Blake's reproductive book illustrations. Most extant impressions in pre-publication states (e.g. **XX**, pl. 1; **XXI**, pl. 6) were probably printed for sale to collectors and are not true working proofs. By the early nineteenth century, booksellers began publishing large-paper issues of illustrated books containing so-called 'proof' impressions with the designs completed but lacking some inscriptions. The 1808 edition of Robert Blair's *The Grave* with Blake's designs was issued in this way, but none of the book illustrations he engraved is known to have been published in such a form.

A copy engraver's fee, usually paid by the bookseller on a per-plate basis, varied according to the craftsman's reputation, the size of the plate, the techniques used, and the degree of finish required. Etchings and outline prints took less time to produce than detailed line engravings, and thus were much cheaper. The lower end of the fee schedule is represented in Blake's career by the 2 Guineas he received for each of his plates in Cumberland's *Thoughts on Outline* (**XXXII**), and the £5 for each plate of Flaxman's classical outlines (**XLVI, LI**). Blake's prices for the small plates he engraved in the 1780s and 1790s were probably equally modest. His larger, quarto-size plates commanded about £30 on at least two occasions later in his career (**XLIV, XLIX**), while the octavo plates for the 1805 Shakespeare (**XLVII**) were worth £25 to the publisher. We can gain some perspective on these prices by turning to the £315 that John and Josiah Boydell paid for many of the large plates based on paintings in their Shakespeare Gallery in the 1790s, with a top fee of £840 going to William Sharpe for his engraving after Benjamin West's *King Lear*.[5] James Parker, one of Blake's fellow apprentices under Basire's direction, received £157 for engraving Richard Westall's *Macbeth* painting. Since Blake's plate after Hogarth (**XX**) is about the same size and degree of finish, he may have received a similar amount for it from the Boydells, although such extrapolations can never be certain. In addition to payment for his skilled labour, an engraver was generally paid a separate amount to reimburse him for the cost of the blank copperplates he initially acquired from a plate-maker. The metal plates were thus the publisher's property and would not be returned to the engraver after printing except by special arrangement.

When the image was nearly completed, or even at some early proofing stage, an engraver would often scratch his own name, and perhaps other inscriptions, into the plate in drypoint. The conventional location for the engraver's name, usually followed by an abbreviation of 'sculpsit', was beneath the lower right corner of the image. The designer's name, followed by an abbreviation of 'invenit', was placed below the lower left corner. If a third person had made a drawing of the original work reproduced, such as an oil painting or sculpture, his name was sometimes given lower left followed by 'delineavit' abbreviated. If the engraver had himself made such an intervening drawing, then both appropriate abbreviations (e.g. 'del. & sc.' (see **L**; **LII**, pl. 6; **LIII**)) would often be added after his name. In some cases, 'delineavit', or some version of both 'inv. & del.', was placed after the original designer's name. Scratched preliminary inscriptions would sometimes be left in the published state (e.g. Blake's signature on **III**, pl. 5) or improved with the burin by the principal engraver himself (e.g. **XLIV**). The more common practice, however, was to send the plate to a writing engraver who would burnish off the scratched inscriptions or engrave right over them in an appropriate formal lettering style. The original engraver was generally not given the opportunity to check the finished inscriptions, and thus any errors (see **VI** for an interesting case in point) were the fault of the publisher and his writing engraver. Elaborate decorative borders were sometimes left for the writing engraver to execute, or yet another craftsman might be employed for such work (see **III**). Besides adding signatures, titles, quotations, and other ordered inscriptions, the writing engraver would cut an imprint (usually the lowest lettering on the plate) giving the publisher's name, place of business, and date, in conformity with the Engravers' Copyright Act (often called 'Hogarth's Act') of 1734. Imprints were sometimes omitted on crude plates in cheap editions, probably because copyright protection was deemed unnecessary. Imprints were generally not altered when the plates were reused in later editions. For example, Blake's plates for C. G. Salzmann's *Elements of Morality* (**XXIII**) were issued over a span of twenty-four years by two different publishers without any imprint changes.

Once a plate was completed and approved, uniform impressions had to be pulled in sufficient numbers to fill the first printing of the text. This task was almost always undertaken by a copperplate printer, a craftsman quite distinct from an engraver or letterpress printer. We know that Blake and his wife printed the plates for two of William Hayley's books (**XLI**, **XLIV**), but there is no reason to assume that either of them printed anything other than a

---

[5] For the extant records of fees, see Winifred H. Friedman, *Boydell's Shakespeare Gallery* (New York: Garland, 1976), 220–45.

few proofs of the vast majority of his reproductive book illustrations. Texts and plates, produced separately using different technologies, would only be brought together physically in the very last stages of production after both had been printed. This procedure can create chronological oddities in the collating of text and prints—for example, the addition of plates to letterpress remainder sheets, printed years earlier, to produce a new illustrated issue (see **I**). Several of the books for which Blake engraved plates were originally issued in periodical parts, and for these the prints would be issued with each part, although frequently not the part of the text illustrated.[6] In volumes first bound and issued in paper-covered boards, all the plates were often gathered at the beginning. An alternative, if somewhat more time-consuming, method was to place each plate between or within gatherings, as near as possible to the passage illustrated without having to cut apart (or 'open') any contiguous and conjugate leaves attached along their outer margins. Either facing-page inscriptions on the plates, generally incised above the images, or a letterpress 'Directions to the Binder' would indicate where each should be positioned when the volume was rebound in finer and more permanent materials.

Even after initial publication, an engraver was sometimes called upon to add further work to plates, thereby transforming them into another 'state'.[7] This work might be done for stylistic reasons, particularly when undertaken in the early stages of printing, but the more common purpose was to restore plates that had suffered from wear in the course of printing. A significant portion of an engraver's business might come from such reclamation activities.[8] Some of this work, such as cleaning solidified ink from lines and slightly deepening incisions already cut, does not register in impressions and thus cannot be recorded as a new state. It seems to have been common practice to hire the original engraver to rework plates whenever possible, but this of course would become increasingly less likely as the time since first execution lengthened. State changes generally, but by no means inevitably, parallel the sequence of issues and editions of the accompanying text. Occasionally a copperplate would crack in the rolling press, or be harmed in some other irreparable way, or lost, and a new plate of the same design would have to be engraved (see **V**, pl. 2; **LII**, pls. 3A–B).

A few general characteristics of the production system outlined above deserve note. From a modern perspective, eighteenth-century engraving might seem to harken back to an era of traditional and independent craftsmanship. Certainly it was an activity demanding disciplined skill, but reproductive engraving was dependent upon a rigorous division of labour and the subordination of individual expression to uniformity and repeatability. All illustrations in a book had to conform to its format, and this mechanical unity was extended to graphic style. If more than one engraver was employed, all had to practise compatible techniques. In spite of an engraver's prerogative to 'sign' his plates, the truly autographic tended to be submerged beneath the anonymity of a corporate and systematic enterprise.

It is no surprise to find Blake, in the first few years after release from apprenticeship,

---

[6] The following catalogue does not detail the bibliographic complexities of parts issues, for which see Bentley 1977.

[7] This term is sometimes used rather loosely to indicate differences in ink colour or paper among impressions, but it should be employed only to indicate that one impression, when compared to another, shows that purposeful changes have been made on the copperplate itself.

[8] A surprisingly large proportion of the bills and receipts of late-eighteenth- and early nineteenth-century English engravers, now in the Lewis Collection, Free Library of Philadelphia, is for reworking plates.

engraving such humble plates as those for the books by Olivier and Emlyn (*Figs. 2, 9*). He may have turned out a good many more illustrations of this sort, but left them unsigned. A better register of Blake's early reputation in the profession and his own youthful expectations is offered by the carefully finished plates for folio volumes (**III, V, VI**). Such commissions indicate booksellers' confidence in Blake's technical competency. But the most significant result of his first decade in the profession is his engravings after designs by Thomas Stothard (1755–1834). Slightly more than half of all the reproductive book illustrations Blake produced between 1780 and 1790 are based on Stothard's work. The two young men met and became close friends by 1780,[9] and Stothard was very probably instrumental in acquiring commissions for Blake. This graphic involvement with Stothard permitted, perhaps even encouraged, Blake's stylistic development, as can be seen in the plates for *The Novelist's Magazine* (**XI**) and Ariosto's *Orlando Furioso* (**XII**) of 1782–3. For these, Blake took the bold linear style he had learned from Basire and developed it into a more various and supple medium particularly suited for the rendering of picturesque, outdoor scenes (*Figs. 27, 29, 35*). The heavy 'worm' lines so characteristic of Basire's shop practice are retained for reticulated surfaces, such as the bark of trees, but integrated with cross-hatching patterns and dot-and-flick work. This style would not be appropriate for drawing-room scenes, and for these Blake used a more rigid and conventional technique with finer lines (*Figs. 32–4*).

It would be wrong to assume that Blake was the single, self-motivated origin of the stylistic developments we witness in his book illustrations of the 1780s. For *The Novelist's Magazine* he was part of a team of engravers that included Charles Grignion, William Walker, his pupils Joseph Collyer and William Angus, and Collyer's student James Heath. Stothard or his publisher, the Harrison family, probably chose these engravers for their compatible styles, the results of similar training. Any engraver added to this 'Walker' circle would have to allow his graver to be guided by the stylistic parameters established for the publications to which they all contributed. This gravitation towards uniformity, voluntary or compelled, makes it particularly difficult to attribute unsigned plates of the 1780s to Blake's hand. For my eyes, it is quite impossible to tell whether Heath or Blake engraved a particular plate from the period without glancing at the inscribed names. Conversely, this difficulty for the modern scholar signifies the inevitable interweaving of economic exigencies and aesthetic norms that shaped eighteenth-century reproductive graphics.

In the 'Public Address' Blake wrote in his *Notebook* c.1810, he implicitly recognized the similarity between his work and Heath's by accusing him of being one of the 'awkward imitators' of 'the style with which' Blake 'set out in life' (E 572, K 592). In the same passage, Blake claims that Stothard 'got his reputation as a Draughtsman' from 'those little prints which I engraved after him five & twenty Years ago'. As Blake himself points out, 'Resentment for Personal Injuries . . . had some share' in shaping 'this Public Address' (E 574, K 594), but there is a core of truth in this allusion to Blake's plates in *The Novelist's Magazine* and others based on Stothard's designs of the 1780s. The team of engravers in which Blake figured was the necessary intermediary between Stothard and his public by translating the designer's monochrome washes or watercolours into uniformly repeatable images. Without such translations and their attendant commercial systems, Stothard could not have become England's

---

[9] See Bentley 1969, p. 19.

most prolific and popular literary illustrator by the end of the eighteenth century.

In 1788 John and Josiah Boydell hired Blake to engrave William Hogarth's painting of a scene in John Gay's *The Beggar's Opera* (*Figs. 65–6*). This commission, from England's greatest printseller for Blake's largest copy plate, is the high-water mark of his career in reproductive graphics. Blake's fee is not known, but it must have been the largest he had received to that time, and quite possibly the most he was ever paid. The work may have provided crucial financial support for Blake's first efforts in relief etching, beginning in about 1788, acquisition of the copperplates for *Songs of Innocence* and *The Book of Thel* in the next year, and his move in 1790 to a substantial house in Lambeth. The plate is also a considerable success in the art and craft of composite etching and engraving. Blake's 'Beggar's Opera' shows greater skill than the plates by Hogarth or his journeymen that accompany it in the Boydells' volume (**XX**), and is a more subtle graphic rendering of an oil painting than the companion print executed by Robert Dodd. In its range of techniques, from fine stipple to bold cross-hatching, its tonal and textural variety, and its evocation of depth and shadow— characteristics only apparent in good impressions of early states—Blake's Hogarth print indicates its indebtedness to, and artistic equivalency with, the work of William Woollett (1735–85), then considered England's finest master of line etching/engraving.[10] Yet the considerable success of Blake's Hogarth plate carries a note of sadness. Never again would Blake receive such a significant commission with the professional standing it conferred, nor would he ever surpass the technical proficiency of the 'Beggar's Opera' in a copy engraving.

Blake's working relations with Stothard in the 1780s established a pattern characterizing later decades in Blake's life as an engraver of book illustrations. His personal and professional relationships with a bookseller, Joseph Johnson, an author, William Hayley, and two fellow artists, Henry Fuseli and John Flaxman, directly or indirectly determined most of his commissions as a reproductive engraver until 1820. Although these associations overlapped chronologically, by tracing each in turn we can perceive the major developments in Blake's career.

By 1790 the liberal publisher Joseph Johnson (1738–1809) had become the most important employer of Blake's graver. Many of the plates produced for Johnson are utilitarian, competent, and of little artistic consequence. Two types of plates, however, deserve more attention. Between 1788 and 1801 Blake engraved a dozen book illustrations after designs by the important Anglo-Swiss artist Henry Fuseli (1741–1825). All appeared in books published by Johnson, to whom Fuseli may have introduced Blake. The graphic styles of the illustrations for Lavater's *Aphorisms* (**XVIII**), Darwin's *Botanic Garden* (**XXI**, pl. 1), and Fuseli's own *Lectures on Painting* (**XL**) are less important than what we learn from a comparison of the engravings with the preliminary drawings. In each case, Blake appears to have been given an unusual amount of responsibility for the completion of the design, not merely its translation to copper, even if we allow for a good deal of consultation between the two friends. The extant preliminaries, two of which remained in Blake's possession for many years, suggest that Fuseli delivered little more than rough sketches to his engraver.[11] Less dramatic instances of artist–

---

[10] Blake's harsh criticisms of Woollett in the 'Public Address' of *c.*1810 do not necessarily reflect his earlier attitudes. Further, disapproval never prevented Blake from borrowing from an artist or writer.

[11] See the individual catalogue entries for more detailed discussions of each instance.

engraver partnerships may have been extended to other volumes among Johnson's publications, at least when the original draughtsman was an amateur. None of the preliminary drawings for Blake's plates in J. G. Stedman's *Narrative* (**XXXIII**) has been traced, but it seems likely that Blake improved Stedman's drawings in the course of engraving them, much as he did for an illustration in John Hunter's *Historical Journal* (**XXVII**). A brief comparison between the preliminary sketch and Blake's plate (*Figs. 137–8*) can reveal how he has converted a rather shabby family group into the eighteenth-century ideal of the noble savage. Ideological configurations—perhaps including Blake's own concept of 'the human form divine' (E 13, K 117)—have in this instance found expression within the space between invention and execution in a reproductive medium. Further, Blake has separated the two adults so that their lineaments do not overlap and has turned the boy's head into profile. Even the fish held by the woman have been spread apart so that we can see the outline of each. While these changes create a more frieze-like composition in accord with neo-classical norms, they also harken back to Blake's training in antiquarian and scientific illustration requiring the separation of forms to delineate their identifying outlines.[12]

Blake's most technically proficient book illustrations of the late 1780s and 1790s, at least from a perspective determined by the graphic hierarchies of that time, are the portrait plates in which variations of tone and surface angle are represented by fine 'dot-and-lozenge' patterns—that is, webs of cross-hatching with dots or flicks in the interstices (e.g. *Figs. 62, 64, 75*). A less conventional and far more significant development can be traced among Blake's humbler book illustrations. In 1791 Blake engraved after his own designs a series of six illustrations for Mary Wollstonecraft's *Original Stories from Real Life*.[13] For these Blake simplified the 'picturesque' style of *The Novelist's Magazine* and used hatching and cross-hatching patterns only slightly less bold than those in the purposefully crude caricature prints he had executed in 1784 for *The Wit's Magazine* (*Figs. 52–6*). The graphic syntax in these plates begins to emerge above the threshold of visual apprehension and become self-referential. As we view such images, we are given both the illusion of three-dimensional objects in space and an awareness of the medium in which that illusion is created. Blake brought much this same style to some of his reproductive plates for Gay's *Fables* of 1793 (*Figs. 125, 127, 129, 131, 133*), for Stedman's *Narrative* of 1796 (*Figs. 155–70*), and to the eight engravings after Fuseli for Charles Allen's two history books of 1798 (*Figs. 173–80*). The last group is clearly indebted to the techniques Blake developed in his *Night Thoughts* illustrations of 1796–7, and thus again shows how experiments in original graphics influenced reproductive styles. In all these plates the syntax is very 'open'. There is a relatively large distance between each line in hatching patterns, and many passages are left unengraved. Some of the plates have an unfinished appearance, like early proofs, as if in reaction against the high finish then regarded as requisite in the best engravings. Rather than trying to disguise a mixed-method etching/engraving as a pure engraving, Blake has allowed the etched lines to declare themselves as such. The evolution of this style may have been influenced by a study of sixteenth-century masters such as Giulio Bonasone and Hendrik Goltzius. George Cumberland, a friend of Blake's since the mid-1780s, had an extensive collection of Bonasone's prints and published

---

[12] I am indebted to Detlef Dörrbecker for his art-historical observations on this plate.
[13] For reproductions, see Bindman 1978, nos. 109–14.

a book about his life and engravings in 1793. On other plates of the 1790s Blake engraved a dark background and left foreground figures in outline with minimal interior shading. This method creates both two-dimensional patterns that call attention to themselves and a relief, sculpturesque quality similar to what we see in the plates for Stuart's and Revett's *Antiquities* of 1794 (*Figs. 139–42*). None of these techniques is unique to Blake, but their orchestration is distinctive. These characteristics allow one to attribute to his graver some unsigned plates of the 1790s, such as those for Salzmann's *Elements of Morality* (*Figs. 76–120*) and three Stedman illustrations (*Figs. 161, 166, 168*), in part on stylistic grounds.

By the last few years of the decade Blake's output of book illustrations waned. The *Night Thoughts* project ended after the publication of less than half the poem, and Johnson's plans for a new edition of Milton, with two of Fuseli's illustrations to be engraved by Blake, came to naught.[14] As Blake told Cumberland in a letter of 26 August 1799, 'Even Johnson & Fuseli have discarded my Graver' (E 704, K 795). After the great promise of the Hogarth plate, the Boydells hired Blake to engrave only one of the smaller illustrations (*Fig. 192*) for their enormous Shakespeare Gallery and edition. Lack of employment may have influenced Blake's decision to leave the business world of London publishing in 1800 and move to Felpham, near the Channel coast, where his livelihood would rest heavily on the patronage of William Hayley (1745–1820). Blake's initial hopes for this relationship and subsequent disappointments are most explicitly recorded in his letters. One of the more cogent declarations of his growing discomfort, in a letter to Thomas Butts of 10 January 1803, makes direct reference to his engraving activities:

> My unhappiness has arisen from a source which if explord too narrowly might hurt my pecuniary circumstances. As my dependence is on Engraving at present & particularly on the Engravings I have in hand for Mr H. & I find on all hands great objections to my doing any thing but the meer drudgery of business & intimations that if I do not confine myself to this I shall not live. This has always pursud me. You will understand by this the source of all my uneasiness This from Johnson & Fuseli brought me down here & this from M^r H will bring me back again ... (E 724, K 812)

Three years earlier, Blake had written that he had 'no objection to Engraving after another Artist', even though 'To Engrave after another Painter is infinitely more laborious than to Engrave ones own Inventions',[15] but the letter to Butts suggests that one of his reasons for moving to Felpham was to free some of his time from the labours of copy engraving. His new patron provided neither surcease from the 'drudgery of business' nor sufficient appreciation for Blake's original compositions, visual and verbal. After his first year or so in Felpham, the tasks for which Blake was kept 'fully Employd & Well Paid' (E 726, K 819) by Hayley were principally reproductive book illustrations.

Blake's personal and professional frustrations in Felpham may account for the deficiencies of the plates he produced for Hayley. Those for *The Triumphs of Temper* (*Figs. 193–8*) are

---

[14] See John Knowles, *The Life and Writings of Henry Fuseli* (London: Colburn and Bentley, 1831), i. 171–2, and the prospectus for a suite of plates reprinted in Bentley 1969, p. 44. A similar project was apparently begun by William Hayley in 1803

(see Blake's letter of 6 July 1803 to Thomas Butts, E 730, K 824), but once again died well short of production.

[15] Letter to John Trusler, 23 Aug. 1799 (E 703, K 794).

stiff, over-laboured, and in some passages simply clumsy. In a letter to Hayley of 23 October 1804, Blake acknowledged these qualities in his work of the recent past:

> O the distress I have undergone, and my poor wife with me. Incessantly labouring and incessantly spoiling what I had done well. Every one of my friends was astonished at my faults, and could not assign a reason; they knew my industry and abstinence from every pleasure for the sake of study, and yet—and yet—and yet there wanted the proofs of industry in my works. (E 756-7, K 852)

The fruitful interchange between original and reproductive graphics characteristic of Blake's best work in the 1790s seems to have broken down. Four of the illustrations for Hayley's *Life of Cowper* (**XLIV**) suffer from a *horror vacui* underscored by contrast with the more open syntax of their two companions, a fine plate in the 'chalk-manner', used to reproduce the qualities of a graphite or chalk drawing (*Fig. 202*), and an engraving after Blake's own design (*Fig. 203*) reminiscent of his etched sketching of the previous decade. Complaints from Hayley and requests for revisions may have led to the over-working of several plates, as well as delays in completing them. Yet, however much Hayley was the external cause, or at least the symbolic epitome, of these problems, they took their internal form as a fundamental disruption in the relationship between conception and execution, mind and act. As Blake wrote in 1801, 'I labour incessantly & accomplish not one half of what I intend because my Abstract folly hurries me often away while I am at work, carrying me over Mountains & Valleys which are not Real in a Land of Abstraction where Spectres of the Dead wander.'[16]

Blake's return to London in the autumn of 1803 did not quickly revive his career as a reproductive engraver. As he confessed after less than a month in the city, 'Art in London flourishes. Engravers in particular are wanted. Every Engraver turns away work that he cannot Execute from his superabundant Employment. Yet no one brings work to me.'[17] Two years later, Blake looked back over his career in commercial printmaking and feared that past failures to attract major commissions would be repeated:

> But my Fate has been so uncommon that I expect Nothing—I was alive & in health & with the same Talents I now have all the time of Boydells Macklins Bowyers & other Great Works. I was known by them & was look'd upon by them as Incapable of Employment in those Works it may turn out so again . . .[18]

---

[16] Letter to Butts, 11 Sept. 1801 (E 716, K 809). In Blake's poem *Milton* of *c*.1804–8, Los gives to Satan 'the Harrow of the Almighty' and the craftsman Palamabron represses his anger at this, 'lest Satan should accuse him of | Ingratitude' (E 100, K 486). The autobiographical context for these poetical acts and personifications is Blake's self-acknowledged error in giving Hayley excessive control over his engraving activities and not expressing his anger because of gratitude for the material support Hayley provided.

[17] Letter to Hayley, 7 Oct. 1803 (E 736, K 829).

[18] Letter to Hayley, 11 Dec. 1805 (E 766–7, K 862). See also Blake's *Notebook* verses of *c*.1810–11 in which he asks if he is 'angry with Macklin or Boydel or Bowyer | Because they did not say O what a Beau ye are' (E 504, K 538). Boydell's two elephant-folios of ninety-six Shakespeare illustrations, none engraved by Blake, had been published in 1805. Thomas Macklin published four of Blake's separate plates in the early 1780s (Essick 1983, nos. XXII–XXV), but did not hire him for the 'Poet's Gallery' series of small folio prints, begun in 1788, or for his six-volume folio Bible (1800) illustrated with seventy-one plates. A 1792 prospectus for Robert Bowyer's illustrated edition of David Hume's *History of England* (five folio volumes completed in 1806) includes Blake among the list of engravers, but none of the 195 plates is signed by him (see Appendix ii, no. 24). For a study of these publications, see G. E. Bentley, jun., 'The Great Illustrated-Book Publishers of the 1790s and William Blake', in William Blissett (ed.), *Editing Illustrated Books* (New York: Garland, 1980), 57–96.

Blake's prospects were indeed cloudy, but his career in reproductive book illustration did not cease. Johnson hired him to engrave two of Fuseli's illustrations for an edition of Shakespeare's plays (XLVII), a task that elicited from Blake something of his former skills at integrating an extended repertoire of linear patterns in relatively high-finish plates (*Figs. 211, 213*). Hayley and his new publisher, Richard Phillips, employed Blake to execute five small plates of his own designs for the 1805 edition of Hayley's *Ballads*.[19] But two of Hayley's other projects demonstrate the professional difficulties Blake was encountering. He began in the summer of 1804 to engrave two plates for Hayley's biography of George Romney (XLIX), but only one was published (*Fig. 215*). Nine of the other eleven plates in the volume, not published until 1809, were engraved in soft, tonal stipple, including seven by Caroline Watson, titled 'Engraver to Her Majesty' on each. She also replaced Blake as the engraver in the 1806 edition of Hayley's life of William Cowper. Watson, her patroness, and her feminine graphic style may lie behind Blake's denunciations of 'Female Space' and an independent 'Female Will' in his later poetry.[20] Blake was a fine stipple engraver, as several of his early separate plates demonstrate, but as an engraver of book illustrations he was closely associated with an older tradition of line work. The popularity of Watson's refined style and growing competition from the new techniques of wood engraving developed by Thomas Bewick and his school probably reduced Blake's professional opportunities.[21]

In the midst of Blake's declining fortunes an old friend from the 1780s, the sculptor John Flaxman (1756–1826), came to his assistance. Of the seventy reproductive book illustrations Blake engraved between 1804 and 1820, forty are based on Flaxman's designs and a further twenty-seven were probably commissioned on Flaxman's recommendation. All sixty-seven of these plates are in outline, or near outline, with a minimum of interior modelling or shading, and thus Blake was led, intentionally or not, into becoming a specialist in that simple and severe style he had first used for the *Thoughts on Outline* (XXXII) by another friend, George Cumberland, in 1796. By 1814, Flaxman could justly claim that Blake was 'the best engraver of outlines'.[22]

Outline engraving would seem to leave little room for innovation, yet even here Blake's inventive spirit found expression. For the Hesiod illustrations (*Figs. 235–71*) Blake developed a stippled-line technique found nowhere else among Flaxman's vastly influential classical compositions. The sources for this technique can be traced back to Basire's habit of signing plates with letters composed of dots (e.g. Appendix i, F, *Figs. 289, 292–4*), a practice Blake followed at least once in the 1780s (III, pl. 3). His stipple book illustrations of the 1790s

[19] For reproductions, see Bindman 1978, nos. 403–7. In comparison to the 1802 *Ballads* plates of some of the same designs (Bindman 1978, nos. 390, 393, 396), the 1805 plates indicate the revivifying effect Blake's return to London had on his engraving skills.

[20] *Milton* (E 104, K 490), *Jerusalem* (E 176–7, K 661). Both images have their source in Blake's earlier poetry (e.g. the 'nameless shadowy female' of *Europe* (E 60, K 238)) written well before Hayley's employment of Watson, but this does not prevent her and what she represented in the arts from entering the circumference of polysemous meaning in the later poetry. Blake associated line with the masculine and colour (including, by implication, colouristic techniques in printmaking) with the feminine. When in *Jerusalem* the blacksmith–artist Los hammers

into shape the outline of being, his wife Enitharmon 'like a faint rainbow waved before him' (E 245, K 732). See also Blake's criticism of Correggio's painterly style as 'soft and effeminate' in the *Descriptive Catalogue* of 1809 (E 548, K 583).

[21] When a new edition of Ritson's *Select Collection of English Songs* (XIV) was published in 1813, wood engravings were substituted for the intaglio engravings by Blake and others. Similarly, Stothard's illustrations for Samuel Rogers's *Pleasures of Memory* were published as copperplate engravings (none by Blake) in 1793 and 1801, but Stothard designed a new group for the 1810 edition specifically for execution in wood by Luke Clennell, one of Bewick's students.

[22] Letter of 19 Aug. 1814 to John Bischoff (Bentley 1969, p. 233).

(*Figs. 144–5, 171*) show the same open format as his line work of the period. Some interior passages in these plates are left free of stipple, but the dots increase in density as they approach outlines, thereby helping to define them. The Hesiod plates take this gradual evolution of line and stipple techniques to its final conclusion, one in which these two contrary styles merge into a single form.

The conceptual implications of stippled lines resonate in intriguing ways with one of Blake's central aesthetic doctrines, the superiority of line over colour and chiaroscuro techniques.[23] Blake's schooling in the traditional methods of line engraving clearly provided the matrix of graphic practice giving shape to his theory of line. To dissolve engraved lines into dots would seem to bring that very practice into conflict with the concept that arose from it, and carry into the graphic arts the same division into abstract particles Blake lamented in atomistic science and the calculus. In the same, crucial letter of 12 April 1827 in which Blake attacks 'Newtons Doctrine of the Fluxions of an Atom', he also claims that 'a Line is a Line in its Minutest Subdivision[s]' and 'is Itself & Not Intermeasurable with or by any Thing Else' (E 783, K 878). Such statements would seem to reject Blake's own practice in the Hesiod plates of ten years earlier, for their lines become points in their minutest subdivisions. To resolve the apparent conflict by proposing that Blake's philosophical ideas and his reproductive practices had nothing to do with each other, the latter being only a method of earning a living, would establish in one's own critical perspective a division between conception and execution of the sort Blake consistently and explicitly rejected. Or can we read the 1827 letter as a defence of the Hesiod technique, an insistence that lines are still lines, even when composed of dots? The possibility of entertaining such a question indicates how complex the relationships between graphic and textual statements, between conception and execution, can become.

By 1818 Blake's career as a reproductive book engraver had substantially ended. He executed six plates in stipple and line (*Figs. 281–6*) for R. J. Thornton's school Virgil of 1821, but these modest contributions are overshadowed by Blake's series of wood engravings of his own designs in the same volumes. The patronage of John Linnell, who met Blake in 1818, allowed Blake to leave his old professional mainstay of copy engraving and devote the remaining decade of his life to original composition. The resulting works in the graphic arts—the Virgil, Job, and Dante engravings—far transcend the commercial productions of earlier years. Yet, these masterpieces, like the earlier illuminated books in relief and white-line etching, would have been impossible without Blake's early training and years of practice in the craft of reproductive engraving. He left behind the more restrictive trammels of his trade, but not the skills it had taught him.

I hope that the foregoing narrative and the comments on individual plates in the following catalogue indicate that Blake's copy engravings published in books are worthy of attention in their own right as a chapter in the history of the commercial arts. Yet this book would never have been written if these were Blake's only works. His reproductive illustrations will continue

---

[23] The fullest study of Blake's theory of line and its epistemological implications is Morris Eaves, *William Blake's Theory of Art* (Princeton: Princeton Univ. Press, 1982).

to have their main importance for Blake scholars because of their relationship to his other productions, both pictorial and verbal.[24]

If we take a very broad view of Blake and the book trade, we find more than financial support for his more private and important endeavours. Reproductive engraving, principally of book illustrations, was Blake's major avenue of contact not only with the world of commerce, but with the intellectual and artistic life of England. The Joseph Johnson circle was a major formative influence on Blake's political and philosophical ideas of the 1790s, but his entry into that social matrix was provided by his craft.[25] Hayley stated that Blake's principal reason for joining him in Felpham in 1800 was to execute the plates for *The Life of Cowper* (**XLIV**). Although Blake probably did not share this view, Hayley's attitude indicates that the major professional relationship of Blake's middle age, one fraught with psychological tensions that shaped the allegorical figures and events in his epics *Milton* and *Jerusalem*, came about through his skills as a reproductive engraver. Flaxman's commissions after 1800 led Blake into an engagement with classical art—Homer, Hesiod, Greek and Roman sculpture (**XLV, XLVI, LI, LII**). These activities form the commercial and quotidian context for Blake's own responses to classicism, ranging from his denunciation of 'The Stolen and Perverted Writings of Homer & Ovid' at the beginning of *Milton* (E 95, K 480) to the use of classical texts and images as the basis of major compositions late in his life.[26] Even Blake's first commission from Linnell was for a copy engraving.[27] Among all of Blake's major patrons, only Thomas Butts did not initially come to Blake because of reproductive graphics.

Copy engraving for other illustrators also introduced Blake to the conventions of text–design relationships of his day. This context, and its possible influence on his own original illustrations, deserve more attention than they have yet been granted in the study of Blake's composite art.[28] Much of the criticism of illustrative methods places individual examples on a spectrum ranging between direct or literal illustration, based on the representation of things and events named in the text, and illumination or interpretive illustration, based on a much freer, even antithetical, perspective on the text. The first type is often assumed to be the conventional approach, while the second is taken to be Blake's. Both assumptions need modification.

Many of Stothard's illustrations range freely beyond textual specifics and approach the condition of book decoration unrelated to the text. In Ritson's *Select Collection of English*

[24] The general issue of how the graphic arts affected Blake's life and thought is beyond the scope of this essay on commercial book illustration. For studies that delve into this larger question, see Robert N. Essick, 'Blake and the Traditions of Reproductive Engraving', *Blake Studies*, 5 (1972), 59–103; Morris Eaves, 'Blake and the Artistic Machine: An Essay in Decorum and Technology', *PMLA*, 92 (1977), 903–29; Essick 1980; Stephen Leo Carr, 'Illuminated Printing: Toward a Logic of Difference', and Robert N. Essick, 'How Blake's Body Means', in Nelson Hilton and Thomas A. Vogler (eds.), *Unnam'd Forms: Blake and Textuality* (Berkeley: Univ. of California Press, 1986), 177–217.

[25] For the members and activities of the Johnson circle, see Gerald P. Tyson, *Joseph Johnson: A Liberal Publisher* (Iowa City: Univ. of Iowa Press, 1979).

[26] See Blake's 'Laocoön' engraving of *c*.1820 (Essick 1983, no. XIX) and two watercolours, *Philoctetes and Neoptolemus at Lemnos* (1812 (Butlin 1981, no. 676)) and *The Sea of Time and*

Space, the latter perhaps based on Homer and Porphyry (1821 (Butlin 1981, no. 803)). For a recently discovered classical composition and a discussion of Blake's responses to Greek and Roman culture, see Robert N. Essick, 'William Blake's *The Death of Hector*', *Studies in Romanticism*, 27 (1988), 97–107.

[27] A portrait of James Upton after Linnell's painting (Essick 1983, no. XL).

[28] The one notable study centring on Blake's responses to conventional illustrative practices is Kay Parkhurst Easson, 'Blake and the Art of the Book', in Robert N. Essick and Donald Pearce (eds.), *Blake in his Time* (Bloomington: Indiana Univ. Press, 1978), 35–52. For a general study of illustrative strategies in the period, see Stephen C. Behrendt, 'The Functions of Illustration—Intentional and Unintentional', in Joachim Möller (ed.), *Imagination on a Long Rein: English Literature Illustrated* (Marburg: Jonas, 1988), 29–44.

Songs (**XIV**) Blake's second plate closely follows one of the poems in the section of love songs for which Stothard's design serves as a tailpiece. The plate, however, is physically distant from its text by over ten pages. The headpiece–tailpiece format dictated the placement of the design, but did not restrict Stothard to illustrating only contiguous passages. Blake's first plate, the headpiece to the same section, is thematically linked to it but not based on any specific passage. To create an eye-catching vignette for Bonnycastle's *Introduction to Mensuration* (**VII**) would test the skill of any illustrator. Stothard's solution is to incorporate geometrical shapes, diagrams, and instruments in his design, but surround them with nude and frolicsome babes (*Fig. 20*). This approach establishes an antithetical relationship between the whimsical illustration and Bonnycastle's earnestly technical book.

Fuseli's work exhibits other pathways to illustrative freedom. Both of his designs for Darwin's *Botanic Garden* (**XXI**, pls. 1, 6) have clear textual cues, but these are almost overwhelmed by the exaggerated theatricality of Fuseli's images and supplemented with motifs not named in the text. In the second design (*Fig. 74*) he divides the personification of 'Tornado', described as a single figure by Darwin, into two combatants. In his Shakespeare illustrations of 1805 (**XLVII**) Fuseli often chose minor or neglected scenes for representation, apparently because they offered subjects compatible with his own repertoire of favourite motifs, invented or borrowed. The single design for *Romeo and Juliet* (*Fig. 213*) illustrates Romeo's visit to the apothecary's shop, hardly the most dramatic event in the play. But the scene gave Fuseli an opportunity to picture a bizarre figure without violating the text, contrast him with a heroically muscled youth, and surround them with slightly threatening paraphernalia. The illustration bodes ill for the potion Romeo is purchasing.[29]

In contrast to the pictorial liberties of Stothard and Fuseli, Blake's illustrations to works by other poets—Young, Gray, Milton, Dante—usually show great fidelity to the text. Direct translation of words into images extends even into the pictorial literalizing of figural expressions in the text—for example, converting Young's personifications of abstractions into fully fleshed human figures.[30] The modern critical conversion of these direct illustrations into commentaries on the text, or even into allegories of Blake's own writings, arises through comparisons of motifs with their appearance elsewhere in Blake's art and other contextualizing strategies.[31]

Blake's designs accompanying his own poetry in illuminated printing embody other responses to contemporary illustrative practices. In his prospectus 'To the Public' of 1793, Blake claimed that his books were 'in a style more ornamental ... than any before discovered' (E 692, K 207). In some instances, the pictorial component of Blake's composite art approaches the independence from the text suggested by the word 'ornamental'. This liberation may have been stimulated by Blake's intimate knowledge of illustrations by Fuseli and Stothard. Book

[29] Recently, Fuseli's illustrations have been criticized for these very characteristics which, in my view, make his work so interesting. In *Five Centuries of English Book Illustration* (London: Scolar Press, 1988), 103, Edward Hodnett finds fault with Fuseli for his 'borrowing' from other artists and his 'eccentric selection of certain moments' that make him 'an imperfect interpretive illustrator'.

[30] For a parallel verbal phenomenon, the literalization of figuration in Blake's poetry, see Robert N. Essick, *William Blake and the Language of Adam* (Oxford: Clarendon Press, 1989), 155,

224–30.

[31] The Dante illustrations are interpreted as representations of ideas in Blake's own writings in Albert S. Roe, *Blake's Illustrations to the Divine Comedy* (Princeton: Princeton Univ. Press, 1953). More recently, David Fuller, 'Blake and Dante', *Art History*, 11 (1988), 349–73, has convincingly demonstrated that the 'Blakean' motifs and their emotional expressiveness can be accounted for as products of a close reading of *The Divine Comedy*.

decoration is usually taken to be devoid of iconographic intention, but in Blake's hands a similar freedom from direct illustration allowed him to develop the pictorial as a medium for symbolic representation interacting with the text but not bound to it. Like Fuseli's illustrations, designs in Blake's illuminated books frequently include motifs or even characters thematically appropriate for the text but not named therein. As in Stothard's designs for Ritson's anthology, the textual point of contact for a design may not be on the same plate. In at least one often cited instance, pl. 9 of *America*, the text speaks of apocalyptic terrors while the design pictures pastoral ease.[32] The opposition exaggerates and complicates the technique hinted at by Stothard's vignette for Bonnycastle. What Blake learnt from his contemporaries about illustrative strategies by engraving their work, and the way in which he both incorporates and diverges from their practices, are more important than his occasional borrowings of specific motifs from their designs.

One further way Blake's activities as a commercial book illustrator could have influenced his original compositions deserves brief attention here. Might the texts for which Blake engraved plates have been read by him and influenced his ideas? My earlier summary of production processes indicates that a reproductive engraver need have no familiarity with the texts his plates will accompany. Yet, it is difficult to believe that Blake, with his wide-ranging interests, did not take every opportunity to peruse books to which he contributed. More specific evidence supports this assumption in several instances. Blake's friendship with several authors, including Fuseli, Stedman, Flaxman, and Hayley, makes it virtually certain that he read their works. Intertextual evidence, even when fairly general, also bespeaks familiarity with several other books catalogued here. For example, the physiological imagery of *The Book of Urizen* suggests the influence of the medical texts published by Johnson for which Blake executed plates (**XIII, XXV, XXIX**). These volumes can also serve as Blake's most likely point of initial contact with a wider range of influence, extending to all of Johnson's publications in theology, the natural sciences, and other subjects within the compass of Blake's allegorical poetry. The following catalogue was written in the hope of providing a factual basis for pursuing these suggested research activities and other attempts to understand the multiple interactions between art and commerce, graphic execution and literary conception, that shaped Blake's life and works.

---

[32] For comments on this *America* plate, see Ronald Paulson, *Representations of Revolution (1789–1820)* (New Haven: Yale Univ. Press, 1983), 95–7. The fullest study of text–design relationships in the illuminated books, including 'the wealth of independent, nonillustrative pictorial significance' and visual/verbal 'syncopation' (pp. 9–10), is W. J. T. Mitchell, *Blake's Composite Art* (Princeton: Princeton Univ. Press, 1978). Important predecessors to Mitchell's work are Northrop Frye, 'Poetry and Design in William Blake', *Journal of Aesthetics and Art Criticism*, 10 (1951), 35–42, and Jean H. Hagstrum, *William Blake Poet and Painter* (Chicago: Univ. of Chicago Press, 1964).

CATALOGUE

I

William Enfield, *The Speaker: or, Miscellaneous Pieces, Selected from the Best English Writers, and Disposed Under Proper Heads, with a View to Facilitate the Improvement of Youth in Reading and Speaking* (London: J. Johnson, 1774 [1780], 1781, 1785, 1795, 1797); *Fig. 1*

Joseph Johnson's edition of Enfield's popular anthology of excerpts contains four plates designed by Stothard. The actual date of issue of the '1774' edition with the plates (perhaps added to letterpress remainder sheets printed in 1774) is given by the 1780 imprints on all four plates. Enfield (1741–79), a dissenting minister of War-rington, was an occasional member of the Johnson circle. Only one plate is signed by Blake as the engraver. For Blake's long association with Sto-thard, see the Introduction and the records in Bentley 1969.

1. Facing p. 300 or 302 (1774 [1780] edn.), p. 289 (1781 and 1785 edns.) and p. 299 or 305 (1795 edn.); 12.5 × 7.3 cm.; *Fig. 1*
Title above border: Clarence's Dream.
Inscription above design, right: *Book VII Chap. 22*
Signatures: *Stothard del.* [left], *Blake sc.* [right]
Inscribed verse below design: see *Fig. 1*.
Imprint: *Publish'd as the Act directs, by J Johnson in S! Pauls Church Yard, 1 Aug. 1780.*

Second State, facing p. 305 (1797 edn.). Hatching has been added to the winged angel's left leg, the ground below the kneeling figure, and to the hair of the lowest fiend. An additional framing line, almost touching the image, has been cut at the top and on both sides. A horizontal scratch cuts through the first line of the inscribed verse.

The design illustrates lines 52–60 of Shakespeare's *Richard III*, Act I, sc. iv. The first six of these lines are inscribed on the plate; a longer selection appears in Enfield's text. Richard's brother, the Duke of Clarence, relates his nightmare to the Keeper of the Tower of London. Clarence dreams that he is in hell, where he is accused by the ghost of Prince Edward of murdering him at the Battle of Tewkesbury. This 'shadow like an angel', pictured as the winged figure upper right, turns to call forth the 'Furies' who will torment Clarence (kneeling lower left) with guilt. One of the three 'foul fiends' pictured by Stothard seems to stop his ears, perhaps to shut out the 'hideous cries' he and his companions have 'howled in' Clarence's 'ears'.

The plate shows considerable wear in the 1793 and 1795 editions and in its second state. A proof before all letters, and with the left side of the winged angel's face pictured rather than the back of his head, is in the BMPR. According to Keynes 1921, p. 226, there were then 'proofs of three states', including one showing the side of the angel's face, and 'Stothard's original sketch of the design', in the collection of W. E. Moss. These were sold from the Moss collection, Sotheby's, 2 March 1937, lot 232, described as '4 states, with Original Sketches by Stothard, for the re-working of the 3rd state' (Dulau, 10s.). I have not been able to locate any of these works from the Moss collection, nor the 'sketch … in the BMPR' noted in Bentley 1977, p. 552.

There are many unillustrated editions of *The Speaker*, including the first (1774), and the 1785 edition was issued both with and without plates. There are at least five anonymous re-engravings of the design: left hand of lowest fiend not pictured, period added after 'Chap 22', lacking 'Shakespeare' after the engraved verses, 'Stothard' signature only, 1798 imprint, known to me only through an unbound impression (RNE); image 0.5 cm. shorter than Blake's plate, the border line extended below the design, without 'Shakespeare' after the verses, 'Stothard' signature only, 1799 imprint, found in a 1799 edition (Bodleian Library); design and framing lines in stipple, face of lowest fiend altered considerably, no signatures, 1800 imprint, found in a 1799 edition (BL); lacking border and both signatures, 1801 imprint, found in an 1801 edition (Princeton University Library, Princeton, New Jersey); 'Stothard' signature only, imprint undated, found in an 1805 edition (BL). According to Bentley 1977, p. 552, there are also illustrated editions of 1807 and 1820, but neither contains Blake's plate.

Literature: Gilchrist 1863, i. 32, ii. 259; Russell 1912, no. 45; Keynes 1921, no. 89; Bentley and Nurmi 1964, no. 364; Bentley 1977, no. 453; Easson and Essick 1979, no. XIII.

II

[J.] Olivier, *Fencing Familiarized* (a new edn.; London: John Bell, 1780); *Fig. 2*

This 'treatise on the art of small sword' (title-page) is illustrated with fourteen plates and a vignette printed twice. One of the folding plates is engraved by Blake after 'J. Roberts' (very probably James Roberts, active 1773–99 as a painter of full-length portraits, principally of actors in character for the same publisher's 'British Theatre'). The text is printed in English and French on facing pages. The [1771] edition, also published by Bell, contains eight different plates of some of the same fencing positions. These may have been used as models for the corresponding 1780 illustrations, including Blake's single plate, or at least as guides for the swordsmen who purportedly posed for Roberts 'ad vivum' (see signatures, below). The attribution of the plate to Blake depends entirely on the signature, for nothing in the execution of this simple etching/engraving indicates his hand. For another 'Blake' plate published by Bell, see **X**.

1. Facing p. 44, or the third plate bound at the end; 15.1 × 20.7 cm.; *Fig. 2*

Signatures: *J. Roberts Del! ad vivum.* [left], *W Blake Sculp* [right]

Title: *4.⁰, Position de l'allongement du Coup de quarte.*

The plate facing p. 45 in the [1771] edition, showing the same fencing position and signed '[T.?] Ovenden Sculp', lacks the wall on the left. The sword is straight, not bent.

Literature: Carl A. Thimm, *A Complete Bibliography of the Art of Fence* (London: Franz Thimm & Co., n.d. [*c*. 1890?]), 127–8; Thimm, *A Complete Bibliography of Fencing and Duelling* (London: John Lane, 1896), 211; Keynes 1921, no. 87; Bentley and Nurmi 1964, no. 398; Bentley 1977, no. 488; Easson and Essick 1979, no. XIV.

III

The Royal Universal Family Bible, with apparatus by John Herries, vol. i (London: Fielding & Walker, 1780; J. Fielding, 1781, 1784); vol. ii (London: J. Fielding, 1781, 1785); *Figs. 3–8*

Five of the 100 plates in the Herries Bible were engraved by Blake. The plate numbers, lightly and crudely scratched upper right and left on fifty-six plates, quickly wore off the copper and do not appear in all impressions. These numbers do not correspond to the actual binding sequence, nor to the plate numbers recorded in the 'Directions for the Binder'. In the single copy located with the title-page for vol. ii dated 1785 (State Library of South Australia, Adelaide), pls. 4 and 5 lack Blake's signature, but this is probably the result of wear rather than purposeful effort.

The Herries Bible was originally issued in weekly parts, and the numbers in the 'Directions' apparently correspond to the part in which each plate was published. According to a prospectus of 1782 (John Johnson Collection, Bodleian Library) for this Bible, the plates 'cost the publisher upwards of Seven Hundred Pounds' and 'the whole [will be] ornamented with Curious borders by Mr. *Clowes*' (Bentley 1977, p. 515). Another prospectus (*c*. 1775) in the same collection, for Henry Southwell's *Universal Family Bible* and *Exposition of the Holy Scriptures*, indicates that Clowes engraved as well as designed the borders for the plates in those two works. Thus the borders on Blake's plates might have been executed not by him, but by the London engraver Butler Clowes (active 1768–82).

The lower right corner of the frontispiece to the Herries Bible is inscribed, very minutely, 'Palmer, scrip.'. This writing engraver may have cut the lettering on other plates, including Blake's. The designers of Blake's pls. 1–4 are not identified on the plates (but see pl. 1 for an unconfirmed attribution). Seven other plates are signed 'Dodd' (probably either Daniel Dodd, active 1761–80, or Robert Dodd, 1748–1816), and three more by the engraver D. Jenkins, as their designers, or at least as the 'delineators' of a design based on some earlier prototype. Bindman 1977 suggests that Blake's work for the Herries Bible and *The Protestant's Family Bible* (**VI**) provided 'the initial impulse' for Blake's turn towards biblical subjects in his drawings of the mid-1780s.

1. Vol. i, facing Numbers 13: 23; 16.5 × 10.7 cm.; *Fig. 3*

Inscribed number, top right: *17*

Title above design: NUMBERS | Chap. 13 Ver. 23

Signature between design and frame, lower right: *Blake sculp*

Dedication below border: see *Fig. 3*.

Imprint: *Published Sept! 16, 1780, by* Fielding & Walker, *Paternoster Row London*

Second State, known only from a single loose impression (RNE) on paper with an 1803 watermark. The central design has been reworked; Moses no longer has rays of light above his head. The inscriptions (except for a few fragments) below the border and its pendant medallion have been eliminated. The plate mark has been reduced from 28.5 × 18.6 cm. to 25.1 × 18 cm. This state was probably executed in anticipation of its use in some other publication, but I have not been able to find any book in which it appears.

The plate is described in the 'Directions for the Binder' as no. 14, 'The Children of Israel stopping at the Brook of Eshcol'. However, the design shows a slightly later event, the presentation to Moses and Aaron of a giant bunch of grapes slung on a pole and other fruits gathered by Jewish scouts in the Holy Land as evidence of its fertility (Numbers 13: 26). Horn-like rays of light emanate from Moses's head; Aaron sits on his left. A proof before the border design and all letters is in the Robert Balmanno Collection, BMPR. This print is inscribed in pencil (by Balmanno?), 'Stothard del', 'Blake sc', and 'The Return of the Jewish Spies from Canaan'. I am unable to confirm this attribution to Stothard. The proof is wrongly described as an unpublished plate in Russell 1912, no. 62, Bentley 1977, p. 589, and Essick 1983, no. LI and fig. 104. The left side of this composition is very similar, even as to Aaron's hand gestures, to an anonymous engraving, probably removed from a seventeenth- or eighteenth-century Bible, in the extra-illustrated Kitto Bible, vol. xiv, leaf 2356 (HEH).

2. Vol. ii, facing Jonah 3: 4; 16.4 × 10.7 cm.; *Fig. 4*

Inscribed number, top left: *73*

Title above design: JONAH | Chap. 3. Ver. 4.

Scratched signature between design and frame, lower right: *Blake. Sc*

Dedication below border: see *Fig. 4*.

Imprint: *Published Octo! 13, 1781 by* J. Fielding, *Paternoster Row, London.*

The plate is described in the 'Directions for the Binder' as no. 49, 'Jonah entering the City of Nineveh'. Jonah, standing in the centre of the composition, has just predicted that 'Nineveh shall be overthrown' (Jonah 3: 4). The citizens around him respond with various gestures of fear, despair, and prayer. In his annotations of c.1798 to Richard Watson's *Apology for the Bible*, Blake noted that 'Jonah was no prophet in the modern sense for his prophecy of Nineveh failed' (E 617, K 392).

3. Vol. ii, facing Judith 13: 10; 16.5 × 10.7 cm.; *Fig. 5*

Inscribed number, top left: *83*

Title above design: JUDITH, | Chap. 13, Ver. 10

Stipple signature between design and frame, lower right: *Blake. Sc:*

Dedication below border: see *Fig. 5*.

Imprint: *Published Dec! 22, 1781, by* J. Fielding, *Paternoster Row.*

The plate is described in the 'Directions for the Binder' as no. 65, 'Judith giving the Head of Holofernes to her Maid'. The three men in the middle distance on the right are not described in the passage illustrated.

4. Vol. ii, facing Matthew 3: 13 (but see note below); 16.4 × 10.9 cm.; *Fig. 6*

Inscribed number, top left: *65*

Title above design: MATTHEW | Chap. 3. Ver. 13

Signature between design and frame, lower right: *Blake Sc*

Dedication below border: see *Fig. 6*.

Imprint: *Published Aug! 18, 1781, by* J. Fielding *Paternoster Row, London*

The plate is described in the 'Directions for the Binder' as no. 85, 'Christ baptized by John in the River Jordan'. There is, however, another plate clearly illustrating that event, inscribed 'Matthew Chap. 3. Ver. 13 & 17'. Blake's plate was very probably wrongly inscribed as to its textual point of reference, for it would be very odd to have two illustrations of the same event. Further, Blake's plate shows an old man anointing the head of a young man holding what may be a shepherd's staff, not a baptism in a river. It was probably intended to be no. 46 in the 'Directions for the Binder', described as showing 'David anointed by Samuel' (I Samuel 16: 13). No other design illustrates this event. In one copy (RNE) the inscription above the design is lined through in ink and the plate bound facing II Samuel 9: 9

through 10: 19 in vol. i, where it has no textual bearing. The figure in the distance on the left is generally similar to one appearing in an illustration to I Samuel 16: 13 by Gaspar Luiken (*c.* 1670–1710) engraved by Christoph Weigel (1654–1725).

5. Vol. ii, facing Revelation 1: 12–13; 16.1 × 10.5 cm.; *Fig. 7*

Title above design: REVELATIONS, | Chap. 1 Ver, 12 & 13

Scratched signature between design and frame, lower right: *Blake. d & sc* [very faint, or even worn off the plate, in some copies]

Dedication below border: see *Fig. 7.*

Imprint: *Published Feb!* 23 1782 by J Fielding *Paternoster Row*

The plate is described in the 'Directions for the Binder' as no. 91, 'The Vision of the seven golden Candlesticks'. St John half kneels on the ground and looks up to behold the seven candlesticks and 'one like unto the Son of man, clothed with a garment down to the foot, and girt about the paps with a golden girdle' (1: 13). This vision of Christ holds 'in his right [left in the design] hand seven stars' and in 'his mouth . . . a sharp two edged sword' (1: 16). The heavy clouds in the sky may have been prompted by the reference to Christ coming 'with clouds' (1: 7), while the rays emanating from His head respond to the statement that 'his countenance was as the sun shineth in his strength' (1: 16). John's book (1: 11), bearing Hebrew letters, rests on a large rock, lower left.

Blake's preliminary pen-and-wash drawing, 16.2 × 10.8 cm., for the plate is now in the BMPR (*Fig. 8*). Right and left are the reverse of the engraving, and only one candlestick is clearly pictured. There are only very slight indications of John's book. An untraced design by Blake of 'The Seven Golden Candlesticks' was last recorded in 1853 as a watercolour, but this work might be the same as the BMPR drawing. Blake frequently dressed Christ in accord with the passage in Revelation illustrated by this design; see, for example, his second design for Robert Blair's *The Grave* (1808), 'Christ Descending into the Grave' (Bindman 1978, no. 466).

Significantly, this is the single plate by Blake in this Bible on which his signature is followed by 'd', indicating that he delineated the design (as the extant drawing proves), although probably after some prototype. That role may have been played by an illustration to the same scene by the French artist and engraver Bernard Picart (1673–1733). His composition was first published in a large collection of plates without text, issued by Picart between 1705 and 1720, but it also appears in several later works, including an English Bible edited by Samuel Clark (London: J. Fuller, 1760). However, the similarities between the two designs are fairly general. John is kneeling in Picart's design, as is traditional in most representations of the scene, but his posture is completely different in other respects. Christ's posture also differs, particularly in arm position, the candlesticks are differently shaped and arranged, and the foreground left and right of John is totally different. Blake was probably influenced by Picart's illustration, but Blake's design may still be considered as his own composition in many respects. At the very least, the image resides in the borderland between an original and a copy.

Literature: Bentley and Nurmi 1964, no. 338; Easson and Essick 1972, no. I (pl. 5 only); Bentley 1977, no. 420; David Bindman, *Blake as an Artist* (Oxford: Phaidon, 1977), 29; Bindman 1978, no. 3 (pl. 5 only); Easson and Essick 1979, no. XV (pls. 1–4 only); Butlin 1981, nos. 120 verso (BMPR drawing for pl. 5), 514 (untraced watercolour).

IV

Henry Emlyn, *A Proposition for a New Order in Architecture* (London: Printed by J. Dixwell [for the author?], 1781, 1784; London: Messrs. Taylor, 1797); *Fig. 9*

The 1781 first edition contains ten plates, the 1784 'Second Edition' twenty-one, and the 1797 'Third Edition' thirty-one. Presumably Emlyn is the designer of all the plates, although only one in the 1797 edition is so signed. Only one plate is signed by Blake as the engraver. No other plates in the first edition are signed. Breman 1971 and Gibson and Minnick 1972 attribute the unsigned plate inscribed 'V' to Blake on the basis of stylistic similarities with the plate he signed. Easson and Essick 1979, p. 20, accept this attribution without comment. Bentley 1977, p. 551, doubts that Blake engraved plate V; I now concur with his view. All the plates are simple outline etchings/engravings without distinctive stylistic features. Plate V shares no more features with Blake's signed plate (inscribed 'II') than with several others in the volume. Indeed, the attribution of plate II to

Blake depends entirely on the signature and the reasonable assumption that he would have had to accept such humble commissions in his first year after apprenticeship. Gibson and Minnick also state that the plates inscribed I, III, IV, and X 'could be by Blake' (p. 14), but they do not argue for this suggestion.

1. The second plate bound after the text (1781 and 1784 edns.); 53.2 × 29.5 cm.; *Fig. 9*

Plate number above design, right: Pl: II.
Measurement inscriptions within design: see *Fig. 9*.
Signature lower right: *Blake Sculp*

Second State, the fourth plate following the text in the 1797 edition. The platemark has been cut down on all four sides from 53.8 × 37 cm. to 44.5 × 28.2 cm., thereby eliminating Blake's signature. The plate is now inscribed 'P. IV.' top centre. Gibson and Minnick 1972, p. 14, and Easson and Essick 1979 claim that these third-edition impressions are from Blake's original plate reworked, but Bentley 1977, p. 551, believes that Blake's work was 'very carefully copied by an anonymous engraver'. Accidental scratches, if found on both 1781–4 and on 1797 impressions, offer the best basis for claiming that they were printed from the same copperplate. Only one such accidental mark presents itself, but I believe it is sufficient to indicate that 1797 impressions represent a second state of Blake's plate. In the 1781–4 plate there are two tiny dots at the centre of the half-circle defining the left end of the first base element just above the large rectangular plinth. These were probably made by the need to adjust the location of the fixed foot of the compass used to delineate the semi-circle. These same two dots appear in 1797 impressions. It would be an extraordinary coincidence if the identical compass adjustment had been required on a second copperplate. Further, a short fragment of the dotted semi-circle upper left on the 1781–4 plate remains in 1797 impressions even though it now serves no purpose. In the second state, many lines in the central medallion have been strengthened and an anchor, rope coils, chains, another shield, and an iron basket have been added to the emblematic design. Many of the dotted measurement lines have been eliminated, but new dotted quarter-circles have been added lower left, upper right, and lower right. The rectangular plinth has been cut down to a narrow footing and the rectangle above the capital has been diminished in height from 3.2 to 2.3 cm.

The proportions of the column represented in the plate are described on p. 9 of Emlyn's 1781 text. His new, sixth 'order' of architecture is decorated with motifs alluding to 'the Most Noble Order of St George' (p. 2). The medallion in Blake's plate shows the 'Knights Shield and Armour, with the Skin of a Wolf, hanging down on each side ...' (p. 3). For a study of archi-tectural motifs in Blake's art and writings, see Paley 1983.

Literature: Paul Breman Ltd., 1971 sale catalogue 14, *English Architecture 1598–1838*, no. 12; William A. Gibson and Thomas L. Minnick, 'William Blake and Henry Emlyn's *Proposition for a New Order in Architecture*: A New Plate', *Blake Newsletter*, 6 (1972), 13–17, with the second state of Blake's plate and the plate inscribed V reproduced; Bentley 1977, no. 452; Easson and Essick 1979, no. XVII, pl. V reproduced; Morton D. Paley, 'The Fourth Face of Man: Blake and Architecture', in Richard Wendorf (ed.), *Articulate Images: The Sister Arts from Hogarth to Tennyson* (Minneapolis: Univ. of Minnesota Press, 1983), 184–215.

V

Edward Kimpton, *A New and Complete Universal History of the Holy Bible* (two issues; London: J. Cooke, *c.* 1781 and later). *The Genuine and Complete Works of Flavius Josephus*, trans. George Henry Maynard (London: J. Cooke, *c.* 1785–6). *The Whole Genuine and Complete Works of Flavius Josephus*, trans. George Henry Maynard (four issues: London: J. Cooke, *c.* 1787–8 and *c.* 1788–9; London: C. Cooke, *c.* 1789–90 and *c.* 1790–1). *Figs. 10–14*

Three of the sixty plates in Kimpton's *History* were engraved by Blake, two after designs by the German engraver Conrad Martin Metz (1755–1827), who worked in London from *c.* 1775 to 1801, and one after Stothard. 'Blake' appears on the title-pages of all issues of Kimpton as one of the 'Capital Performers' who engraved the plates. Revised states of most of the Kimpton plates, including all three by Blake, were published in Maynard's Josephus. The reworking of the plates may have been executed by someone other than Blake, particularly if he had not been responsible for the first-state borders (as seems likely for the Herries Bible, **III**). The publication history of both titles is complicated by the lack of dates on title-pages and plates. I am grateful to G. E. Bentley, jun., for the conjectural dates of the second and subsequent Josephus issues recorded here.

   The revisions in the plates indicate that the Kimpton prints were pulled prior to those in Josephus. This sequence also suggests the publication priority of Kimpton's volume. At least one late reissue of Kimpton (RNE) contains a mixture of Kimpton and Josephus states, with the 'Josephus' inscriptions above the designs in the latter either masked during printing or burnished off the plate (as in the fourth state of pl. 3). Apparently there was an insufficient stock of first states for this reissue, and thus new pulls had to be taken from the very worn plates which had already been converted to their later (Josephus) states. Both Kimpton and Josephus were originally issued in weekly parts, a genre in which the publisher John Cooke (1731–1810) and his son and successor, Charles Cooke, specialized. The numbers given the plates in the 'Directions to the Binder' recorded below apparently correspond to the part in which each was published.

Versions of Blake's pls. 1 and 2, re-engraved by 'American artists', appear in *The Whole Genuine and Complete Works of Flavius Josephus* (New York: William Durrell, 1794).

1. Facing p. 19 in Kimpton; 17.3 × 11.3 cm.; *Fig. 10*

Inscription above border: *Engraved for Kimpton's History of the Bible.*
Signatures between design and frame: *C M. Metz del.* [left], *Blake sc* [right]
Inscription below design: Genesis, XIII. 11.
Title: The Parting of Lot and Abraham, | *after seperating their Flocks, &c.*

Second State,   facing p. 13 in Josephus, all issues. The border has been replaced by a completely different design featuring leaves and, at the top, flower garlands. '*Engraved for* | Maynard's | *Josephus.*' now appears in a circular medallion in the upper border. The Bible reference below the design and the signatures have been removed. New signatures ('*Metz Delin.*' left, '*Blake sculp.*' right) have been added below the border. The title inscription remains. Hatching and cross-hatching patterns have been added throughout the central design. This new work is particularly evident in the sky upper left and on the clothing of Lot and Abraham, the woman on a donkey, and the man left of her.

The plate is listed in Kimpton's 'Directions to the Binder' as no. 9, 'The parting of Lot and Abraham', and as no. 32, similarly described, in Josephus. Lot, the younger man on the right, is departing for the land he has chosen, 'the plains near Sodom and Gomorrah' (Kimpton, p. 19). Abraham will remain at Bethel. A generally similar woman and donkey appear in an illustration of the same event by Gerard Hoet (1648–1733) engraved by 'Van Der Gucht' (father and son active in London *c.* 1680–1776). The vignette in the top border would seem to represent a greeting or reunion, contrary to the parting in the main design.

2. Facing p. 110 in Kimpton; 17.3 × 10.9 cm.; *Fig. 11*

Inscription above border: *Engraved for Kimpton's History of the Bible.*
Signatures between design and frame: *Stothard del* [left], *Blake sc* [right]
Inscription below design: Joshua, VIII. 20.
Title: The Battle of Ai, *with the* Destruction of | the City, *by the Army of* Joshua.

Second State, facing p. 65 in Josephus, all issues except as noted below for the third state. The border has been replaced by a different design retaining elements of the inner frame but with new decorations featuring leaves and, at the top, flower garlands. '*Engraved for* | Maynard's | *Josephus.*' now appears in a circular medallion in the upper border. The Bible reference below the design and the signatures have been removed. New signatures ('*Stothard delin.*' left, '*Blake sculp.*' right) have been added below the border. The first line of the title has been changed to '*The* Battle *of* Ain, *&* the Destruction *of*'. This revision was prompted by the spelling 'Ain' in Josephus's text ('Ai' in Kimpton and the King James Bible). In the central design, hatching and cross-hatching have been added to the head, neck, leg, and chest of the fallen horse, lower right, and to the neck, shoulder, haunch, and flank of the horse bearing the archer. The ground in the immediate foreground has been cross-hatched.

Third State, facing p. 65 in at least one copy (RNE) of the final issue of Josephus. The smoke forming a flattened cloud along the top of the design in the first and second states now billows out to the right. Some of the hatching on the archer's horse has been strengthened and covers more of the animal's haunch.

A print (17.4 × 10.8 cm.) of the same design, probably by Blake but without letters and a frame different from either published version, is in the LC (*Fig. 12*). This must have been printed from a different copperplate, for right and left are the reverse of the published version, in which all the soldiers are left-handed. The most likely explanation for the production of two plates is that the properly right-handed copperplate was damaged or lost, and a substitute quickly prepared. Stothard's pen-and-grey-wash preliminary drawing, 17.8 × 10.5 cm., is also in the LC (*Fig. 13*). Right and left are as in the unpublished, and presumably earlier, plate. Blake has followed Stothard's design very closely in his engraving.

The plate is listed in Kimpton's 'Directions to the

Binder' as no. 13, 'The Battle of Ai', and as no. 26, 'The battle of Ain and destruction of the city', in Josephus. Joshua's army is on the right, about to 'cut to pieces' (Kimpton, p. 110) the army of the King of Ai, whose city burns upper left. The helmets in the upper border denote the military theme. In his annotations of *c.* 1798 to Richard Watson's *Apology for the Bible*, Blake comments that 'The Earthquakes of Lisbon &c were the Natural result of Sin. but the destruction of the Canaanites by Joshua was the Unnatural design of wicked men' (E 614–15, K 388). Ai was one of the royal cities of Canaan.

3. Facing p. 131 in Kimpton; 17.5 × 10.5 cm.; *Fig. 14*

Inscription above border: *Engraved for Kimpton's History of the Bible.*

Signatures between design and frame: *C. M Metz del.* [left], *Blake sc.* [right]

Inscription below design: JUDGES IX–46.

Title: THE FUGITIVE SHECHEMITES | *Burnt and Suffocated in the Holds of their Idol Berith,* | *by order of King Abimelech.*

Second State, facing p. 76 in Josephus, all issues except as noted below for the third state. The border has been replaced by a completely different design featuring leaves and, at the top, flower garlands. '*Engraved for* | MAYNARD'S | *Josephus.*' now appears in a circular medallion in the upper border. The Bible reference below the design and the signatures have been removed. New signatures ('*Metz delin.*' left, '*Blake sculp.*' right) have been added below the border. The second line of the title now reads '*Burnt and Suffocated in the Holds of their Retreat,*'. The central design has received only minor reworking. Hatching has been added to the left thigh of the man holding a lance, lower left, and to the semi-circle (of vegetation?) hanging from the cliff, centre right. Some of the cross-hatching strokes in the foreground, lower left corner, have been extended further into the design.

Third State, facing p. 76 in at least one copy (RNE) of the final issue of Josephus. The eyes of the woman holding a child near her face in the cave above the fire lower right have been darkened and enlarged. Many hatching lines throughout the image have been strengthened.

Fourth State, facing p. 131 in at least one copy (RNE) of a late reissue of Kimpton. All letters have been removed from the central medallion in the top border.

The plate is listed in Kimpton's 'Directions to the Binder' as no. 2, 'The Fugitive Shechemites burnt in the holds of their Idol Berith, by order of king Abimelech', and in Josephus as no. 23, 'The fugitive Shechemites burnt and suffocated'. Abimelech's army has begun to immolate the defeated Shechemites who have sought refuge in 'a cluster of strong holds, belong-

ing to the temple of their idol Berith' (Kimpton, p. 130), represented in the design as caverns in a rocky cliff. The snake holding a firebrand in the top border underscores the evil of this massacre. Brown 1938, p. 458, describes an impression then in his collection 'even prior to the state appearing in Kimpton. The plate is unsigned, and the frame, entirely different from those published, contains at the top a circle suitable for an inscription, which is, however, blank. The title is the same as in Kimpton.' I have not been able to locate any such impression.

Literature: Gilchrist 1863, ii. 259 (pl. 2 in Josephus only); Russell 1912, no. 63 (Josephus only); Keynes 1921, no. 100 (Josephus only); Allen R. Brown, 'Unrecorded Engravings of Blake', *The Colophon*, NS 3 (1938), 457–8 (discovery of the Kimpton plates); Bentley and Nurmi 1964, nos. 386–7; Paul Grinke, 1972 sale catalogue 5, no. 32 (drawing for pl. 2), with a note on the alternative pl. 2 by Ruthven Todd; Bentley 1977, nos. 477–8; Easson and Essick 1979, nos. XVIII–XIX (second states reproduced); Essick 1983, no. LIII (alternative pl. 2).

VI

The Protestant's Family Bible (London: Harrison and Co., *c.* 1781); *Figs. 15–19*

Five of the fifty-eight plates are signed by Blake as the engraver. Three of them are credited on the plates to Raphael (1483–1520) and two to Peter Paul Rubens (1577–1640) as their designers, but all are in fact based, somewhat loosely, on the frescoes in the Vatican Loggias traditionally called 'Raphael's Bible' but actually executed by his assistants. Blake must have been working from copies of the originals, such as the suite of twenty-eight rather crude etchings by Giovanni Lanfranco (1581–1647), the suite of engravings by Nicolas Chapron published in Rome in 1649, or *The Gallery of Raphael, Called His Bible ... Engraved in the Academy of Arts at Glasgow* (Glasgow, 1770). Blake may have been responsible for changing Raphael's horizontal format to the vertical and for the other major modifications noted for each plate below. None of these changes appears in the earlier engravings I have seen. Right and left are the reverse of the frescoes in pls. 1–2.

Raphael was one of Blake's great artistic heroes,

but Rubens was for Blake 'a Fool' (E 513, K 546) and 'a most outrageous demon' (*Descriptive Catalogue* (E 547, K 582)). In his annotations of *c.* 1808 to Joshua Reynolds's *Discourses*, Blake comments on these two artists: 'I am happy I cannot say that Rafael Ever was from my Earliest Childhood hidden from Me. I saw & I Knew immediately the difference between Rafael & Rubens' (E 637, K 447). Apparently the writing engraver who added the designers' names was not so adept at making this distinction. Reynolds's text makes no mention of Rubens in the passage annotated, and thus Blake's comment may have been motivated by a recollection of this odd error.

This Bible was first issued in weekly parts. The conjectural date of publication is based on a 1781 imprint on the plate illustrating Acts 7: 59.

1. Facing Genesis 18: 2; 14.6 × 10.7 cm.; *Fig. 15*

Inscription in upper border: Genesis. | XVIII. 2.

Title: *Abraham & the Three Angels.*

Signatures: *Raphael de Urbin Del!* [left], *Blake Sculp.* [right]

Imprint: *Publish'd as the Act directs by Harrison & C.º N.º 18, Pater-noster. Row.*

Abraham's 'tent' (Genesis 18: 2) is pictured as a wooden building. His wife Sarah waits just inside the door. The large tree is not in Raphael's fresco. Bindman 1977 suggests that this design influenced the postures and gestures of the figures in Blake's watercolour of 1783, *The Witch of Endor Raising the Spirit of Samuel* (Butlin 1981, no. 144). A closer parallel, including a similar placement of a building with a pitched roof, foliage, a kneeling old man, and an angelic figure in a flowing gown, is presented by Blake's watercolour of *Manoah's Sacrifice*, *c.* 1780–5 (Butlin 1981, no. 116 recto).

2. Facing Genesis 19: 26; 14.9 × 10.4 cm.; *Fig. 16*

Inscription in upper border: Gen: | XIX. 26.

Title: *Lot's Escape.*

Signatures: *Rubens del.* [left], *Blake sculp.* [right]

Imprint: Publish'd as the Act directs, by Harrison & C.º N.º 18, Pater noster Row.

Lot leaves behind the burning city of Sodom or Gomorrah, his 'two daughters with him' (Genesis 19: 30). His wife, on the left, looks back to the city a moment before she becomes 'a pillar of salt' (19: 26). The lightning and river do not appear in Raphael's fresco. The design bears general similarities to the family group lower left in Blake's *America*, pl. 5,

although John Singleton Copley's 1783 painting, *The Death of Major Peirson*, may have been a stronger influence. Blake frequently used thistles and briars, like those lower left in this plate, to symbolize a state of bondage to fallen nature—see, for example, the lower border designs in the Job engravings, pls. 6 and 8. Behrendt 1987–8 suggests a 'thematic association' between the subject of this plate and the final plate of Blake's *Europe*. Blake's drawing of *The Departure of Lot* has been untraced since 1854 (Butlin 1981, no. 841). Its compositional relationship to this plate is not known.

3. Facing Genesis 37: 28; 14.6 × 10.5 cm.; *Fig. 17*

Inscription in upper border: Gen, | XXXVII, 28.

Title: *Joseph sold to the | Ishmeelites.*

Signatures: *Rubens: del.* [left], *Blake sculp.* [right]

Imprint: as on pl. 2.

The plate is mistitled. The selling of Joseph (Genesis 37: 28) is represented in Raphael's next fresco in the series. This design shows Joseph (centre) telling his dreams to his brethren. The circular vignettes in the sky represent these dreams: the sheaves of Joseph's brethren making 'obeisance' to his sheaf (37: 7), and 'the sun and the moon and the eleven stars' making 'obeisance' to Joseph (37: 9). The large central palm in the middle distance of Raphael's fresco is omitted in this plate. Its vertical format has necessitated the displacement of the flock of sheep from the right margin of the fresco to a position between Joseph and the three figures on the right. Butlin 1981, no. 155, attributes to 'Bindman' the suggestion that this design was 'Blake's immediate source' for his series of three watercolours illustrating the life of Joseph, exhibited in 1785 (Butlin 1981, nos. 155–9). In *Milton* Blake refers to Joseph's sale into bondage and transforms his coat of many colours into swaddling bands 'of emblematic texture' (E 120, K 508). *Jerusalem* also alludes to Joseph's sale 'into Egypt' (E 204, K 686) and to his coat (E 220, 239; K 704, 724).

4. Facing Exodus 32: 19; 15.1 × 10.7 cm.; *Fig. 18*

Inscription in upper border: Exodus. | XXXII. 19.

Title: *The Israelites Idolatry.*

Signatures: *Raphael de Urbin del.* [left], *Blake sculp.* [right]

Imprint: Publish'd as the Act directs, by Harrison & C.º N.º 18 Pater noster Row.

The Israelites dance about the golden calf made by Aaron (Exodus 32: 5, 19). Moses, standing upper left with Joshua, is about to 'cast the tables out of his hands, and brake them beneath the mount' (32: 19). In Raphael's fresco, Moses and Joshua are much larger figures and the calf is placed on a much lower base, closer to the biblical 'altar' (32: 5) than the column with an ionic capital that is in Blake's plate. The woman near the right margin with one arm raised is a man raising both arms in the fresco, which also pictures three kneeling figures lower left which are omitted from the plate. Blake's tempera painting of *Moses Indignant at the Golden Calf*, c. 1799–1800 (Butlin 1981, no. 387), shows a basically similar calf but shares no other features with this plate.

5. Facing Joshua 4: 16; 14.6 × 10.3 cm.; *Fig. 19*

Inscription in upper border: Joshua, | IV. 16.

Title: *Joshua passing over Jordan*

Signatures: *Raphael de Urbin, del.* [left], *Blake sculp.* [right]

Imprint: Publish'd as the Act directs, by Harrison & C? N? 18 Paternoster Row.

'Priests . . . bare the ark of the covenant' (Joshua 4: 18) towards the River Jordan. Some of the 'forty thousand prepared for war' (4: 13) stride forwards on the right. The conversion of Raphael's design to a vertical format has eliminated Joshua, seated on the far left in the fresco. The flags are not as large and are differently positioned in the painting, which lacks the shell and starfish (rather odd for a river bank).

Literature: Russell 1912, no. 73; Keynes 1921, no. 88; Bentley and Nurmi 1964, no. 337; Bindman 1977 (see **III**, *Literature*), pp. 29–30; Bentley 1977, no. 419; Easson and Essick 1979, no. XX; Stephen C. Behrendt, '*Europe* 6: Plundering the Treasury', *Blake: An Illustrated Quarterly*, 21 (1987–8), 90.

VII

John Bonnycastle, *An Introduction to Mensuration* (London: J. Johnson, 1782, 1787, 1791, 1794); *Fig. 20*

The only engraving is an uninscribed vignette on the title-page. Its attribution to Blake depends on a proof on laid India paper (BMPR) signed in the plate '*Stothard, del*' (left) and '*Blake, Sc*' (right) just beneath a line border, 7.2 × 9.4 cm., cut from the plate when it was trimmed to a platemark of 6.9 × 9.3 cm. prior to publication. This proof is reproduced in Keynes 1963, facing p. 207, and Essick 1980, fig. 23.

The subject of Bonnycastle's handbook and the habits of mind it represents may have influenced Blake's characterization of Urizen, his desire for 'one weight, one measure', and his use of 'a line & a plummet | To divide the Abyss' in *The Book of Urizen* (E 72, 80; K 224, 233). For what Blake may have learnt from another of Bonnycastle's scientific studies, *An Introduction to Astronomy*, see Dörrbecker 1989.

1. Vignette on the title-page, 1782 edn.; 6.3 × 8.7 cm.; *Fig. 20*

Second State (1787 and 1791 edns.). The image has been trimmed on the bottom and left sides to 5.8 × 8.2 cm. and the platemark reduced to 6 × 8.5 cm. Horizontal hatching has been added to the ground, the pyramid on the left, and the sky right of the pyramid. The vertical hatching on the rectangular block beneath the three children on the right has been strengthened. Reproduced, from a copy of the 1791 edition, in Ryskamp 1969, pl. [3], bottom.

Third State (1794 edn.). Horizontal crossing strokes have been added to the left end of the cylinder projecting from the right margin, and to the left end of the block beneath the three children on the right.

Stothard's design indicates the youthful audience for which the book was intended, and perhaps also plays upon Bonnycastle's allusion to the 'origin' of mensuration 'in those remote ages of antiquity' (p. v) by picturing science in its infancy. The pyramid may have been prompted by the reference to 'Egypt' as the 'fruitful mother of almost all the liberal sciences', while the classical columns are appropriate for a book based in part on 'the Elements of Euclid' (p. v). The diagram on the ground to which one boy points and the drawing on the block behind him both demonstrate the Pythagorean theorem (not dealt with in the text). Russell 1912, p. 137, suggests that Fuseli, a friend of Bonnycastle, may have played a role in acquiring the commission for Stothard and Blake. See also the Introduction for further comments on this illustration, very probably influenced by Hogarth's etching, 'Boys Peeping at Nature' (1730–1, revised state 1751).

Several later editions, including those of 1798 and 1802, contain Stothard's vignette re-engraved by another, unidentified, hand. The version in the 1807 and 1816 editions is signed by J. Dudley; the 1823 edition has the design engraved on steel by C. Cooke.

Literature: Gilchrist 1863, ii. 259; Russell 1912, no. 47; Keynes 1921, no. 90; Geoffrey Keynes, 'A Blake Engraving in Bonnycastle's *Mensuration*, 1782', *The Book Collector*, 12 (1963), 205–6; Bentley and Nurmi 1964, no. 351;

Charles Ryskamp, *William Blake Engraver: A Descriptive Catalogue of an Exhibition* (Princeton: Princeton Univ. Library, 1969), no. 11; Bentley 1977, no. 436; Bindman 1978, no. 2; Easson and Essick 1979, no. XXI; D. W. Dörrbecker, '*The Song of Los*: The Munich Copy and a New Attempt to Understand Blake's Images', *Huntington Library Quarterly*, 52 (1989), 43–73.

VIII

William Nicholson, *An Introduction to Natural Philosophy* (2 vols.; London: J. Johnson, 1782, 1787); *Fig. 21*

This introductory student text on physics, astronomy, and chemistry contains twenty-five unsigned folding plates and a vignette, the latter signed by Blake as the engraver and printed on the title-page to each volume. Nicholson (1753–1815) was a member of the Joseph Johnson circle. His *Natural Philosophy*, particularly its first section 'Of Matter in the Abstract', epitomizes the rational materialism Blake parodies and criticizes in *There is No Natural Religion* (c. 1788) and continued to attack throughout his life. Baine and Baine 1976 suggest that 'Inflammable Gass the Wind finder' (E 449, K 44) in Blake's *An Island in the Moon* of c. 1784–5 is a caricature of Nicholson, but the older identification of this figure with Joseph Priestley is still generally accepted.

1. Vignette on the title-page to both volumes (1782 edn.); 3.9 × 6.7 cm.; *Fig. 21*

Inscription on banner: QUIS: BASIN: DEMONSTRET:

Signature: *Blake sc*

Second State, both title-pages (1787 edn.). Cross-hatching has been added to the cloud band second from the bottom on the left. A few lines have been recut on the clouds far right, but the plate shows considerable wear and Blake's signature has almost disappeared.

The signature, not discovered until Heppner 1978–9, is very small and only lightly scratched into the plate, 2 mm. below the 'S' and 'T' of 'DEMONSTRET' in the banner inscription. The unattributed design would seem to be an emblem of the sciences both as light and as a classical rotunda in the heavens. Yet this temple of reason has its foundation in the clouds, a situation that makes the motto on the banner (roughly, 'Who

would demonstrate the foundation?') difficult to answer. There may be an ironic relationship between this emblem and Blake's image of 'Air' (a subject to which Nicholson devotes section IV of his book) personified as a melancholy man seated on clouds in *For Children: The Gates of Paradise* (1793). When he revised and reissued this work c. 1818 as *For the Sexes: The Gates of Paradise*, Blake inscribed the plate 'On Cloudy Doubts & Reasoning Cares' (E 261, K 763).

An unsigned, crude engraving of the same design appears in the editions of 1790, 1796, and 1805.

Literature: Rodney M. Baine and Mary R. Baine, 'Blake's Inflammable Gass', *Blake: An Illustrated Quarterly*, 10 (1976), 51–2; Christopher Heppner, 'Another "New" Blake Engraving: More about Blake and William Nicholson', *Blake: An Illustrated Quarterly*, 12 (1978–9), 193–7 (with reproductions of the signature, magnified, and the re-engraved vignette in the 1805 edition).

IX

John Scott, *The Poetical Works* (London: J. Buckland, 1782, 1786; London: Alexander Cleugh and John Dolfee, 1795); *Figs. 22–5*

Four of the fourteen plates were engraved by Blake after Stothard. These illustrations are fine examples of the designer's sentimental neo-classicism and the engraver's skill at translating such images to copper. John Scott of Amwell (1730–83) was a Quaker poet praised by Samuel Johnson. He was a close friend of John Hoole, the translator of the edition of Ariosto's *Orlando Furioso* illustrated by Stothard (**XII**). The publisher James Buckland (1710–90) specialized in dissenting literature. The reissue of 1795 substitutes a typographic title-page for the engraved version in the earlier editions. The text of 1782 appears in some copies (RNE) of this reissue, whereas others have the 1786 text (collection of G. E. Bentley, jun.). The placement of the plates follows whichever remainder sheets were employed.

Keynes 1921, p. 228, notes 'a series of proofs of these plates before letters printed on India paper', then in the collection of W. E. Moss. These are not listed in the Moss sale, Sotheby's, 2 March 1937, but may have been included in the miscellaneous group of plates by Blake sold as lot 218 (£11 to Rosenbach Co.). I have not been able to trace these Moss impressions, but the LC proof of pl. 2, noted below, may be one of them. In the *European Magazine, and London Review*, 2 (Sept. 1782), 195, the anonymous reviewer of the 1782 edition notes 'that the plates with which this publication is adorned, are designed and executed with skill and elegance'.

1. P. 21 in all edns.; 5.3 × 8.4 cm.; *Fig. 22*
Signatures: *Stothard del* [left], *Blake sc* [right]
Title: ECLOGUE IV
The design illustrates the beginning of the eclogue that concludes on p. 21. The 'moon' has just begun 'to rise' (p. 17). In the background on the right, Damon leans in a melancholy posture against 'Delia's tomb' and laments her death 'in the cypress gloom' (p. 18). Two shepherds, old Lycoron and youthful Milo, have just entered the sorrowful scene on the left. There is a proof before all letters in the BMPR and an impression of the published state in the Royal Academy, London, printed on a thick card.

2. Facing p. 23 (1782 edn.), and p. 25 (1786 edn.) (the first page of elegies in both); oval, 6.7 × 9.7 cm.; *Fig. 23*
Number upper right: *3*
Signatures: *Stothard del.* [left], *Blake sc* [right]
Title: *There is, who deems all climes, all seasons fair | Contentment, thankful for the gift of life. | Elegy IV.*
The design illustrates the inscribed passage from Elegy IV printed on p. 45. A personification of Contentment sits below the Seasons dancing on a cloud. Winter (far right) heralds a 'sounding storm', Spring wears 'gay bloom[s]' in her hair, Summer looks to the 'chearful skies', and Autumn holds a sprig from her 'corn-clad field' (p. 46). A proof before all letters is in the BMPR. Another, in the same state but printed on laid India paper, is in the LC.

3. Facing p. 247 (1782 edn.), and p. 249 (1786 edn.) (first page of 'The Mexican Prophecy' in both); oval, 6.7 × 9.8 cm.; *Fig. 24*
Number upper right: *7*
Signatures: *Stothard del.* [left], *Blake sc.* [right]
Title: *Warriors! let the Wretches live! | Christians! pity and forgive.*
'Cortes' conquering army' (p. 247) arrives on the right. Within the grove on the left, 'Motezume's magicians' pay homage to the idol Tlcatlepuca, before which 'magic fires' blaze (p. 249). Olmedo, 'chaplain to Cortes' (p. 251), stands in the centre of the design and

stops the Spanish soldiers from attacking the Aztec priests. Proofs before all letters are in the BMPR and the LC.

4. P. 335 (1782 edn.), and the page mis-numbered '322' (verso of 337) (1786 edn.); 8.2 × 8.1 cm.; *Fig. 25*
Inscription on monument: SACRED | TO | SIMPLICITY
Signatures: *Stothard, d* [left], *Blake sc* [right]
This picture of an elegantly clad lady depositing a manuscript on a garlanded monument seems to lack any specific textual source, although it may refer to Scott's plea to the reader to 'accept' his poetry (p. 335). His poems frequently praise 'simple Nature' (p. 314) and a life of retirement. Russell 1965 claims, without supporting evidence, that this plate 'was no doubt specifically commissioned by Scott to illustrate his belief that "classical simplicity", as opposed to the flowery inanities of Hayley and other popular versifiers, was the sole criterion of merit in poetry' (p. 353). An impression in the BMPR is printed on a thick card. Russell 1912, p. 138, notes that 'a volume of miscellaneous Blake items, sold at Sotheby's, 9th Dec. 1905 (Lot 921, No. 42), and again, 15th Dec. 1906 (Lot 482, No. 42), contained a pencil drawing (with some ink outline) by Blake (measuring $9\frac{1}{2} \times 6\frac{1}{2}$ in.) of a quasi-classical figure looking at a tombstone with "Sacred to . . ." on it, probably to be connected with this engraving'. Both sale catalogues list this item simply as 'an original sketch by Blake', sold to 'Paul' in 1905 and to 'Abbey' in 1906. This may have been a variant design by Stothard, not Blake. Not seen by Russell and now untraced.

Literature: Gilchrist 1863, i. 51, ii. 258 (pl. 4), 259; Russell 1912, no. 48; Keynes 1921, no. 94; Bentley and Nurmi 1964, no. 404; Norma Russell, 'Some Uncollected Authors XL: John Scott of Amwell 1710–1782', *The Book Collector*, 14 (1965), 350–60; Bentley 1977, no. 494; Easson and Essick 1979, no. XXIII.

X

Geoffrey Chaucer, *The Poetical Works*, vol. xiii (Edinburgh: Apollo Press, 1782 [1783]); *Fig. 26*

This edition of Chaucer's poems in fourteen volumes is part of John Bell's edition of the poets of Great Britain in 109 volumes, 1777–87, each with an engraved (as well as letterpress) title-page. Several of these title-plates, including the one in vol. xiii of the Chaucer, were designed by

Stothard. In some, presumably early, copies, this plate is signed by Blake as the engraver; in others, a different plate of the same design is signed '*Cooke Sculp!*' (probably the J. Cook who engraved other plates for Bell's series) and has an imprint dated 16 February 1787. Later issues of Bell's Poets contain Cooke's plate.

1. Bound as the first printed leaf in the volume, preceding the letterpress title-pages to the poet and to the individual volume; 10.7 × 6.5 cm. (border to border); *Fig. 26*

Title above design: BELL'S EDITION | The POETS of GREAT BRITAIN | *COMPLETE FROM* | CHAUCER to CHURCHILL.

Inscription below design: CHAUCER VOL XIII. | Sampson yhad experience | That Women were ful trew ifound | *In praise of Women L 81. 82.*

Signatures: *Stothard del* [left], *Blake Sculp!* [right]

Imprint: London Printed for John Bell British Library Strand May 24.ᵗʰ 1783.

The design illustrates a pseudo-Chaucerian ballad 'in the praise or rather dispreise of women for ther doublenes' (p. 106), lines 81–5 on p. 109 of this volume. Samson rests his head in Delilah's lap just after his locks were cut by the Philistines (Judges 16: 19). The stylized head with long hair above the vignette suggests Samson's earlier condition. Blake's second of two watercolours illustrating the story of Samson (*c.* 1800–3 (Butlin 1981, no. 455)) has some general compositional similarities with this plate in the placement, but not the postures, of the figures. 'Two states' of the plate are listed in *Examples of the English Pre-Raphaelite School of Painters ... Together with a Collection of the Works of William Blake* (Philadelphia: [Pennsylvania] Academy of the Fine Arts, 1892 exhibition catalogue), no. 202. Perhaps one of these 'states' was actually Cooke's re-engraving. A plate bearing the signatures of Stothard and Blake, showing a winged figure flying through clouds, may have been intended for Bell's Poets but never published (see Essick 1983, no. LII). For Blake's large engraving of 1810, 'Chaucers Canterbury Pilgrims', see Essick 1983, no. XVI.

Literature: Russell 1912, no. 51; Keynes 1921, no. 93; Bentley and Nurmi 1964, no. 358; Bentley 1977, no. 442; Easson and Essick 1979, no. XXIV.

XI

The Novelist's Magazine (London: Harrison and Co.). Vol. viii, engraved general title-pages of 1782 and 1792; typographic title-pages to *Don Quixote* of 1782, 1784, and 1792. Vol. ix, engraved general title-pages of 1782 and 1793; typographic title-pages to *A Sentimental Journey, The Adventures of David Simple*, and *The Adventures of Sir Launcelot Greaves* of 1782, 1785, 1787, and 1792. Vol. x, engraved general title-page of 1783; typographic title-pages to *Sir Charles Grandison* of 1783, 1785, 1793, and n.d. [*c.* 1800?]. Samuel Richardson, *The History of Sir Charles Grandison* (2 vols.; London: C. Cooke, n.d. [plates dated 1811]; vol. i only, London: T. Kelly, 1818. *Figs. 27–34*

All forty-nine plates in vols. viii–x of *The Novelist's Magazine* were designed by Stothard, of which eight were engraved by Blake. Proofs before all letters of pls. 1, 2, 3 (two impressions), 5–7 are in the BMPR. The various engraved and typographic title-pages, the former for each volume and the latter for each novel, appear in a bewildering number of combinations. The co-ordination between these and the first two states of each plate is recorded for each below, but it would not be surprising to find other combinations. The *Magazine* was issued in weekly parts *c.* 1780–8 and included approximately sixty novels in twenty-three volumes. See the Introduction for additional comments.

Third states of pls. 6–8 appear in the [1811] edition, and fourth states in at least some copies of the 1818 edition, of *Sir Charles Grandison*. These volumes have no connection with *The Novelist's Magazine* other than the use of plates originally executed for it. The existence of some of these states was first noted in Heppner 1977 (third state of pl. 6, and fourth of pls. 7–8, reproduced). Heppner (p. 101) and Bentley 1977–8 state that pl. 7 is a new copperplate, but close comparison of hatching patterns and accidental features in the border designs indicates that Blake's original pl. 7, like pls. 6 and 8, was extensively reworked and reprinted. Blake probably did not make these rather crude alterations.

1. Vol. viii (Cervantes, *Don Quixote*), facing p. 256 in copies with title-pages dated before 1792; 11.7 × 7.1 cm.; *Fig. 27*

Title: DON QUIXOTE

Signatures: *Stothard del.* [left], *Blake sculp.* [right]

Imprint: Published as the Act directs by Harrison & C⁰ May 4, 1782.

Plate number lower left: Plate IX.

Second State, facing p. 256 in copies with either title-page dated 1792. Further hatching and cross-hatching have been added to the clothing of all figures except the man looking back, far right. The face of the man holding the basin has been darkened with hatching and stipple. Wavy lines have been added to the sunburst in the top border.

Quixote, centre left, holds aloft Mambrino's barber's basin and proclaims it to be a knight's helmet. The curate stands to the left of Quixote, with other townspeople gathered about. Sancho Panza stands lower left.

2. Vol. viii (*Don Quixote*), facing p. 587 in copies with title-pages dated before 1792; 11.9 × 7.1 cm.; *Fig. 28*

Title: DON QUIXOTE

Signatures: *Stothard del.* [left], *Blake Sculp.* [right]

Imprint: Published as the Act directs, by Harrison & C⁰ June 15, 1782.

Plate number lower left: Plate XV.

Second State, facing p. 587 in copies with either title-page dated 1792. The cross-hatching (lower right only in the first state) has been extended across the entire floor. Crossing strokes have been added to the hatching on the bed curtain, upper left, to the pillows and the margin of the sheet where it falls over the side of the bed, and to the clothing of all figures except the man in the bed and the man second from the right. Wavy lines have been added to the sunburst in the top border.

Don Quixote lies stricken in his bed. The curate (third from right) has received Quixote's confession; the tearful Sancho (fourth from the right) and the notary (lower left) have entered the room. The housekeeper arranges Quixote's pillow, and behind her on the left is his niece. Quixote's now discarded armour hangs above the bed.

3. Vol. ix, facing p. 52 of Laurence Sterne's *Sentimental Journey* in copies with engraved title-page dated 1782; 11.6 × 7.1 cm.; *Fig. 29*

Title: SENTIMENTAL JOURNEY

Signatures: *Stothard del.* [left], *Blake Sculp.* [right]

Imprint: Published as the Act directs by Harrison & C⁰ July 6, 1782.

Plate number lower left: Plate II.

Second State, facing p. 52 of *Sentimental Journey* in copies

with engraved title-page dated 1793. Crossing strokes have been added to the hatching on the dancing man's right leg below the knee, the arm of the girl behind him, the shawl of the seated woman raising her left hand, and to the right arm and shoulder of the violinist. The dotted hatching on the seated woman's left knee has been recut as continuous lines. Wavy lines have been added to the sunburst in the top border.

The design illustrates Sterne's passing reference to the harvesting of grapes by the French peasantry, when 'Musick beats time to Labour' (p. 52). Yorick sits just left of the violinist.

4. Vol. ix, facing p. 66 of Sarah Fielding's *David Simple* in copies with engraved title-page dated 1782; 11.7 × 7.1 cm.; *Fig. 30*

Title: DAVID SIMPLE

Signatures: *Stothard del.* [left], *Blake Sculp.* [right]

Imprint: Published as the Act directs, by Harrison & C⁰ Aug. 10, 1782.

Plate number lower left: Plate I.

Second State, facing p. 66 of *David Simple* in copies with engraved title-page dated 1793. Patches of cross-hatching have been added to the foot of the bed, the pillow left of the man's head, and to the folds of the seated woman's dress below and to the left of her right elbow. Wavy lines have been added to the sunburst in the top border.

David Simple enters on the right to see 'a most moving scene' (p. 66) of abject poverty and misery—a sick young man being cared for by a young woman and dunned for the rent by the landlady. The walls are 'broken in many places' (p. 67).

5. Vol. ix, facing p. 45 of Tobias Smollett's *Sir Launcelot Greaves* in copies with engraved title-page dated 1782; 12 × 7.4 cm.; *Fig. 31*

Title: LAUNCELOT GREAVES

Signatures: *Stothard del.* [left], *Blake sculp.* [right]

Imprint: Published as the Act directs by Harrison & C⁰ Sep. 21, 1782.

Plate number lower left: Plate III.

Second State, facing p. 45 of *Sir Launcelot Greaves* in copies with engraved title-page dated 1793. Crossing strokes have been added to the thighs of the man far left, the right side of the back of the man second from the left, the left thigh of the central man lacking a right leg, and to the clothing of the three men right of the horse's head. A patch of cross-hatching now appears on the right elbow of the raised man on the left. Wavy lines have been added to the sunburst in the top border.

Sir Launcelot, in armour, has ridden into 'the midst of the multitude' assembled for the election campaign (p. 44). The flag reveals the last word of one of their slogans, 'Old England For Ever' (p. 43). On the left, one of the candidates, Mr Vanderpelft, has been 'hoisted . . . on the shoulders of four strong weavers' (p. 45) who prepare for battle with members of the other party on the right.

6. Vol. x of *The Novelist's Magazine* (Samuel Richardson's *Sir Charles Grandison*), facing p. 328 in copies with typographic title-page dated 1783 or 1785; 11.9 × 7.2 cm.; *Fig. 32*

Title: GRANDISON.

Signatures: *Stothard del.* [left], *Blake sculp.* [right]

Imprint: Published as the Act directs, by Harrison & Cº Apr. 5, 1783.—

Plate number lower left: Plate XXIII.

Second State, facing p. 328 in copies with typographic title-page dated 1793 or undated. A few crossing strokes have been added to the arms of the centre woman and to the left arm of the woman on the left. Wavy lines have been added to the sunburst in the top border.

Third State, vol. i, facing p. 173, [1811] edition of *Sir Charles Grandison* and some copies (e.g. McGill University, Montreal) of the 1818 edition. The imprint has been replaced by '*Printed for C. Cooke, Paternoster Row, July 6. 1811*', the left signature replaced by '*Scatchard del.*', and an additional title has been cut below the border: 'Letter 6. Vol. II.| *Miss Byron paying a visit to* | *Emily in her Chamber.*' The plate number lower left has been removed. The design has been reworked extensively. The hair on the left and central women has been piled on their heads in stylish coiffures without hats and their dresses altered to a neo-classical style with narrower skirts. A circle has been added below the lips of the head in the top border.

Fourth State, vol. i, facing p. 173, in some copies (e.g. RNE) of the 1818 edition of *Sir Charles Grandison*. The plate has been substantially reworked once again. The hat worn by the woman on the right no longer forms a peak above her forehead. The ribbon in the hair of the central figure has been eliminated and a decorative line has been added just above the hem of her apron. The dresses worn by the women left and centre have been given a scoop neck-line with a ruffle border. The carpet has been replaced by boards (left) and a small carpet next to the bed. A large swag has been added to the bed curtain, upper right, but the chinoiserie design on the back wall has been eliminated. Fine lines have been added between the bold hatching in the border. Vertical hatching has been added to the face in the top border.

Miss Byron is greeted by Emily, whose maid (right) has just opened the door.

7. Vol. x of *The Novelist's Magazine (Sir Charles Grandison)*, facing p. 351 in copies with typographic title-page dated 1783 or 1785; 11.8 × 7.2 cm.; *Fig. 33*

Title: GRANDISON

Signatures: *Stothard del.* [left], *Blake sculp.* [right]

Imprint: Published as the Act directs, by Harrison & Cº Dec. 7, 1782.

Plate number lower left: Plate VI.

Second State, facing p. 351 in copies with typographic title-page date 1793 or undated. Diagonal crossing strokes have been added to the woman's dress and to the wall between the left margin and the right hand of the combatant on the left. The hatching on his lower left leg has been darkened and extended to the knee. The dotted horizontal lines in the white cloud seen through the door have been made continuous. Wavy lines have been added to the sunburst in the top border.

Third State, vol. i, facing p. 193, [1811] edition of *Sir Charles Grandison*. The imprint has been replaced by '*Printed for C. Cooke, Paternoster Row, June 8, 1811.*', the left signature replaced by '*Scatchard del.*', and an additional title has been cut below the border: 'Letter 13. Vol. II.| *Sir Charles Grandison, discerning* | *Captain Salmonet.*' The plate number has been removed. The design has been radically altered, particularly the man on the left. His face, hair, and coat have been completely re-engraved. The coat now fits closely, without a tail flying to the left. The woman's hat has been changed to a bonnet and the raised sword is much longer.

Fourth State, vol. i, facing p. 193, 1818 edition of *Sir Charles Grandison*. The standing man's tricorn has been changed to a bicorn hat. The swirling pattern in the carpet has been changed to one composed of circles and diamonds.

Grandison (left) has drawn his sword and 'laid' Salmonet 'on the floor' (p. 351). Major O'Hara, sword drawn, waits for a chance against Grandison while Mrs Jervois begins to run 'into the hall' (p. 351).

8. Vol. x of *The Novelist's Magazine (Sir Charles Grandison)*, facing p. 442 in copies with typographic title-page dated 1783 or 1785; 11.7 × 7.3 cm.; *Fig. 34*

Title: GRANDISON

Signatures: *Stothard del.* [left], *Blake sculp* [right]

Imprint: Published as the Act directs by Harrison & Cº Jan. 18, 1783.

Plate number lower left: Plate XII.

Second State, facing p. 442 in copies with typographic title-page dated 1792 or undated. Patches of cross-hatching have been added to the skirt folds, right shoulder, and hat of the woman in the centre. The hatching on the right woman's breast has been strengthened.

Third State, vol. i, facing p. 217, [1811] edition of *Sir Charles Grandison*. Fragments of the original imprint remain, but it has been replaced by '*Printed for C. Cooke, Paternoster Row June 1. 1811.*' The plate number has been removed and the left signature changed to '*Stothard R. A. del.*' An additional title has been cut below the border: 'Letter.

19. Vol II.|*Charlotte and Caroline's affecting interview with*|*their Brother Sir Charles Grandison.*'

Fourth State, vol. i, facing p. 217, 1818 edition of *Sir Charles Grandison*. The man's coat and the women's dresses have been narrowed and the women's snoods changed to turban-like hats. The bodice worn by the woman on the right has been changed to a simple collar and the cross has been eliminated.

Grandison enters. Clementina, holding a book, rises, while the Marchioness turns away, 'holding her handkerchief at her eyes' (p. 442). In the [1811] and 1818 editions of *Grandison* the plate is used to illustrate an earlier episode, as the title added in the third state indicates.

Literature: Gilchrist 1863, i. 32, ii. 259; Russell 1912, no. 49; Keynes 1921, no. 92; Bentley and Nurmi 1964, nos. 395–7; Bentley 1977, nos. 485–7; Christopher Heppner, 'Notes on Some Items in the Blake Collection at McGill with a Few Speculations around William Roscoe', *Blake Newsletter*, 10 (1977), 100–8; G. E. Bentley, jun., 'A Supplement to *Blake Books*', *Blake: An Illustrated Quarterly*, 11 (1977–8), 149–50; Easson and Essick 1979, no. XXII; Essick 1980, pp. 46–9.

XII

Lodovico Ariosto, *Orlando Furioso*, trans. John Hoole (5 vols.: London: For the Author, 1783; London: George Nicol, 1785; 2 vols.: London: J. Dodsley, 1791; 5 vols.: London: Otridge and Son, Vernor and Hood, *et al.*, 1799); *Figs. 35–6*

Of the six plates in these editions, Blake engraved one after Stothard. John Hoole (1727–1803), translator and dramatist, was a friend of Samuel Johnson and John Scott (see **IX**). In a letter of 26 November 1800 to William Hayley, Blake states that he is 'absorbed' in the study of several poets, including 'Ariosto' (E 714, K 806). This activity was probably in preparation for painting eighteen portrait panels of famous authors as decorations for Hayley's library, but Ariosto was not included in the series.

1. Vol. iii, facing p. 164 (1783 and 1785 edns.); 15.3 × 10.9 cm.; *Fig. 35*

Inscriptions above design: *Vol. 3.* [left], *Page 164* [right]

Signatures: *Stothard del.* [left], *Blake sc* [right]

Second State, vol. i, facing p. 461 (1791 edn.). The inscriptions above the design have been changed to '*Vol. I.*' (left) and '*facing Page 461*' (right).

Third State, vol. iii, facing p. 164, 1799 edition. The central figure's face has been smoothed with stippled hatching, his beard has been highlighted with burnishing, and hatching now shades the cloth where it falls over his right thigh. Flicks have been added between the crossing strokes on the horse's neck. The rock lower left and the foliage left of the central figure's right knee have been darkened. The inscriptions above the design have been removed and a new one cut upper right, '*Vol. 3. Page 164.*' An imprint has been added: '*Published by Vernor & Hood, Dec.*' *1. 1798.*'

Orlando, in his fury, casts off his armour and weapons and 'a lofty pine up-tears'. In the background, two 'rustic swains . . . the wonder view' (p. 164). Stothard's pen-and-wash preliminary drawing, 15.1 × 10.7 cm., is in the LC (*Fig. 36*). The plate reverses the image, darkens Orlando's beard slightly, and adds much larger roots to the pine. Bentley 1977, p. 513, records a 'proof' in the Royal Academy, London, but the two impressions I have been able to locate in that collection are in the first published state. Some unbound impressions of the first state (New York Public Library; Pierpont Morgan Library, New York; RNE) are on sheets (up to 27.7 × 20.5 cm.) considerably larger than those found in uncut copies of the first edition (approx. 22.8 × 14.3 cm.).

Literature: Gilchrist 1863, ii. 260 (1791 edn. only); Russell 1912, no. 53; Keynes 1921, no. 96; Bentley and Nurmi 1964, no. 335; Bentley 1977, no. 417; Easson and Essick 1979, no. XXV; Essick 1980, pp. 50–1.

XIII

Thomas Henry, *Memoirs of Albert de Haller* (Warrington: J. Johnson, 1783); *Fig. 37*

The only plate is the frontispiece, a portrait of the Swiss physiologist Albrecht von Haller (1708–77), signed by Blake as the engraver. Thomas Henry (1734–1816) was a surgeon and chemist, a friend of Joseph Priestley, and an occasional member of the Joseph Johnson circle. In a letter of 13 April 1783 to Johnson, Henry refers to the progress of Blake's engraving: 'Pray hasten the head of Haller—The Book is finished, and very neat; and the Season is advancing rapidly' (Bentley 1977, p. 580). Bentley 1988, p. 1, suggests that this delay, and perhaps others, may have been the cause of Johnson doing without Blake's services as a copy engraver between 1783 and 1788.

This and other medical texts for which Blake engraved plates (**XXV, XXIX**) may have influenced the physiological imagery in his poetry. Henry's praise of Haller's 'inquiries into the laws by which man is formed' and how he 'beheld the arteries and veins unfold themselves' (pp. 54, 64) touches on subjects Blake presents in his account of the creation of the human body in *The Book of Urizen* (1794).

1. Frontispiece; circle, 5.8 cm. diameter; *Fig. 37*
Signatures: *Dunker. d* [left], *Blake. sc* [right]
Title: ALBERT DE HALLER.

I have not been able to trace the original portrait by the Swiss artist Balthasar Anton Dunker (1746–1807), but Blake very probably worked from an engraved copy, such as the one executed by Christian Geyser for the *Almanach der deutschen Musen* (1776) or the one published in Haller's *Poesies* (Paris, 1775).

Literature: *Exhibition of the Works of William Blake* (London: Burlington Fine Arts Club, 1876), no. 271 (first attribution of the plate to Blake); Russell 1912, no. 54; Keynes 1921, no. 95; Bentley and Nurmi 1964, no. 381; Bentley 1977, no. 472; Easson and Essick 1979, no. XXVI.

XIV

Joseph Ritson, *A Select Collection of English Songs* (3 vols.; London: J. Johnson, 1783); *Figs. 38–46*

Seven of the seventeen plates are signed by Blake as the engraver and Stothard as the designer. Unsigned pls. 3 and 4 are attributed to both on the basis of proofs noted for each below. Two other unsigned plates in the first volume, the frontispiece (based on a design by Fuseli) and p. 107, may have been executed by Blake, although James Heath, whose name appears in the plate on p. 77 of vol. ii, might also be their engraver. Gilchrist 1863, i. 51–2, praises the 'Blake-like feeling and conception' of these designs, particularly pls. 2 and 7 and 'one at the head of the *Love Songs*, a Lady singing, Cupids fluttering before her'. Several plates serve as headpieces to groups of love songs, but none fits Gilchrist's description. In the 1813 edition, revised by Thomas Park, unsigned wood engravings were substituted for the first-edition plates.

Ritson (1752–1803) was a leading anthologizer of regional verse and early English poetry. He was known to several members of the Joseph Johnson circle, including William Godwin, and was active in a number of political and literary disputes in the 1780s and 1790s.

1. Vol. i, p. 1, headpiece to 'Love-Songs. Class I'; 6.3 × 8.7 cm.; *Fig. 38*
Signatures: *Stothard del* [left], *Blake sc* [right]
This scene of a supplicant lover and a decidedly disdainful lady does not illustrate any specific passage but would appear to represent the whole first section of love songs. Unrequited love is a central theme in most of the poems in this group.

2. Vol. i, p. 85, tailpiece to 'Love-Songs. Class I'; 6.3 × 8.6 cm.; *Fig. 39*
Signatures: *Stothard del* [left], *Blake sc* [right]
The design illustrates John Gay's 'Song LXV' from his *What d'ye Call It* (1715), here printed on pp. 73–4. A 'damsel' sits on a 'rock' and casts 'a wistful look' towards the sea, hoping for the return of her lover. Instead, 'his floating corpse she spied'. Stothard drew several other designs showing distressed figures beside the sea, a theme Blake also pictured on pls. 1, 7, and 11 of *Visions of the Daughters of Albion* (1793) and pl. 38 of *Milton* (c. 1804–8). For another floating corpse, see *The Marriage of Heaven and Hell* (c. 1790–3), pl. 11, lower left. Gilchrist 1863, i. 52, and Russell 1912, p. 144, claim that this plate is based on the story of Hero and Leander, but that is true only in the sense that Gay's poem may have been influenced by that tale. An impression on a paper card, thicker than the paper used in the book and lacking the verso text, is in the RNE collection.

3. Vol. i, p. 86, headpiece to 'Love-Songs. Class II'; 6.3 × 8.5 cm.; *Fig. 40*
Cupid plays a lyre for four women, perhaps Venus (seated) and the Graces. The design has no specific textual reference, although Cupid and Venus are mentioned in the first song in the group, Dryden's 'Address to Britain'. The attribution is based on a proof in the BMPR, signed in the plate 'Stothard d.' (lower left) and 'Blake sc.' (lower right). An earlier proof in the collection of G. E. Bentley, jun., has a line border removed from later states, lacks the signatures (added in ink), and lacks the flick work on the tree trunk, the hatching on the drapery on the seated woman's shoulder, and some of the hatching strokes on the

dresses, shoulders, and faces of the two women furthest to the right.

4. Vol. i, p. 108, headpiece to 'Love-Songs. Class III'; 5.9 × 8.2 cm.; *Fig. 41*

A youth and a lady part. Her left glove and necklace lie on the ground, and she (or perhaps the man) has just discarded a letter. The ruined tower on the right suggests the condition of their love. This scene of parting generally accords with several poems in the group, including Thomas Carew's 'Disdain Returned', beginning just below the plate, but none mentions a glove, necklace, or letter. The attribution is based on a proof in the BMPR, signed in the plate '*Stothard del*' (lower left) and '*Blake sc*' (lower right).

5. Vol. i, p. 156, tailpiece to 'Love-Songs. Class III'; 6.3 × 8.6 cm.; *Fig. 42*

Signatures: *Stothard del.* [left], *Blake sc.* [right]

Swains and maidens dance around a maypole to the tune of a violinist, lower right. The design may have been prompted by 'Song XXXVII. The Country Wedding' (pp. 145–6), set in May but lacking any reference to a maypole or violin. Bindman 1977, p. 60, suggests the influence of this design on Blake's headpiece to 'The Ecchoing Green' in *Songs of Innocence* (1789); the similarities seem slight to me.

6. Vol. i, p. 157, headpiece to 'Love-Songs. Class IV'; 6.1 × 8.6 cm.; *Fig. 43*

Signatures: *Stothard del.* [left], *Blake sc.* [right]

A cupid holds a lamp for a lady writing. A full moon shines through an open doorway. The design has no specific textual reference, but befits the mood of this group of songs spoken by or about lovelorn women.

7. Vol. i, p. 170, tailpiece to 'Love-Songs. Class IV'; 6.2 × 8.6 cm.; *Fig. 44*

Signatures: *Stothard del.* [left], *Blake sc.* [right]

A melancholy woman holds a large stone, or perhaps a skull, in her right hand. This figure, particularly if she holds a skull, suggests portrayals of the repentant Magdalen. Behind her is a large open book. Two cupids sport in the air, one with a bow, the other with a torch. The design may have been prompted by Mary Jones's 'The Lass of the Hill', pp. 168–70, whose lover has betrayed her. However, only one 'Cupid' is mentioned in that poem, and 'the lass on the brow of the hill' (p. 170) has no stone, skull, or book. Butlin 1981, no. 257, calls attention to the parallels between the cupids in this plate and the two figures on the left in Blake's *The Good and Evil Angels*, first executed as a watercolour

c. 1793–4. Wilton 1973–4, pp. 62–3, claims a relationship between these same cupids and those flanking the central vignette in Blake's design for a fan of *c.* 1795 (Butlin 1981, no. 223A verso).

8. Vol. i, p. 171, headpiece to 'Love-Songs. Class V'; 6.2 × 8.7 cm.; *Fig. 45*

Signatures: *Stothard del.* [left], *Blake sc.* [right]

A youth addresses a lady in an arbour and points with his right hand toward a distant (church?) steeple. The design serves as a general emblem for this section of poems, most of which are professions of constancy and devotion, but a few specific passages may have influenced the composition. In 'Song I' by Barton Booth, the lover proclaims that his love will be eternal, even though time will devour 'marble tow'rs' (p. 172). In 'Song XLV' by Mary Whateley, the lover invites his lady into an 'artless maple bower, | With blooming woodbines twin'd' (p. 221).

9. Vol. ii, p. 1, headpiece to 'Drinking Songs'; 6.2 × 8.7 cm.; *Fig. 46*

Signatures: *Stothard del.* [left], *Blake sc.* [right]

Six men drink at a table; one lifts his glass to make a toast. The design represents the genre of this section, but may take a specific cue for the toast-making from 'Song I. The Honest Fellow', p. 2. Blake's design for 'Laughing Song' in *Songs of Innocence* (1789) pictures a generally similar scene of figures arranged around a table drinking. The raised goblet and plumed hat of the central figure in Stothard's design are given to a standing man, seen from the back, in Blake's illustration. This is one of the clearest examples of Blake borrowing from another artist's design he had engraved.

Literature: Gilchrist 1863, i. 51–2, ii. 359; Russell 1912, no. 55; Keynes 1921, no. 97; Bentley and Nurmi 1964, no. 401; Andrew Wilton, 'A Fan Design by Blake', *Blake Newsletter*, 7 (1973–4), 60–3; Bentley 1977, no. 491; Bindman 1977 (see **III**, *Literature*), pp. 59–60; Easson 1978 (see Introduction, n. 28), 44–5; Easson and Essick 1979, no. XXVII; Essick 1980, pp. 46, 139.

XV

John Seally and Israel Lyons, *A Complete Geographical Dictionary* (2 vols.; London: John Fielding, *c.* 1784; London: Scatcherd and Whitaker, 1787). Michael Adams, *The New Royal Geographical Magazine* (London: Alexander Hogg, *c*. 1793). Adams, *The New Royal System of Universal Geography* (London: Hogg, *c*. 1794). *Figs. 47–9*

Three of the thirty-two plates of 'views' in the first edition of Seally and Lyons bear 'Blake' signatures very lightly scratched into the copper (and thus not clearly visible in the present reproductions). The engraver's prototypes were probably prints in some other geographical study, but I have not been able to trace such a source. The plates are Blake's least proficient—far less skilled than his work of about the same time for *The Novelist's Magazine*, Ariosto, and Ritson (**XI, XII, XIV**). The poor quality makes one suspect that these plates were executed by some other 'Blake', but perhaps a small fee determined the technique. Each view simply decorates the text's description of the city named on the plate. All the publications containing these prints were originally issued in weekly parts. The Seally and Lyons volumes are not paginated. The presence of the reworked plates in Adams's two titles (the latter a reissue of the former) was first reported in Essick 1984, pp. 133–8. Blake's plates are listed by Adams as nos. 6, 19, and 42 in the 'Directions to the Binders'.

1. Vol. ii, illustrating the article on Lyons in Seally and Lyons (both edns.); 14.2 × 20.2 cm.; *Fig. 47*

Scratched signature lower right between design and border: *Blake sc*
Title: *Lyons.*
Imprint: *Publish'd May 4 1782 by J. Fielding, N.º 23 Paternoster Row.*

Second State, facing p. 857 in Adams, *New Royal Geographical Magazine*. The imprint has been removed and the title changed to '*View of Lyons, in France*'. The low hills, near side of the river on the right, have been cross-hatched on their right sides. The clump of trees below and to the left of the left hillock has been partly darkened with horizontal hatching. The shadowed area below these hills has been darkened with diagonal strokes. Small patches of cross-hatching have been added to some of the smaller buildings. Blake's signature has been removed—or has simply worn off the plate. The thin border line below the signature has been strengthened, perhaps to repair inadvertent damage caused during removal of the signature.

Third State, facing p. 857 in Adams, *New Royal System of Universal Geography*. Cross-hatching has been added over the sketchy lines indicating vegetation in the centre and right foreground (particularly evident below the short tree stump). The shady areas on the far side of the river, and many roofs on the near side, have been darkened with cross-hatching. Reproduced in Essick 1984, p. 135.

2. Vol. ii, illustrating the article on Osnaburg in Seally and Lyons (both edns.); 14.5 × 21.4 cm.; *Fig. 48*

Scratched signature lower right between design and border: *Blake sc*
Title: *Osnaburg in Westphalia.*
Imprint: *Published Jan.º 12, 1782, by I. Fielding, N.º 23, Pater-noster Row.*

Second State, facing p. 745 in Adams, *New Royal Geographical Magazine*. Imprint removed. Blake's signature has been erased from the plate—or simply worn off.

Third State, facing p. 745 in Adams, *New Royal System of Universal Geography*. Hatching and cross-hatching have been added to the shaded sides of many roofs. The most easily observed revision appears on the city wall to the left of the archway leading to it, about 2.5 cm. above the horse and cart in the foreground. Horizontal crossing strokes have been added to the vertical hatching in this area and to the right side of the tower immediately to the left. Reproduced in Essick 1984, p. 137.

3. Vol. ii, illustrating the article on Presburg in Seally and Lyons (both edns.); 15.3 × 21.1 cm.; *Fig. 49*

Scratched signature lower right between design and border: *Blake sc*
Title: *Presburg in Hungary.*
Imprint: *Published April 6, 1782, by I. Fielding, N.º 23, Pater-noster Row.*

Second State, facing p. 765 in Adams, both titles. The imprint has been removed, although small fragments of it are still visible in some impressions. A faint shadow of Blake's signature remains.

Literature: Bentley and Nurmi 1964, no. 405; Bentley 1977, no. 495; Easson and Essick 1979, no. XXVIII; Robert N. Essick, 'Some Unrecorded States, Printings, and Impressions of Blake's Graphic Works', *Blake: An Illustrated Quarterly*, 17 (1984), 130–8.

XVI

The Wit's Magazine, vol. 1 (London: Harrison & Co., 1784); *Figs. 50–6*

Blake engraved five folding frontispiece designs for the January through May issues of the magazine, the only plate in each. The first, engraved after Stothard, is found in two versions printed from two different copperplates. The first plate may have been damaged during printing or lost, thereby necessitating the production of a second. An alternative explanation is suggested by the fact that pl. 1B, found in most copies examined, is much closer in graphic style to the other plates. Perhaps it was created as the substitute for the sake of this pictorial compatibility with its companions. This sequence is also suggested by the fact that pl. 1A follows Stothard's preliminary drawing much more closely. Pls. 2–5 were designed by the caricaturist Samuel Collings, known to be active only during the 1780s. The title-pages for the February through May issues note 'a Large Quarto Engraving ... [title and/or text illustrated] ... designed by Mr. Samuel Collings, and engraved by Mr. W. Blake, purposely for this Work'. Collings also wrote the poem illustrated by pl. 5. According to an advertisement on the back wrapper for the November 1784 issue, separate hand-coloured impressions of the plates were available (6*d*. each), as well as copies of the monthly issues with two impressions, one coloured and one plain (1*s*.). The only hand-coloured impressions I have seen are crude examples probably tinted at a later date.

Thomas Holcroft (1745–1809), the dramatist who in the 1790s became a member of the pro-revolutionary Society for Constitutional Information and was indicted for treason, edited the first four issues of the magazine. Schorer 1946 suggests that, since Holcroft's editorship coincides with Blake's participation, except for the month of May, Holcroft may have been responsible for hiring Blake. It is also possible that Blake's friendship with Stothard played a crucial role in gaining the initial commission for the January issue. Gilchrist 1863, i. 92, states that Blake met Holcroft in the early 1790s when both were part of the Joseph Johnson circle, but it seems likely that Blake would have met the editor of a work for which he was engraving plates in 1784. In December 1807 Holcroft received from R. H. Cromek the promise of a copy of Robert Blair's *The Grave* (1808) with Blake's illustrations in partial payment for a manuscript (Bentley 1969, p. 576). Holcroft's name also appears in the list of subscribers in the book.

The Wit's Magazine may have influenced Blake's own excursion into social satire, *An Island*

in the Moon of *c*. 1784–5. A brief essay in the August 1784 issue, pp. 294–5, entitled 'Expedition to the Moon' and signed with the initial 'C', explores the same vein of British humour and attacks some of the same intellectual pretensions as Blake's farce (see Essick 1989).

These are the only caricature prints engraved by Blake. The graphic style is appropriately broad and rugged, particularly in the barnyard scene of pl. 2. In August 1799 Blake wrote to John Trusler that 'I percieve that your Eye is perverted by Caricature Prints, which ought not to abound so much as they do. Fun I love but too much Fun is of all things the most loathsom' (E 702, K 793; see also the letter to Cumberland of 26 Aug. 1799, E 704, K 975). Blake may have felt that the great rage for caricature prints in the 1790s was a hindrance to the sale of his own original graphic works.

1A. Frontispiece (Jan. issue), one of two alternative plates of the same design; 17.5 × 22.8 cm.; *Fig. 50*
Signatures: *Stothard del.* [left], *Blake sculp.* [right]
Title: THE TEMPLE OF MIRTH.
Imprint: Published as the Act directs, by Harrison & C? Feb? 1. 1784.

Second State. Heavy cross-hatching now darkens the floor, lower left. The wall on each side of the boy's right leg, lower left, has been cross-hatched. Further crossing strokes have been added to the coat-tail of the man seated below Mirth (centre), to the middle of the right sleeve of the man to the right of Mirth, and to the lower reaches of the woman immediately to the right of this man. The lettering under the two busts on the right has been recut in darker block letters ('FIELD[ING]' illegible in the first state). Reproduced, and described as the only state, in Easson and Essick 1979. Both states were published with the magazine (RNE copy, first state; BMPR copy, second state).

A female personification of Mirth reigns over the jovial company. She holds a book in her left hand—*The Wit's Magazine* perhaps? Portraits of comic figures decorate the back wall: Don Quixote and Sancho Panza on the left, probably Falstaff on the right. Busts of comic writers reside in niches on the side walls. From left to right on the left wall are 'VOLT[AIRE]', 'STERN[E]', and an unnamed wit; 'RABEL[AIS]', 'FIELD[ING]', and another (unnamed) are on the right, reading right to left. Although the assembled children and adults may be the 'family of Wit' mentioned in the 'Preface', p. iv, the design functions less as an illustration of any specific passage than as an introductory emblem for the genre of the whole. The 'Contents' page notes that the issue contains 'a Large Quarto Engraving of the Temple of Mirth, designed by Stothard, and engraved by Blake, purposely for this Work'. Stothard's preliminary pen-and-watercolour drawing, 18.1 × 22.9 cm., is now in the National Gallery of Canada, Ottawa (*Fig. 51*). Other than the reversal of right and left, Blake's pl. 1A follows the drawing closely. The names under the busts centre right and far left in the drawing match those in pl. 1A; the other names are illegible. A proof in the BMPR lacks all letters.

1B. Frontispiece (Jan. issue), one of two alternative plates of the same design; 17.1 × 22.7 cm.; *Fig. 52*

Signatures: as on pl. 1A, but in smaller letters.
Title: as on pl. 1A.
Imprint: as on pl. 1A, but without the comma between 'directs' and 'by'.

The design is basically the same as pl. 1A, but with many small differences in the relative sizes of figures, their placement, and expressions. The foremost woman on the right wears a dress with vertical stripes in this plate; a watch fob now dangles from the waistcoat of the man closest to the viewer on the left. An open pamphlet rests on the left thigh of the man seated below Mirth. There is only a single man, rather than two, behind the man wearing a black hat on the left. The tops of the niches in the walls end in arches close to each bust rather than extending to the top margin. The man second from Mirth on the right has straight hair, not a wig, and his hand touching his chin is no longer present. In all these respects, pl. 1A is closer to Stothard's drawing (*Fig. 51*). The position of Don Quixote's horse in the painting on the left back wall, and the circular decorations on the floor rather than plain boards, also indicate that pl. 1B strays a good deal further from the drawing than does pl. 1A. The names under the busts on the left wall now read, left to right, 'STERNE', 'SWIFT', and 'VO[LTAIRE]'. Phillips 1987 identifies the unnamed bust on the right wall as Pope, on the basis of unstated (physiognomic?) evidence. There are proofs before signatures in the LC (imprint area trimmed off) and HEH (title and imprint areas trimmed off). Bentley 1977, p. 634, records a proof in the RNE collection, but there is none.

2. Frontispiece (Feb. issue); 16.3 × 21.9 cm.; *Fig. 53*

Signatures: *Collings del.* [left], *Blake sculp.* [right]
Title: TYTHE IN KIND; OR THE SOW'S REVENGE.

Imprint: Publish'd as the Act directs, by Harrison & C.º March 1. 1784.

The plate illustrates a poem, 'Tythe in Kind; or, the Sow's Revenge. A Tale', signed 'F—', pp. 71–2. The vicar has come to collect his tythe, a new piglet. The sow objects to his pursuit of one of her young and pulls him down into 'the mire'. Farmer Hodge, his wife, and children look on in amusement; the man coming into the sty (to rescue the vicar?) is not mentioned in the text. Although playful, the poem has an antiprelatical tone.

3. Frontispiece (Mar. issue); 15.7 × 21.1 cm.; *Fig. 54*

Signatures: *Collings del.* [left], *Blake sculp.* [right]
Title: THE DISCOMFITED DUELLISTS.
Imprint: Published as the Act directs, by Harrison & C.º April 1, 1784.

The plate illustrates an essay, 'Preservative Against Duelling', signed 'H—' (Holcroft?), pp. 89–92. Two 'young fellows, both ensigns in the army' have insulted the 'young woman … officiating in the bar' (p. 89) of a coffee house and caused a disturbance. The author–speaker of the essay, second from left, has 'snatched … the poker from the fire', destroyed one of the ensign's swords, and driven 'him to the wall' (p. 90). The other ensign, his sword drawn, approaches our hero from behind, but is held back by other patrons. The map of the 'Pacifico Ocean' on the back wall comments ironically on the rowdy proceedings. The story has a mildly anti-military bias.

4. Frontispiece (Apr. issue); 16.7 × 21.4 cm.; *Fig. 55*

Signatures: *Collings del.* [left], *Blake sculp.* [right]
Title: THE BLIND BEGGARS HATS.
Imprint: Published as the Act directs, by Harrison & C.º May 1. 1784.

The plate illustrates a poem, 'The Beggars Hats; or, the Way to Get Rich. A Tale. By Mr. Holcroft', pp. 151–3. A statue of the Virgin stands on the left side of a square in Florence, ready to receive prayers and money from the faithful. Two blind beggars, who feign to be lame for added profit, have had their hats, wherein they hid their money, stolen by the 'Signior' who skulks away in the background. The beggars begin to fight, each thinking the other the thief. The Christ child in the statue's arms, the dogs, and the three people in the building on the right are not mentioned in the text. The poem is crudely anti-Catholic.

5. Frontispiece (May issue); 15.9 × 21.1 cm.; *Fig. 56*

Signatures: *Collings del.* [left], *Blake sculp.* [right]

Title: MAY-DAY in LONDON.
Imprint: Publish'd as the Act directs, by Harrison & C⁰ June 1. 1784.

The plate illustrates a poem, 'May-Day. An Epistle from Sammy Sarcasm in Town, to his Aunt in the Country. By Mr. Collings', p. 191. The residents and street vendors of Milk Street, Cheapside, celebrate the first of May. Two revellers carry 'pots and platters' on their heads. Three 'milk-maids' dance to a song by 'their Minstrel, blind, legless, that struts in the middle, | And tortures to discord a broken–back'd fiddle'. 'A group of young Clergy' (i.e. the street urchins left of the musician and in the right foreground) 'are hopping between; | With just as much wig as to make them look arch'. Two chimney 'sweeps' (a London type important to Blake's poems about them in *Songs of Innocence* and *Songs of Experience*) prance lower left. Collings refers to his 'Sketch' (with a footnote added, 'See the Print') as a further description of the festival. This is one of the few examples from the late eighteenth century, other than Blake's illuminated books, in which the same person designed and wrote an interdependent text and illustration. Russell 1912, p. 147, states that 'Mr Rimmell (of Shaftesbury Avenue) has Collings' original drawing for this plate'. This is probably the drawing recorded by the Art Gallery of New South Wales, Sidney, as being in its collection, although the curator has not yet been able to track it down.

Literature: Gilchrist 1863, i. 53–4, ii. 259; Russell 1912, no. 58; Keynes 1921, no. 98; Mark Schorer, *William Blake: The Politics of Vision* (New York: Holt, 1946), 158; Bentley and Nurmi 1964, no. 420; Bentley 1977, no. 513; Easson and Essick 1979, no. XXIX; Essick 1983, no. LX; Michael Phillips (ed.), *An Island in the Moon* (Cambridge: Cambridge Univ. Press, 1987), 16; Robert N. Essick, review of Phillips 1987, *Huntington Library Quarterly*, 52 (1989), 139–42.

XVII

Daniel Fenning and Joseph Collyer, *A New System of Geography*, ed. Frederick Hervey (2 vols.; London: J. Johnson and G. and T. Wilkie, 1785–6, 1787); *Figs. 57–8*

One of the forty-four plates in the 1785–6 edition is signed by Blake as the engraver (pl. 2). Pl. 1 is tentatively attributed to Blake on the basis of the evidence cited below. Some copies of earlier editions of the book have Blake's pl. 2 inserted (see Bentley 1977, pp. 555–6).

1. Frontispiece to vol. i (1785–6 edn.); 17.5 × 12.4 cm.; *Fig. 57*

Inscription above border: *Engraved for Hervey's New System of Geography.*
Inscription in top border: *FRONTISPIECE* | VOL. I.
Title: *ASIA and AFRICA | Characterised by a representation of their | Various Inhabitants.*
Imprint: *Published June 6.ᵗʰ 1784; by G. Wilkie, S.ᵗ Pauls Church Yard.*

Second State, 1787 edition. The date in the imprint has been changed to '*July 16.ᵗʰ 1787*' and the semi-colon after the year changed to a comma.

The attribution of this unsigned plate to Blake is based on a proof of the central design only in the BMPR, reproduced in *Blake Newsletter*, 5 (1972), 241. It is inscribed in pencil (by Robert Balmanno?) '*Stothard del.*' (left), '*Blake sc*' (right), and '*The four quarters of the World. Frontispiece to a system of Geography—1779*'. At the very least, the date is wrong, for there seems to be no 1779 edition of Fenning and Collyer. Gilchrist 1863, i. 32, claims, probably on the basis of this same proof, that Blake executed 'a well-engraved frontispiece after Stothard, bold and telling in light and shade ("The four Quarters of the Globe"), to a *System of Geography* (1779)'. The list of engravings in Gilchrist 1863, ii. 259, titles this plate 'Asia and Africa', thereby indicating that Gilchrist was referring in vol. i to the Fenning and Collyer illustration. It is difficult to support this attribution on the basis of stylistic evidence. Only the modest claim that the graphic technique is compatible with Blake's more refined style of the 1780s seems certain. The lion, although attributed to Stothard as the designer, bears some similarity to the equally tame lion in Blake's second plate of 'The Little Girl Lost', first published in *Songs of Innocence* (1789). The only impression of the first state I have been able to locate (BL, reproduced here) is damaged lower left. The plate serves as a general frontispiece to the first volume, a companion to the representations of Europe and America pictured in the frontispiece to vol. ii.

2. Vol. i, facing p. 583 (1785 edn.); 20.5 × 17.4 cm.; *Fig. 58*

Inscription above design: *Engraved for Hervey's New System of Geography.* | *Vol. I. page 583.*
Inscriptions within design: see *Fig. 58*.
Scratched signature: *Blake Sc* [right]

Imprint: *Publish'd April 16.th 1785 by G. & T. Wilkie, St Pauls Church Yard.*

Number lower right: N.° 16.

Second State, vol. i, facing p. 583 (1787 edn.). The year in the imprint has been changed to '*1787*'.

The plate illustrates several natives mentioned in the narrative of Captain James Cook's third voyage through the Pacific. The chest of the man lower left shows the ritual scarring described on p. 577. The central portrait is referred to on p. 583: 'See the print of Poulaho with one of these feathered head-dresses.' The top two portraits are similarly mentioned on p. 599: 'See the prints of a man and woman of this Sound, taken from Mr. Webber's drawings.' This note indicates that these two vignettes were based on designs by John Webber (1752–98), the official artist on Cook's third voyage. All the portraits in Blake's plate are in fact copied from engravings of Webber's designs in James Cook [and James King], *A Voyage to the Pacific Ocean* (London: G. Nicol and T. Cadell, 1784), pls. 6, 7 (two vignettes at the bottom of Blake's plate), 18 (centre vignette), 46, 47 (two top vignettes). All but the portrait top left are reversed in Blake's plate. For reproductions of the 1784 plates and the drawings on which they were based, see Rüdiger Joppien and Bernard Smith, *The Art of Captain Cook's Voyages* (New Haven: Yale Univ. Press, 1988), iii. 270–3, 275, 314–15, 473–5, 480–3.

Literature: Gilchrist 1863, i. 32, ii. 259; Russell 1912, no. 43; Keynes 1921, nos. 86, 99; Bentley and Nurmi 1964, no. 366; Bentley 1977, no. 455; Easson and Essick 1979, no. XXX.

XVIII

John Caspar Lavater, *Aphorisms on Man* (London: J. Johnson, 1788, 1789, 1794); *Figs. 59–60*

The frontispiece, the only plate in the volume, was engraved by Blake after a design by Fuseli, who also translated the aphorisms from the German. Fuseli had been a close associate of Lavater's, the Zurich poet, preacher, and physiognomist (1741–1801), in the early 1760s. For Blake's long association with Fuseli, see the Introduction and the records in Bentley 1969.

1. Frontispiece (1788 and 1789 edns.); 12 × 7.4 cm.; *Fig. 59*

Signature: *Blake. sc* [right]

Second State, some copies (e.g. HEH, LC, RNE) of the 1794

edition. Crossing strokes have been added on the fore-edge of the book's leaves, lower right, and on the floor just to the left of the hourglass. The cross-hatchings on the sky-borne figure's neck, and on the cloud below the lower right corner of the tablet, have been extended upwards a few millimetres.

Third State, some copies (e.g. BL, RNE) of the 1794 edition. The crossing strokes on the floor have been extended to the left edge of the image. Cross-hatching now appears on the side of the bench on which the man sits (just right of his right ankle), on the lower edge of the man's left forearm and on both legs (particularly evident from ankle to knee), across the upper portion of his left hip, and on the right side of his chest. The many fine hatching lines on his left shoulder (first state) have been replaced by fewer and bolder strokes. A series of horizontal crossing strokes have been cut in the man's cloak just to the right of his right calf.

The second and third states appear with about equal frequency in copies of the 1794 edition. It is possible that copies with the third state are a slightly later printing, but there is no physical evidence for this. The second state was first identified in Essick 1988, where all three states are reproduced. Bentley 1977, p. 593, refers to 'proofs . . . in three different states' in the LC, but these would appear to be two impressions of the first state, and one of the second, with slight differences in wear and inking. A 'proof' was sold as part of a large collection of Blake's engravings, Sotheby's, 9 December 1905, lot 921 no. 46 (to 'Paul'), and again on 15 December 1906, lot 428 no. 46 (to 'Abbey'). Another 'proof' is listed in the *Catalogue of Books, Engravings Water-Colors & Sketches of William Blake* (Grolier Club, New York, 1905), no. 68, but this seems unlikely since the impression is bound in a copy of the 1794 edition. The same frontispiece design appears in the 1790 editions published in Dublin (re-engraved in stipple by Patrick Maguire) and Boston (crudely re-engraved). The Maguire plate is reproduced in Shroyer 1977, p. 25.

The design does not illustrate a specific passage in the *Aphorisms*, but pictures the moment of their transmundane inspiration. Thus, the seated figure represents Lavater composing his aphorisms—and perhaps also Fuseli in the act of translating and editing his friend's words. The hovering presence is the muse, revealing the insights into human nature communicated by the aphorisms in the volume. Rather than offering a representational portrait of the sort so frequently used for frontispieces, Fuseli and Blake have created a spiritual portrait commenting, in a most complimentary manner, on the origin and composition of the book. This arrangement of authorial persona and inspiring muse may have influenced Blake's disposition of similar figures in the frontispiece to *Songs of Innocence* (1789). The Greek inscription on the tablet ('Know thyself', from the Temple of Delphi and Juvenal's eleventh satire: 'from heaven descends the saying, "Know thyself"') refers to Lavater's final aphorism: 'If you mean to know yourself, interline such of these aphorisms as affected you agreeably in reading, and set a mark to such as left a sense of uneasiness with you; and then shew your copy to whom you please' (p. 224, no. 643). Blake followed these instructions in his marked and extensively annotated copy of the 1788 edition (HEH). For these annotations and excerpts from the aphorisms they respond to, see E 583–601, K 65–88. Lavater's aphorisms very probably influenced Blake's composition of the 'Proverbs of Hell' in *The Marriage of Heaven and Hell* (*c.* 1790–3).

Fuseli's pen-and-ink preliminary drawing, 11.1 × 7.5 cm. with the image the reverse of the plate, is in the RNE collection (*Fig. 60*). This quick and energetic sketch is inscribed in pencil on the verso, in the hand of John Linnell or a member of his family, 'given by W. Blake to J. Linnell | by Fuseli'. Blake must have retained the drawing for many years, for he did not meet Linnell until 1818. Although the verso inscription suggests a gift, the drawing may have been one of 'two by Fuseli' Linnell purchased from Blake's widow on 26 January 1829 (Bentley 1969, p. 596; see also **XL**). It is, of course, possible that Blake worked from a far more detailed preliminary drawing, of the type conventionally supplied by an artist to a copy engraver, but no record of such an intervening work exists. If, as Todd 1971–2 was the first to suggest, Blake worked only from this rough sketch, then Fuseli must have had an unusually close and trusting working relationship with Blake, and allowed the engraver to develop much of the design on his own. It is reasonable to assume, however, that some consultation took place, including the submission of proofs. It is also possible that Blake prepared a more finished drawing of the design, as he did for one of Fuseli's illustrations for Erasmus Darwin's *Botanic Garden* (see **XXI**, pl. 1). Only the first letter of the Greek inscription on the tablet is indicated in the drawing. The hourglass and book, lower right in the plate, do not appear in the preliminary. The slight indications of wings on the hovering figure are not retained in the engraving. The curious objects (masks? artist's palettes?) in the niche below the seated man in the drawing have been converted into books in the print.

The sheet, 22.5 × 18.2 cm., bearing the pen drawing also contains in the left margin two physiognomic profiles, apparently of the same man in youth and age. These are probably loose portraits of Lavater (see Blake's engraved profile of 1787; Essick 1983, no. XXIX), or of Fuseli, or an attempt to articulate the similarities between the two men's features. A pencil sketch, 13.5 × 11 cm., on the verso of Fuseli's portrait of Michelangelo (see **XL** and *Fig. 189*), may represent an earlier stage in the development of the *Aphorisms* design. At the very least, the pencil drawing contains a similar arrangement of hovering head and torso (but holding a book or scroll rather than a tablet) above a seated and contemplative figure. This drawing is also linked to the *Aphorisms* through the presence of a profile sketched in ink that may be an earlier version of the heads on the *Aphorisms* preliminary drawing.

Literature: Gilchrist 1863, i. 61, ii. 260; Russell 1912, no. 68; Keynes 1921, no. 101; Bentley and Nurmi 1964, no. 389; Ruthven Todd, 'Two Blake Prints and Two Fuseli Drawings', *Blake Newsletter*, 5 (1971–2), 173–81, both Fuseli sketches reproduced; Schiff 1973, nos. 789, 831; Bentley 1977, no. 480; Richard J. Schroyer, 'The 1788 Publication Date of Lavater's *Aphorisms on Man*', *Blake: An Illustrated Quarterly*, 11 (1977), 23–6; Easson and Essick 1979, no. XXXII; Essick 1980, pp. 19–20, 51–2; Lavater, *Aphorisms on Man*, ed. R. J. Schroyer (Delmar: Scholars' Facsimiles and Reprints, 1980), a reproduction of Blake's annotated copy; Carol Louise Hall, *Blake and Fuseli* (New York: Garland, 1985), 127; Robert N. Essick, 'Blake in the Marketplace, 1987', *Blake: An Illustrated Quarterly*, 22 (1988), 10–11.

XIX

John Caspar Lavater, *Essays on Physiognomy*, trans. Henry Hunter (3 vols. in 5; London: John Murray, *et al.*, 1789–98, 1792; London: John Stockdale, 1810); *Figs. 61–4*

Lavater's lengthy study of the pseudo-science of physiognomy contains over 500 plates, of which four are signed by Blake as the engraver. Henry Fuseli played a significant role in the editing and illustrating of this translation and may have helped secure Blake's commission for the engravings. The work was originally issued in forty-one parts. According to a prospectus (noted in Bentley 1977, p. 595), all the copperplates were auctioned by 'Mr. Saunders' on 29 January 1818, but I have not located either the plates or a sale catalogue.

Blake's own efforts as a portraitist, particularly the 'Visionary Heads' he drew for John Varley *c.* 1819–25, may have been influenced by physiognomical and phrenological theories (see Mellor 1978). In his *Descriptive Catalogue* of 1809, Blake describes his painting of Chaucer's Canterbury Pilgrims as representing 'the physiognomies or lineaments of universal human life' (E 532–3, K 567). In 1787 Blake engraved a separate plate of Lavater's head in physiognomic profile (see Essick 1983, no. XXIX). Although this portrait was published by Johnson as a separate print, not by Murray or the others involved in publishing the *Essays*, the plate may have had some connection with the book. A profile of Fuseli, engraved by William Bromley (ii, facing p. 280), is very similar in conception and graphic style to Blake's Lavater portrait.

1. Vol. i, p. 127; 5.2 × 7.2 cm.; *Fig. 61*

Scratched signature lower right among the foliage: *Blake sc*

This vignette of two elderly men planting and watering saplings serves as a tailpiece to an essay on 'The Physiognomist', pp. 116–27, but may not be related to any specific passage. The text immediately above the plate indicates that this is 'not a complete Treatise, but merely Fragments of Physiognomy'. Perhaps, as Bentley 1972, p. 49, suggests, the design indicates that such incomplete works, like young trees, need nurturing. The very small signature, probably not visible in the reproduction, was first noticed in Bentley 1972.

2. Vol. i, facing p. 159; 16.7 × 13.8 cm.; *Fig. 62*

Signatures: *Rubens delin.* [left], *Blake sculp.* [right]
Title: DEMOCRITUS.
Number far lower right: *25* [not reproduced; almost completely worn away in the 1810 edition]

The full-page plate is based on a portrait (now in the Prado, Madrid) of the Greek philosopher by Peter Paul Rubens (1577–1640). Blake may have based his plate on the engraving of the portrait by Lucas Vorsterman (1595–1675). For Blake's opinion of Rubens, see VI. The essay illustrated, 'Democritus', pp. 159–61, concentrates on the man's 'sarcastic grin'.

3. Vol. i, p. 206; 13.2 × 5.4 cm.; *Fig. 63*
Scratched signature: *Blake sc* [right]
This plate, showing several flies hovering around a

flame, is the tailpiece to an essay of 'General Reflections on the Objections against Physiognomy', pp. 200–6, which centres on the ability to see things clearly. The design would seem to take its cue from two distinct passages in the text, the 'female butterfly and the winged ant' (p. 202) and 'persons' who 'have eyes, and the faculty of seeing when they open them to the light' (p. 203), but these images join into a single emblem only in the plate. In an earlier section, p. 117, Lavater makes passing reference to a time 'when the bright shining of a candle doth give thee light'. Perhaps the design represents the truths of physiognomy to which all should be attracted. A traditional emblematic meaning of these motifs—it is unwise to be attracted to that which can destroy you—seems inappropriate, or at least oddly contrary to the thrust of the text, in this context.

4. Vol. i, p. 225; 9.5 × 6.3 cm.; *Fig. 64*

Scratched signature: *Blake sculp* [right]

This profile is described in the text on the same page as having a 'forehead ... of a thinker who embraces a vast field; a sweet sensibility is painted in the eye, and the man of taste is discernible in the nose and the mouth. However, the drawing of the nostril is defective: it is too small, and the trait which forms it is indifferently marked'.

Literature: Gilchrist 1863, ii. 260; Russell 1912, no. 69; Keynes 1921, no. 102; Bentley and Nurmi 1964, no. 390; G. E. Bentley, jun., 'A "New" Blake Engraving in Lavater's *Physiognomy*', *Blake Newsletter*, 6 (1972), 48–9; Bentley 1977, no. 481; Anne K. Mellor, 'Physiognomy, Phrenology, and Blake's Visionary Heads', in Robert N. Essick and Donald Pearce (eds.), *Blake in his Time* (Bloomington: Indiana Univ. Press, 1978), 53–74; Easson and Essick 1979, no. XXXIII; Essick 1980, pp. 27–8, 60–1.

XX

The Original Works of William Hogarth (London: John and Josiah Boydell, 1790). *The Original and Genuine Works of William Hogarth* (London: Boydell and Company, *c.* 1795). *The Works of William Hogarth, from the Original Plates Restored by James Heath* (London: Printed for Baldwin, Cradock, and Joy by J. Nichols and Son, 1822; London: Baldwin and Cradock [three undated issues, the last two perhaps published by H. G. Bohn and/or Chatto & Windus]; London: Printed for Baldwin, Cradock, and Joy by Nichols and

Son, 1822 [actually Bernard Quaritch, *c*. 1880]). 'The Beggar's Opera' *by Hogarth and Blake*, a portfolio compiled by Wilmarth S. Lewis and Philip Hofer (Cambridge, Massachusetts: Harvard Univ. Press, and New Haven, Connecticut: Yale Univ. Press, 1965). *Figs. 65–6*

The first Boydell edition of Hogarth's works contains 103 plates, the second 108 plates, the 1822 edition 119 leaves of plates, and all later nineteenth-century editions 116 leaves of plates. Only one plate was engraved by Blake. The undated Baldwin and Cradock edition can be divided into three issues on the basis of different colophons on p. 42 of the letterpress text. The issue with 'G. Woodfall, Angel Court, Skinner Street, London' is evidently the first, for it contains the fifth state of Blake's plate and Woodfall (active at the Angel Court address *c*. 1812–40) is named as the printer on the title-pages of all three issues. The other two undated issues, both with the sixth state of the plate, have on p. 24 'G. Norman, Printer, Maiden Lane, Covent Garden' (where he was active *c*. 1824–71) or 'Jas. Wade, 18, Tavistock-street, Covent Garden, London'. The severe wear on the plates in the Wade issue indicates that it was printed after Norman's. The '1822' edition, with 'Nichols and Son' rather than 'J. Nichols and Son' on the title-page, also bears Wade's colophon on p. 42. This volume contains the seventh state of Blake's plate and thus is the last nineteenth-century issue. For the probable dating of these later editions, see the comments below on the history of the Hogarth copperplates.

1. Pl. 103 in some copies of the 1790 edition (see explanation below); 40.1 × 54.2 cm.; *Fig. 65*

Signatures: *Painted by W*^m*. Hogarth.* [left], *Engraved by W*^m *Blake.* [right]

Title, open letters: BEGGAR'S OPERA, ACT III.

Inscription below title: *"When my hero in Court appears, &c."* | *From the Original Picture, in the Collection of his Grace the Duke of Leeds.*

Imprint: *Publish'd July 1*st *1790, by J. & J. Boydell, Cheapside, & at the Shakspeare Gallery Pall Mall London.*

Second State, pl. 103 in some copies of the 1790 edition (see explanation below). The lightly scratched inscriptions of the first state have been more darkly cut and the open

letters of the title have been filled with horizontal hatching strokes. An inscription has been added left of the imprint: '*Size of the picture 24,! by 30,! long.*' All impressions inspected of the first and second states are on laid paper.

Third State, pl. 102 in the undated Boydell edition of *c*. 1795. The highlight on the left knee of the standing man, lower right, has been darkened with fine crossing strokes. All impressions inspected of the third and subsequent states are on wove paper.

Fourth State, pl. 19 in the 1822 edition. The long diagonal highlight on the dress of the woman kneeling lower right, where it falls over her lower right leg, has been darkened by extending contiguous hatching strokes through the area. A bit more cross-hatching has been added to this woman's dress 7 mm. left of the lower end of her handkerchief. This work (and other slight touches?) was probably executed by James Heath (1757–1834), as the 1822 title-page announces.

Fifth State, pl. 19 in the undated Baldwin and Cradock issue with Woodfall named as the printer on p. 42. In previous states, the right cheek of the central man in shackles is illuminated with a subtle highlight. Re-engraving of the hatching strokes has eliminated this highlight except for a small, round patch just left of his right eye. The highlight on the woman's dress lower right, darkened in the fourth state, has been burnished back into the plate. This work was probably not executed by Heath, who retired in 1822, even though his name continues to appear on the title-pages of this and all subsequent nineteenth-century issues. See comments below on the reworking of *c*. 1835 attributed to Ratcliff of Birmingham.

Sixth State, pl. 19 in the undated Baldwin and Cradock issues with Norman or Wade named as the printer on p. 42. Many hatching patterns, particularly on faces and dresses, have been more deeply, and very crudely, recut on the worn plate. The cross-hatching on the dress of the woman kneeling lower left has worn away and has been replaced by careless hatching strokes that hinder the illusion of depth and volume. Many of the highlights on the dress of the woman kneeling lower right have been narrowed or eliminated by cutting hatching through them. All sixth-state impressions inspected are on machine-made paper.

Seventh State, pl. 19 in the '1822' (i.e. *c*. 1880) edition and unbound pl. 11 in the 1965 portfolio. Cross-hatching has been returned to the lower left folds of the dresses of both kneeling women. Diagonal crossing strokes have been added to the folds of material left of the right upper arm of the kneeling woman on the right and to her dress below the lace on her right sleeve. Some crossing strokes have been added to the left hand and lower collar of the woman seated far left holding a closed fan.

There are two pre-publication proof states of the plate, both printed on laid paper in all impressions inspected. The earliest, an etched proof, lacks most (perhaps all) of the finishing work executed with the graver, but does contain some sketching with a stipple burin (*Fig. 66*). This state bears scratched signatures ('*Painted by Willm. Hogarth 1729*', left, and '*Etch'd by Willm Blake 1788*', right) and an imprint: '*Publishd October 29: 1788: by Ald^m Boydel & C° Cheapside*'. The presence of an imprint and the number of extant impressions of this state (BMPR; HEH; Houghton Library, Harvard University, Cambridge, Massachusetts; RNE; Rosenwald Collection, National Gallery of Art, Washington) strongly suggest that this is not a true working proof but a state published as a separate print for connoisseurs. In the second proof state (reproduced Essick 1980, fig. 48) the design has been engraved to a state of finish approaching that of the first published state and the signature lower right accordingly changed to '*Engravd by Willm Blake 1788*'. However, this proof still lacks a title, the inscription beneath it, and some finishing strokes, particularly on the dress of the woman kneeling lower right. I have been able to locate only one impression (RNE) of this proof state, but it too was probably printed for sale.

When the Boydells acquired Hogarth's copperplates from his widow's cousin in 1789 (Paulson 1970, i. 71), they apparently also received a number of remainder impressions, some in early states, printed on a variety of papers. This speculation would seem the best explanation of why some copies of the 1790 edition contain such a variety of impressions mounted on large sheets. Both such copies examined (Metropolitan Museum of Art, New York; Princeton University Library, Princeton, New Jersey) contain the first published state of Blake's plate. Other copies of the 1790 edition (e.g. LC) contain new impressions from Hogarth's plates and the second published state of Blake's print. Both the Boydell editions indicate in the 'Catalogue' of plates that the prints could be purchased individually, including 'Beggar's Opera' (15*s*. in 1790, 10*s*. 6*d*. in the *c*. 1795 edition). The latter price, with 'Blake' named as the engraver, is also given in *An Alphabetical Catalogue of Plates ... which Compose the Stock of John and Josiah Boydell* (London: Boydell, 1803), p. 21, pl. 104. The 1790 'Catalogue' states that Blake's plate was 'never before inserted in this Collection'. The word 'inserted', and the fact that the proofs are dated one year before the Boydells acquired Hogarth's own copperplates, suggest that the 'Beggar's Opera' was originally commissioned as a separate plate. The choice of subject may have been influenced by John Nichols's comment, in his *Biographical Anecdotes of William Hogarth* (London: Nichols, 1781), 16, that an engraving of Hogarth's

painting 'would prove a valuable present to the Publick'. The Boydells also published a companion print, based on Hogarth's painting of a scene from John Dryden's *The Indian Emperour*, engraved by Robert Dodd (1748–1816). Blake's engraving is mentioned, and the events pictured are briefly described, in an essay 'On Splendour of Colours, &c.' by 'Juninus' (identity not known) in *The Repository of Arts*, 4 (1810), 130–1 (excerpt in Bentley 1988, pp. 62–3).

Hogarth's copperplates, presumably including Blake's, were sold as lot 226 in the 1–6 June 1818 R. H. Evans auction of the Boydell estate. All were acquired at or shortly after this sale by Baldwin, Cradock, and Joy. Their 1822 edition was originally issued in twenty-four monthly parts and contains a description of the 'Beggar's Opera', without reference to Blake, on p. 6 of the letterpress text (included on p. 5 in all later nineteenth-century issues). The Hogarth plates passed into the possession of the banking firm, Salt & Co., which sold them to the publisher Henry G. Bohn in about 1835, who 'had them thoroughly repaired by Ratcliff, of Birmingham' (Tuer 1882, i. 59). Presumably Ratcliff was responsible for the fifth and/or sixth state revisions. All the plates were sold by Bohn *c*. 1864 to Chatto & Windus, and then 'at a later date' to Quaritch (Paulson 1970, i. 72; see also Tuer 1882, i. 59). In his *General Catalogue of Books* (1880), item 3523, Quaritch offers a set of Hogarth's works 'printed for me from the restored coppers', but 'with a text dated 1822', and claims that 'nearly 1000 guineas have been lately expended on the restoration of the original coppers, from which this issue is printed'. This is clearly the '1822' issue with the seventh state of the 'Beggar's Opera'.

Quaritch offered Blake's copperplate in his catalogue of 1921, *A Collection of Relics of William Hogarth Consisting of Actual Copper-Plates*, p. 16 (£100), and again in catalogue 500 of 1935, no. 66 (£100). The plate was acquired (according to E. M. Dring of Quaritch) in 1935 by a Mr. Crabtree, who died shortly thereafter. Blake's copperplate was probably among those which, according to Paulson 1970, i. 73, 'came up again at Christie's in 1937' (no catalogue located). The plate was acquired at or shortly after this sale by E. Weyhe, the New York dealer, who in turn sold it to Philip Hofer. He had the restrikes pulled for the 1965 portfolio. Upon Hofer's death in 1984, the plate entered the collection of the Houghton Library, Harvard University, Cambridge, Massachusetts, where it had been on deposit for over twenty years. It is unlikely that any more impressions will be pulled from the worn plate that has yielded so many over a span of 177 years.

Blake's print is a faithful reproduction of Hogarth's painting of 1729, now in the Yale Center for British Art, New Haven, Connecticut. The design represents Act III, sc. xi, of John Gay's *The Beggar's Opera* as first performed at Lincoln's Inn Fields on 29 January 1728. The highwayman Macheath (centre, in shackles, played by Thomas Walker) has been arrested and is now in Newgate Prison under penalty of hanging. To the left, his mistress Lucy Lockit (Mrs. John Egleton [Jane Giffard]) kneels and pleads with her father (John Hall), warden of Newgate, to help free her lover. On the right, Macheath's wife, Polly Peachum (Lavinia Fenton), pleads the same cause to her father (John Hippisley). The line from the play inscribed on the plate indicates that Polly has begun to sing 'Air XIV'. Distinguished members of the audience sit and stand behind tables on both sides of the stage, almost as though they were a jury at a trial. According to an outline engraving of the design (published by Boydell, July 1790) identifying the actors and members of the audience, the play's author is immediately to the right of Peachum. The next figure to the right is John Rich (*c*. 1682–1761), the theatre's manager and a famous pantomimist, who repeats Peachum's cutting or hanging gesture at the throat of 'M.ʳ Cock, The Auctioneer'. Seated far right is the Duke of Bolton (1685–1754), who fell in love with Lavinia Fenton (playing Polly and looking toward the Duke), later made her his mistress, and married her in 1751.

In the prospectus of 1809 for his engraving of 'Chaucers Canterbury Pilgrims', Blake refers to 'the Works of our own Hogarth' as evidence that 'no other Artist can reach the original Spirit so well as the Painter himself' (E 567, K 586; see also the *Public Address*, E 576, K 595). This general opinion may lie behind Blake's criticism of Thomas Cook's engravings after Hogarth (*Notebook* verses of *c*. 1809 (E 505, K 554–5, 595)), but a belief in the superiority of original over reproductive graphics would also imply that Blake's own 'Beggar's Opera' plate, in spite of its technical excellence, is necessarily inferior to Hogarth's engravings of his own designs. For further comments on this plate, see the Introduction.

The 1965 portfolio containing the modern restrike reproduces Hogarth's painting, his five other versions of it, one of his preliminary sketches, a photograph of Blake's copperplate, impressions of the first proof and second published states, and the outline engraving identifying the figures.

Literature: [J. B. Nichols (ed.)], *Anecdotes of William Hogarth* (London: Nichols, 1833), 174–5, 323 (describing four states only, including proofs); Gilchrist 1863, ii. 260; Andrew W. Tuer, *Bartolozzi and his Works* (London: Field and Tuer, *c*. 1882), i. 59 (history of Hogarth's copperplates); Russell 1912, no. 71 (four states); Geoffrey Keynes, *Engravings by William Blake: The Separate Plates* (Dublin: Emery Walker, 1956), no. XXXII (four states); Bentley and Nurmi 1964, no. 384; Ronald Paulson, *Hogarth's Graphic Works* (rev. edn., New Haven: Yale Univ. Press, 1970), i. 71–3 (history of Hogarth's copperplates); Bentley 1977, no. 475; Easson and Essick 1979, no. XXIV (five states); Essick 1980, pp. 18–19, 58–9; Essick 1983, no. LXI; Elizabeth Einberg and Judy Egerton, *The Age of Hogarth: British Painters Born 1675–1709* (London: Tate Gallery Publications, 1988), 74–81 (versions of the painting), 145 (Blake's plate); Ronald Paulson, *Breaking and Remaking: Aesthetic Practice in England, 1700–1820* (New Brunswick: Rutgers Univ. Press, 1989), 175–81, 185, 190 (iconography of Hogarth's painting).

XXI

Erasmus Darwin, *The Botanic Garden* (London: J. Johnson, 1791; 'Second Edition', 1791; 'Third Edition', 1795; 'Fourth Edition', 1799). *The Poetical Works of Erasmus Darwin* (3 vols.; London: J. Johnson, 1806). *Figs. 67–74*

The Botanic Garden is divided into two parts, 'The Economy of Vegetation' (containing Blake's plates), and 'The Loves of the Plants' (first published separately without plates in 1789). The poem's two parts are frequently bound in separate volumes, particularly in the 1799 edition. The first and second editions of Part I, both dated 1791, contain ten plates, one of which is signed by Fuseli as the designer and Blake as the engraver (pl. 1). Fuseli's involvement in the project may date back to 1784, since in a letter probably of that year Darwin told Johnson that Fuseli had been 'so kind as to promise some ornament for the work' (Fuseli 1982, p. 23). One further plate (6) by the same two artists was added in 1795. Four unsigned plates (2–5), appearing in all three editions through 1795, are views of the famous Roman cameo-glass vase then in the collection of the Duke of Portland and now in the British Museum. Apparently the fashionable engraver Francesco Bartolozzi (1725–1815) was the first to produce engravings of the vase, but these were found to be unsatisfactory by both Darwin and Johnson. As Darwin wrote on 9 July 1791 to Josiah Wedgwood, who had been lent the vase to make basalt-ware copies, 'Mr. Johnson's engraver [i.e. Blake] now wishes much to see Bartolozzi's plates of the vase, & will engrave them again if necessary—I told Johnson in my own name, *not in yours*, that I thought the outlines too hard, & in some places not agreeable' (Bentley 1988, p. 10). The identity of 'Johnson's engraver' is indicated by Johnson's letter of 23 July 1791 to Darwin: 'Blake is certainly capable of making an exact copy of the vase, I believe more so than Mr. B[artolozzi], if the vase were lent him for that purpose, & I see no other way of its being done, for the drawing he had was very imperfect—this you will determine on consulting Mr. Wedgwood, & also whether it should be copied as before, or reduced & brought into a folding plate' (Bentley 1969, pp. 43–4). Although this letter only proposes that Blake should receive the commission, there is no reason to think that the work was assigned to anyone else, particularly since (as the signatures indicate) Blake engraved two other plates for the book. Johnson's letter would seem to propose that the original vase should be lent to Blake, but he may have worked from one of Wedgwood's fine copies, first produced in the late 1780s (see L for Blake's later, and possibly earlier, contacts with the Wedgwoods). Blake must have prepared preliminary drawings, but none has survived. They may have been destroyed during counter-proofing on to the copperplates. The designs on the vase are interpreted in 'The Economy of Vegetation', Canto 2, lines 319–40, but Blake's plates are bound with the lengthy 'Note XXII' in which Darwin explains his analysis further.

Part I of the 1791 edition of *The Botanic Garden* was not entered at Stationers' Hall until 10 May 1792 (Bentley 1977, p. 547). According to an anonymous reviewer in *The Monthly Review*, 11 (June 1793), 182, Part I 'was kept back, as we are informed, for the execution of some of the engravings'. King-Hele 1981, p. 215, asserts, without providing any evidence, that publication was delayed until June 1792 because Blake's Portland Vase engravings were not ready until then.

The 1793 reviewer suggests in a footnote that the vase engravings were based on one of the Wedgwood facsimiles. Darwin could have provided it, for he owned one of the early Wedgwood copies, now in the Fitzwilliam Museum, Cambridge (King-Hele 1981, p. 193). The first three editions of *The Botanic Garden* were printed as quartos with non-folding plates, although the lower margins of the Portland Vase plates were folded over in a few copies during rebinding and trimming. The 1799 edition was reduced to octavo size, with reduced re-engravings of pls. 1–5, listed below as pls. 7–11. Pl. 10 is signed by Blake, and thus it seems likely that he engraved all the reduced plates based on those he had engraved for the quarto volumes. Bentley 1977, p. 548, states that the octavo plates 'were evidently commissioned and executed at the same time as those for the first edition' since they repeat the same imprint dates. But Blake—or, more probably, a writing engraver—may have simply repeated the old imprints at a later date. The reduced plates were used again in Darwin's *Poetical Works* (1806).

Darwin's versified natural history and comparative mythology attracted a large and respectful readership in the 1790s. His influence on the major Romantic poets, including Blake, is discussed in King-Hele 1986. A good deal of Blake's nature imagery in his poetry of 1789–95 may have been shaped by *The Botanic Garden*. Darwin's poem and its illustrations have received more critical attention from Blake scholars than any other work for which he engraved plates after designs by another artist—see the commentaries under *Literature*.

1. Facing p. 127, 'The Economy of Vegetation' (1791–5 edns.); 19.8 × 15.4 cm.; *Fig. 67*

Scratched signatures: *H Fuseli. RA: inv* [left], *W Blake. sc.* [right]

Title: *Fertilization of Egypt.*

Imprint: *London, Publish'd Dec!. 1ˢᵗ 1791. by J. Johnson, S! Pauls Church Yard.*

The design illustrates Canto 3, pp. 126–7, lines 129–34, but the image is also explained in Darwin's note on p. 127. 'Sirius, or the dog-star' has risen 'at the time of the commencement of the flood' of the Nile. The dog-headed god Anubis straddles the river, colossus-like, and lifts his hands in prayer to the star. A winged storm god (not mentioned in the text) hovers over the distant cataract. Roe 1969 offers a detailed reading of the design's iconography in terms of Blake's own mythological poetry and his criticism of Egypt as a land of geometric logic and death, but Beer 1973 has disputed several of Roe's specific interpretations.

There are two drawings of the design in the BMPR. One in pencil, 24.1 × 19.4 cm., is inscribed by Frederick Tatham in ink, 'Sketched by Fuseli for Blake to engrave from' (*Fig. 68*). Roe 1969 and David Bindman (as reported in Butlin 1981, no. 173) have suggested that Blake was actually the author of this drawing, but Tatham's ascription has been generally accepted. The second drawing, 19.4 × 15 cm., was executed by Blake in pen-and-monochrome wash (*Fig. 69*), probably in direct preparation for the engraving. The sistrum, lower left in the plate, might be vaguely suggested by a few lines forming a rough triangle in Fuseli's sketch, lower right, but does not appear in Blake's drawing. A few lines in the pencil sketch hint at pyramids, lower left; these have been rendered clearly as two pyramids in the engraving, lower right. Blake has lowered the storm god's arms to the horizontal and lengthened his beard—features that strongly suggest the influence of an engraving of Jupiter Pluvius from the Column of Marcus Aurelius in Bernard de Montfaucon, *Antiquity Explained* (Eng. edn., London, 1721), i, facing p. 25 (noted in Blunt 1959). Very similar figures appear again in Fuseli's 1793 painting, *The House of Death* (untraced, but engraved 1813) and in Blake's 1795 colour-printed drawing (Butlin 1981, nos. 320–2) based on the same passage in Milton's *Paradise Lost*, Book II, lines 477–93. Blake borrowed the posture of Fuseli's Anubis for his watercolour of *c.* 1803–5, *The Great Red Dragon and the Woman Clothed with the Sun* (version in the Brooklyn Museum, New York; Butlin 1981, no. 519). Four other illustrations of Revelation (Butlin 1981, nos. 518, 520–2) are related compositionally.

Taken together, the two drawings for this plate suggest that Fuseli relied on Blake not simply to reproduce his design, but to develop it from a loose sketch into a finished, and significantly altered, image. For apparently similar circumstances, see **XVIII** and **XL**. Fuseli must have been pleased with Blake's efforts, for he suggests in a letter of 17 August 1798 to his patron William Roscoe that the engraver Moses Haughton should 'look at the Anubis in the first part of the Botanic Garden' to find a 'Clue' as to how Fuseli's designs should be rendered in a print (Bentley 1988, p. 15).

2. Facing p. 53 of 'Additional Notes' to 'The Economy of Vegetation' (1791–5 edns.); 25.4 × 17.9 cm.; *Fig. 70*

Title: *The Portland Vase.*

Imprint: *1. London, Published Decr 1.st 1791, by J. Johnson, St Paul's Church Yard.*

Darwin explains that the central figure holding an 'expiring torch' is 'an hieroglyphic or Eleusinian emblem of Mortal Life' (p. 54). On each side are 'emblems of Humankind, with backs toward the dying figure of Mortal Life, unwilling to associate with her' (p. 55).

3. Facing p. 54 of 'Additional Notes' to 'The Economy of Vegetation' (1791–5 edns.); 15.9 × 27.2 cm.; *Fig. 71*

Title: *The first Compartment.*

Imprint: *2. London, Published Decr 1.st 1791, by J. Johnson, St Paul's Church Yard.*

For Darwin's interpretation of these figures, see pl. 2.

4. Facing p. 55 of 'Additional Notes' to 'The Economy of Vegetation' (1791–5 edns.); 15.6 × 25.7 cm.; *Fig. 72*

Title: *The second Compartment.*

Imprint: *3. London, Published Decr 1.st 1791, by J. Johnson, St Paul's Church Yard.*

Darwin interprets this scene as 'an emblem of immortality' (p. 55). The man on the left is 'the Manes or Ghost . . . descending into a dusky region' and dragging 'after him a part of his mortal garment'. The 'beautiful female' is 'a symbol of Immortal Life'. The serpent, because it annually renews its skin, 'has from great antiquity . . . been esteemed an emblem of renovated youth' (pp. 55–6). The cupid, with a 'torch' in his right hand, represents the 'divine Love' (p. 57) that conducts 'the manes or ghost to the realms of Pluto' (p. 56), who stands far right. The woman and serpent very probably influenced Blake's disposition of the same motifs on pl. 16 of *America* (1793). Blake also draws upon the association of the snake with renewal in his use of serpent imagery in *America*, much of which is metonymically related to Orc, the youthful embodiment of revolutionary regeneration in Blake's mythology.

5. Facing p. 58 of 'Additional Notes' to 'The Economy of Vegetation' (1791–5 edns.); 13.8 × 24.6 cm.; *Fig. 73*

Title: *The Handles & Bottom of the Vase.*

Imprint: *4. London, Published Decr 1.st 1791, by J. Johnson, St Paul's Church Yard.*

Darwin believes that the figure on the bottom of the vase is 'a Priestess or Hierophant, whose office it was to introduce the initiated' into the mysteries represented in the other designs (p. 58). 'The masks, hanging to the handles of the vase [left and right in the plate], seem to indicate that there is a concealed meaning in the figures besides their general appearance' (pp. 57–8). The bottom is now known to be a replacement piece taken from another vase.

6. Facing p. 168, 1795 edition of 'The Economy of Vegetation'; 21.2 × 17 cm.; *Fig. 74*

Scratched signatures: *H. Fuseli RA: inv:* [left], *W Blake: sc:* [right]
Title: *Tornado.*
Imprint: *London, Published Aug.ᵗ 1ˢᵗ 1795, by J. Johnson, S.ᵗ Paul's Church Yard.*

The design illustrates Darwin's personification of 'Tornado', his 'serpent-train' and 'forked lightning' (p. 168). Darwin is describing a single figure, whereas Fuseli represents two distinct combatants. Schiff 1973, no. 976, entitles this design *Zeus im Kampf mit Typhon*, thereby suggesting that Fuseli is interpreting Darwin's text in terms of the story of the struggle between Zeus and the giant Typhon (see Hesiod, *Theogony*). The twining of the serpent's tail about the man's body may have influenced Blake's somewhat different uses of this arrangement in pl. 6 of *The Book of Urizen* (1794) and the 1795 colour-printed drawings, *Elohim Creating Adam* and *Satan Exulting over Eve* (Butlin 1981, nos. 289–92). In several portrayals of Satan in his *Paradise Lost* illustrations, Blake similarly divides a single character in the text into a human figure entwined with his own serpent form (Butlin 1981, nos. 529.4–5, 536.4, 537.1).

Five proof impressions of the plate lack the same work in the design, including the diagonal crossing strokes in the sea and air lower left. The figure's left knee has not yet been covered with curved hatching lines and flicks. The lightning bolts and the serpent's body lack some hatching strokes. The edge of the cloud, upper right, and the serpent's wing above the man's right arm are much lighter in the proofs. One such print, with signatures but lacking title and imprint, is in the RNE collection. A proof in the BMPR has the signatures with the title and imprint areas trimmed off. Another in the same collection has the signatures and title with the imprint area trimmed off. A third BMPR proof has the signatures but lacks the title (imprint area trimmed off) and bears pencil indications on the lightning and serpent where crossing strokes and other

work were added in the published state. The proof in the collection of Raymond Lister has all letters. The number of such proof impressions, and the presence of an imprint on one of them, suggest that they were printed for use in the book or sale to collectors.

7. Reduced re-engraving, reversed, of pl. 1; Part I, facing p. 145, 1799 edition of *The Botanic Garden*; and vol. i, facing p. 145, *The Poetical Works* (1806); 13.1 × 8 cm.

Title: as on pl. 1.
Imprint: as on pl. 1, but with '*Publish'd*' changed to '*Published*' and a comma, rather than a period, following '*1791*'.

8. Reduced re-engraving of pl. 2; Part I, facing p. 352, 1799 edition of *The Botanic Garden*; and vol. i, facing p. 335, *The Poetical Works* (1806); 11 × 7.7 cm.

Title and imprint: as on pl. 2, but with the title placed above the image and the number preceding the imprint removed.

9. Reduced re-engraving of pl. 3; Part I, facing p. 355, 1799 edition of *The Botanic Garden*; and vol. i, facing p. 338, *The Poetical Works* (1806); 9.1 × 16 cm.

Title and imprint: as on pl. 3, but with the title placed above the image and the number preceding the imprint removed.

10. Reduced re-engraving of pl. 4; Part I, facing p. 357, 1799 edition of *The Botanic Garden*; and vol. i, facing p. 340, *The Poetical Works* (1806); 9 × 15.6 cm.

Added signature, lower right border: *Blake*
Title and imprint: as on pl. 4, but with the title placed above the image and the number preceding the imprint removed.

11. Reduced re-engraving of pl. 5; Part I, facing p. 362, 1799 edition of *The Botanic Garden*; and vol. i, facing p. 344, *The Poetical Works* (1806); 8.7 × 10.6 cm.

Title and imprint: as on pl. 5, but with '*Handles*' changed to '*Handle*' in the title, now placed above the image, and the number preceding the imprint removed.

Literature: Gilchrist 1863, i. 92, ii. 260–1 (pls. 1 and 6 only, the latter taken to be a separate plate of a 'subject apparently from the Scandinavian Mythology'); Basil de Selincourt, *William Blake* (London: Duckworth, 1909), 218–19 (on pl. 1); Russell 1912, no. 76 (pls. 1 and 6, with 2–5 only suggested as 'possibly' by Blake); Keynes 1921, nos. 103 (attributing pls. 2–5 to Blake on stylistic grounds), 108, 118; Anthony Blunt, *The Art of William Blake* (Morningside Heights: Columbia Univ. Press, 1959), 41 (drawing for pl. 1); Bentley and Nurmi 1964, no. 363; S. Foster Damon, *A Blake Dictionary* (Providence: Brown Univ. Press, 1965), 116–17 (on pl. 1); Kathleen Raine, *Blake and Tradition* (Princeton: Princeton Univ. Press, 1968), i. 126–35 (on pls. 2–5); A. S. Roe, 'The Thunder of Egypt', in Alvin H. Rosenfeld (ed.), *William Blake: Essays for S. Foster Damon* (Providence: Brown Univ. Press, 1969), 159–69 (on pl. 1); Kathleen Raine, *William Blake* (London: Thames and Hudson, 1970), 30–2; Keynes 1971, pp. 59–61; John Beer, 'Blake, Coleridge, and Wordsworth: Some Cross-Currents and Parallels', in Morton D. Paley and Michael Phillips (eds.), *William Blake: Essays in Honour of Sir Geoffrey Keynes* (Oxford: Clarendon Press, 1973), 247–55 (on pls. 1 and 6); Schiff 1973, nos. 974, 976, 1038; David V. Erdman, *The Illuminated Blake* (Garden City: Anchor Books, 1974), 33–4, 39, 107 (Darwin's influence on *The Book of Thel* and *The Marriage of Heaven and Hell*); Thomas A. Reisner and Mary Ellen Reisner, 'A Blake Reference to Goldsmith's "Citizen of the World"', *Notes and Queries*, NS 21 (1974), 264–5 (on the sistrum in pl. 1); D. E. L. Haynes, *The Portland Vase* (London: British Museum, 1975), with detail reproductions of the vase and summaries of interpretations, including Darwin's; David Worrall, 'William Blake and Erasmus Darwin's *Botanic Garden*', *Bulletin of the New York Public Library*, 78 (1975), 397–417 (parallels between Darwin's poem and Blake's writings of *c*.1791–5); Bentley 1977, no. 450; David Charles Leonard, 'Erasmus Darwin and William Blake', *Eighteenth-Century Life*, 4 (1978), 79–81 (Darwin's possible influence on *The Book of Urizen*); Easson and Essick 1979, nos. XXXVI, XXXVII; Gerald P. Tyson, *Joseph Johnson: A Liberal Publisher* (Iowa City: Univ. of Iowa Press, 1979), 110–13; Essick 1980, pp. 33, 51, 64; Butlin 1981, no. 173 (Blake's drawing for pl. 1); Nelson Hilton, 'The Spectre of Darwin', *Blake: An Illustrated Quarterly*, 15 (1981), 36–48 (general influence, and comments on pls. 2–6); Desmond King-Hele (ed.), *The Letters of Erasmus Darwin* (Cambridge: Cambridge Univ. Press, 1981), 214–15; Henry Fuseli, *The Collected English Letters*, ed. David H. Weinglass (Millwood: Kraus, 1982), 22–3, 187; Desmond King-Hele, *Erasmus Darwin and the Romantic Poets* (London: Macmillan, 1986), 35–61 (general survey of Darwin's influence on Blake); Albert Boime, *Art in the Age of Revolution, 1750–1800* (Chicago: Univ. of Chicago Press, 1987), 291–4, 330–4; Desmond King-Hele, 'A Twist in the Tale of "The Tyger"', *Blake: An Illustrated Quarterly*, 23 (1989), 104–6 (verbal echoes of Darwin's poetry in Blake's 'The Tyger').

XXII

David Hartley, *Observations on Man* (London: J. Johnson, 1791); *Fig. 75*

The only plate is the frontispiece portrait engraved by Blake. The work was issued in both a one-

volume quarto and a three-volume octavo format (the latter also issued without the plate). The 1810 edition contains the same portrait engraved by James Heath. An announcement in *The St. James's Chronicle* (5–7 April 1791) states that the book 'will be published . . . with a Head of the Author, engraved by Mr. Blake' (Bentley 1977, p. 570).

Hartley's influential philosophical treatise, first published in 1749, would seem to epitomize everything Blake most strongly criticized in eighteenth-century rational materialism. This assessment is supported by a note Blake wrote *c*.1798 in his copy of Richard Watson's *Apology for the Bible*. Watson introduces a quotation from the *Observations on Man* as an example of what has 'been conjectured by men of judgment' about the authorship of the Bible. Blake retorts, 'Hartley a Man of Judgment then Judgment was a Fool what Nonsense' (E 619, K 394).

1. Frontispiece; oval, 14.8 × 11.1 cm.; *Fig 75*

Scratched signature: *Blake. sc:*

Title: *David Hartley, M. A.* | *From a Painting, by Shackelton.*

Imprint: *Published by J. Johnson, in St. Paul's Church-yard, March 1st 1791.*

A proof before all letters is in the BMPR. There are two impressions (LC; Princeton University Art Gallery, Princeton, New Jersey) of a proof state lacking only Blake's signature. A proof lacking his signature and with the imprint area trimmed off is in the HEH. A review of the book, signed 'QQ', in Johnson's *Analytical Review*, 9 (Apr. 1791), 361, states that the 'Head [of Hartley] is sold alone, pr. 2s.6d.'. I have not been able to locate any impression which, because of paper size or type, can be identified as a separate issue, but the proofs noted here may have been pulled for sale as individual prints. The original portrait by John Shackleton (or 'Shackelton' (d. 1767)) is mentioned in 'The Bookseller's Advertisement' bound in the book: 'For the use of a portrait, from which an engraving has been taken by Mr. Blake . . . the bookseller returns his thanks'. This painting or drawing is now untraced.

Literature: Russell 1912, no. 78; Keynes 1921, no. 105; Bentley and Nurmi 1964, no. 373; Bentley 1977, no. 464; Easson and Essick 1979, no. XXXVIII; Essick 1983, no. LXII.

XXIII

Christian Gotthilf Salzmann, *Elements of Morality* (3 vols.: London: J. Johnson, 1791, 1792, 1799, 1805; 2 vols.: London: J. Johnson, 1793; 'Juvenile Library' edn., 2 vols., London: John Sharpe, *c.* 1815); *Figs. 76–120*

All the English illustrated editions of the *Elements of Morality* recorded here contain a frontispiece to vol. i and fifty numbered plates. The first English edition, published by Johnson in 1790, is unillustrated even though the title-page states that the two volumes are 'Illustrated with Copper Plates'. The imprint dates on the plates, beginning with 1 October 1790, suggest that they may not have been ready in time for the first edition, issued without them and without altering the title-page. The work is a translation by Mary Wollstonecraft of Salzmann's *Moralisches Elementarbuch*, first published in Leipzig in 1782. In her 'Advertisement', pp. i-iv, Wollstonecraft points out that she has 'altered many parts' of the original work and compares it to her own *Original Stories from Real Life*, first published by Johnson in 1788 and again in 1791 with six plates designed and engraved by Blake (Bentley 1977, no. 514; Bindman 1978, nos. 109–14).

The plates fall into at least two categories. One type, represented by the frontispiece and the plates inscribed 1, 7, 10 (signed, rather mysteriously, '*W. P: C fec¹ 1790*'), 11, and 27, is characterized by fine, closely spaced lines. The remaining forty-five plates have much bolder linear patterns and larger areas of the plate left free of all lines. This graphic style, sometimes characterized as 'picturesque' because of its purposeful ruggedness and simplicity (see Essick 1980, pp. 46–7), is a less refined cousin to Blake's technique in his plates for Wollstonecraft's *Original Stories*. The first to claim that Blake engraved at least some of the unsigned plates was Gilchrist 1863, i. 91–2, perhaps relying on information from someone who knew Blake. Gilchrist's general statement that Blake 'illustrated' *Elements of Morality* leaves it uncertain as to whether Blake designed the plates, engraved them, or both. The matter is clarified by Locker 1880, where it is pointed out that all but two of the illustrations are based on designs by the German artist Daniel Nicolaus Chodowiecki (1726–1801). These were first published as a series of sixty-seven designs without text in *Kupfer zu Herrn Professor Salzmanns Elementarwerk nach den zeichnungen Herrn Dan. Chodowiecki, von Herrn Nussbiegel, Herrn Penzel und Herrn Crusius sen. gestocken* (Leipzig, 1784). These plates plus a frontispiece were used in the 1785 Leipzig edition of Salzmann's book. The engraving style is basically similar to the fine-line, minority style in the English translation.

Ever suspicious of Gilchrist's casual attributions, Russell 1912 lists only fourteen of the English plates as Blake's work, including eight 'possibly, but not certainly, by Blake' (pp. 157–8). Keynes 1921 expands the list to sixteen; Bentley and Nurmi 1964 and Bentley 1977 increase the attribution to seventeen. But once any of the 'picturesque' style plates are attributed to Blake, it is difficult to exclude the others because they all seem to be by the same hand. The final step is taken in Essick 1978 and Easson and Essick 1979, where the forty-five plates listed here are ascribed to Blake. In my 1978 essay I based the attribution in part on the addition to pls. 2, 29, 33, 40, and 41 of a carpet with a swirled pattern also found in Blake's engraving after Hogarth (XX), 'Moore & Co's Advertisement' designed and engraved by Blake *c.* 1797–8 (Essick 1983, no. XII), and in the final plate in the 1802 *Designs to a Series of Ballads* by William Hayley (Bentley 1977, no. 466; Bindman 1978, no. 398). These and other differences between the German plates and those ascribed to Blake are briefly noted for each below. Some of these changes may have been made to conform to English conventions in costume and interior decor. The attribution of these plates to Blake is far from certain; I continue to be very tentative in the attribution of pl. 43 to his hand.

All but pls. 3 and 23 were altered for the 1792 edition and again in 1793; pls. 3 and 23 were reworked in 1793. The most significant features of these revisions are the filling in of open areas with hatching and cross-hatching and the addition of stipple to hands and faces. The latter brings

Blake's plates slightly closer to the appearance of the fine-line work by the other engraver and would seem to violate the picturesque aesthetic implicit in Blake's graphic style. Since this three-step revision process was undertaken over a relatively short, three-year period, it was probably motivated not by a need to repair worn plates but by stylistic considerations. This care is rather unexpected for unsigned copy engravings in a book for children. The location of the illustrations in the three-volume editions of 1791, 1792, and 1799 is established by the 'Directions for placing the Plates' at the end of each volume. At least one copy of the 1791 edition (RNE) contains pls. 12, 13, 18, 19, and 27–45 in their second states. A copy of the 1799 edition in the RNE collection has the plates crudely hand coloured.

Locker 1880 notes that the plates inscribed 27 and 28 (pl. 23 below) are not based on Chodowiecki's illustrations. These are both attributed to Blake as his 'own designing' in the 1905 Grolier club catalogue. This seems unlikely for the first of these plates since it is engraved in the fine-line (non-Blake) style. In Essick 1978 I attribute the design of pl. 23 to Blake because it includes several motifs found in his work, including a climbing vine almost identical to one in the frontispiece to Wollstonecraft's *Original Stories*.

The titles inscribed on the plates are quoted (with a few minor variations) from lines in the text printed in italic. The only copies of the 1805 edition I have located lack vols. ii–iii. The number and placement of the plates in vol. i match the 1799 edition. In the listings below, I have assumed that the same pattern would continue in a complete copy of the 1805 edition. The 1796 Philadelphia edition contains twenty of the designs re-engraved by another hand. The London 1793 edition was apparently also issued without plates, as a copy in that condition in the BL suggests. An anonymous review of the first volume of 1791 in *The Analytical Review*, 9 (Jan.–Apr. 1791), 102, notes that 'the prints are far superior, both with respect to design and engraving, to any we have ever seen in books designed for children'.

1. Vol. i, facing p. 15 (1791 edn.); 12.4 × 7 cm.; *Fig. 76*

Inscription top right: *Pl. 2, Vol. I.*
Title: *Health is dearer to me than a whole | Sack full of Gold.*
Imprint: *Published by J. Johnson, Oct! 1, 1790.*

Second State (1792 edn.). Cross-hatching has been added to the ground lower right, the right leg and foot and left forearm of the seated man, both men's hats, the standing man's coat below his right elbow, and the tree on the right. More diagonal hatching now appears on the seated man's clothing, the standing man's coat and legs, and the child's pants. Vertical lines, indicating stripes, have been added to the seated man's hose.

Third State, vol. i, facing p. 10 (1793 and Juvenile Library edns.); and facing p. 15 (1799 and 1805 edns.). All hands and faces, except the right hand of the standing man, have been shaded with stipple.

Mr and Mrs Jones and their son Charles have come upon a labourer eating his dinner in Sir William's garden. The title words are spoken by the poor but contented workman.

2. Vol. i, facing p. 20 (1791 edn.); 12.2 × 7 cm.; *Fig. 77*

Inscription top right: *Pl. 3, Vol. I.*
Title: *Of what use are all these things to me | when I have not Health?*
Imprint: as on pl. 1.

Second State (1792 edn.). Cross-hatching has been added to the right figure's coat above the pocket.

Third State, vol. i, facing p. 14 (1793 and Juvenile Library edns.); and facing p. 20 (1799 and 1805 edns.). Crossing strokes have been added to the hatching on the seat of the chair and the hands and faces of the men on the right and second from the left have been shaded with stipple.

Mr Jones (second from left?), young Charles, and Sir William stand 'at a bow-window' and drink coffee (p. 19). The servant (left) holding a tray is not mentioned in the text. The title words are spoken by the wealthy but unhealthy Sir William. In the German plate, the floor is divided into squares, replaced in Blake's plate by a carpet with decorative swirls.

3. Vol. i, facing p. 24 (1791 and 1792 edns.); 12.4 × 7 cm.; *Fig. 78*

Inscription top right: *Pl. 4, Vol. I.*
Title: *What will become of me!*
Imprint: *Published by J. Johnson, Oct! 1. 1790.*

Second State, vol. i, facing p. 16 (1793 and Juvenile Library edns.); and facing p. 24 (1799 and 1805 edns.). A very small amount of stipple has been added to the child's face.

Charles is lost in a wood and thinks the words quoted on the plate.

4. Vol. i, facing p. 28 (1791 edn.); 12.5 × 7.1 cm.; *Fig. 79*

Inscription top right: *Pl. 5, Vol. I.*
Title: *Stop! Stop!*
Imprint: *Published by J. Johnson Oct.¹ 1 1790.*

Second State (1792 edn.). The cross-hatchings on the man's coat near his left thigh and on his left lower leg have been extended further to the left. Crossing strokes have been extended up his right thigh. Short but heavy hatching lines have been added to the upper trunk and limbs of the large tree on the left.

Third State, vol. i, facing p. 20 (1793 and Juvenile Library edns.); and facing p. 28 (1799 and 1805 edns.). More hatching lines have been added to the man's coat, particularly on his shoulder, and his hair has been darkened with short strokes. More stipple has been added to both faces.

The village Curate finds Charles in the wood. In his fear, the boy ran from his rescuer, who had to cry out the words quoted on the plate. The position of the figures is similar to the arrangement of child and adult in the lower right corner of 'The Chimney Sweeper' in *Songs of Innocence* (1789). The 1790 date on this Salzmann illustration does not exclude a possible influence of the German plate on Blake's own composition. The man's posture is also similar to the woman's on the frontispiece to *For Children: The Gates of Paradise*, Blake's emblem series of 1793. Raine 1968 claims that the story in *Elements of Morality* illustrated by this and the preceding plate provided 'the raw material' (i. 16) for Blake's 'The Little Boy lost' and 'The Little Boy Found' in *Songs of Innocence*. However, children lost and found is one of the commonest motifs in eighteenth-century children's literature.

5. Vol. i, facing p. 41 (1791 edn.); 12.5 × 7 cm.; *Fig. 80*
Inscription top right: *Pl. 6, Vol. I.*
Title: *There he is! There comes our dear Father.*
Imprint: as on pl. 1.

Second State (1792 edn.). Long vertical lines have been added to the woman's skirt, many diagonals to the clothing of the boy far left, and cross-hatching to the man's right forearm.

Third State, vol. i, facing p. 28 (1793 and Juvenile Library edns.); and facing p. 41 (1799 and 1805 edns.). Several of the hatching lines on clothing and the stipple on faces have been darkened. A few strokes have been added to the man's hair.

The Curate is greeted by his family. Charles follows, lower right.

6. Vol. i, facing p. 60 (1791 edn.); 12.6 × 7 cm.; *Fig. 81*
Inscription top right: *Pl. 8, Vol. I.*

Title: *Pompey is dead!*
Imprint: as on pl. 1.

Second State (1792 edn.). Diagonal strokes have been added to the knees of the child second from the left and crossing strokes to the hatching on the floor, ceiling, and wall.

Third State, vol. i, facing p. 40 (1793 and Juvenile Library edns.); and facing p. 60 (1799 and 1805 edns.). More stipple has been added to faces and hands. Some of the cross-hatching on the man's gown has been extended and a few short lines have been added to his collar.

The curate consoles his son George, whose dog Pompey has died. Other members of the family gather around.

7. Vol. i, facing p. 81 (1791 edn.); 12.8 × 7.2 cm.; *Fig. 82*

Inscription top right: *Pl. 9, Vol. I.*
Title: *Patience can soften every pain.*
Imprint: as on pl. 1.

Second State (1792 edn.). Cross-hatching has been extended into the top edge of the bed canopy and along the floor lower left. Fine horizontal lines have been added to the ceiling beams and vertical crossing strokes to the bed curtain above the woman's arm on the right.

Third State, vol. i, facing p. 54 (1793 and Juvenile Library edns.); and facing p. 81 (1799 and 1805 edns.). Stipple has been added to hands and faces, except for the face of the man in bed. Some of the hatching on the blanket has been strengthened.

The Curate and Charles (lower right) visit a sick man whose mouth and nose, masked in the plate, 'were almost eaten away by a cancer' (p. 80). The invalid utters the words inscribed on the plate. His family gathers around. In the German plate, the floor is divided into squares.

8. Vol. i, facing p. 124 (1791 edn.); 12 × 7.1 cm.; *Fig. 83*

Inscription top right: *Pl. 12, Vol. I.*
Title: *Is there any Hope?*
Imprint: as on pl. 3.

Second State (1792 edn.). Crossing strokes have been added to the wall upper left, the entire floor, to the coat, leg, and shoes of the man far left, the upper arm and shoe of the man second from the left, and to the left hand and sleeve of the boy reaching up to this man.

Third State, vol. i, facing p. 82 (1793 and Juvenile Library edns.); and facing p. 124 (1799 and 1805 edns.). Stipple has been added to all faces and much of the hatching on clothing has been darkened.

Mr Jones's coachman, John, lies injured in the house of the Curate (second from left). Mr and Mrs Jones, their son Charles, their other coachman Nicholas (far left), and Mr Smith, the surgeon (right-most standing man) gather around the bed as Mr Jones (the head seen behind the two women?) asks the question inscribed on the plate. The surgeon holds a feather he has just used to see if John was still breathing.

9. Vol. i, facing p. 130 (1791 edn.); 12.7 × 7.2 cm.; *Fig. 84*

Inscription top right: *Pl. 13, Vol. I.*
Title: *Your Compassion has saved my life.*
Imprint: as on pl. 1.

Second State (1792 edn.). Crossing strokes have been added to the wall on the left, the left portion of the wall seen between the bed curtains, the coat of the man on the left below his right arm, the bed seen between this man's legs, the floor just right of the empty shoes, and to the shirt beneath the tail of the jacket and the back of the third figure from the right. Fine horizontal lines have been added to the cross-hatching on the ceiling beam on the left.

Third State, vol. i, facing p. 86 (1793 and Juvenile Library edns.); and facing p. 130 (1799 and 1805 edns.). Stipple has been added to all faces and the men's hands, and the hatching on all clothing has been darkened, particularly on the shoulders and arm of the man in bed.

John, still in his sick bed, holds Mr Jones's hand and utters the words of thanks inscribed on the plate. The Curate, his wife, and Mrs Jones are on the right; Charles stands far left.

10. Vol. i, facing p. 136 (1791 edn.); 13 × 7.1 cm.; *Fig. 85*

Inscription top right: *Pl. 14, Vol. I.*
Title: *I hate you!*
Imprint: as on pl. 1.

Second State (1792 edn.). Further crossing strokes have been added to the side of the middle ceiling beam, the entire beam on the right, the left figure's arm and upper coat, the right figure's cuff and hat, the circular container left of the candle, and to the entire floor. Horizontal lines have been added to the hatching on the door and to the front of the right figure's coat.

Third State, vol. i, facing p. 90 (1793 and Juvenile Library edns.); and p. 136 (1799 and 1805 edns.). Stipple has been added to all hands and faces. The vertical hatching beneath the right figure's shoulder has been extended to the right.

The Curate (left) visits his eldest brother at the village inn. The older man hates the younger because he believes that the Curate prevented his marriage to the Curate's sister-in-law.

11. Vol. i, facing p. 144 (1791 edn.); 13.1 × 7.2 cm.; *Fig. 86*

Inscription top right: *Pl. 15, Vol. I.*
Title: *If we love others, they will love us in return.*

Imprint: as on pl. 1.

Second State (1792 edn.). Crossing strokes have been added to the back of the boy on the left, the entire floor, the ceiling near the back corner, the left lapel of the man far left, the hat of the woman in the background, the right arm and upper chest of the man behind those shaking hands, the collar and shoulder of the man on the right, and the legs and shirt of the boy far right.

Third State, vol. i, facing p. 94 (1793 and Juvenile Library edns.); and facing p. 144 (1799 and 1805 edns.). Many hatching lines have been strengthened; stipple has been added to hands and faces except for those of the boy on the right and the right hand of the boy on the left.

Mrs Benson, the Curate's wife, greets the brother (right) with whom the Curate is now reconciled. Mr and Mrs Jones stand in the background. The two boys bring their uncle, who speaks the words inscribed on the plate, his nightcap and slippers; young Caroline gives him a piece of cake. In the German plate there are beams in the ceiling.

12. Vol. ii, facing p. 6 (1791 edn.); 12.2 × 7.2 cm.; *Fig. 87*

Inscription top right: *Pl. 16, Vol. II.*
Title: *An Idle Man will never be Content.*
Imprint: as on pl. 1.

Second State (1792 edn.). Crossing strokes have been added to the ground lower left and below the horse and cart, to the sky upper right, the clouds upper left, the hats worn by the boy and the man holding his hand, and this man's right leg, coat-tail, and coat collar.

Third State, vol. i, facing p. 114 (1793 and Juvenile Library edns.); and vol. ii, facing p. 6 (1799 and 1805 edns.). Diagonal crossing strokes have been added to the cloud above the horse and cart. The hands and faces of the foreground figures have been shaded with stipple.

Charles and his parents speak with a countryman about farmer Brown (background) and his idle ways.

13. Vol. ii, facing p. 10 (1791 edn.); 12.5 × 7.1 cm.; *Fig. 88*

Inscription top right: *Pl. 17, Vol. II.*
Title: *While I live I never will disobey you.*
Imprint: *Published by J. Johnson, Jan.ᵉ 1, 1791.*

Second State (1792 edn.). Crossing strokes have been added to the man's breeches, hat, shoes, right arm, waistcoat, and coat lapels, almost all of the sky and clouds, the ground, the horse's legs and flank, the door, sides of the coach seen through the wheel, back of the bed of the coach, the boy's left arm and leg, coat-tail, and face, and the inner brim of the hat worn by the figure in the coach.

Third State, vol. i, facing p. 118 (1793 and Juvenile Library edns.); and vol. ii, facing p. 10 (1799 and 1805 edns.).

Some of the hatching lines have been darkened and all hands and faces shaded with more stipple.

Charles promises his father never to disobey him. Mrs Jones looks out of the coach.

14. Vol. ii, facing p. 16 (1791 edn.); 12.3 × 7.2 cm.; *Fig. 89*

Inscription top right: *Pl. 18, Vol. II.*
Title: *Prodigality has made me poor.*
Imprint: as on pl. 13.

Second State (1792 edn.). Cross-hatching has been added to the right edge of the left figure's coat. Crossing strokes have been added to the boy's coat beneath his left arm and to the ground beneath and between the men. A few short hatching strokes have been added to the central figure's lower right arm.

Third State, vol. i, facing p. 120 (1793 and Juvenile Library edns.); and vol. ii, facing p. 16 (1799 and 1805 edns.). Diagonal crossing strokes have been added to the lower part of the sky. The hatching lines on the back of the central figure's coat have been darkened and all faces and hands have been shaded with more stipple.

Charles and his father (centre) come upon Mr Noel, who remarks upon the spendthrift ways that have reduced him to his tattered condition. Noel's words, inscribed on the plate, are quoted from p. 13 (1791 edn.).

15. Vol. ii, facing p. 24 (1791 edn.); 13.1 × 7.2 cm.; *Fig. 90*

Inscription top right: *Pl. 19, Vol. II.*
Title: *Now I see that you love Truth, I shall always | in future believe you.*
Imprint: as on pl. 13.

Second State (1792 edn.). Horizontal crossing strokes have been added to the walls and floor, and diagonal strokes to the table top, the woman's face, and the man's arms and pants. A few vertical lines have been added to the woman's lower skirt and the man's lower left leg.

Third State, vol. i, facing p. 126 (1793 and Juvenile Library edns.); and vol. ii, facing p. 24 (1799 and 1805 edns.). The hatching on the woman's apron has been darkened and all faces and the man's hands have been shaded with stipple.

Upon his return home, Mr Jones congratulates his daughter Mary on her truthfulness in confessing that she had broken a cup. The writing and hat she had been working on lie on the table. Mary's aunt stands on the left.

16. Vol. ii, facing p. 49 (1791 edn.); 12.4 × 6.8 cm.; *Fig. 91*

Inscription top right: *Pl. 20, Vol. II.*

Title: *Amongst all our Pleasures the most | delightful is that of doing Good.*
Imprint: as on pl. 13.

Second State (1792 edn.). Horizontal crossing strokes have been added to the wall and floor, vertical strokes to the man's coat, and diagonal hatching to the children's clothing and the floor in the foreground.

Third State, vol. i, facing p. 144 (1793 and Juvenile Library edns.); and vol. ii, facing p. 49 (1799 and 1805 edns.). Hatching strokes have been added to the woman's left upper arm. Hatching patterns on the table and the man's coat have been darkened and all hands and faces have been shaded with stipple.

Mr Jones explains that 'doing good' is even sweeter than the fine after-dinner wine his wife has just served him. The children are not pictured in the German plate, which shows place settings on the table and a floor in squares rather than a carpet.

17. Vol. ii, facing p. 54 (1791 edn.); 12.1 × 7 cm.; *Fig. 92*

Inscription top right: *Pl. 21, Vol. II.*
Title: *Oh that I could call back the years that are passed.*
Imprint: as on pl. 13.

Second State (1792 edn.). Horizontal crossing strokes have been added to the back wall, floor, and cupboard door, vertical strokes to the side of the cupboard, and a few diagonal strokes to the table top next to the left margin.

Third State, vol. i, facing p. 146 (1793 and Juvenile Library edns.); and vol. ii, facing p. 54 (1799 and 1805 edns.). The man's face has been shaded with more stipple.

A young clerk laments his poor work and the chiding Mr Jones, his employer, has just given him. A woman, not mentioned in the text, reaches into the cupboard in the German plate. She is dressed like Mrs Jones in earlier designs.

18. Vol. ii, facing p. 57 (1791 edn.); 12.1 × 7.1 cm.; *Fig. 93*

Inscription top right: *Pl. 22, Vol. II.*
Title: *I am a very poor unhappy man.*
Imprint: as on pl. 13.

Second State (1792 edn.). Crossing strokes have been added to the brim of the woman's hat, the door beneath her hand, and the floor below the corner of the door. Vertical hatching has been added to the man's lower left leg.

Third State, vol. i, facing p. 148 (1793 and Juvenile Library edns.); and vol. ii, facing p. 57 (1799 and 1805 edns.). Stipple has been added to hands and faces.

Mrs Jones enters the dwelling of the avaricious, but now poverty-stricken, Mr Skinpenny. In the German plate, the floor is divided into squares.

19. Vol. ii, facing p. 66 (1791 edn.); 12 × 7.5 cm.; *Fig. 94*

Inscription top right: *Pl. 23, Vol. II.*

Title: *The Industry which my Mother taught me remains | with me still, & supports me & my Children.*

Imprint: as on pl. 13.

Second State (1792 edn.). Horizontal crossing strokes have been added to the floor and diagonal strokes to the walls, the table top below the centre woman's right hand, the dresses of the three figures on the left, the necks and faces of the first and second figures on the left, and the cloak of the woman on the right just below her hair.

Third State, vol. i, facing p. 156 (1793 and Juvenile Library edns.); and vol. ii, facing p. 66 (1799 and 1805 edns.). Faces (except for the woman's far right) and hands have been shaded with stipple. A line now delineates the right edge of the upper arm of the girl far left; the lower edge of her cap has been recut.

Mrs Sanford, a milliner, explains her industrious habits to Mrs Jones (right). Two of the milliner's daughters are 'busily employed making hats and caps' (ii. 61). In the German plate the floor is divided into squares.

20. Vol. ii, facing p. 69 (1791 edn.); 11.4 × 7.2 cm.; *Fig. 95*

Inscription top right: *Pl. 24, Vol. II.*

Title: *It is hard to suffer Want.*

Imprint: as on pl. 13.

Second State (1792 edn.). Vertical lines have been added to the woman's skirt near the right margin, and horizontal and diagonal crossing strokes to the floor, ceiling, and walls.

Third State, vol. i, facing p. 158 (1793 and Juvenile Library edns.); and vol. ii, facing p. 69 (1799 and 1805 edns.). Vertical hatching has been added to the table top and the front side of the open box on it. Stipple has been added to all faces, the right figure's right hand and left arm, the seated woman's right hand, and the left-most figure's right arm.

The milliner (right) continues to describe her difficult life to Mrs Jones, now seated. The industrious daughters have increased from two (pl. 19) to three. In the German plate the floor is divided into square blocks, five containers are on top of the cupboard, and wainscoting is on the walls.

21. Vol. ii, facing p. 77 (1791 edn.); 11.6 × 7.3 cm.; *Fig. 96*

Inscription top right: *Pl. 25, Vol. II.*

Title: *You are my Benefactor, my Preserver.*

Imprint: as on pl. 13.

Second State (1792 edn.). Diagonal crossing strokes have been added to the central man's coat, both of his legs, the right leg of the man on the right, the woman's skirt far right, and the wall and ceiling. Vertical strokes have been added to the side and legs of the chair, far left.

Third State, vol. i, facing p. 164 (1793 and Juvenile Library edns.); and vol. ii, facing p. 77 (1799 and 1805 edns.). Stipple has been added to the faces and hands of the men shaking hands. The hatching on the woman's jacket has been darkened.

Mr Noel greets Mr Goodman, his former tutor. The Jones family stands on the right. In the German plate the floor is divided into squares, not covered with a rug.

22. Vol. ii, facing p. 86 (1791 edn.); 11.5 × 6.9 cm.; *Fig. 97*

Inscription top right: *Pl. 26, Vol. II.*

Title: *Through Perseverance we may do many | things, which we thought impossible.*

Imprint: as on pl. 13.

Second State (1792 edn.). Diagonal crossing strokes have been added to the back wall, the woman's left elbow and skirt, the man's left leg and shoe, and the left shoulder and jacket front of the second figure from the right.

Third State, vol. i, facing p. 168 (1793 and Juvenile Library edns.), and vol. ii, facing p. 86 (1799 and 1805 edns.). All faces and the woman's right hand have been shaded with stipple. The hatching on the cloth in the basket has been darkened.

Mary (right) has brought her work basket to her parents, Mr and Mrs Jones, and speaks the words inscribed on the plate. Her brother Charles looks on. In the German plate a large curtain with finials above it is on the left. The back wall is plain and the floor is divided into squares.

23. Vol. ii, facing p. 104 (1791 and 1792 edns.); 12.5 × 6.8 cm.; *Fig. 98*

Inscription top right: *Pl. 28, Vol. II.*

Title: *Through Impatience we always make | things worse.*

Imprint: as on pl. 3.

Second State, vol. i, facing p. 180 (1793 and Juvenile Library edns.); and vol. ii, facing p. 104 (1799 and 1805 edns.). The very faint hatching lines on the boy's pants and hose have been darkened. His face and neck have been shaded with stipple.

William, one of Charles's schoolmates, has been locked in a garden. In his impatience, he 'kicked against the door' (ii. 101) and injured his foot on a nail. The words inscribed on the plate are spoken by Mr Jones after the incident. The very different German plate illustrates this later point in the narrative when 'Mr. Jones and his whole family' (ii. 103) had come to rescue William. For the attribution of the English plate to Blake as the designer, see the discussion above and Essick 1978, pp. 13–14.

24. Vol. ii, facing p. 113 (1791 edn.); 12 × 6.8 cm.; *Fig. 99*

Inscription top right: *Pl. 29, Vol. II.*

Title: *Gratitude exalts a Man much higher | than Learning.*

Imprint: as on pl. 13.

Second State (1792 edn.). Crossing strokes have been added to the wall, part of the sofa's back, the legs and right shoe of the central figure, the right figure's forehead, hair below the bow, and left arm and hand. Short hatching lines now shade the centre figure's upper left arm.

Third State, vol. i, facing p. 186 (1793 and Juvenile Library edns.); and vol. ii, facing p. 113 (1799 and 1805 edns.). The faces of the left and centre figures have been shaded with more stipple and the hatching on the right figure's coat-tail has been darkened.

Mr Jones (right) shakes the hand of the 'professor', who has just promised his benefactor, the elderly man sitting on the sofa, that he will help Mr Goodman and his large family out of gratitude for the benefactor's past assistance. Mr Jones speaks the words inscribed on the plate. In the German plate the floor is divided into squares and there are curved patterns on the back of the sofa and chair.

25. Vol. ii, facing p. 139 (1791 edn.); 12.2 × 6.9 cm.; *Fig. 100*

Inscription top right: *Pl. 30, Vol. II.*

Title: *Whoever will enjoy Health and Content, | must be moderate.*

Imprint: as on pl. 13.

Second State (1792 edn.). Crossing strokes have been added to the pillows on the couch, the standing man's coat-tail, and the seated man's robe just right of his right foot and along the right edge of his left arm.

Third State, vol. ii, facing p. 8 (1793 and Juvenile Library edns.); and facing p. 139 (1799 and 1805 edns.). Stipple has been added to both faces, the standing man's left hand, and the seated man's right hand. Many hatching lines on the figures have been darkened.

Mr Jones (left) visits one 'of the persons, with whom he had been in company the evening before' (ii. 135–6) and speaks his words of moderation to the man suffering from a hangover. In the German plate the sofa and pillows are decorated in a swirling pattern and the floor is divided into squares.

26. Vol. ii, facing p. 153 (1791 edn.); 11.8 × 6.8 cm.; *Fig. 101*

Inscription top right: *Pl. 31, Vol. II.*

Title: *All this Vexation has been occasioned by | your Tattling.*

Imprint: as on pl. 13.

Second State (1792 edn.). Crossing strokes have been added to the floor, ceiling, wall, front of the cabinet, front edge of the sofa and its cushion just left of the woman's right arm, the right side of her hat brim, the child's right calf, and the man's coat left of his left elbow.

Third State, vol. ii, facing p. 18 (1793 and Juvenile Library edns.); and facing p. 153 (1799 and 1805 edns.). More hatching has been added to the woman's skirt, lower left. A few crossing strokes have been added to the shaded area of the boy's coat where it touches the woman's thigh. Stipple has been added to both faces and the man's hands.

Charles sinks in his mother's lap as his father, Mr Jones, accuses him of being a gossip. In the German plate the floor is plain with no suggestion of a carpet.

27. Vol. ii, facing p. 177 (1791 edn.); 12.1 × 6.6 cm.; *Fig. 102*

Inscription top right: *Pl. 32, Vol. II.*

Title: *We loathe a Slanderer as we do a Viper.*

Imprint: as on pl. 13.

Second State (1792 edn.). More horizontal lines have been added to the sky and crossing strokes to the hatching on both women's skirts and the right woman's hat near its top.

Third State, vol. ii, facing p. 34 (1793 and Juvenile Library edns.); and facing p. 177 (1799 and 1805 edns.). Stipple has been added to the women's arms, hands, faces, and necks. The very light hatching strokes on the right woman's skirt have been darkened.

Mrs Jones (right) cautions Hannah, sister of the Professor's new bride, about her propensity for vicious gossip.

28. Vol. iii, facing p. 12 (1791 edn.); 12.2 × 6.8 cm.; *Fig. 103*

Inscription top right: *Pl. 33, Vol. III.*

Title: *Welcome dear Henry, & good Catherine.*

Imprint: *Published by J. Johnson, March 15, 1791.*

Second State (1792 edn.). Crossing strokes have been added to the right leg and foot of the boy and to the man's coat lapel. Some of the horizontal lines in the floor near the lower margin have been darkened.

Third State, vol. ii, facing p. 50 (1793 and Juvenile Library edns.); and vol. iii, facing p. 12 (1799 and 1805 edns.). Stipple has been added to all faces.

The Jones children, Mary and Charles, greet their returning servants Catherine and, behind her, Henry. In the German plate the woman wears a bonnet folding over her ears and the floor is divided into squares.

29. Vol. iii, facing p. 23 (1791 edn.); 12.2 × 7 cm.; *Fig. 104*

Inscription top right: *Pl. 34, Vol. III.*
Title: *How sad is life without a friend!*
Imprint: as on pl. 28.

Second State (1792 edn.). Crossing strokes have been added to the wall and door, floor, sofa beneath and to the right of the cushion, table top and legs, seat of the chair, and the boy's right thigh. A third layer of hatching lines has been added to the tablecloth where it falls below the edge of the table.

Third State, vol. ii, facing p. 58 (1793 and Juvenile Library edns.); and vol. iii, facing p. 23 (1799 and 1805 edns.). Stipple has been added to the child's face and neck.

Charles, suffering from a toothache, is left alone at home while the rest of the Jones family goes on an excursion. In the German plate the back of the chair is curved and much higher and the floor is divided into squares.

30. Vol. iii, facing p. 30 (1791 edn.); 12.2 × 6.9 cm.; *Fig. 105*

Inscription top right: *Pl. 35, Vol. III.*
Title: *In every religion there are good people.*
Imprint: as on pl. 28.

Second State (1792 edn.). More crossing strokes have been added to the floor (it is now completely cross-hatched) and wall. A few additional strokes have been added to the boy's coat-tail.

Third State, vol. ii, facing p. 62 (1793 and Juvenile Library edns.); and vol. iii, facing p. 30 (1799 and 1805 edns.). A little stipple has been added around the mouth of the boy on the right.

Ephraim (left), a Jew, has cured Charles (right) of his toothache, and thus the boy learns a lesson in religious tolerance. Mr Noel, clerk to Charles's father, works in the background. The other boy, presumably Charles's brother, is not mentioned in the text. In the German plate the floor is divided into squares.

31. Vol iii, facing p. 37 (1791 edn); 12.4 × 7 cm.; *Fig. 106*

Inscription top right: *Pl. 36, Vol. III.*
Title: *He who can torment a little helpless | animal, has certainly a bad heart.*
Imprint: as on pl. 28

Second State (1792 edn.). Crossing strokes have been added to the males' hat brims, the man's left thigh, and the shadow beneath the boy's right foot. Short horizontal lines have been added to the foreground stubble.

Third State, vol. ii, facing p. 66 (1793 and Juvenile Library edns.); and vol. iii, facing p. 37 (1799 and 1805 edns.).

More stipple has been added to the faces of the three figures on the left.

James has tortured a mouse, held in his left hand, with the knife in his right hand. His sister Mary points this out to their father, Mr Jones, who offers the words of admonishment inscribed on the plate.

32. Vol. iii, facing p. 50 (1791 edn.); 12.2 × 6.9 cm.; *Fig. 107*

Inscription top right: *Pl. 37, Vol. III.*
Title: *A wicked man is more to be pitied | than a cripple.*
Imprint: as on pl. 28.

Second State (1792 edn.). Crossing strokes have been added to the floor, upper drawers of the chest, the wall on each side of the chest, the back and seat of the chair, the man's coat on the left, right hip, and left arm, the hats of the children, and the boy's sleeves.

Third State, vol. ii, facing p. 76 (1793 and Juvenile Library edns.); and vol. iii, facing p. 50 (1799 and 1805 edns.). Stipple has been added to all faces, the boy's hands, and the woman's left hand.

Mr Jones offers the inscribed precept to his son James after having witnessed the vicious behaviour of the landlord towards his wife. Mrs Jones and Mary are also pictured. In the German plate the chest of drawers has large round knobs, not handles, and the floor is divided into squares.

33. Vol. iii, facing p. 68 (1791 edn.); 12.6 × 6.8 cm.; *Fig. 108*

Inscription top right: *Pl. 38, Vol. III.*
Title: *What wicked children must they be | who can vex their parents.*
Imprint: as on pl. 28.

Second State (1792 edn.). Crossing strokes have been added to the wooden floor, the wicker cradle centre left, the bed cover, the arms and collar of the man far right, the surface just below his right elbow, and the skirt of the front-most girl on the right.

Third State, vol. ii, facing p. 86 (1793 and Juvenile Library edns.); and vol. iii, p. 68 (1799 and 1805 edns.). Stipple has been added to faces except for those of the two standing children on the right.

The Jones family visit the Curate (far right), his wife (in bed), and his children suffering from smallpox. The lines inscribed on the plate are spoken by young George Jones in a later conversation with no direct reference to the pictured scene. In the German plate the cradle is wooden, not wicker, and the floor is divided into squares without a carpet.

34. Vol. iii, facing p. 76 (1791 edn.); 12.4 × 7 cm.; *Fig. 109*

Inscription top right: *Pl. 39, Vol. III.*
Title: *See how much good a Single man can do!*
Imprint: as on pl. 28.

Second State (1792 edn.). Crossing strokes have been added to the floor, wall, ceiling, base of the spinning wheel, table side and legs on the left, and the vertical moulding on the cabinet. Hatching has been added to the man's shoes, the top of the table on the left, the man's left thigh, the upper leg of the boy lower left, and the woman's skirt below and to the right of her right hand.

Third State, vol. ii, facing p. 92 (1793 and Juvenile Library edns.); and vol. iii, facing p. 76 (1799 and 1805 edns.). Stipple has been added to the faces of all four foreground figures and to the face and right hand of the boy far right.

The Jones family (foreground) visits the parlour of an innkeeper, whose children work industriously in the background.

35. Vol. iii, facing p. 86 (1791 edn.); 12.4 × 6.7 cm.; *Fig. 110*

Inscription top right: *Pl. 40, Vol. III.*
Title: *Her honesty has gained my entire | confidence.*
Imprint: as on pl. 28.

Second State (1792 edn.). Small amounts of hatching have been added to the sky, the adults' hats, the woman's skirt, and the boy's hat and leg near the right margin.

Third State, vol. ii, facing p. 98 (1793 and Juvenile Library edns.); and vol. iii, facing p. 86 (1799 and 1805 edns.). Diagonal crossing strokes have been added to the sky and a few more hatching strokes to the adults' hats. Faces have been shaded with more stipple.

The girl on the left has returned Mrs Jones's lost purse. Mrs Jones speaks the words inscribed on the plate as she prevents her husband from rewarding the girl and offers to do so herself.

36. Vol. iii, facing p. 93 (1791 edn.); 11.9 × 6.9 cm.; *Fig. 111*

Inscription top right: *Pl. 41, Vol. III.*
Title: *How happy it is that there are rich men | in the world.*
Imprint: as on pl. 28.

Second State (1792 edn.). Horizontal crossing strokes have been added to the wall, floor, and doors. Small clusters of crossing lines have been added to the coat of the man far right, coat and forehead of the seated man, and the right leg and coat-tail of the man second from the left.

Third State, vol. ii, facing p. 104 (1793 and Juvenile Library edns.); and vol. iii, facing p. 93 (1799 and 1805 edns.). A little more stipple has been added to all faces.

Mr Jones, seated, pays his weavers, one of whom (left) expresses the capitalist principle inscribed on the plate. In the German plate the floor is divided into squares.

37. Vol. iii, facing p. 101 (1791 edn.); 12 × 6.9 cm.; *Fig. 112*

Inscription top right: *Pl. 42, Vol. III.*
Title: *Act honestly, and your very enemies | will contribute to your happiness.*
Imprint: as on pl. 28.

Second State (1792 edn.). Crossing strokes have been added to the front of the cabinet on the right, the curtains, the standing man's right calf, and the spaces between the railing columns.

Third State, vol. ii, facing p. 108 (1793 and Juvenile Library edns.); and vol. iii, facing p. 101 (1799 and 1805 edns.). Stipple has been added to the seated man's face and hand.

Jackson, the weaver who speaks in the previous illustration, is promoted by Mr Jones (seated). In the German plate the floor is divided into squares and the seated man's chair can be seen behind the railing.

38. Vol. iii, facing p. 105 (1791 edn.); 12.4 × 7 cm.; *Fig. 113*

Inscription top right: *Pl. 43, Vol. III.*
Title: *Sorrow is very beneficial.*
Imprint: as on pl. 28.

Second State (1792 edn.). Crossing strokes have been added to the wall pillars, moulding and picture on the left, the shoulder of the child centre left, the coat of the man left foreground, the floor beneath his coat-tail far left, the right leg and left thigh of the boy choking the girl, the backs of the chairs centre and right, the skirt of the girl on the right, the coats of the men on the right, and the area right of the dog.

Third State, vol. ii, facing p. 112 (1793 and Juvenile Library edns.); and vol. iii, facing p. 105 (1799 and 1805 edns.). Stipple has been added to faces except the child's centre left, to the left hand of the man seated on the right, and to the left arm of the child at his knee.

The Curate, who speaks the line inscribed on the plate, and his family are visiting the Jones family. The text, unlike the illustration, gives no hint of a fight among the children. In the German plate the floor is divided into squares.

39. Vol. iii, facing p. 122 (1791 edn.); 11.9 × 6.8 cm.; *Fig. 114*

Inscription top right: *Pl. 44, Vol. III.*
Title: *O God, how great art Thou!*
Imprint: as on pl. 28.

Second State (1792 edn.). Crossing strokes have been added to the side of the cart, the coats of the figures except the second from the left, the left haunch of the horse on the right, and the neck of the next horse to the left.

Third State, vol. ii, facing p. 122 (1793 and Juvenile Library edns.); and vol. iii, facing p. 122 (1799 and 1805 edns.).

A few short hatching strokes and some stipple have been added to the faces of the girls holding muffs.

The two families (see pl. 38) have gone for a ride through the winter landscape. The Curate (third from the left) looks to the stars and speaks the words inscribed on the plate. In the German plate the people ride in a sleigh, rather than the 'cart' specified in the English text, and another sleigh appears to the right where a horse and rider are pictured in Blake's plate. Turbaned heads decorate the front of the sleighs and the front-most horse is draped with a large sash.

40. Vol. iii, facing p. 145 (1791 edn.); 11.9 × 6.7 cm.; *Fig. 115*

Inscription top right: *Pl. 45, Vol. III.*
Title: *O God, how good art Thou!*
Imprint: as on pl. 28.

Second State (1792 edn.). Crossing strokes have been added to the back wall, ceiling, upper right arm of the standing woman, coat of the seated man on the left, skirt of the girl far left, and the left sleeve, lapel, and coat-tail of the man on the right.

Third State, vol. ii, facing p. 138 (1793 and Juvenile Library edns.) and vol. iii, facing p. 145 (1799 and 1805 edns.). The hatching on the left man's coat has been darkened and stipple has been added to all faces.

Charles responds, with the words inscribed on the plate, to the Curate's lecture on how perfectly God has made the pike and goose brought in for dinner. In the German plate there is no cloth on the table, the back of the chair is higher, and the floor is divided into squares.

41. Vol. iii, facing p. 156 (1791 edn.); 12.1 × 7 cm.; *Fig. 116*

Inscription top right: *Pl. 46, Vol. III.*
Title: *O God, Thou knowest all things, how | wonderfully hast Thou brought my innocence | and this man's wickedness to light!*
Imprint: as on pl. 28.

Second State (1792 edn.). Crossing strokes have been added to the wall, carpet, stretcher of the chair, right shoulder of the man far left, and skirt of the standing woman below her right hand. Dotted hatching lines have been added to her throat.

Third State, vol. ii, facing p. 146 (1793 and Juvenile Library edns.); and vol. iii, facing p. 156 (1799 and 1805 edns.). Many hatching lines have been darkened and stipple has been added to all faces.

Mrs Sandford, seated right, thanks God for the discovery, by the standing girl, of a promissory note from Mr Skinpenny that will prove the lawsuit against him.

The Jones family gathers around. In the German plate the back wall contains some panels and forms a corner with a contiguous wall; the floor is divided into squares.

42. Vol. iii, facing p. 164 (1791 edn.); 11.5 × 7.1 cm.; *Fig. 117*

Inscription top right: *Pl. 47, Vol. III.*
Title: *O God! Thou art just!*
Imprint: as on pl. 28.

Second State (1792 edn.). Crossing strokes have been added to the floor, parts of the bottom sides of the ceiling beams, the left shoe, calf, and hair bow of the man second from left, and the bed just above the table and to the right of the man's cane.

Third State, vol. ii, facing p. 150 (1793 and Juvenile Library edns.); and vol. iii, facing p. 164 (1799 and 1805 edns.). More stipple has been added to the face of the man far left.

Mr Jones (with cane) visits old Martin, one of his weavers, who lies sick in bed. The man far left is his son, Thomas, who has sadly neglected his father, but reproaches him for once having treated his father similarly. The old man speaks the words inscribed on the plate. In the German plate the back wall and floor boards are smooth. The condition of the room in Blake's plate suits this 'miserable garret' (iii. 161).

43. Vol. iii, facing p. 173 (1791 edn.); 12.9 × 7.1 cm.; *Fig. 118*

Inscription top right: *Pl. 48, Vol. III.*
Title: *O God, Thou hast had compassion on me! | Thou hast heard my prayer!*
Imprint: as on pl. 28.

Second State (1792 edn.). Diagonal hatching lines have been added to the water just above the bottom margin. Crossing strokes have been added to the back and left and upper right legs of the right-most figure, the wall on the right, the glass panes of all three windows, the hat of the left-most figure, and the coat of the figure second from the right below his left forearm.

Third State, vol. ii, facing p. 156 (1793 and Juvenile Library edns.); and vol. iii, facing p. 173 (1799 and 1805 edns.). Many of the hatching patterns on the figures, most noticeably on the right leg of the right-most figure, have been darkened. A bit more stipple has been added to the three figures on the left.

The Severn has flooded the countryside. Mr Jones (standing centre) and some boatmen have rescued the praying Henry from the open window of the summer house. In the German plate the man on the left wears a tricorn hat. The graphic style of the English plate clearly sets it apart from the others attributed to Blake. It is at once both more conventional and less skilfully executed than its companions and may be the work of yet a third engraver (see discussion above). It is included here on the slight possibility that it is by Blake.

44. Vol. iii, facing p. 180 (1791 edn.); 12.8 × 7.4 cm.; *Fig. 119*

Inscription top right: *Pl. 49, Vol. III.*
Title: *See Children how powerful God is!*
Imprint: as on pl. 28.

Second State (1792 edn.). More hatching has been added to the man's right boot and crossing strokes have been added to his left boot and to the top of the boy's hat.

Third State, vol. ii, facing p. 162 (1793 and Juvenile Library edns.); and vol. iii, facing p. 180 (1799 and 1805 edns.). Stipple has been added to all faces.

Mr Jones uses the flood's damage (see pl. 43) to exemplify the point of the inscribed line to his children.

45. Vol. iii, facing p. 195 (1791 edn.); 12.9 × 7.6 cm.; *Fig. 120*

Inscription top right: *Pl. 50, Vol. III.*
Title: *My Spirit is immortal, and goes to God.*
Imprint: as on pl. 28.

Second State (1792 edn.). Crossing strokes have been added to the wall centre and lower left, the back wall on the right, the floor, the boy's back and thighs, the bed canopy lower right, the front and back edges of the man's gown, and the bed just below the girl's chest.

Third State, vol. ii, facing p. 172 (1793 and Juvenile Library edns.); and vol. iii, facing p. 195 (1799 and 1805 edns.). Stipple has been added to all faces (except the boy's on the left), the hand of the boy on the left, and the left arm and hand of the woman.

Mrs Jones, on her deathbed, utters the inscribed words to her weeping husband and children. In the German plate there are no decorative patterns on the curtain seen between the sections of the bed canopy; the floor is divided into squares.

Literature: Gilchrist 1863, i. 91–2, ii. 260; 1880, i. 91; Frederick Locker, 'The Illustrations in Mrs. Godwin's "Elements of Morality"', *Notes and Queries*, 6th ser. 1 (19 June 1880), 493–4; Grolier Club, *Catalogue of Books, Engravings Water-Colors and Sketches by William Blake* (New York, 1905), no. 67; Russell 1912, no. 77; Keynes 1921, no. 104; Joseph H. Wicksteed, 'Blake's Songs of Innocence', *Times Literary Supplement* (18 Feb. 1932), 112 (influence of the *Elements* on some of Blake's lyrics); Bentley and Nurmi 1964, no. 402; Raine 1968 (see **XXI**, *Literature*), I. 15–17; Bentley 1977, no. 492; Robert N. Essick, 'The Figure in the Carpet: Blake's Engravings in Salzmann's *Elements of Morality*', *Blake: An Illustrated Quarterly*, 12 (1978), 10–14; Easson and Essick 1979, no. XXXV; Essick 1980, pp. 49–50; Essick 1984 (see **XV**,

Literature), pp. 130–3 (on the 1793 edn.); J.R. Windle, *Mary Wollstonecraft (Godwin): A Bibliography of her Writings, 1787–1982* (Los Angeles: privately printed, 1988), no. 3.

XXIV

Bellamy's Picturesque Magazine, vol. 1 (London: T. Bellamy, 1793); *Fig. 121*

The first (and only recorded) volume of this magazine contains eleven plates plus an engraved title-page. The attribution of the tenth plate to Blake rests almost entirely on the signature, for nothing in the very conventional engraving technique provides a basis for ascription. The editor of the magazine, Thomas Bellamy (1745–1800), tried his hand at several periodicals, but none achieved much success.

1. Facing p. 37; 16.5 × 11.4 cm. (including frame and clouds above it); *Fig. 121*

Title in frame: F: REVOLUTION
Signatures: *C. R. Ryley del.* [left], *Blake sc* [right]
Imprint: *Publish'd by T,, Bellamy Aug 1,ˢᵗ, 1793*

The plate illustrates an 'Account [pp. 37–40, 50–1, 61–2] of the Revolution in France, from its Commencement to the Death of Louis XVI', extracted from James White's translation of Jean Paul Rabaut Saint-Étienne, *History of the Revolution of France* (London: J. Debrett, 1792). The design by Charles Reuben Ryley (*c.* 1752–1798) pictures Louis XVI and Marie Antoinette protected by loyal troops from a revolutionary mob which stormed the palace at Versailles on 6 October 1789. The extract from Rabaut, 'to be continued' (p. 62), does not describe this incident, but it does appear in White's complete translation, from which Ryley was evidently working: 'The King and Queen, alike alarmed, were seeking for each other; but by the zeal and prudence of the life-guards they met; the Queen had merely time to throw certain garments on her, and to gain the King's apartments' (p. 130). The anti-revolutionary tenor of the text may not have pleased Blake, but the engraving is his most direct and explicit engagement as a pictorial artist with the events unfolding in France.

Literature: Bentley and Nurmi 1964, no. 336; Bentley 1977, no. 418; Easson and Essick 1979, no. XL.

XXV

James Earle, *Practical Observations on the Operation for the Stone* (London: J. Johnson, 1793, 1796, 1803); *Figs. 122–4*

Both plates in the 1793 edition bear Blake's scratched signature. Chard 1975, p. 155, suggests that 'the possibility exists' that Blake also engraved a third plate, included in the 'Appendix' added to the 'Second Edition' of 1796 and its reissue in 1803. This possibility is taken as a virtual certainty by Keynes 1973, who learnt of Chard's discovery of the plates in Earle's book but had not seen his forthcoming essay. Keynes accurately points out that 'the engraving technique' of pl. 3 'is the same as that of the first plate' (note particularly the use of long hatching lines, free of crossing strokes, to depict polished metal surfaces) and that the inscriptions on the second state are typical of Blake's scratched lettering (compare, e.g., **XXXII**, *Figs. 147–54*). The evidence of the inscriptions persuades me that Keynes is probably right in his attribution of pl. 3. No designer is named on the plates, and Blake probably worked directly from the objects pictured. Earle (1755–1817) was a leading surgeon of his day and an associate of other physicians published by Johnson (see Chard 1975).

1. Facing p. 52; 17.9 × 10.9 cm. (border to border); *Fig. 122*

Inscription top right: *p. 52.*
Scratched signature: *Blake: sc:* [right]

The instruments pictured are a 'staff' and a 'gorget' (right) for performing lithotomies. The small object in the centre is a detail of the grooved end of the staff.

2. Facing p. 74; 20 × 12 cm. (border to border); *Fig. 123*

Inscription top right: *p. 74.* [partly trimmed off in the copy reproduced]
Scratched signature: *Blake: sc:* [right]

The plate pictures four urinary tract stones 'remarkable for their size or shape' (p. 74). Keynes 1973 states that this plate is 'wholly etched', but there are a few crossing strokes on the left end of the lowest stone that were probably cut with the graver. It may only be a coincid-

ence that the rugged surfaces of the top and bottom stones resemble the lichens or undersea creatures covering the rock in Blake's colour-printed drawing, *Newton* (Butlin 1981, nos. 306–7), first executed in 1795. If reduced in scale, these surfaces would also resemble the maculations produced by Blake's colour-printing process. If these similarities do carry iconographic significance, then the stone on which Newton sits in the colour print is the macrocosmic projection of both the biological microcosm operated on by Earle and the graphic microcosm produced by the very technique used to picture Newton's world. Or, to reverse the perspectival shift, Newton inhabits an interior space—mental, biological, artistic.

3. Folding plate facing p. 8 of the 'Appendix', some copies of the 1796 edition; 12.5 × 26.7 cm.; *Fig. 124*

Inscription top left: *To face p. 8, Appendix.* [partly trimmed off in the copy reproduced]

Second State, most copies of the 1796 edition and the 1803 edition. Two details of the right ends of the instruments at the top of the plate have been added below the other objects. Two scratched inscriptions have been added: '*fig. 2.*' (bottom centre) and '*Fig. 2.* | *See last page*' (bottom right). Reproduced in Chard 1975, p. 65.

The plate pictures alternative designs, described on p. 22 of the 'Appendix', for the types of instruments pictured in pl. 1. I have found the first state only in the copy of the 1796 edition at the National Library of Medicine, Bethesda, Maryland.

Literature: Geoffrey Keynes, 'William Blake and Bart's', *Blake Newsletter*, 7 (1973), 9–10; Leslie F. Chard, 'Two "New" Blake Engravings: Blake, James Earle, and the Surgeon's Art', *Blake Studies*, 6 (1975), 153–65; Bentley 1977, no. 451; Easson and Essick 1979, no. XLI.

XXVI

John Gay, *Fables* (2 vols.; London: John Stockdale, 1793, *c.* 1811); *Figs. 125–36*

Blake engraved twelve of the sixty-eight plates in this handsome edition of the verse fables by John Gay (1685–1732). The somewhat worn but otherwise unaltered plates were used again in a second edition printed on paper watermarked 1809, 1810, and 1811. It contains the engraved title-pages of the 1793 edition, but can be distinguished from it by the absence of the long 's' found throughout the first-edition text.

All the plates are copied after the designs by William Kent (1685–1748) and John Wootton (*c*. 1678–1765) appearing in the first edition of the *Fables* (1727), and the additional designs by Henry Gravelot (1699–1773) in the second volume of new fables published in the fifth edition (1738). These sources for the 1793 plates were first discussed in Keynes 1972. The publisher, John Stockdale (*c*. 1749–1814), allowed his engravers some liberty in their re-engraving of the earlier illustrations. They very probably prepared drawings for transfer on to the new copperplates, and this procedure gave Blake the opportunity to invest his renditions with something of his own sensibility. The more significant differences between Blake's plates and their prototypes are noted for each below. Some of the plates by other engravers show an equal range of variation from their sources. The most remarkable difference is in the illustration to Fable XIV, 'The Monkey Who Had Seen the World' (i. 63), engraved by 'Lovegrove'. The monkey dressed as a man has been replaced by a caricature of Thomas Paine holding a book inscribed 'Rights of Man'.

The inscriptions on the plates far lower right, about 9.5 cm. below the designs, are binder's directions and are usually bound into the spines. These are not included in the reproductions. The fact that three of Blake's plates have right and left as in the earlier prints, whereas the others are reversed, suggests that he used two different methods of transferring the designs to his copperplates. The Boston 1891 catalogue lists seven unidentified 'unfinished proofs' of the Gay plates, lent by R. C. Waterston and E. W. Hooper, but these are untraced. Another edition of the *Fables*, printed by Darton & Harvey in 1793 and sold by F. & C. Rivington, *et al.*, contains plates clearly copied, rather stiffly, after those in the Stockdale edition. Each plate contains two designs in an oval format.

1. Vol. i, facing p. 1, 'Introduction to the Fables, the Shepherd and the Philosopher'; 7.7 × 9.4 cm.; *Fig. 125*

Scratched signature: *Blake sc*
Inscription lower right: V 1. P 1

The design is based loosely on the beginning of the fable when the philosopher asks the seated shepherd about his 'learning'. The sheep dog and cottage are not mentioned in the text. Blake's plate differs considerably from the rather crude engraving of Kent's design by Peter Fourdrinier (d. 1758) in the 1727 edition. In the earlier version, the cottage is further in the distance and has a conical roof. The sheep look undernourished and are differently arranged. The philosopher is a far less noble personage, with a short beard and a cloak over his head. Blake's rendition of the two men foreshadows his presentation of Thenot and Colinet in several of his wood engravings for R. J. Thornton's 1821 edition of Virgil's *Pastorals* (Bindman 1978, nos. 602–18). The large spreading tree and cottage are products of the same stylistic orientation represented by these motifs in the Virgil designs. The philosopher is typical of Blake's patriarchal figures so frequently pictured in his art. The huddled sheep are a familiar element in many of Blake's own designs, including the frontispiece, 'The Shepherd', 'The Lamb', and 'Spring' in *Songs of Innocence* (1789), and the frontispiece to *Songs of Experience* (1794). A close relative of the dog, differently positioned, appears in pls. 1 and 21 of Blake's Job engravings (1826). The statement in Keynes 1972 that this illustration to the *Fables* should 'be regarded as an original design by Blake' (p. 62) is only a slight overstatement. Russell 1912, p. 161, notes a proof in the 'Print Room' (apparently the BMPR), but the only impressions I can locate in that collection are in the published state.

2. Vol. i, facing p. 29, 'Fable VI, the Miser and Plutus'; 7.6 × 9.3 cm.; *Fig. 126*

Scratched signature: *Blake: sc*
Inscription lower right: V 1. P 29

The miser has just opened 'the chest with treasure stor'd'. 'Plutus, his god', rebukes the miser and points to 'Heaven'. Blake has followed Kent's design, engraved by Fourdrinier in the 1727 edition, fairly closely. In the earlier plate both figures wear loose cloaks, Plutus's wings are smaller, and the background is much lighter. A proof of Blake's plate in the BMPR lacks the signature, some lines on the figure's wings, some dot work in the background, on the left end of the chest on the left, and on the floor, and some of the cross-hatching on the miser's thigh and on the strip of cloth just below Plutus's right shoulder. A light brown wash has been painted over part of the god's wings and his strip of cloth.

3. Vol. i, facing p. 59, 'Fable XIII, the Tame Stag'; 7.5 × 9.7 cm.; *Fig. 127*

Scratched signature: *Blake: sc:*
Inscription lower right: V1. P 59

The stag 'attacks again' his captors. Blake's plate varies only in minor respects from Wootton's design engraved by John Van der Gucht (1697–1776) for the 1727 edition. Left and right are the reverse of Blake's plate, there is a wall on the far left, the tree trunk is smaller, and the background figure far right (left in Blake's plate) wears a hat and holds a staff. Here and elsewhere in Blake's plates for the *Fables*, the loose and baggy clothing pictured in the earlier plates has been replaced by the tightly fitted breeches and shirts Blake favoured in his own designs.

4. Vol. i, facing p. 73, 'Fable XVI, the Pin and the Needle'; 7.6 × 9.3 cm.; *Fig. 128*

Scratched signature: *Blake: sc:*
Inscription lower right: V 1. P 73

The 'interpreter' in 'Gresham hall' points to the upright pin, which then enters into dialogue with the 'needle' lying on the table. The 'loadstone' is pictured as a round compass placed to the right of the pin. The vase, shield and spear, mummy, busts, bottles, fish, deer skeleton, and partly covered globe decorating the room are the artist's imaginative responses to the unspecified 'wonders of the show' that amaze the inquisitive pin. Blake's plate is very close to Fourdrinier's version of Kent's design in the 1727 edition, except that the interpreter's wand is shorter in the earlier plate.

5. Vol. i, facing p. 99, 'Fable XXII, the Goat without a Beard'; 7.6 × 9.6 cm.; *Fig. 129*

Scratched signature: *Blake: sc:*
Inscription lower right: V 1. P 99

The 'vain' goat is about to lose his beard at the hands of the 'flippant monkey'. Blake's plate, with right and left reversed, is very close to Van der Gucht's print of Wootton's design in the 1727 edition. The coffee pot is rounder and more elegant in Blake's plate, but he has failed to reproduce the back leg of the table on the left.

6. Vol. i, facing p. 109, 'Fable XXIV, the Butterfly and the Snail'; 7.7 × 9.8 cm.; *Fig. 130*

Scratched signature: *Blake: sc:*
Inscription lower right: V 1. P 109

The 'gardener' stands in the left middle-ground, while the fable's two titular characters make their complaints on the right. Blake has reversed right and left and altered several motifs in Kent's design, engraved by

Fourdrinier for the 1727 edition. The terms of the arbour are more clearly delineated in the earlier plate, the gardener's right hand touches his chest, a low wall extends towards us in the middle foreground, a corner of a ruined wall or pediment rises from the ground in front of the snail, and large cumulus clouds billow above the arbour. The snail is slightly larger, and the butterfly much larger, in Blake's plate.

7. Vol. i, facing p. 125, 'Fable XXVIII, the Persian, the Sun, and the Cloud'; 7.6 × 9.5 cm.; *Fig. 131*

Scratched signature: *Blake sc:*
Inscription lower right: V 1. P 125

The Persian is 'prostrate' in prayer to the sun, temporarily hidden by the envious cloud. Blake has reversed right and left and made a few changes in Kent's design, engraved by Fourdrinier for the 1727 edition. Much larger shafts of light break around the darker and larger cloud in the earlier plate, there is only one tree behind the Persian, there are small stones in front of the bank on which he leans, and his gown and turban are more rumpled.

8. Vol. i, facing p. 133, 'Fable XXX, the Setting-Dog and the Partridge'; 7.6 × 9.5 cm.; *Fig. 132*

Scratched signature: *Blake: sc:*
Inscription lower right: V. 1 P. 133

The prone dog spies the partridge. On the left, 'the men in silence, far behind | Conscious of game, the net unbind'. Blake's plate, with right and left reversed, closely follows Wootton's design, engraved by Bernard Baron (*c.* 1700–62) for the 1727 edition.

9. Vol. i, facing p. 181, 'Fable XLI, the Owl and the Farmer'; 7.6 × 9.6 cm.; *Fig. 133*

Scratched signature: *Blake: sc:*
Inscription lower right: V 1. P 181

The farmer replies to the 'owl, of grave deport and mien', who roosts in the barn 'upon a beam aloft'. Blake has reversed right and left and made several minor changes in Wootton's design, engraved by Van der Gucht in the 1727 edition. The floor is made of stone blocks in the earlier plate, rather than Blake's boards, the owl squats lower and has prominent ears, the doors have heavy horizontal braces rather than Blake's stylish hinges, and the farmer's coat has a pocket below the belt. In the 1727 plate the owl perches on top of a large pile of straw. Blake has placed him on a beam, in accord with Gay's text. This is the clearest indication in the series that Blake was consulting the poem when preparing his plates.

10. Vol. ii, facing p. 1, 'Fable I, the Dog and the Fox'; 7.7 × 9.4 cm.; *Fig. 134*

Scratched signature: *Blake: sc:*
Inscription lower right: V 2. P. 1

'A shepherd's Dog' and 'Reynard' continue their 'chat' as the latter drops 'his bushy tail in fear'. On the left, the 'farmer's wife' with her 'poultry-ware' rides a 'pie-ball'd mare' to market. Blake has reversed right and left and changed Gravelot's vertical design, engraved by Louis Gerard Scotin (active in London 1733–50) in the 1738 edition, to a horizontal format. Blake has altered the shape of the large tree and the position and configuration of the foreground foliage.

11. Vol. ii, facing p. 105, 'Fable XII, Pan and Fortune'; 7.7 × 9.3 cm.; *Fig. 135*

Scratched signature: *Blake: sc:*
Inscription lower right: V 2. P. 105

Pan tramples 'the dice' beneath 'his hoof' and tears the 'cards'. Fortune, 'that false, fickle jade', stands on her wheel (a traditional emblem not mentioned in the text) and objects to these acts. In the background 'stern clowns' with 'brawny arms' attack 'the elm and rev'r-end oak' to pay for the owner's gaming losses. A fool's rattle rests on the ground lower right. Blake has reversed right and left and changed Gravelot's vertical design, engraved by Scotin in the 1738 edition, to a horizontal format. Pan now has less of a scowl than in the earlier plate and the woodcutters are in slightly different postures.

12. Vol. ii, facing p. 145, 'Fable XVI, the Ravens, the Sexton, and the Earth-Worm'; 7.5 × 9.3 cm.; *Fig. 136*

Scratched signature: *Blake: sc:*
Inscription lower right: V 2. P. 145

The Sexton 'suspends his spade' to scold the 'two Ravens' perched in the churchyard's 'venerable yew'. The funeral for the 'squire' continues on the left, with his 'fair hall' behind. The 'Earth-worm, huge in size', is pictured just to the left of the spade. Blake has reversed right and left and changed Gravelot's vertical design, engraved by Scotin in the 1738 edition, to a horizontal format. The worm is even larger in the earlier plate, the Sexton scowls rather than smiles, there are two chimneys on the hall (reduced to one by Blake), and the large tomb is differently decorated.

Literature: Gilchrist 1863, ii. 257 (nine plates only, mistakenly credited to Blake as the designer); Boston Museum of Fine Arts, *Exhibition of Books, Water Colors, Engravings, Etc. by William Blake* (Boston, 1891), nos. 110a–b; Russell 1912, no. 80; Keynes 1921, no. 106; Bentley and Nurmi 1964, no. 371; Geoffrey Keynes, 'Blake's Engravings for Gay's Fables', *The Book Collector*, 21 (1972), 59–64 (eight plates from the 1727 and 1738 edns. reproduced); Bentley 1977, no. 460; Easson and Essick 1979, no. XLII; Essick 1980, pp. 228–9, 238 (Fourdrinier's plate of the first design reproduced).

XXVII

John Hunter, *An Historical Journal of the Transactions at Port Jackson and Norfolk Island* (London: John Stockdale, quarto and octavo edns., 1793); *Figs. 137–8*

The quarto edition contains eleven plates, plus an engraved title page and five maps; the evidently later octavo edition has only two plates, the engraved title-page, and one map. Both editions contain one plate engraved by Blake. John Hunter (1738–1821) was captain of the *Sirius* on its voyages to New South Wales, 1787–92. His *Historical Journal* is an important account of the early exploration and history of Australia.

1. Facing p. 414 (quarto edn.); 18.9 × 16 cm.; *Fig. 137*

Signatures: *From a Sketch by Governor King* [left], *Blake. Sculp!* [right]
Title: A FAMILY OF NEW SOUTH WALES
Imprint: *Publish'd by I. Stockdale Piccadilly, Nov! 15 – 1792*

Second State, a folding plate facing p. 372 (octavo edn.). The title and imprint have been re-engraved in smaller letters. The title, 10.3 cm. long in the first state, is now 8.3 cm. long, and is 1.1 cm. below the design (2 cm. in the first state). The imprint is similarly raised closer to the image. These changes may have been made so that the plate would fit into an octavo format, although the folding of the plate made such alterations unnecessary.

The illustration is not described in the text, although the aborigines' habit of carrying 'a piece of lighted wood in their hand' (p. 414, quarto edn.) is noted in passing. Blake's plate is based on a wash drawing, 23.5 × 15.8 cm., now in the Mitchell Library, New South Wales (*Fig. 138*). As the signature in the plate indicates, this drawing has traditionally been attributed to Philip Gidley King (1758–1808), appointed lieutenant-governor of Norfolk Island in January 1790, although this ascription is not certain. Blake has made a number of significant alterations in the design. The woman in the plate walks with her right (rather than left) leg forward, thereby matching the man's gait. The boy's face is turned to a profile view, vegetation added below him, and the man and woman spread apart so that their limbs no longer overlap. Blake has made the woman less fat and parted the two fish she holds. The background shrubbery has changed. Smith 1985 compares the attitudes towards the aborigines expressed by some of these alterations with Blake's 'The Little Black Boy' in *Songs of Innocence*. Gott 1989, p. 90, suggests that Blake worked from an 'idealized finished copy-drawing ... from another journeyman's hand'. If such a drawing did exist, it is more likely to have been by Blake than anyone else—see **XXI**, pl. 1, for an analogous instance. For other comments, see the Introduction.

Literature: Bentley and Nurmi 1964, no. 385; Bentley 1977, no. 476; Easson and Essick 1979, no. XXXIX; Essick 1980, p. 53; Bernard Smith, *European Vision and the South Pacific* (2nd edn., New Haven: Yale Univ. Press, 1985), 173–5; Ted Gott, ' "Eternity in an Hour": The Prints of William Blake', in Martin Butlin and Ted Gott, *William Blake in the Collection of the National Gallery of Victoria* (Victoria: National Gallery of Victoria, 1989), 88–91.

XXVIII

James Stuart and Nicholas Revett, *The Antiquities of Athens*, vol. iii (London: Printed by John Nichols [for the authors?], 1794); *Figs. 139–42*

This monumental and influential study of the ancient buildings and statues of Athens by Stuart (1713–88) and Revett (1720–1804) was published in four large folio volumes between 1762 and 1816. All four of Blake's plates are among the 107 in the third volume and are based on drawings by William Pars (1742–82), the official draughtsman on Revett's expedition to Ionia in 1764–6. Pars's drawings for Blake's plates are now in the British Museum, Department of Greek and Roman Antiquities. The illustrations engraved by Blake, which follow the drawings closely, are briefly described on p. 9 of the text. All four show portions of the battle of the Centaurs and Lapithae represented on the frieze above the entrance to the pronaos (anti-temple) of the Temple of Theseus, Athens. The entire wall is pictured in the unsigned 'Pl. IV'. Along with Blake's work on Cumberland's *Thoughts on Outline* (**XXXII**), these plates for Stuart and Revett are Blake's most direct

engagement with the type of antiquities that shaped late-eighteenth-century neo-classicism.

Blake's commission for the plates is documented in a letter to him of 18 October 1791 from Willey Reveley, editor of the third volume: 'Mr Reveley's Compt^{ts} to Mr Blake [;] if he wishes to engrave any of Mr Pars's drawings for the Antiquities of Athens, & can do them by the end of January Mr Reveley will be glad to [send] some to him' (Bentley 1969, p. 44). Blake replied in an undated letter: 'Mr Blakes Compt^{ts} to Mr Reveley tho full of work (as M^r R said he should be by then [tho] the plates were put in hand) he is glad to embrace the offer of engraving such beautiful things. & will do what he can by the end of January' (E 699, K 790). In May 1808 George Cumberland wrote in his notebook that he 'Got Blake to Engrave for Athens' (Bentley 1969, p. 189), perhaps in reference to the Stuart and Revett plates Blake had engraved some sixteen years earlier. But the commission may have also come as a result of Blake having been an art student of Pars's elder brother (suggested by Bentley 1969, p. 44 n. 3) or a recommendation from Blake's former master, James Basire, who had engraved plates for Stuart's and Revett's first volume. In a letter to Prince Hoare of 25 December 1803, John Flaxman commented that Blake's plates in 'Stuart's Athens' were executed 'in a very masterly manner' (Bentley 1969, p. 136).

The plate inscriptions along their right margins are horizontal in the volume since the plates are bound vertically. The edition of 1825–30 contains the illustrations re-engraved in outline on a much reduced scale.

1. The twenty-first plate following p. 10; 14.3 × 37.6 cm.; *Fig. 139*

Inscription along right margin: Vol. III. Chap. I. Pl. XXI.

Signatures: *W. Pars delin^t* [left], *Blake. Sculp.* [right]
Imprint: *Pub,^{d} as the Act directs, April 3^d 1792—*

The text, p. 6, notes that the figure far right, standing above a fallen centaur, may be Theseus.

2. Following pl. 1; 14.2 × 36 cm.; *Fig. 140*

Inscription along right margin: Vol. III. Chap. I. Pl XXII.

Signatures: *W. Pars, Delin.* [left], *Blake, Sculp.* [right]
Imprint: *Pub.* *as the Act directs, April 3.ᵈ 1792.*

The text, p. 9, identifies the figure lower right, beneath a rock held by two centaurs, as Caeneus.

3. Following pl. 2; 14.3 × 38.1 cm.; *Fig. 141*

Inscription along right margin: Vol. III. Chap. I. Pl. XXIII.
Signatures: *W. Pars, Delin.* [left], *Blake Sculp.* [right]
Imprint: *Pub.ᵈ as the Act directs, April 3.ᵈ 1792.*

4. Following pl. 3; 14.3 × 38.3 cm.; *Fig. 142*

Inscription along right margin: Vol III Chap I Pl XXIV
Signatures: *W, Pars delin.* [left], *Blake, Sculp.* [right]
Imprint: *Pub,.ᵈ as the Act directs April 3.ᵈ 1792.*

Literature: Bentley and Nurmi 1964, no. 409; Bentley 1977, no. 500; Easson and Essick 1979, no. XLIII; Essick 1980, pp. 33, 143.

XXIX

John Brown, *The Elements of Medicine* (2 vols.; London: J. Johnson, 1795); *Fig. 143*

The frontispiece to the first volume, the only plate in the book, was engraved by Blake after a portrait by John Donaldson (1737–1801). The author and subject of the plate, Dr John Brown (1735–88), was the founder of the important 'Brunonian' system of medicine. In 1786 he moved from Edinburgh to Golden Square, London, about two blocks from the home of Blake's brother James, but there is no record of contact between the physician and the engraver.

1. Frontispiece, vol. i; oval, 13.1 × 10.8 cm.; *Fig. 143*

Signatures: *Donaldson Pinx.* [left], *Blake Sculp.* [right]
Title: JOHN BROWN, M. D.
Imprint: *London, Published May 1. 1795, by J. Johnson, S.ᵗ Paul's Church Yard.*

According to Charles Creighton's article on Brown in the *Dictionary of National Biography*, iii. 16, Donaldson's original 'miniature' portrait, copied in Blake's plate, was then in the collection of the artist Ford Madox Brown, but this work is now untraced. An engraving by James Caldwall of the same miniature, but with slight changes in the costume, was published by Thomas Cox in 1799. Edward Evans, *Catalogue of a Collection of Engraved Portraits* (c. 1835–6), no. 1401,

lists an impression of Blake's plate for sale (1*s*. 6*d*.). Perhaps a few impressions were issued as a separate plate or simply left unbound after the publication of the book.

Literature: Russell 1912, no. 83, without reference to the plate's appearance in the book; Keynes 1921, no. 109; Bentley and Nurmi 1964, no. 354; Bentley 1977, no. 438; Easson and Essick 1979, no. XLIV.

XXX

The Poems of Caius Valerius Catullus, in English Verse [by John Nott] (2 vols.; London: J. Johnson, 1795); *Figs. 144–5*

The only two plates, the frontispiece to each volume, were engraved in stipple by Blake after statues of Catullus and his friend, Cornelius Nepos, which stand 'over the *Palazzo di Consiglio*, or Council-house at Verona' ('Preface', i, p. xii). The 'Xaverius Della Rosa' whose name appears on the plates evidently made drawings of these statues, perhaps on commission for Nott (1751–1825), the editor and translator of the work, while Nott was in Italy. I can find no information about Della Rosa.

1. Frontispiece, vol. i; 16.8 × 10 cm.; *Fig. 144*

Inscription top right: *Frontispiece to Vol. 1.*
Signatures: *Xaverius Della Rosa, Veronæ, delin.* [left], *Blake sculpsit.* [right]
Title: C: VAL: CATVLLVS. | Apud effigiem antiquam curiæ senatûs veronensi superpositam.
Imprint: *London Published March 19, 1795 by J. Johnson, S.ᵗ Pauls Church Y.ᵈ*

2. Frontispiece, vol. ii; 17 × 10.5 cm.; *Fig. 145*

Inscription top right: *Frontispiece to Vol. 2.*
Signatures: as on pl. 1.
Title: CORNEL: NEPOS. | as on pl. 1
Imprint: *London Published March 19, 1795, by J. Johnson, S.ᵗ Pauls Church Yard.* [not reproduced]

Literature: Gilchrist 1880, ii. 283; Russell 1912, no. 82, recorded as loose impressions only, the book untraced; Keynes 1921, no. 110; Bentley and Nurmi 1964, no. 357; Bentley 1977, no. 441; Easson and Essick 1979, no. XLV.

XXXI

George Cumberland, *An Attempt to Describe Hafod* (London: sold by T. Egerton [for the author], 1796); *Fig. 146*

The only plate in this small volume, a folding map, was first attributed to Blake by David V. Erdman (as reported in Keynes 1970, pp. 39, 58–9) on the basis of the left-pointing serif on the lower case 'g' in the map's inscriptions (see for example 'Cardigan' in the box lower left, *Fig. 146*). This is an unusual feature of Blake's etched or engraved writing in the 1790s (see Erdman, 'Dating Blake's Script: The "g" Hypothesis', *Blake Newsletter*, 3 (1969), 8–13). More generally, the style of all the letters, their shape and method of stroking, is the same as in Blake's other, and reasonably distinctive, scratched inscriptions, such as those on the plates he executed for Cumberland's *Thoughts on Outline* of the same year (**XXXII**). Bentley 1975 and 1977 questions the attribution because the plates in *Thoughts on Outline* signed by Cumberland also contain the sinister 'g'. These inscriptions, however, are in my view also by Blake—see discussion under **XXXII**. I find Erdman's argument, supplemented by a consideration of all the letter forms, convincing. The attribution pertains only to the inscriptions. Blake may have engraved the entire plate; but it is also possible that Cumberland, an amateur engraver, executed the map (after his own drawing?) and then turned to Blake for his skill in reverse lettering—just as Cumberland did for his own plates in *Thoughts on Outline*.

Cumberland (1754–1848) was a close friend of Blake, perhaps from as early as the mid-1780s. The many documents regarding their relationship are printed or summarized in Bentley 1969; Blake's six extant letters to Cumberland are printed in E and K. Cumberland's *Attempt to Describe Hafod* presents a tour of the picturesque environs of the estate of Thomas Johnes in Wales. Johnes owned a copy of *Song of Innocence* (Bentley 1977, p. 409) and is probably the figure referred to as 'Hereford, ancient Guardian of Wales' (E 188, K 676) in *Jerusalem* pl. 41 (as pointed out by

Paley 1969 and Todd 1975). The two men may have known each other, but there is no documentary record of direct contact between them.

1. Folding map, facing p. 1; 15.5 × 35.2 cm.; *Fig. 146*

Title lower left: *A Map of part of the Estate of Thomas Johnes Esq: MP | at Havod in the County of Cardigan: Jan.ᵞ 1796.*

Other inscriptions: see *Fig. 146*.

Literature: Morton D. Paley, 'Thomas Johnes, "Ancient Guardian of Wales"', *Blake Newsletter*, 2 (1969), 65–7; Geoffrey Keynes, 'Some Uncollected Authors XLIV: George Cumberland 1754–1848', *The Book Collector*, 19 (1970), 31–65 (repr. in part and with revisions in Keynes 1971, pp. 230–52); G. E. Bentley, jun., *A Bibliography of George Cumberland* (New York: Garland, 1975), 12–15; Ruthven Todd, 'The Identity of "Hereford" in *Jerusalem*', *Blake Studies*, 6 (1975), 139–51; Bentley 1977, no. 445; Easson and Essick 1979, no. XLIX; Malcolm Andrews, *The Search for the Picturesque* (Stanford: Stanford Univ. Press, 1989), 145–50 (on the Hafod estate).

XXXII

George Cumberland, *Thoughts on Outline* (London: Messrs. Robinson and T. Egerton, 1796); *Outlines from the Antients* (London: Septimus Prowett, 1829); *Figs. 147–54*

Thoughts on Outline contains twenty-four plates bound following Cumberland's essay. Fifteen are signed by Cumberland as the designer and engraver, eight are signed by Cumberland as the designer and Blake as the engraver, and the engraved title-page to the plates is unsigned (but presumably by Cumberland). The subjects for the plates Blake engraved are based (in some cases very loosely) on the story of Cupid and Psyche in *The Golden Ass* of Apuleius (pls. 1–5), Ovid's *Metamorphoses* (pl. 6), *The Clouds* of Aristophanes (pl. 7), and Anacreon's *Odes* (pl. 8). According to Cumberland's letter of 10 January 1804 to the publisher Longman & Rees, Blake was paid 'Two guineas each and the coppers' for his work (Bentley 1969, p. 569).

Second states of pls. 3, 4, 7, and 8 were published in an appendix to Cumberland's *Outlines from the Antients* (1829). In a letter of 24 May 1824 to his son George, Cumberland expressed the hope that his new publisher, Prowett, 'will put the 4 Plates into Blakes hands to reenter the lines & repair, as he will do it, I know carefully having engraved them for me' (Bentley 1969, p. 286). And in a letter of 17 June 1824, also to his son, Cumberland refers 'particularly' to pls. 3 and 7 and hopes that these will be 'repaired by Blake if they are worn by Printing' (Bentley 1969, p. 287). The four plates in *Outlines from the Antients* show no clear evidence of reworking other than the change in inscribed plate numbers noted below. Blake may only have removed solidified ink from the lines, if indeed he worked on the plates at all. The renumbering may have been done by someone other than Blake.

According to Bentley 1977, p. 543, 'proofs for pl. 2–24' (as numbered on the plates) are in the BMPR, but the only such group I have located in that collection is in the published states (but see pl. 7 for one proof). Folio copies of *Outlines from the Antients* (e.g. RNE) are printed on a paper (1825 watermark) much thicker than the stock used in quarto copies. A reissue of the 1829 work (RNE) contains a new 'Contents' leaf, listing 'IV. Plates, from Compositions by G. Cumberland, outlined by Blake'; this issue contains only the plates without Cumberland's essay.

Thoughts on Outline participates in the neo-classical linearism, inspired by Greek vase paintings, sculpture, and antique gems, of which John Flaxman's compositions were the most famous exemplars (see **XLVI, LI**). The aesthetic implicit in such severe images, discussed by Cumberland in his text, had much in common with Blake's own linear graphic style and neo-classical predilections of the 1780s and 1790s. In a letter to Cumberland of 2 July 1800 Blake welcomed the 'flood of Grecian light & glory which is coming on Europe' and noted how 'artists of all ranks', including Flaxman, had 'praise' for Cumberland's 'outlines' (E 706, K 797–8), which had also received commendation in William Hayley's *Essay on Sculpture* (see **XXXIX**). Soon thereafter, Blake's response to classicism shifted dramatically towards harsh criticism. As he wrote *c.* 1804–8 in the 'Preface' to *Milton*, 'we do not want either Greek or Roman Models if we are but just & true to our own Imaginations' (E 95, K 480). This change, however, did not dislodge 'firm and determinate outline' (*Descriptive Catalogue* of 1809 (E 549, K 585)) from its central position in Blake's concepts of perception and creation.

In *Thoughts on Outline* Cumberland commends Blake's efforts on the book:

> ... one thing may be asserted of this work, which can be said of few others that have passed the hands of an engraver, which is, that *Mr. Blake* has condescended to take upon him the laborious office of making them, I may say, facsimiles of my originals: a compliment, from a man of his extraordinary genius and abilities, the highest, I believe, I shall ever receive:— and I am indebted to his generous partiality for the instruction which encouraged me to execute a great part of the plates myself; enabling me thereby to reduce considerably the price of the book.   (pp. 47–8)

This 'instruction' appears to have extended to Blake's execution of the lettering on the plates signed by Cumberland, as Keynes 1971 was the first to contend (p. 237). In a 1795 description of his own method of engraved writing, Cumberland indicates that the letters were not reversed on the plates and thus impressions would have backwards writing (Keynes 1971, pp. 231–2). This would indicate that he had not learnt the art of writing and engraving in reverse, a skill for which he praises Blake in an article of 1811 (Essick 1980, p. 90). The most direct evidence that Cumberland turned to Blake as his writing engraver is provided by the same lettering style used on the plates signed by both men and the appearance of a reverse serif on the 'g' in Cumberland's plates— a characteristic of Blake's engraved and etched hands in the 1790s (see David V. Erdman, 'Dating Blake's Script: The "g" Hypothesis', *Blake Newsletter*, 3 (1969), 8–13). These Cumberland plates should be included in Blake's graphic œuvre, or a subset of it devoted to 'Plates by Others Bearing Blake Inscriptions'. His contribution, however, was minor in this instance, and thus Cumberland's plates have not been catalogued here.

Cumberland was for many years a friend of Blake's—see **XXXI** and the records in Bentley

1969. In a letter of 6 December 1795 to Cumberland, Blake notes that he has 'not been able to send a proof of the bath [i.e. pl. 8] tho I have done the corrections [perhaps suggested by Cumberland]. my paper [for printing] not being in order' (E 700, K 791). This letter also contains a description of how to transfer a drawing to a copperplate, probably to assist Cumberland in the preparation of his own plates for the book. Blake wrote to Cumberland on 23 December 1796, thanking him for his 'beautiful book' (E 700, K 791), and again on 26 August 1799, stating that he studies Cumberland's 'outlines as usual just as if they were antiques' (E 704, K 795). In his manuscript account of Cumberland, written sometime before 1850, Thomas Dodd criticizes Cumberland's plates but compliments Blake's as being 'decidedly more correct' (Bentley 1969, p. 12).

1. The twelfth plate following the text, *Thoughts on Outline*; oval, 11.1 × 14 cm.; *Fig. 147*

Number top right: 12
Title top left: PSYCHE DISOBEYS
Signatures and imprint: *From an original Invention by G. Cumberland. Engᵈ by W Blake: Publishd as the Act directs November 5: 1794*

Psyche, disobeying Cupid's commands, brings forth a lamp to see his face and form. Chayes 1970, pp. 218–19, points out the similarities between Cumberland's design, an engraving of the 'Discovery of Cupid' by Agostino Veneziano after Michiel van Coxie, pl. 7 of Blake's *Europe*, and a pencil sketch in *The Four Zoas*, p. 28. The oval shapes of the designs in pls. 1 and 2 suggest cameos, while their densely hatched backgrounds 'imitate' the red-figure paintings on 'Greek vases', as Cumberland pointed out in a letter of 17 June 1824 (Bentley 1969, p. 287).

2. The thirteenth plate, *Thoughts on Outline*; oval, 11.2 × 14.3 cm.; *Fig. 148*

Number top right: 13
Title top left: PSYCHE REPENTS
Signatures and imprint: *From the original invention by G: Cumberland. Engᵈ by W Blake. Publish'd as the Act directs Nov. 5: 1794*

Psyche, regretting her disobedience (pl. 1), grasps Cupid by the ankle in an attempt to prevent his leaving her.

3. The fourteenth plate, *Thoughts on Outline*; 14.1 × 11.1 cm.; *Fig. 149*

Number top right: 14
Title at top: VENUS COUNCELS CUPID
Signatures and imprint: *From an original Invention by G Cumberland. Engᵈ by W. Blake. Publishd as the Act directs Nov 5: 1794*

Second State, first plate in the 'Appendix', *Outlines from the Antients*. The number top right has been removed and '78' inscribed in open letters below the title.

The design appears to be based on the passage in *The Golden Ass* when Venus disarms Cupid and chastises him for falling in love with Psyche. In his note to the 'Appendix' in *Outlines from the Antients*, Cumberland states that this and pl. 4 are based on designs 'made at the request of the celebrated *Pickler* [Johann Pichler, 1734–91], of Rome, in 1789, for two cameos in imitation of the Antique, and in which the mode of composition of the Greeks was aimed at: one of them represents the sufferings from the passion of love, the other their conjugal union' (p. 45).

4. The fifteenth plate, *Thoughts on Outline*; 14.9 × 11.3 cm.; *Fig. 150*

Number top right: 15
Title at top: THE CONJUGAL UNION OF CUPID
Signatures and imprint: *From an original Invention by G. Cumberland. Engᵈ by W Blake. Publishd as the Act directs Nov: 5. 1794*

Second State, the second plate in the 'Appendix', *Outlines from the Antients*. The number top right has been removed and '79' inscribed in open letters below the title.

Although Apuleius mentions several conjugal unions of the couple, his text does not contain a description of this scene. Psyche is now given her customary wings; beneath her are two butterflies or moths, her traditional emblems. Cupid bound to a tree is also a traditional motif with a history extending into early Greek art. One of the first literary uses of this motif is the *Cupido cruciatus* of Ausonius. For Cumberland's note on this design, see pl. 3.

5. The sixteenth plate, *Thoughts on Outline*; 15.6 × 21.6 cm.; *Fig. 151*

Number top right: 16
Title on base of column, left: CUPID & PSYCHE
Signatures and imprint: *From an original Invention by G. Cumberland. Engᵈ by W Blake. Publish'd as the Act directs | Nov. 5: 1794*

The same subject as pl. 1. Cumberland's pencil, pen, and grey-wash preliminary drawing, 17 × 22.9 cm., is in an album in the BMPR. The mounting sheet is inscribed in pencil by Cumberland, 'This was the design I alluded to in my thoughts on outline when I said there was one among them stolen from Antique models, and which I inserted as a crust for the critics, but which they failed to discover it was taken from two separate statues in the Vatican.'

6. The eighteenth plate, *Thoughts on Outline*; 13.2 × 23.1 cm.; *Fig. 152*

Number top right: *18*

Title top left: IRON AGE

Inscription upper right: *Then cursed steel & more accursed gold | Gave mischief birth & made that mischief bold. | Ovid. Iron Age*

Signatures and imprint: *From an original Invention by G: Cumberland: Eng.ᵈ by W Blake. Publishd as the Act directs. Nov.ʳ 5: 1794.*

The design is based loosely on Ovid's description, Book I of his *Metamorphoses*, of how the discovery of gold brought chaos even to the gods during the Iron Age. Jupiter, observing the conflict between Furies and Satyrs with disapproval, stands on the left, with his eagle (perched on his staff) and a stylized thunderbolt in his right hand. The text quoted upper right is from the 1717 translation edited by Samuel Garth. In his text, Cumberland notes that this plate exemplifies how 'a flowing Outline gives motion' (p. 28) and how the lines delineating one of the Furies 'violate the system' of outline composition he has described (p. 47). Cumberland's preliminary pen-and-ink drawing (13.2 × 23.1 cm.), tinted in imitation of a red-figure vase painting, is in an album in the BMPR. The mounting sheet is inscribed by Cumberland in pencil, 'The female figure on the right hand was especially designed to show how easily the beauty of a composition might be destroyed by a miss-application of both form and lines.'

7. The nineteenth plate, *Thoughts on Outline*; 14.3 × 20.5 cm.; *Fig. 153*

Number top right: *19*

Title at top: ARISTOPHANES CLOUDS. SCENE. I.

Greek inscriptions above figures of their names: see *Fig. 153.*

Signatures and imprint: *From an original Invention by G: C: Eng.ᵈ by W. B: Published January. 1: 1795—*

Second State, the third plate in the 'Appendix', *Outlines from the Antients*. The number top right has been removed and '80' inscribed in open letters below the title.

The design illustrates the opening scene of *The Clouds*. Pheidippides (right) sleeps under a sheepskin while his father Strepsiades (centre) rises to read his ledger and call for his servant (the 'Therapon', left) to light the lamp. Strepsiades mentions that his son dreams of driving his horses in tandem, as in the picture on the wall to which Pheidippides points. In his note to the 'Appendix' in *Outlines from the Antients* Cumberland states that this design is 'intended as a specimen of the proper mode of embellishing the classics' (p. 45). A proof of the plate, lacking a few strokes on the jug lower left and the flame before the boy, is in an album of Cumberland drawings in the BMPR. In the picture upper right, there are trees rather than columns right of the chariot, the reins are not present, and a large feather or leaf projects from the lower right corner of the frame. The impression has been trimmed to the edges of the image and tinted in imitation of red-figure vase painting. The Greek inscriptions within the design, if present, have been painted over in black.

8. The twenty-third plate, *Thoughts on Outline*; 12.1 × 16.4 cm.; *Fig. 154*

Number top right: 23

Title at top: ANACREON ODE LII

Signatures and imprint: *From an Original Invention by G: C: Eng.ᵈ by W. B: Publishd Jan.ʸ 1: 1795*

Second State, the fourth plate in the 'Appendix', *Outlines from the Antients*. The number top right has been removed and '81' inscribed in open letters below the title.

Anacreon's fifty-second ode, 'Grapes, or the Vintage', describes wine-making and the love-making that follows. Apparently the figures in the vat are pressing grapes, while the winged Cupid (right) is lifting the girl from the bath to protect her from the Satyrs. Cumberland's composition bears only a loose relationship to its titular subject. In his note in the 'Appendix' in *Outlines from the Antients* Cumberland states that 'the Bath, with Innocence protected, was for the same purpose' (p. 45) as pl. 3. Cumberland's preliminary pen-and-ink drawing (14.1 × 17.2 cm.), tinted in imitation of red-figure vase painting, is in the BMPR.

Literature: Gilchrist 1863, ii. 261 (*Thoughts on Outline* only); Russell 1912, no. 85 (*Thoughts on Outline* only); Keynes 1921, nos. 112, 133; Bentley and Nurmi 1964, nos. 361–2; Raine 1968 (see **XXI**, *Literature*), i. 180–203; Irene H. Chayes, 'The Presence of Cupid and Psyche', in David V. Erdman and John E. Grant (eds.), *Blake's Visionary Forms Dramatic* (Princeton: Princeton Univ. Press, 1970), 214–43; Keynes 1970 (see **XXXI**, *Literature*), pp. 15–17, 20, 39–40; Bentley 1977, nos. 446–7; Easson and Essick 1979, nos. XLVII–XLVIII; Essick 1980, pp. 53–4; Gott 1989 (see **XXVII**, *Literature*), pp. 99–108.

XXXIII

John Gabriel Stedman, *Narrative, of a Five Years' Expedition, against the Revolted Negroes of Surinam* (2 vols.; London: J. Johnson and J. Edwards, 1796; London: J. Johnson and T. Payne, 1806, 1813); *Figs. 155–70*

The 1796 and 1806 editions, and the reissue of the latter in 1813, contain a frontispiece to vol. i, an engraved vignette on each title-page, and eighty numbered full-page plates (including three maps). Thirteen of the numbered plates are signed by Blake as the engraver. Two plates (7, 14) are unsigned, but were first attributed to Blake on stylistic grounds by Russell 1912. Keynes 1921, Bentley and Nurmi 1964, and Bentley 1977 accept Russell's opinion and ascribe another unsigned plate (12) to Blake. The attribution of all three unsigned plates to Blake is justified, for they exhibit the bold worm lines and cross-hatching patterns that distinguish his work from the plates signed by other engravers in the volumes. Since Blake signed one of the botanical illustrations (pl. 11), executed in a somewhat less distinctive style than his others, it is possible that other, merely workmanlike unsigned plates of flora and fauna are also from his hand. An untraced '*Proof* of an illustration designed and engraved by Blake for "Stedman's Surinam"' was sold at Sotheby's, 9 December 1905, lot 921 no. 53 (to 'Paul') and again on 15 December 1906, lot 482 no. 53 (to 'Abbey'). Johnson's co-publisher for the 1796 edition, James Edwards, was the brother of Richard Edwards, publisher of the 1797 edition of Young's *Night Thoughts* with illustrations designed and engraved by Blake. James Edwards may have played a role in introducing Blake or his work to his brother.

Although only two plates bear Stedman's name as the designer, there is no reason to doubt the statement on the title-pages that the '80 elegant Engravings' are all based on 'drawings made by the Author'. Unfortunately, only one of Sted-man's drawings for the book has survived, a water-colour for the plate numbered 73, 'Manner of Sleeping &c. in the Forest', engraved by J. Barlow (drawing and plate reproduced in Price and Price 1988, fig. 7). Barlow has changed the format from vertical to horizontal and made many alterations in the placement and configuration of motifs. It is reasonable to assume that the other engravers were permitted similar liberties. Stedman's amateur drawing is not without charm, but his figures lack grace and his sense of composition (although perhaps faithful to the scene portrayed) falls below contemporary standards of proportion and balance. Thus it seems fair to believe that the dignified postures and expressiveness of the figures in Blake's plates were in part the work of the engraver. Blake's improvements, and in particular the dignity imparted to people then thought to be primitive, may have followed the same course observable in his plate for Hunter's *Historical Journal (***XXVII**, Figs. 137–8).

On 1 December 1791 Stedman wrote in his journal that he had received 'about 40 Engravings from London'—no doubt proofs of the illustrations for his book—and had written 'to the Engraver Blake to thank him twice for his excellent work but never received any answer' (Bentley 1969, p. 45). In June 1794 Stedman visited Blake and their publisher, Joseph Johnson, and Blake subsequently undertook 'to do business' for Stedman when he was 'not in London' (Bentley 1969, pp. 48–9). These favours may have included dealings with Johnson, about whose slowness and printing errors Stedman often complained.

Stedman's narrative of the brutalities of slavery very probably influenced Blake's own anti-slavery position, particularly as expressed in *Visions of the Daughters of Albion* of 1793 (see Erdman 1952). The figure being broken on a rack in pl. 14 resembles, and may have influenced the con-figuration of, the figure bound to a rock on pl. 3 of Blake's *America* (1793). Erdman 1954 (p. 216 n. 11), Bogan 1976, and Keynes 1979 have independently concluded that Stedman's description of 'the Vampire [bat] or Spectre of Guiana' and its representation in the plate numbered 57, engraved by Anker Smith, helped shape Blake's conception of the 'Spectre' in *Jerusalem* and its bat-winged portrayal on pls. 6 and 37 of the illuminated book. Price and Price 1988, p. XLII, interestingly suggest that Stedman's description of a 'red tyger' with 'eyes ... sparkling like stars' and of a 'tyger-cat' with 'eyes emitting flashes like lightning' (ii. 50–1) influenced the imagery of stars and their 'spears' (i.e. lightning?) in Blake's most famous lyric, 'The Tyger', first composed as a draft in his *Notebook c.* 1793 (K 172–3).

Several unsigned reviews of Stedman's *Narrative* take notice of the plates. Johnson's own *Analytical Review*, 24 (Sept. 1796), 237, comments that the 'numerous plates ... are neatly engraved, and are, we have great reason to believe, faithful and correct delineations of objects described in the work'. *The Critical Review*, 19 (Jan. 1797), 60, claims that the plates are 'executed in a style of uncommon elegance', but *The British Critic*, 8 (Nov. 1796), 539, is more circumspect: 'The plates are very unequal; some would do honour to the most elegant, whilst others would disgrace the meanest, performances. The representations of the negroes suffering under various kinds of torture [pls. 2, 14], might well have been omitted, both in the narrative and as engravings, for we will not call them embellishments to the work.' See also comments on pl. 5, below.

The 1796 edition was issued in both large- (approx. 30 × 23.5 cm.) and small-paper formats. At least a few, and perhaps all, of the large-paper copies (e.g. James Ford Bell Library, University of Minnesota, Minneapolis; HEH; Keynes Collection, Cambridge University Library) were very effectively hand coloured, some with touches of liquefied gold or silver. Price and Price 1988, p. XLVIII, compare the extant watercolour with the coloured plate and conclude that all the hand colouring was probably based on Stedman's originals. There are also coloured copies of the 1806 and 1813 editions, but these are less skilful and may have been tinted at later dates (e.g. RNE). A hand-coloured impression of pl. 16 from the 1796 edition is reproduced in colour in Price and Price 1988, facing p. 618. There are several translations of Stedman's book containing some of Blake's plates re-engraved: Hamburg 1797 (pls. 1, 5, 15),

Paris 1798 (pls. 1, 2, 4, 5, 8–10, 12, 13, 15), Amsterdam 1799–1800 (same plates as Paris 1798), Stockholm 1800 (pl. 5), and Milan 1818 (pls. 1, 2, 5, 8, 10, 12, 13, 15). For details on these editions, and reproductions of the copies of pl. 8 in the Paris, Amsterdam, and Milan editions, see Price and Price 1988, pp. LXXIII–LXXX and fig. 13.

1. Vol. i, facing p. 80 (1796 edn.); and facing p. 87 (1806 and 1813 edns.); 17.7 × 13.5 cm.; *Fig. 155*

Signature right: *Blake Sculp!*

Title: *A Coromantyn Free Negro, or Ranger, armed.*

Imprint and number: *London, Published Dec! 2ᵈ 1793, by J. Johnson, S! Paul's Church Yard.* | 7

The Rangers, a 'corps of manumitted slaves', were recruited to fight against the 'rebel negroes' (p. 79). Their dress, including 'a scarlet cap, the emblem of liberty, on which is their number', and arms are described on p. 80. The Ranger in this plate also bears tribal scarring on his cheeks, not noted in the text.

2. Vol. i, facing p. 110 (1796 edn.); and facing p. 116 (1806 and 1813 edns.); 18 × 12.9 cm.; *Fig. 156*

Signature right: *Blake Sculp!*

Title: *A Negro hung alive by the Ribs to a Gallows.*

Imprint and number: *London, Published Dec! 1ˢᵗ 1792, by J. Johnson, S! Pauls Church Yard.* | 11

The torture represented was not witnessed by Stedman, but described to him by 'a decent looking man', pp. 108–9. The victim 'never complained', even though he was 'kept alive three days'.

3. Vol. i, facing p. 132 (1796 edn.); and facing p. 140 (1806 and 1813 edns.); 18.7 × 13.4 cm.; *Fig. 157*.

Signature right: *Blake Sculp!*

Title: *A private Marine of Col. Fourgeoud's Corps.*

Imprint and number: *London, Published Dec! 2ᵈ 1793, by J. Johnson, S! Pauls Church Yard.* | 13

The dress (but not the hat decorations) and arms of the Marines are described on p. 132. Fourgeoud, with whom Stedman served, led the colonial defence against the rebel slaves.

4. Vol. i, facing p. 166 (1796 edn.); and facing p. 174 (1806 and 1813 edns.); 18 × 13.2 cm.; *Fig. 158*

Signature right: *Blake Sculp!*

Title: *The Mecoo & Kishee Kishee Monkeys.*

Imprint and number: *London, Published Dec! 2ⁿᵈ 1793, by J. Johnson, S! Pauls Church Yard.* | 18

Stedman describes these two varieties of monkey, seen

during his trip up the Cottica and Patamaca rivers, on p. 166. The Mecoo monkeys are at the top of the tree.

5. Vol. i, facing p. 174 (1796 edn.); and facing p. 182 (1806 and 1813 edns.); 18.1 × 13 cm.; *Fig. 159*

Signature right: *Blake Sculp.*

Title: *The skinning of the Aboma Snake, shot by Cap. Stedman.*

Imprint and number: as on pl. 1 | *19*

The 'negro David' (p. 174) climbs up the boa constrictor, 'twenty-two feet and some inches' long (p. 173), to begin skinning the snake. Like the man similarly hung from the gallows in pl. 2, the victim is still alive. The figure lower left is probably Stedman. This plate attracted the notice of two anonymous reviewers of the book. *The British Critic*, 8 (Nov. 1796), 540, notes that 'the snakes in the plate must be greatly out of proportion with respect to the man. In the narrative it is expressly affirmed to have been about the thickness of the boy Quace; but in the plate it far exceeds that of the man David'. *The London Review and Literary Journal* (Jan.–Apr. 1797), 118, comments more simply that this is 'a very good print' (no copy located; quoted from Bentley 1977, p. 623). Price and Price 1988, p. XLII, suggest that Stedman's design influenced Blake's picture of a snake with three children riding it in *America* pl. 13 (1793). This seems unlikely, for Blake had already used a very similar version of the motif in 1789, before any recorded involvement with Stedman's book, on pl. 8 of *The Book of Thel*.

6. Vol. i, facing p. 200 (1796 edn.); and facing p. 209 (1806 and 1813 edns.); 18.1 × 13.4 cm.; *Fig. 160*

Signature right: *Blake Sculp.*

Title: *Group of Negros, as imported to be sold for Slaves.*

Imprint and number: as on pl. 1 | *22*

Stedman described these slaves, just disembarking from a ship, as 'walking skeletons' (p. 200). Blake's tendency to idealize these figures, particularly the woman holding the child's hand, runs counter to the thrust of the narrative. The man behind the group is a 'sailor' with a 'bamboo-rattan' stick used to shepherd the slaves along (p. 201).

7. Vol. i, facing p. 227 (1796 edn.); and facing p. 237 (1806 and 1813 edns.); 18.2 × 12.9 cm.; *Fig. 161*

Title: *The Sculls of Lieu. t Leppar, & Six of his Men.*

Imprint and number: as on pl. 1 | *25*

Colonial troops have come upon 'seven *human* skulls stuck upon stakes . . . and part of the garments, (as may be seen in the annexed plate) and which proved them

to be the remains of the unfortunate Lieutenant *Lepper* [of the colonial Rangers], with six of his unhappy men' killed by the rebels (p. 227). The event is not witnessed by Stedman but reported to him.

8. Vol. i, facing p. 326 (1796 edn.); and facing p. 339 (1806 and 1813 edns.); 18.1 × 13.2 cm.; *Fig. 162*

Signature right: *Blake Sculp.*

Title: *Flagellation of a Female Samboe Slave.*

Imprint and number: as on pl. 1 | *35*

Stedman (lower left?) tries to stop the overseer and his 'two negro-drivers' (p. 325) from whipping the girl any further. Instead, they double their efforts, and Stedman flees back to his boat, lower left. The disproportionate sizes of the figures may have been deployed for expressive purposes.

9. Vol. ii, facing p. 10 (all edns.); 18.2 × 13.1 cm.; *Fig. 163*

Signature right: *Blake Sculp.*

Title: *The Quato & Saccawinkee Monkeys.*

Imprint and number: as on pl. 4 | *42*

These rather comic creatures are described on pp. 10–13. The Saccawinkee monkeys are at the top of the tree.

10. Vol. ii, facing p. 56 (1796 edn.); and facing p. 58 (1806 and 1813 edns.); 18 × 13.1 cm.; *Fig. 164*

Signature right: *Blake Sculp.*

Title: *A Surinam Planter in his Morning Dress.*

Imprint and number: as on pl. 1 | *49*

'To give a more complete idea of this fine gentleman, I in the annexed plate present him to the reader with a pipe in his mouth, which almost every where accompanies him, and receiving a glass of Madeira wine and water, from a female quaderoon slave, to refresh him during his walk' (p. 56). 'Fine' is ironic here, for Stedman describes the self-corrupting brutality of such planters. Boime 1987, p. 341, claims that 'Blake added to the engraving a black female servant', but I can find no evidence that the 'female . . . slave', mentioned in Stedman's description of the plate, did not appear in his untraced drawing.

11. Vol. ii, facing p. 74 (1796 edn.); and facing p. 76 (1806 and 1813 edns.); 18 × 13.1 cm.; *Fig. 165*

Signature right: *Blake Sculp.*

Title: *Limes, Capsicum, Mammy Apple &c.*

Imprint and number: *London, Published Dec.r 2.nd 1793, by J. Johnson, S.t Pauls Church Yard.* | *52*

The letters beside each item are keyed to their brief

descriptions in the text, p. 74, where Stedman also compliments himself on the accuracy of his botanical drawings 'taken from nature'.

12. Vol. ii, facing p. 104 (1796 edn.); and facing p. 107 (1806 and 1813 edns.); 18 × 13.1 cm.; *Fig. 166*

Title: *March thro' a swamp or Marsh, in Terra-firma.*
Imprint and number: *London, Published Dec.ʳ 1ˢᵗ 1794, by J. Johnson, St. Paul's Church Yard.|55*

'Having so frequently had occasion to speak of marching through a swamp, it may not be improper to illustrate the description by the *annexed drawing*. The first figure represents Colonel Fourgeoud (preceded by a negro slave, as a guide, to give notice by his swimming when the water deepens) followed by myself [Stedman], some other officers and marines, wading through the marsh above our middle, and carrying our arms, ammunition, and accoutrements above our heads, to prevent their being damaged by the wet. In the back-ground may be seen the manner in which the slaves carry all burdens whatever on the head, and the mode of the rebel negroes [top left] firing upon the troops from the tops of high palm-trees, &c.' (pp. 103–4).

13. Vol. ii, facing p. 280 (1796 edn.); facing p. 291 (1806 and 1813 edns.); 17.9 × 13 cm.; *Fig. 167*

Signature right: *Blake Sculp.ᵗ*
Title: *Family of Negro Slaves from Loango.*
Imprint and number: *London, Published Dec.ʳ 1ˢᵗ 1792, by J. Johnson, St. Pauls Church Yard.|68*

Stedman describes this supposedly contented and healthy slave family, p. 280, including 'the marks on the man's body', indicating that he is from 'the Loango nation', and the '*J. G. S.* in a cypher' on his right breast, 'by which his owner may ascertain his property'. The woman, 'spinning a thread of cotton', is 'pregnant'. Erdman 1952, p. 244, compares Stedman's initials branded on the man to a speech by the tyrant Bromion in *Visions of the Daughters of Albion* (1793): 'Thy soft American plains are mine, and mine thy north & south: | Stampt with my signet are the swarthy children of the sun: | They are obedient, they resist not, they obey the scourge' (E 46, K 190). Smith 1985, p. 175, points out the caricature-like aspects of the woman's portrayal.

14. Vol. ii, facing p. 296 (1796 edn.); and facing p. 307 (1806 and 1813 edns.); 17.8 × 13 cm.; *Fig. 168*

Title: *The Execution of Breaking on the Rack.*
Imprint and number: as on pl. 1|71

A freed 'negro, whose name was *Neptune*' is being '*broken alive upon the rack*' for having killed an overseer. The 'executioner, also a black man, having now with a hatchet chopped off his left hand, next took up a heavy iron bar, with which, by repeated blows, he broke his bones to shivers ... but the prisoner never uttered a groan nor a sigh' (p. 295). Erdman 1952, p. 244, describes the executioner's look of 'bitter concern', an expression not noted in Stedman's text.

15. Vol. ii, facing p. 348 (1796 edn.); and facing p. 361 (1806 and 1813 edns.); 18.2 × 13.1 cm.; *Fig. 169*

Signature right: *Blake Sculp.ᵗ*
Title: *The celebrated Graman Quacy.*
Imprint and number: *London, Published Dec.ʳ 2ⁿᵈ 1793, by J. Johnson, St. Paul's Church Yard.|76*

The 'Graman', or 'Great-man Quacy' (p. 346), was a powerful sorcerer who aided the slave masters and freed slaves. His coat and gold medal were gifts from the Prince of Orange. 'Having taken a portrait of this extraordinary man, with his grey head of hair, and dressed in his blue and scarlet with gold lace, I, in the annexed plate, beg leave to introduce it to the reader' (p. 348).

16. Vol ii, facing p. 394 (1796 edn.); and facing p. 409 (1806 and 1813 edns.); 18 × 12.9 cm.; *Fig. 170*

Signature right: *Blake Sculp.ᵗ*
Title: *Europe supported by Africa & America.*
Imprint and number: as on pl. 2|80

'I will close the scene with an emblematical picture of *Europe supported by Africa and America*, accompanied by an ardent wish that in the friendly manner as they are represented, they may henceforth and to all eternity be the props of each other' (pp. 394–5). Erdman 1952, p. 244, finds that Blake's plate does not accord with Stedman's ameliorative intentions, for 'Europe is *supported* by her darker sisters, and they wear slave bracelets while she has a string of pearls—a symbolism rather closer to the historical fact'. Price and Price 1988, p. XLI, reject this interpretation that establishes an ironic displacement between Stedman's text and Blake's graphic performance.

Literature: Gilchrist 1863, i. 136, ii. 260 (fourteen unspecified plates only); Russell 1912, no. 84; Keynes 1921, no. 111; David V. Erdman, 'Blake's Vision of Slavery', *Journal of the Warburg and Courtauld Institutes*, 15 (1952), 242–52, summarized in part in Erdman, *Blake: Prophet against Empire* (Princeton: Princeton Univ. Press, 1954), 213–16; Bentley and Nurmi 1964, no. 408; Geoffrey Keynes, 'William Blake and John Gabriel Stedman', *Times Literary Supplement* (20 May 1965), 400 (repr. with revisions in

Keynes 1971, pp. 98–104); James Bogan, 'Vampire Bats and Blake's Spectre', *Blake Newsletter*, 10 (1976), 32–3; Bentley 1977, no. 499; Geoffrey Keynes, 'Blake's Spectre', *The Book Collector*, 28 (1979), 60–6; Essick 1980, pp. 52–3; Thomas V. Lange, 'Blake in American Almanacs', *Blake: An Illustrated Quarterly*, 14 (1980), 94–6 (on the woodcuts based on pls. 5 and 7 in *The People's Almanac* (Boston, 1834, 1836)); Mary Lynn Johnson, 'Coleridge's Prose and a Blake Plate [2] in Stedman's *Narrative*: Unfastening the "Hooks & Eyes" of Memory', *The Wordsworth Circle*, 13 (1982), 36–8; Smith 1985 (see **XXVII**, *Literature*), pp. 174–5; Boime 1987 (see **XXI**, *Literature*), pp. 339–42; Richard Price and Sally Price, introduction to Stedman, *Narrative of a Five Years Expedition against the Revolted Negroes of Surinam* (Baltimore: Johns Hopkins Univ. Press, 1988).

XXXIV

Leonard Euler, *Elements of Algebra*, trans. from the French [by Francis Horner] (2 vols.; London: J. Johnson, 1797, 1810); *Fig. 171*

The only plate is the frontispiece portrait in vol. i, signed by Blake as the engraver. Euler (1707–83), the Swiss mathematician, was one of Europe's most prolific and famous scientists of his time.

1. Vol. i, frontispiece; 10.6 × 6.4 cm.; *Fig. 171*

Signature: *Blake Sculp.*

Title: LEONARD EULER. | *From a Medalion, as large as life, | by Ruchotte, in the possession of | John Wilmot Esq.,*

Blake executed the plate in an unusual combination of line (mostly for the hair) and stipple patterns of various densities. For an earlier and less innovative prelude to this technique, see **XXX** (*Figs. 144–5*). The careful articulation of the forehead suggests the influence of physiognomic and phrenological theories (see **XIX**), although Blake may simply be trying to render accurately the undulating surfaces of a medallion in low relief. In a letter of 4 May 1804 to William Hayley, Blake proposed 'to etch' some of George Romney's designs 'in a rapid but firm manner, somewhat, perhaps, as I did the *Head of Euler*' (E 749, K 844; see also L). I have found no information about 'Ruchotte', and his medallion portrait, then in the collection of the author and Whig politician John Eardley-Wilmot (1750–1815), is untraced. A very similar profile of Euler, lacking the segmentation of the forehead and with eyes more open, was engraved by J. Thornthwaite and published in the *Literary Magazine & British Review*, 2 (Nov. 1789), facing p. 321. A note on p. 328 of the magazine states that 'the head of him [Euler] here given, is taken from the model sent by the Academy at Petersburgh to the Academy of Sciences at Paris'. This may be another cast by Ruchotte or the basis for it.

Literature: Gilchrist 1880, i. 210 (transcription of Blake's 1804 letter), ii. 283; Russell 1912, no. 86; Keynes 1921, no. 113; Bentley and Nurmi 1964, no. 365; Bentley 1977, no. 454; Joseph Viscomi, *Blake at Cornell: An Annotated Checklist of Works by and about William Blake in the Cornell University Libraries and the Herbert F. Johnson Museum* (Ithaca: Cornell Univ., 1984), no. 12 (first notice of Blake's plate in the 1810 edn.).

XXXV

The Monthly Magazine, and British Register, 4/23 (Oct. 1797), printed for R. Phillips, sold by J. Johnson; *Fig. 172*

Blake's plate illustrates an unsigned essay, 'Memoirs of the Life and principal Works of the late Joseph Wright, Esq. of Derby', pp. 289–94, in a section of 'Original Anecdotes and Remains of Eminent Persons'.

1. Facing p. 289; 8.7 × 6 cm.; *Fig. 172*

Inscription above design: *For the Monthly Magazine, Sept. 1797.*

Scratched signature: *Blake: s*

Title: The late MR WRIGHT | of Derby.

The subject of the portrait, Joseph Wright (1734–Aug. 1797), was one of eighteenth-century England's great painters, known chiefly for his scientific and industrial subjects dramatically illuminated. I have not been able to trace the drawing, painting, or print on which Blake's plate is based.

Literature: Russell 1912, no. 87; Keynes 1921, no. 114; Bentley and Nurmi 1964, no. 392; Bentley 1977, no. 483.

XXXVI

Charles Allen, *A New and Improved History of England* (London: J. Johnson, 1798); *Figs. 173–6*

All four plates (excluding an unsigned folding chart at the end of the volume, frequently missing) are signed by Blake as the engraver. Although no designer's name is given, all authorities have confidently ascribed the designs to Henry Fuseli on stylistic grounds (see comments on pl. 3 and **XXXVII**). Fuseli's drawings are untraced. The rather unusual choice of subjects for illustration expresses an anti-monarchical position, either by suggesting the submission of a king to some other authority (humorously so in pl. 1, seriously in pl. 2) or by portraying a challenge to royal authority (pls. 3–4). The story of Wat Tyler and his rebellion (pl. 3) had considerable symbolic significance for political radicals in the 1790s as a precedent for the popular uprising they hoped might come to England as it had to France. It is difficult, however, to reconcile these ideological implications with evidence that, in the late 1790s, Fuseli had no deep political commitments. The author or his decidedly liberal publisher, indicted for sedition in January 1798, may have chosen the subjects of the illustrations.

1. Facing p. 15; 14.7 × 8.1 cm.; *Fig. 173*

Inscription top right: *P. 15.*
Scratched signature right: *Blake: s*
Title: *Alfred and the Neat-herd's Wife.*
Imprint: *London, Published Dec.ʳ 1, 1797 by, J. Johnson, Sᵗ Paul's Church Yard.*

King Alfred, while hiding in 'the house of a neat-herd' (p. 14) from the Danes, is 'amusing himself by the fireside in trimming his bow and arrows'. The 'neat-herd's wife, who was ignorant of his quality', berates Alfred for neglecting her orders by not looking after the 'cakes' to which she points (p. 15). Two early drawings by Blake (Butlin 1981, nos. 100–1) may have as their subjects an associated story, *King Alfred and the Swineherd's Wife.* In a list of incidents from English history that Blake wrote in his *Notebook* (*c.* 1793), he included what may be the same general subject as Fuseli's design, 'Alfred in the countrymans house' (E 672, K 208).

2. Facing p. 78; 14.6 × 8.2 cm.; *Fig. 174*

Inscription top right: *P. 78.*
Scratched signature right: *Blake. sc*
Title: *King John absolved by Pandulph.*
Imprint: as on pl. 1.

King John has given up his struggle against Church authority and bows before Pandolf, the Pope's legate. The mitred figure in the background on the right is the archbishop of Dublin, displeased with Pandolf's 'insolence' (p. 79). The design is based closely on an engraving of 'Pope Coelestin Crowning Emperor Henry VI' published in Johann Wirz, *Romae animale exemplum* (Zurich, 1677), a source pointed out and reproduced in Schiff 1973, no. 938.

3. Facing p. 128; 14.7 × 8.3 cm.; *Fig. 175*

Inscription top right: *P. 128.*
Scratched signature right: *Blake: s.*
Title: *Wat Tyler and the Tax-gatherer.*
Imprint: *London Published Dec.ʳ 1, 1797, by J. Johnson, Sᵗ Paul's Church Yard.*

A tax gatherer (bottom) had attacked the daughter (fleeing upper left) of a 'blacksmith'. In response, the father has 'knocked out the ruffian's brains with his hammer' (p. 128). Allen does not indicate that this blacksmith was Wat Tyler, the leader of the subsequent rebellion against Richard II, but the plate's inscription makes this traditional identification, now known to be a mistake stemming from the fact that the smith and the rebel shared the same last name. Fuseli, or whoever else devised the caption, thereby gives to Allen's book a more specifically political thrust than is provided by the text alone. Fuseli's painting of the same basic design is now in a private collection (Schiff 1973, no. 879). It is probably not a preliminary for the plate and has been dated by Schiff to 1799. Blake's work on this engraving may have stimulated his interest in the incident when drawing the 'Visionary Heads' *c.* 1819. On leaf 65 of the recently rediscovered Blake–Varley Sketchbook (see Christie's, London auction catalogue, 21 March 1989), Blake drew a head inscribed by John Varley, 'Wat Tyler | in the act of striking the Tax Gatherer'. A female visage on leaf 67 verso is inscribed 'Wat Tylers daughter | striving to get loose from the Tax gatherer'. For counter-proofs and replicas of these drawings, see Butlin 1981, nos. 737–41. A drawing of about the same date, *The Tax-Gatherer Killed by Wat Tyler*, was sold at auction in 1885, but is now untraced (Butlin 1981, no. 742).

4. Facing p. 224; 14.6 × 8 cm.; *Fig. 176*

Inscription top right: *P. 224.*
Scratched signature right: *Blake: s.*
Title: *Queen Elizabeth and Essex.*
Imprint: *London, Published Dec.ʳ 1, 1797, by J. Johnson, Sᵗ Paul's Church Yard.*

In the midst of a heated argument with the Queen, Robert Devereux, Earl of Essex, 'clapped his hand to his sword, and swore, that he would not bear such treatment, were it from Henry VIII himself' (p. 224). The Queen's gesture commands Essex to withdraw from the court. The bat-like wings of Elizabeth's collar and her tightly-curled hair may have influenced Blake's presentation of the Wife of Bath in his painting (*c.* 1803) and engraving (1810) of 'Chaucers Canterbury Pilgrims' (Butlin 1981, no. 653; Essick 1983, no. XVI).

Literature: Gilchrist 1863, ii. 260 (listing the plates by title without reference to the book); Russell 1912, no. 89; Keynes 1921, no. 115; Bentley and Nurmi 1964, no. 333; Schiff 1973, nos. 936–9; Bentley 1977, no. 415; Essick 1980, pp. 79–80.

XXXVII

Charles Allen, *A New and Improved Roman History* (London: J. Johnson, 1798); *Figs. 177–80*

All four plates are signed by Blake as the engraver. Although no designer's name is given, all authorities have confidently ascribed the designs to Henry Fuseli on stylistic grounds (see also **XXXVI**). Fuseli's drawings are untraced. A copy in original boards (RNE) has the plates printed on a single conjugate sheet folded and bound at the front of the volume. The continuous platemark running along the bottom of all plates indicates that they were engraved on a single piece of copper. The erotic violence of Fuseli's art finds expression in pls. 1–2, and 4, for all have as their subject the violation and/or suicide of women.

1. Facing p. 2; 14.5 × 8.1 cm.; *Fig. 177*
Inscription top right: *P. 2.*
Scratched signature right: *Blake: s.*
Title: *Mars and Rhea Silvia.*
Imprint: *London, Published Dec.[!] 1, 1797 by, J. Johnson, S.[!] Paul's Church Yard.*

Allen begins with the mythic history of the kings of Alba, one of whom forced his niece, 'Ilia, or Rhea Silvia', to become a vestal virgin. In the illustrated incident, Mars comes upon the virgin 'in the sacred grove' (p. 2) before impregnating her with Romulus and Remus. The text describes Rhea Silvia as fetching water, not langorously seated as in the plate.

2. Facing p. 33; 15 × 8.3 cm.; *Fig. 178*
Inscription top right: *P. 33.*
Scratched signature right: *Blake: sc*
Title: *The Death of Lucretia.*

Imprint: *London, Published Dec.[!] 1, 1797, by J. Johnson, S.[!] Paul's Church Yard.*

After being raped, Lucretia has stabbed herself to death with the dagger now held aloft by Junius Brutus, who swears to avenge her. Collatinus, Lucretia's husband, holds her, while Lucretius, her father, stands behind.

3. Facing p. 174; 14.6 × 8.4 cm.; *Fig. 179*
Inscription top right: *P. 174*
Scratched signature right: *Blake: sc*
Title: *C. Marius at Minturnum.*
Imprint: *London, Published Dec.[!] 1, 1797, by Johnson, S.[!] Paul's Church Yard.*

Marius, fleeing from his rival Cinna, had hidden in the marshes of Minturnum. 'He was then seized, and conducted to prison, and a Cimbrian slave was sent to dispatch him; but the barbarian had no sooner entered the prison for this purpose, than he was so struck with the awful look of the fallen general, that he threw down his sword, exclaiming, at the same time, that he found himself incapable of executing his orders' (p. 174).

4. Facing p. 292; 14.6 × 8.1 cm.; *Fig. 180*
Inscription top right: *P. 292.*
Scratched signature right: *Blake: s*
Title: *The Death of Cleopatra.*
Imprint: *London, Published Dec.[!] 1, 1797, by J. Johnson, S.[!] Paul's Church Yard.*

The asp continues to bite the right breast of the dead Egyptian queen. Iris sits dead at her feet, while Charmion, dressed in a most un-Egyptian costume, places a cloth 'diadem' (p. 292) on Cleopatra's head and turns to look at one of Octavius's soldiers entering through the doorway.

Literature: Gilchrist 1863, ii. 260 (listing the plates by title without reference to the book); Russell 1912, no. 88; Keynes 1921, no. 116; Bentley and Nurmi 1964, no. 334; Schiff 1973, nos. 932–5; Bentley 1977, no. 416.

XXXVIII

John Flaxman, *A Letter to the Committee for Raising the Naval Pillar* (London: T. Cadell, W. Davies, T. Payne, and R. H. Evans, 1799); *Figs. 181–4*

In 1799 a committee sponsored by the Duke of Clarence called for the submission of plans for building by subscription a public monument to recent British naval victories, such as the Battle of the Nile. Flaxman's fifteen-page *Letter to the Committee* is his proposal. Neither Flaxman's monument of Britannia, nor any of the plans submitted by other artists, was selected or built. In his *Letter to . . . the Committee . . . in Answer to the Letter of John Flaxman* (London, 1800), Alexander Dufour criticizes Flaxman's proposal and objects that the sculptor tried to prejudice the committee against alternatives by submitting poor 'drawings' (p. 11) of columns and arches (see pl. 2).

Flaxman's response to the surge of British patriotism may have stimulated Blake both to appeal to and to criticize militant nationalism in his 1809 exhibition of paintings, a show that included his tempera of *The Spiritual Form of Nelson Guiding Leviathan* (Butlin 1981, no. 649). The *Letter* may also have been one of Flaxman's many works that influenced Blake's interest in, and use of imagery drawn from, architecture and sculpture. For general surveys of these concerns, see Stephen A. Larrabee, *English Bards and Grecian Marbles* (New York: Columbia Univ. Press, 1943), 99–119; Andrew Wilton, 'Blake and the Antique', *The British Museum Yearbook 1: The Classical Tradition* (1976), 187–218; Paley's two essays, 1978 (**LII**, *Literature*) and 1983 (**IV**, *Literature*); and Chayes 1990 (**LII**, *Literature*). Flaxman's advocacy of public support for works of art dedicated to national interests is complemented by Blake's sense that 'Art is the glory of a Nation' and that he is meeting 'the greatest of Duties to [his] Country' by exhibiting his works (Advertisement to the exhibition of 1809 (E 528, K 561)).

Only the first of the three plates is signed by Blake as the engraver. The others could be ascribed to him on stylistic grounds alone, but his receipt for payment for work on all three plates makes this attribution certain: 'Received Decr 14 1799 of Mr Flaxman the Sum of Eight pounds Eight shillings for Engraving Three Plates for the Statue of Britannia & Twelve shillings & Eight pence for Copper' (Bentley 1969, p. 570). Blake's three copperplates, now untraced, were sold from Flaxman's collection, Christie's, 1 July 1828, lot 170 (with a 'manuscript Letter'). For Blake's long association with Flaxman, see the Introduction and the records in Bentley 1969. Blake very prob-

ably gained the commissions to execute these and other plates after Flaxman because of his friendship with the artist rather than through business dealings with the publishers.

1. Frontispiece; 18.8 × 14.9 cm.; *Fig. 181*

Inscription top right: *Frontispiece*
Scale along right margin: see *Fig. 181.*
Inscription on pedestal: BRITANNIA | BY DIVINE PROVIDENCE | TRIUMPHANT
Scratched signature right: *Blake sculp*
Title: *A Colossal Statue 230 feet high: proposed to be erected on Greenwich hill*

An unpaginated 'Explanation of the Plates' at the end of the *Letter* describes the frontispiece: 'STATUE of Britannia Triumphant, with its pedestal and basement, 230 feet high; the pedestal decorated with the Portraits of His Majesty, and the Naval Heroes, Howe, St. Vincent, Duncan, Nelson, &c. with Wreaths of Laurel on the altars, at the corners of the basement, to contain the names of Captains, &c.' Flaxman's ink-and-pencil preliminary drawing, 19 × 15.2 cm., in the Victoria and Albert Museum (*Fig. 182*), shows two significant differences from the plate: reverse-buttress projections from the corner columns rather than wreaths, and a trident rather than a lance in Britannia's right hand. Blake may have been working from a now-lost drawing embodying these revisions, which were undoubtedly authorized by Flaxman. A sheet of pencil sketches, 19.8 × 23.4 cm., by Flaxman in the LC bears several versions of the monument with a variety of column lengths and an equestrian statue placed in front of the plinth (reproduced in *Blake Newsletter*, 9 (1975–6), 82). These, or other drawings noted here, may be the 'sketches for the Naval Pillar' mentioned in Sidney Colvin, *The Drawings of Flaxman in the Gallery of University College London* (London: Bell and Sons, 1876), 45, then in the collection of William Russell. A 'related drawing' is located in the possession of Edward Croft-Murray, without specifying which plate it is related to, by Croft-Murray, 'An Account-Book of John Flaxman', in *The Twenty-Eighth Volume of the Walpole Society* (Oxford: Univ. Press, 1940), 71. Bentley 1977, p. 564, notes that 'four sketches for Britannia triumphant are in Princeton', but there are in fact only three drawings and these are for an alternative design, a triumphal arch surmounted by a seated figure of Britannia (reproduced in Campbell 1958). An ink-and-pencil drawing by Flaxman, 14 × 25.5 cm., 'for the base of a statue to Commemorate British victories', was sold at Sotheby's, 19 June 1975, lot 54, but I have not been able to determine the precise relationship of this untraced sketch to Blake's plate. The catalogue for the Royal Academy exhibition of 1801 lists, as no. 1037, a 'sketch' by Flaxman 'for a colossal statue of Britannia triumphant, proposed to be erected upon Greenwich-hill'. Since this work is in the section reserved for the 'Model Academy', it was probably the plaster model of the monument, almost five feet high, now in Sir John Soane's Museum, London (reproduced in Campbell 1958, p. 66). This model has the projections from the corner columns as in the Victoria and Albert Museum drawing.

2. Facing p. 6; 18.8 × 15 cm.; *Fig. 183*

Inscription top right: *Plate 2*
Inscription beneath monuments: see *Fig. 183*.

The plate illustrates Flaxman's survey of monument types he rejects in favour of the statue presented in pl. 1. The 'Explanation of the Plates' lists this as 'PLATE III' and describes the numbered monuments as follows:

> 1. The Egyptian Obelisk, from Stuart's Obelisk of the Sun. 2. A Column in honour of Antoninus Pius, from a Consecration Medal of that Emperor; possibly a first thought for the Column of the same name now existing in Rome. 3. The Meta of the Circus—Piranesi's bases, Plate 14. 4. The Arch of Titus—Bartoli's Triumphal Arches. 5. The Pharos, or Light-house, of Alexandria, from Smeaton's Preface to the Eddistone Light-house. 6. One of the Temples of Paestum.

On 18 November 1799 Flaxman visited Joseph Farington and sketched for him versions of the six monuments pictured on this plate and a view of Greenwich Hospital (with his monument installed) basically the same as pl. 3. Farington labelled this sheet of drawings 'Flaxmans notes' and included it in his *Diary* (reproduced in Farington 1979, iv. 1304).

3. Facing p. 12; 9.7 × 18.7 cm.; *Fig. 184*

Inscription top right: *Plate 3*
Title: *A View of Greenwich Hospital with the Statue of Britannia on the Hill*

The 'Explanation of the Plates' lists this as 'PLATE II' and repeats the title inscription. For the sketch in Farington's *Diary*, see pl. 2.

Literature (including comments on Flaxman's project without reference to Blake): Allan Cunningham, *The Lives of the Most Eminent British Painters, Sculptors, and Archi-*

tects (London: John Murray, 1830), iii. 322–4; Gilchrist 1863, i. 144 (all three plates), ii. 260 (pl. 1 only); Russell 1912, no. 91; Keynes 1921, no. 119; W. G. Constable, *John Flaxman, 1755–1826* (London: Univ. of London Press, 1927), 59–60; Malcolm Campbell, 'An Alternative Design for a Commemorative Monument by John Flaxman', *Record of the Art Museum, Princeton University*, 17 (1958), 65–73; Bentley and Nurmi 1964, no. 369; John Physick, *Designs for English Sculpture, 1680–1860* (London: Stationery Office, 1969), 165, 167–9; *The Age of Neo-Classicism* (exhibition catalogue, Royal Academy and Victoria and Albert Museum; London: Arts Council, 1972), no. 571; Bentley 1977, no. 458; David Bindman (ed.), *John Flaxman* (London: Thames and Hudson, 1979), no. 139; *The Diary of Joseph Farington*, ed. Kenneth Garlick and Angus Macintyre (New Haven: Yale Univ. Press, 1979), iv. 1266, 1304–6, 1331; David Irwin, *John Flaxman, 1755–1826* (London: Studio Vista, 1979), 163–6; Essick 1980, p. 177; Alison Yarrington, *The Commemoration of the Hero, 1800–1864: Monuments to the British Victors of the Napoleonic Wars* (New York: Garland, 1988), 57–9.

XXXIX

William Hayley, *An Essay on Sculpture: In a Series of Epistles to John Flaxman* (London: T. Cadell and W. Davies, 1800); *Figs. 185–7*

Hayley's verse epistle is illustrated with three plates. Two are signed by Blake as the engraver, but both stylistic features and documentary evidence make it certain that he also executed pl. 1. According to J. T. Smith (Bentley 1969, p. 461), Flaxman 'introduced' Blake 'to his friend Hayley'. It is apparently on this basis that Bentley 1969, p. 63, concludes that 'Flaxman had recommended Blake to do the engravings' for this book (see also Bentley 1959, p. 168). For Blake's interest in sculpture, see **XXXVIII**. For Hayley's patronage of Blake, see the Introduction and the records in Bentley 1969. Hayley's emphasis on classical sculpture may have had an antithetical influence on Blake's denunciation of 'Greek and Roman Models' at the beginning of *Milton* (c. 1804–8 (E 95, K 480)).

1. Frontispiece; circle, 6.5 cm. diameter; *Fig. 185*

Inscription top right: *To face the Title*
Title: PERICLES. | *from a Bust in the Possession of Charles Townley Esq.*

Scratched imprint: *Publishd June 14. 1800 by Cadell & Davis Strand*

Pericles is mentioned in the text as the patron of Phidias, pp. 56, 236, 243. The pictured bust of the Athenian leader, then in the possession of the great antiquarian collector Charles Townley (or 'Towneley', 1737–1805), was acquired as part of the 'Townley Gallery' by the British Museum in 1805 (for illustration and description, see *The Townley Gallery* (London: Charles Knight, 1836), ii. 3–6). Letters by Hayley to Flaxman of 21 December 1799 and to Samuel Rose of 7 March 1800 (Bentley 1969, pp. 62–3) make it clear that Blake was working from a drawing of the bust by Hayley's beloved (and mortally ill) natural son, Thomas Alphonso Hayley (1780–1800), who was studying sculpture under Flaxman's direction. On 26 March 1800 Flaxman wrote to Hayley that 'the head of Pericles' is 'most likely done by this time' (Bentley 1969, p. 64), but Blake did not send a 'proof' to Hayley for his 'Remarks' until 6 May (E 705, K 797).

2. Facing p. 126; 12.8 × 18 cm.; *Fig. 186*

Inscription top right: *To face Page 126*
Greek inscription on plinth: see *Fig. 186*.
Signatures: *T. H. invenit.* [i.e. Thomas Hayley—see pl. 1], *W. Blake sc.* [right]
Title: The DEATH of DEMOSTHENES. | *He views this Outrage with indignant Eyes,* | *And at the Base of Neptunes Statue dies.* | *Epistle 5 Verse 61.*
Scratched imprint: as on pl. 1.

The pictured event is described on the facing page of text. In his letter of 21 December 1799 to Flaxman, Hayley states that the scene was 'described expressly . . . in the poem' so that his son's design could be used as an illustration (Bentley 1969, p. 62). The youth against whom the orator leans may be a portrait of Thomas Hayley (see pl. 3). Philip of Macedonia's soldiers enter on the right. An ink drawing of the design, 12 × 17.8 cm., is now in the Keynes Collection, Fitzwilliam Museum (reproduced in William Wells and Elizabeth Johnston, *William Blake's 'Heads of the Poets'* (Manchester: City Art Gallery, 1969), fig. 4). This drawing is attributed to Thomas Hayley in Keynes 1964; but, in a letter of 21 December 1799, William Hayley asked Flaxman 'to retouch for Him [Thomas] his Demosthenes in such a manner, that it may form an engrav'd outline, & yet still remain very fairly his own design' (Bentley 1969, p. 62). Thus, the drawing may have a joint authorship, particularly if it is the direct preliminary for Blake's engraving. He might

have worked from another, slightly later drawing, for, in a letter of 29 January 1800 to Hayley, Flaxman noted that the drawing he had delivered to Blake had 'the right orthography of the Dedication to Neptune' (Bentley 1969, p. 63). In the Keynes drawing the faint Greek inscription in pencil ('To Poseidon') on the plinth follows the Homeric spelling, changed to the Attic form on the plate. Thomas Hayley, Flaxman, or both working together may have drawn the slight pencil sketch, 14.7 × 19.1 cm., of the design in the Rosenwald Collection, National Gallery of Art, Washington (reproduced in *Blake Newsletter*, 9 (1975–6), 82).

Blake sent Hayley a proof of the plate, 'approved . . . by Mr. Flaxman', on 18 February 1800 (extract from Blake's untraced letter in Gilchrist 1880, i. 143). Hayley seems to have been pleased with Blake's efforts, for in a letter to Samuel Rose of 7 March 1800 he commented on how 'delightfully' Blake 'has done the outline of dear Toms Demosthenes' (Bentley 1969, p. 63). For an impression printed in red, see comments on pl. 3. Blake used this design for the motifs left and right on his panel portrait of Demosthenes, painted as part of the 'Heads of the Poets' series for Hayley's library *c.* 1800–3 (Butlin 1981, no. 343.2).

3. Facing p. 163; circle, 6.5 cm. diameter; *Fig. 187*

Inscription top right: *To face Page 163*
Signature: *Blake. sc*
Title: THOMAS HAYLEY, | *the Disciple of* | *John Flaxman.* | *from a Medallion.*
Imprint: as on pl. 1.

Hayley's letter to Flaxman of 21 December 1799 indicates that the original 'medallion' was designed by Flaxman, who was asked to have the artist Henry Howard (1769–1847) prepare a drawing of the work in preparation for the engraving (Bentley 1969, p. 62). Hayley complained in subsequent correspondence about Howard's delay in performing this task, but learned from Flaxman on 26 March 1800 that Howard had 'finished a beautiful drawing from the medallion [both now untraced] . . . four weeks ago, since which time it has been in the hands of M.ʳ Blake' (Bentley 1969, p. 64). Blake sent a proof, 'approved' by Flaxman, to Hayley on 1 April (E 705, K 769), but the recipient did not like the portrait and asked for revisions in a long letter of 17 April (Bentley 1969, pp. 65–6). Blake sent a proof from the reworked plate with his letter to Hayley of 6 May (E 705, K 797). Hayley seems never to have been pleased with the results, for, in a letter of 16 July 1800 to Flaxman, Hayley hoped that Blake's 'two next prints' (not further identified) would 'atone for all the defects of the engraved Medallion' (Bentley 1969, p. 70). And, in a letter of 13 September 1800 to Lady Hesketh, Hayley referred to 'the miserably unjust Medallion' of his dead son 'in the Essay on Sculpture' (Bentley 1969, p. 73). Nevertheless, Hayley had in July commissioned Blake to prepare a drawing 'from a most wonderful portrait, as large as Life, which my dear crippled child contrived to execute of Himself in crayons' (Bentley 1969, pp. 68–9, 71). This lost work (Butlin 1981, no. 344; see also no. 345) may have been a preliminary for Blake's profile of Thomas Hayley among the 'Heads of the Poets' series of c. 1800–3 (Butlin 1981, no. 343.18).

An impression in sanguine is in the RNE collection, printed on laid paper clearly distinct from the wove stock used in the book. Since the plate has been cut down from the 22.5 × 16.3 cm. platemark in the book to 14.5 × 11.2 cm., thereby trimming off the inscription top right and the imprint, this separate impression must have been pulled after the printing of the plate in black ink used in the book. Bentley 1977, p. 575, reports a 'proof' of pl. 2 'printed in Red' in the collection of Mr Walter Fancutt, but I have been unable to locate this impression. Hayley may have had these separate impressions printed as memorials of his son, although they could have been created many years later by someone else.

Literature: Gilchrist 1880, i. 143–4, ii. 283 (pls. 1–2 only); Russell 1912, no. 94; Keynes 1921, no. 120; G. E. Bentley, jun., 'Blake's Engravings and his Friendship with Flaxman', *Studies in Bibliography*, 12 (1959), 167–70; Bentley and Nurmi 1964, no. 376; Geoffrey Keynes, *Bibliotheca Bibliographici: A Catalogue of the Library Formed by Geoffrey Keynes* (London: Trianon Press, 1964), no. 634; Bentley 1977, no. 467.

XL

Henry Fuseli, *Lectures on Painting* (London: J. Johnson, 1801); *Figs. 188–9*

The book has only two plates, a title-page vignette after Fuseli, signed by Francis Legat as the engraver, and Fuseli's portrait of Michelangelo on the final page, signed by Blake as the engraver.

1. P. 151; 12 × 7.5 cm.; *Fig. 188*
Scratched signature right: *Blake: sc*
Title: *Ancora imparo. | M: Angelo Bonarroti.*

Fuseli discusses Michelangelo's art in his second and third lectures, pp. 61–3, 117, 124–32, but these passages provide only the most general context for the portrait. The fact that Sir Joshua Reynolds ended his fifteenth and final *Discourse* (1791) with 'the name of— Michael Angelo' may have prompted Fuseli to end his lectures with a pictorial equivalent. Proofs before the title inscription are in the RNE collection (reproduced Essick 1980, fig. 37) and in the Keynes Collection, Cambridge University Library (pasted into a copy of Hayley, *An Essay on Sculpture* (1800) (**XXXIX**)). Bentley and Nurmi 1964, p. 117, and Todd 1971–2, p. 175, state that there is a 'proof' bearing Fuseli's name in the BMPR, but a thorough search has been unable to locate it. These references may simply be a misreading of the statement in Keynes 1921, p. 249, that there is in the BMPR such a proof of the title-page vignette.

Fuseli's pen-and-ink preliminary sketch on a sheet 22.4 × 18.8 cm. is in the RNE collection (*Fig. 189*). The crude pencil sketch top right is probably Blake's attempt to develop the lower half of Michelangelo's body for inclusion in the plate. The presence of this pencilwork lessens the possibility that Fuseli prepared a more detailed drawing, but it is certainly possible that Blake did, as in the case of one of Fuseli's illustrations for Darwin's *Botanic Garden* (**XXI**, pl. 1). None the less, the extant evidence suggests a close and trusting relationship between designer and engraver. The wall of the Colosseum was probably added to the plate at Fuseli's suggestion, or at least with his approval. The relative sizes of the figure and wall embody the superiority of Michelangelo even over the monuments of ancient Rome.

The drawing is inscribed in pencil, lower left, by John Linnell or a member of his family, 'Mich: Angelo | by Fuseli | original Drawing had from Wᵐ Blake'. Blake must have retained the drawing for many years, for he did not meet Linnell until 1818. This may have been one of 'two [drawings] by Fuseli' Linnell purchased from Blake's widow on 26 January 1829 (Bentley 1969, p. 596). The drawing is on the same type of laid paper as the drawing for Blake's plate in Fuseli's translation of Lavater's *Aphorisms* (**XVIII**, *Fig. 60*) and may even be half of the same sheet separated along the right or left side. These two works are further linked by the presence, on the verso of the Michelangelo portrait, of a pencil sketch and a profile in ink similar to the *Aphorisms* drawing. Because of these connections, Todd 1971–2, pp. 175, 178, offers the tantalizing speculation that the portrait of

Michelangelo, both drawing and engraving, was executed *c.* 1788 for Fuseli's 'Aphorisms on Art', the proof sheets of which were destroyed in a fire. In no. 168 of these aphorisms, finally published in John Knowles, *The Life and Writings of Henry Fuseli* (London: Colburn and Bentley, 1831), iii. 129, Fuseli notes that 'the crook-back of Michael Angelo strikes with awe', a comment that could have provided a textual cue for his slightly hunched posture in the portrait. Keynes 1921, p. 248, reports having seen a 'wash drawing' of the design, but no such work has come to light. The portrait was re-engraved by Francis Engleheart and published in the 1820 edition of Fuseli's *Lectures*.

Literature: Gilchrist 1863, i. 160, ii. 260; Russell 1912, no. 95; Keynes 1921, no. 122; Bentley and Nurmi 1964, no. 370; Todd 1971–2 (see **XVIII**, *Literature*); Schiff 1973, no. 873; Bentley 1977, no. 459; Essick 1980, pp. 51–2; Butlin 1981, no. 172.

XLI

Designs to a Series of Ballads, Written by William Hayley (Chichester: J. Seagrave, P. Humphry, and R. H. Evans, for W. Blake, 1802); *Figs. 190–1*

According to Hayley's 'Preface', p. ii, his stories in verse about animals were 'vehicles contrived to exhibit the diversified talents of my Friend [Blake] for original design, and delicate engraving'. The series of four ballads, each published separately and sold mostly to the author's friends, is known principally for the twelve plates both designed and engraved by Blake (reproduced Easson and Essick 1972, no. VI, and Bindman 1978, nos. 385–98). In addition, there are tailpieces to the first and third ballads engraved by Blake after antique gems. In his letter of 10 June 1802 to Lady Hesketh about the publication of the *Ballads*, Hayley notes that Blake and 'his excellent Wife (a true Helpmate!) pass the plates thro' a rolling press in their own cottage together' (Bentley 1969, p. 97). Blake had brought his rolling press with him when he moved to Felpham in 1800, and thus was able to print his *Ballads* plates on sheets provided by the Chichester printer of the letterpress, Joseph Seagrave. In all copies seen, the

two gem plates, executed in stipple, are very lightly printed. The considerable correspondence among Hayley and his friends about the *Ballads* is recorded in Bentley 1969, pp. 92–118.

Blake twice refers to antique gems in his writings. In his annotations of *c.* 1808 to Joshua Reynolds's *Discourses*, Blake notes that the 'Greek Gems are in the Same Style as the Greek Statues' (E 651, K 463). In the 'Laocoön' inscriptions he proposes that such classical works are based on ancient Hebraic originals: 'What we call Antique Gems are the Gems of Aarons Breast Plate' (E 274, K 777).

1. P. 9, tailpiece to 'The Elephant, Ballad the First'; oval, 6.3 × 8.4 cm.; *Fig. 190*

Inscription above oval, left: *Size of the Gem*
Signature right: *Blake. sc*
Title: *From an Antique Gem*
Imprint: *Publish'd June 1 1802, by W Blake Felpham*

In a letter of 3 April 1803 to the bookseller R. H. Evans, Hayley makes passing reference to 'the *small Elephant* at the close of the first' ballad (Bentley 1969, p. 115). Keynes 1921, p. 204, states that this 'study of an elephant [is] after a drawing by Thomas Hayley'. Keynes gives no evidence for this attribution to William Hayley's son, who died in 1800, but he may simply be reasoning by analogy with pl. 2, signed by 'T. H.' as the designer. Bentley 1977, p. 573, notes that 'Hayley used this gem [or a stamp made from it?] to seal his letters with'. For an equally massive beast with a similar tail, see Behemoth in pl. 15 of Blake's Job illustrations, first executed as a watercolour *c.* 1805–6 (Butlin 1981, no. 550.15).

2. P. 39, tailpiece to 'The Lion, Ballad the Third'; oval, 5.7 × 8.3 cm.; *Fig. 191*

Signatures: *T. H. del:* [i.e. Thomas Hayley], *Blake. sc* [right]
Title: *From an Antique* [probably an antique gem, like pl. 1]
Imprint: *Publishd Aug^st 5 1802 by W Blake Felpham*

Literature: Russell 1912, no. 19; Keynes 1921, no. 72; G. E. Bentley, jun., 'William Blake as a Private Publisher', *Bulletin of the New York Public Library*, 61 (1957), 539–60; Bentley and Nurmi 1964, no. 375; Bentley 1977, no. 466.

XLII

The Dramatic Works of Shakspeare Revised by George Stevens (9 vols.; London: John and Josiah Boydell, George and W. Nicol, 1802 [i.e. 1803]). *Boydell's Graphic Illustrations of the Dramatic Works, of Shakspeare* (London: Mess.rs Boydell & Co., *c.*1803, 1813). *The Dramatic Works of William Shakspeare*, ed. Charles Henry Wheeler (London: Moon, Boys, & Graves, 1832). *Fig. 192*

Boydell's folio edition of Shakespeare's plays, issued in parts beginning in 1791, contains 100 plates reproducing the oil paintings by various artists he commissioned for his Shakespeare Gallery (for the history of which, see Friedman 1976). The 1803 imprint dates on some plates provide a *terminus a quo* for the publication of the complete work. The date of *Boydell's Graphic Illustrations*, in which the same plates appear without texts of the plays, is conjectural, and thus it is uncertain as to which publication was the first to contain the single plate engraved by Blake.

1. Vol. ix, facing p. 101 of *Romeo and Juliet* in *Dramatic Works* ([1803]); the ninety-fifth plate in *Boydell's Graphic Illustrations* (*c.*1803 and 1813); and facing the leaf bearing pp. 251–4 in *Dramatic Works* (1832); 16.5 × 25.5 cm.; *Fig. 192*

Signatures: *Painted by J. Opie.* [left], *Engrav'd by W. Blake.* [right]

Title: Variation. | SHAKSPEARE. | *Romeo and Juliet,* | ACT IV. SCENE V.

Imprint: *Pub.d March 25, 1799, by John & Josiah Boydell, at the Shakspeare Gallery Pall Mall, & N.o 90, Cheapside.*

Blake's plate is a 'variation' (see inscribed title) of the immediately preceding etching with aquatint by Peter Simon, also reproducing the oil painting executed in the late 1780s by John Opie (1761–1807) for Boydell's Shakespeare Gallery. The painting is listed, with a two-page quotation of the scene illustrated, in *A Catalogue of the Pictures, &c. in the Shakspeare Gallery* (London: [Boydell], 1790), 66–8. In the 'Descriptive Index' of the *Graphic Illustrations* Blake's plate is listed as no. XCV and the reader is referred to the description of Simon's plate (no. XCIV):

A Chamber in Capulet's House.—Juliet [lying on the bed], to avoid marrying Paris [holding Juliet], her parent's choice, and preserve her hand for Romeo, having swallowed an opiate furnished her by Friar Lawrence [with left hand raised, right of Juliet's mother], the effect of which is to produce the temporary semblance of death—is found by her Nurse [above Juliet's head], &c. apparently dead, on the morning of her intended nuptials. A universal lamentation takes place; and Friar Lawrence, with a view to moderate it, and prove his friendship for Romeo, recommends her immediate interment.

Simon's version contains the same principal figures, including Juliet, her father [far right] and mother, Paris, and Friar Lawrence; but the Nurse turns her back with left hand raised to her face in sorrow, and there are only three subsidiary figures on the left and none on the right. These differences are explained by an anonymous review of the Shakespeare Gallery in *The Public Advertiser* for 2 July 1789 (see Friedman 1976, p. 171). Opie had originally painted the design with many figures, but subsequently repainted the canvas and eliminated inessential characters. Thus, Blake's 'variation' returns to the earlier version. The large (44.3 × 59.5 cm.) plate of Opie's design, engraved by George and John G. Facius in 1791 and published in Boydell's *Collection of Prints . . . Illustrating the Dramatic Works of Shakspeare* (1803), also preserves the earlier version and probably served as the model for Blake's plate. The copperplate of 'Romeo and Juliet, after Opie, by Blake' was offered in lot 302 in the 1–6 June 1818 R. H. Evans auction of the Boydell estate. Both Opie's painting, last recorded in an 1892 Christie's auction, and Blake's copperplate are now untraced. 'Prints' (4s.) and 'Proofs' (7s. 6d.) of the 'Trance of Juliet' by 'Blake' were offered for sale in the catalogues of Moon, Boys, & Graves of 1829 and Hodgson & Graves of 1836 (p. 159 in both).

Literature: Keynes 1921, no. 123 (*Boydell's Graphic Illustrations* only); Bentley and Nurmi 1964, nos. 353, 406; Winifred H. Friedman, *Boydell's Shakespeare Gallery* (New York: Garland, 1976), 171–2, 231; Bentley 1977, nos. 437, 497; Essick 1983, no. LXIII (separate sale of Blake's print).

XLIII

William Hayley, *The Triumphs of Temper* (12th edn.: Chichester: T. Cadell and W. Davies, 1803; 13th edn.: 1807); *Figs. 193–8*

Hayley's moralizing poem in six 'cantos' was first published in 1781. The sixth edition of 1788 includes seven plates after designs by Stothard. For the twelfth edition (1803) Hayley and his publishers substituted six plates, signed by Blake as the engraver, after designs by Maria Flaxman (1768–1833), the half-sister of the sculptor John Flaxman, a close friend of both the author and the engraver. Her contribution is noted on the title-pages of 1803 and 1807: 'With New Original Designs, | By Maria Flaxman'. Two of her drawings were exhibited at the Royal Academy in 1800, no. 665 in the catalogue, and all were sold from John Flaxman's collection at Christie's, 26 February 1883, lot 295 (now untraced). According to his letter to Thomas Butts of 10 January 1803, Blake was then 'engaged in Engraving' the plates 'for a New Edition' of the *Triumphs* (E 723, K 811–12). Blake gave his brother James the same information in a letter of 30 January, and added that he would receive '10 Guineas each' for the six plates (E 726, K 820). Hayley apparently sent a copy of the new edition to Lady Hesketh by late June, for her letter to him of 1 July 1800 notes that she was 'disappointed in the Prints'. This response apparently led Hayley to mention that 'the Ladies ... find fault with the Engravings' in his letter to John Flaxman of 7 August 1803, where he also reports Blake's fee and that one plate lacks a 'Figure (the tall *Minerva*)' in Maria's drawing (see pl. 5) 'that Blake & I thought it would be better to omit' (Bentley 1969, p. 121). In his reply on 24 August, Flaxman regretted that one of his sister's drawings, showing 'Serena veiwing herself in the Glass when dressed for the Masquerade whilst her Maid adjusts her train', was not chosen for engraving, and also complains that 'the prints for Serena seem ... to be worse than the drawings' (Bentley 1969, p. 130). Apparently the additional drawing had been an issue between the two men earlier in the month, for in his letter of 7 August Hayley noted that there were only six drawings, although he had 'a faint confused Recollection of having once beheld' another (*The Letters of William Blake*, ed. Geoffrey Keynes (Oxford: Clarendon Press, 1980), 59–60).

Blake's plates, all bearing scratched inscriptions in his hand, are sometimes bound with pl. 1 as a frontispiece and the others facing the lines illustrated; but their placement at the start of the canto illustrated, as in an unopened copy of the 1803 edition in original boards (RNE) and all copies seen of the much rarer 1807 edition, is recorded below. The 1803 edition was issued in both large- (24.5 × 14.7 cm.) and small-paper formats. The best impressions are generally found in large-paper copies; the plates are quite worn in the 1807 edition. There is another 1807 edition, lacking the title-page reference to Maria Flaxman's designs and with the plates after Stothard. A copy of the 1803 edition in the collection of George Goyder has the plates hand coloured, possibly by Blake.

1. Facing p. 1; 11.2 × 7.6 cm.; *Fig. 193*
Title: *Canto. I. Verse 29*
Signatures: *Maria Flaxman. inv & del.* [left], *W Blake. sculp* [right]
Imprint: *Publish'd May 1. 1803. by Cadell & Davies. Strand*

Serena pays 'passive obedience' (p. 3) to her father, Sir Gilbert, seated in his 'elbow-chair' (p. 2). The basket of flowers may have been suggested by Hayley's comparison of Serena to 'a rose-bud' (p. 2). Neither the lily (an emblem of Serena's virgin purity?) nor Sir Gilbert's book is mentioned in the text.

2. Facing p. 24; 10 × 7.9 cm.; *Fig. 194*
Title: *Canto II^d Verse 471.*
Signatures: *Maria Flaxman inv & del.* [left], *W Blake. sculp* [right]
Imprint: *Publishd May 1. 1803. by Cadell & Davies. Strand*

Serena, in 'her chamber' (p. 48), offers a prayer of thanks to her guardian spirit, Sophrosyne, for having stilled Sir Gilbert's anger.

3. Facing p. 50; 10.4 × 7.9 cm.; *Fig. 195*
Title: *Canto. III. Verse. 201.*
Signatures: *Maria Flaxman. inv & del:* [left], *W Blake. sc* [right]
Imprint: *Publish'd May 1. 1803 by Cadell & Davies. Strand*

Serena enters into the cave of Spleen. 'O'er an arch'd cavern, rough with horrid stone' are the words 'all ye who enter, every hope forego' (p. 53), barely indicated in the plate by a few marks on a tablet or block of stone at the top of the cave's mouth. Various spectres within the cave battle 'in the blazing air' (p. 61). Flaxman has amalgamated two distinct, but clearly parallel, incidents in the text into a single design.

4. Facing p. 81; 10.3 × 7.4 cm.; *Fig. 196*

Title: *Canto. IV. Verse 328*
Signatures: *Maria Flaxman inv: & del* [left], *W Blake. sculp.* [right]
Imprint: *Publishd May 1. 1803. by Cadell & Davies' Strand*

Sir Gilbert at the breakfast table reads with growing anger some scandalous gossip in the newspaper about his daughter Serena. She turns to read a comforting book by 'Chesterfield' (p. 97) while her 'prudish aunt' (p. 96) looks on with an expression of sorrow that seems out of character with her descriptions as a 'malignant crone' (p. 96).

5. Facing p. 103; 11 × 7.9 cm.; *Fig. 197*

Title: *Canto V. Verse 43*
Signatures: *Maria Flaxman inv & del* [left], *W Blake sculp* [right]
Imprint: *Publishd May 1. 1803. by Cadell & Davies Strand*

A personified 'Quiet' lays 'her lightest mantle' (p. 105) over the sleeping Serena. The guardian spirit, Sophrosyne, enters immediately thereafter and is compared to 'Jove's favourite daughter' (p. 105). Thus, the drawing for this plate may have been the one to which Hayley refers as containing a 'Minerva' figure omitted from the engraving (see letter quoted above).

6. Facing p. 139; 10.3 × 7.9 cm.; *Fig. 198*

Title: *Canto. VI. Verse 294.*
Signatures: *Maria Flaxman. inv & del.* [left], *W Blake. sculp.* [right]
Imprint: as on pl. 1.

Serena, dressed as 'Ariel' (p. 147), attends a 'masquerade' (p. 141). Sir Gilbert, holding a club, is dressed as 'Caliban', while Serena's aunt (right foreground) plays 'Sycorax' (p. 144) in the 'habit of a witch' (p. 145). The figure just left of Sir Gilbert is probably the youthful Edwin, wearing 'the minstrel dress of yore' (p. 152). To the left of Edwin we can see the turban of the host, Earl Filligree, dressed 'in the semblance of a Moorish prince' (p. 150). Serena has just 'thrown aside' her mask, which she holds in her hand in the plate, and reveals her beauty 'in all her blushing pride' (p. 154). The 4 cm. horizontal scratch, running 2.5 cm. above the lower margin of the design, wore off the plate

in the course of the 1803 printing and thus appears as only a faint shadow line in the 1807 edition.

Literature: Gilchrist 1863, i. 171–2, ii. 260; Russell 1912, no. 97; Keynes 1921, no. 125; Bentley and Nurmi 1964, no. 380; Bentley 1977, no. 471; Essick 1980, pp. 170–1.

XLIV

William Hayley, *The Life, and Posthumous Writings, of William Cowper* (3 vols., London: J. Johnson, 1803 (vols. i–ii), 1804 (vol. iii); 2nd edn. of vols. i–ii, 1803); *Figs. 199–206*

Hayley's biography of his friend, the poet William Cowper (1731–1800), contains six plates, all signed by Blake as the engraver. Pl. 4 is also signed by him as the designer, but it includes a medallion probably based on someone else's design, and thus is included here for the sake of completeness. The scratched inscriptions on all the plates were no doubt cut by Blake, and it seems unlikely that a writing engraver was employed to execute even the more carefully engraved letters. Blake states in his letter to Thomas Butts of 11 September 1801 that his 'Principal labour' at that time was 'Engraving Plates for Cowpers Life' (E 716, K 809). On 30 January 1803 Blake wrote to his brother James that his 'Wife has undertaken to Print the whole number of the Plates for [vols. i–ii of] Cowper's work' under Blake's supervision (E 726, K 821). Bentley 1969, p. 606, calculates that the Blakes probably received about £21 for this plate-printing work. In a letter of 7 August 1803 Hayley implies that Blake received '30 Guineas' for one of the plates 'for the Cowper', but it is unclear as to which plate (perhaps pl. 1?) he is referring (Bentley 1969, p. 121). Other documentary records of Blake's work on these plates are printed in Bentley 1969, pp. 78–94, 112–13, 137–8, 149–51, and are summarized for each plate below. See Bentley 1988, pp. 21–3, 26, 60, for further contemporary references.

The plates for vols. i–ii are much more clearly and darkly printed in the second edition (so indicated on the title-pages) than the first. Perhaps many of the lines were cut more deeply when the plates were converted into their second states, but more careful inking and printing could account for the considerable tonal differences. One hesitates to blame Mrs Blake for the poor impressions of the first states, but that may indeed be the case. Bentley 1977, p. 577, notes 'an early proof of one [unidentified] plate in the Rosenwald Collection', but I have not been able to find it. Pls. 1, 3, and 4 were re-engraved by Peter Rushton Maverick for the 1803 New York octavo edition. The Chichester 1806, 1809, and 1812 octavo editions in four volumes (the last two retitled *The Life and Letters, of William Cowper*) contain a reduced (10.2 × 7.8 cm.) re-engraving of pl. 1 by Caroline Watson as the frontispiece to vol. i. Hayley must have told Blake of his plans to employ Watson, for in his letter to Hayley of 22–5 March 1805 Blake claims that the 'Idea of Seeing an Engraving of Cowper by the hand of Caroline Watson is I assure you a pleasing one to me it will be highly gratifying to see another Copy by another hand & not only gratifying but Improving' (E 764, K 859). It is, however, unlikely that Blake was actually pleased to be replaced by Watson at a time when he needed further employment for his graver. Perhaps it was polite letters of this sort that prompted Blake to write more privately and honestly in his *Notebook* about his relationship with Hayley: 'I write the Rascal Thanks till he & I | With Thanks & Compliments are quite drawn dry' (E 506, K 549). Watson also engraved the frontispiece, 'Judith, or Cowper's Oak', for Hayley's *Supplementary Pages to the Life of Cowper* (1806). A re-engraving by J. W. Cook of pl. 3, 10.7 × 8.5 cm., appears as the frontispiece to vol. i of *The Life and Letters* (London: Baldwin, Cradock, & Joy, *et al.*, 1824) and was used again in the one-volume edition of 1835 published by Longman, Rees, and Co., *et al.*

Blake's work on the *Life of Cowper* apparently had a significant impact on his relationship with the book's author. The importance of the project to both men is indicated by Hayley's comment in his *Memoirs* that Blake settled in Felpham 'to execute various works of art, & particularly the prints, with which He [Hayley] hoped to decorate the projected Life of Cowper' (Bentley 1969, p. 74). The arduous work on the plates, and criticism of them by Hayley's friends, probably taxed Blake's patience and contributed to his 'irritability' for which Flaxman commiserated with Hayley in August 1803 (Bentley 1969, p. 130). Hayley's attitude towards Cowper may have given Blake insights into his own increasingly strained relationship with his patron. Hayley was the sort of practical man who took pleasure in assisting unworldly geniuses and directing their artistic endeavours. In a revelatory letter to Lady Hesketh of 3 August 1805 Hayley offers an implicit comparison between Blake and Cowper in the form of a diagnosis: 'I have also every wish to befriend Him [Blake] from a motive, that, I know, our dear angelic Cowper would approve, because this poor man with an admirable quickness of apprehension & with uncommon powers of mind, has often appeared to me on the verge of Insanity:—' (Bentley 1969, p. 164). Blake's awareness of Hayley's proclivities is registered in a *Notebook* poem, entitled 'William Cowper Esqre' but also referring to Hayley's relationship with Blake: 'For this is being a Friend just in the nick | Not when hes well but waiting till hes sick' (E 507, K 551). Cowper's madness was a fatally exaggerated form of the personality traits that attracted Hayley's solicitousness—an extreme to which Blake did not want to descend. Nor did he wish to receive the kinds of directions from Hayley that had, in Blake's view, harmed George Romney, the designer of pl. 1. As Blake told his brother James in a letter of 30 January 1803, Hayley 'thinks to turn me into a Portrait Painter as he did Poor Romney, but this he nor all the devils in hell will never do' (E 725, K 819). For a study of how such attitudes may have prompted Blake's formulation of the 'Spectre' in his poetry, see Paley 1968.

1. Vol i, frontispiece (1st edn.); 18.5 × 14.4 cm.; *Fig. 199*

Scratched inscription and signature below design: *From a Portrait in Crayons Drawn from the Life by Romney in 1792 Engravd by W Blake 1802*

Title: WILLIAM, COWPER. | Carmine Nobilem | Hor:

Imprint: *Publish'd Novemb^r: 5. 1802. by J. Johnson St Pauls Church Yard*

Second State (2nd edn.). Small patches of cross-hatching have been added to the hat far right and just right of the man's ear. A few hatching strokes have been added to the scarf just below the man's neck and along the top of the right loop of the bow. A serif has been added to the 'g' of '*engravd*'.

Hayley mentions in his text (ii. 69) that he saw George Romney (1734–1802) draw this portrait, an event to which Cowper refers in letters of 25 and 26 August 1792 printed by Hayley (ii. 78, 82). Hayley also prints Cowper's sonnet 'To George Romney' (ii. 95) about this drawing in pastels, 57.2 × 47 cm., now in the National Portrait Gallery, London (reproduced in Bishop 1951, following p. 160). Blake drew a carefully finished copy (Butlin 1981, no. 351) in pen and wash, 18.8 × 14.7 cm. (LC, *Fig. 200*). Hayley refers to this or some similar drawing 'from which he [Blake] will also make an engraving' in his letter to Romney of 3 February 1801 (Bentley 1969, p. 78). The face is very close to Romney's original, but Blake has altered the bow at the neck. The LC drawing is inscribed by Hayley in ink, 'William Cowper Esqr | Given by the Poet; to his friend Hayley'. As Butlin 1981 points out, p. 305, this 'inscription, which implies that Cowper gave the drawing to Hayley before the former's death in 1800, would rule out Blake's participation but presumably is the result of a later confusion with Romney's original'. The LC drawing may also have been the basis for Blake's two watercolour miniatures of Cowper (Butlin 1981, nos. 353–4). There is as well a pencil sketch based on the Romney portrait (Butlin 1981, no. 352), but in my view its attribution to Blake is not certain. Blake based his portrait of Cowper among the 'Heads of the Poets' series, painted to decorate Hayley's library *c*. 1800–3, on Romney's drawing (Butlin 1981, no. 343.17). For other engravings of Romney's portrait, see Russell 1963, pp. 289–90.

Hayley sent a proof of this plate or pl. 3 to Flaxman for his comments (letter of 18 January 1802 (Bentley 1969, p. 88)). Although Lady Hesketh had intensely disliked both Romney's portrait and Blake's miniature of it, she confessed in a letter to Hayley of 29 December 1802 that she admired Blake's engraving because it was now 'softened' (Bentley 1969, p. 113). Blake expressed his pleasure at finally satisfying Lady Hesketh in a letter to his brother James on 30 January 1803 (E 726, K 820). Lady Hesketh was always on guard against any portrait of her cousin which, in her view, showed the slightest hint of his insanity.

2. Vol. i, facing p. 4 (1st edn.); 15.7 × 12.9 cm.; *Fig. 201*
Scratched signatures: *D. Heins Pinx* [left], *W Blake sculp* [right]

Title: Mrs COWPER | Mother of the Poet
Imprint: *Publish'd Novemb^r 5. 1802 by J. Johnson St Pauls Church Yard*

Second State (2nd edn.). The highlights in the hair on top of the woman's head have been enlarged slightly with burnishing. A few hatching strokes on the woman's breast just above the centre of the lace bodice may have been deepened.

Hayley refers (i. 4) to the oil-portrait miniature of Anne Donne Cowper (1703–37) by D. Heins, a German artist active in Norfolk *c*. 1725–56. Blake's plate is based closely on this painting, 15.9 × 12.7 cm., now in the collection of Miss Mary Barham Johnson (reproduced in Charles Ryskamp, *William Cowper of the Inner Temple* (Cambridge: Cambridge Univ. Press, 1959), pl. 1). This is probably the portrait that occasioned Cowper's poem of 1790, 'On the Receipt of My Mother's Picture out of Norfolk'. Hayley evidently borrowed the painting from Cowper's friend Anne Bodham, for in a letter of 15 January 1803 he thanked her for the loan (Bentley 1969, p. 113). In a letter of 25 July 1801, Hayley states that Blake 'is at this moment engraving' the 'portrait of the poets mother', and reports in a letter of 3 September that 'Blake is finishing' the plate (Bentley 1969, p. 81). Another engraving of the portrait, 9.8 × 7.8 cm., by 'H. Robinson' (probably John Henry Robinson) was published in *The Life and Works of William Cowper*, ed. Robert Southey (London: Baldwin and Cradock, 1835), i, facing p. 5. The engraving by Edward Finden, 8.8 × 8.2 cm., appears as the frontispiece to *The Works of William Cowper*, ed. T. S. Grimshawe (London: Saunders and Otley, 1835–6), vii.

3. Vol. ii, frontispiece (most copies of the 1st edn.); 22.8 × 16.5 cm.; *Fig. 202*

Signatures: *T Lawrence R A: ad vivum del: 1793* [left], *W. Blake sculp 1802* [right]
Title: *William Cowper— | Author of "The Task"*
Imprint: *Publish'd Novr 5. 1802 by J Johnson St Pauls Church Yard*

Second State (some copies of the 1st edn. and the 2nd edn.). The dots of stipple shading left of the man's mouth and nose have been extended further to the left. A few dots have been added to the collar below his ear. Some of the stipple lines on the hat, upper left, have been extended downwards. His face has been darkened considerably with more stipple in the shadow areas. Reproduced in Essick 1980, fig. 180.

Blake has engraved this plate in stippled lines, probably with the aid of a roulette, in imitation of a pencil or chalk drawing. Cowper refers to his portrait by Sir

Thomas Lawrence (1769–1830) in letters to his cousin John Johnson and to Hayley of 29 September and 5 October 1793, both printed by Hayley in this work (ii. 155). The portrait was exhibited at the Royal Academy in 1795, no. 596 in the catalogue. Francesco Bartolozzi had engraved the portrait in 1799 for Samuel Rose, who distributed the print privately to Cowper's friends (Garlick 1964, reproduced Ryskamp 1959 and Russell 1963, pl. XII), but in November 1801 Hayley borrowed the original drawing from Lady Hesketh so that Blake could engrave it (see Hayley's letters of 1 and 14 November and 7 December 1801 (Bentley 1969, pp. 85–7)). Ryskamp 1959 argues that the original from which Bartolozzi and Blake worked is the pencil-and-wash drawing, 20 × 14.9 cm., acquired in 1910 by the Cowper and Newton Museum, Olney (reproduced in Ryskamp 1959). There is also a pencil drawing, 21 × 16.5 cm., acquired by John Fremantle (later Lord Cottesloe) in 1950 but now untraced (reproduced in Goldring 1951, facing p. 80). A note on the back of the frame (quoted in Goldring 1951, p. 103, and Russell 1963, p. 292) by Louisa Margaret Harris states that she acquired the drawing from 'Lady Clarges' (a friend of Lady Hesketh, according to Russell 1963, p. 291) in 1809. This comment at least indicates that the drawing is not a later copy. Goldring, in the caption to his reproduction, refers to this work as a copy of the drawing exhibited in 1795, or a 'variant of it', while Garlick 1964 attributes the Fremantle drawing to Lawrence, lists it as the basis for Blake's engraving, and states that the drawing is 'said to have belonged to Cowper's cousin, Harriet, Lady Hesketh'. Garlick describes the Cowper and Newton Museum drawing as a 'repetition' of the Fremantle version, and has informed me in correspondence that he finds none of Lawrence's stylistic traits in the Museum's drawing, which he believes was probably copied after one of the prints. There is also a small pencil drawing of Cowper, 12 × 12 cm., in the Beinecke Library, Yale University, New Haven, Connecticut, which has been attributed to Lawrence (Garlick 1961, no. 48). A pencil-and-wash drawing, '8 × 5¼ inches', of Cowper is attributed to Lawrence in the Anderson Galleries auction catalogue, New York, 5–6 January 1920, lot 208 (sold from the collection of George S. Hellman but now untraced).

William Ridley engraved three versions of Lawrence's portrait of Cowper, all printed in periodicals beginning with *The Lady's Monthly Magazine*, 6 (Feb. 1801). A revised state of Bartolozzi's plate, with title and signatures, bears a J. Johnson imprint dated January 1806. There is also a much revised state, with a frame added, the lower areas of Cowper's arms and chest completed, re-engraved inscriptions, and a William Miller imprint of May 1805. Russell 1963, p. 75, notes that this version was intended for the J. Johnson 1806 edition of Cowper's *Poems* but not published in it. However, a copy of the *Poems* at the HEH has this print bound as a frontispiece. A small engraving, approx. 10 × 8.4 cm., appears as the frontispiece to *The Works of William Cowper*, ed. T. S. Grimshawe (London: Saunders and Otley, 1835–6), vi. This plate, signed by Edward Finden as the engraver, is reproduced in *The Poems of William Cowper*, ed. J. C. Bailey (London: Methuen, 1905), facing p. 552, where it is described as a copy of a drawing by William Harvey after Lawrence's 'original painting [*sic*]'. Perhaps one of the drawings noted above is this copy by Harvey. For other engravings of the portrait, including plates that combine elements of both the Lawrence and Romney (pl. 1) portraits, see Russell 1963, pp. 293–8.

Keynes 1921, p. 251, records a proof of Blake's plate in his collection, but this is simply an impression of the first state with the imprint cut off. In a letter to Lady Hesketh of 20 December 1802, Hayley comments that Blake's plate was 'infinitely superior to Bartolozzi's' (Bentley 1969, p. 112), an opinion also given by Samuel Greatheed in *The Eclectic Review*, 1 (1805), 923 (Bentley 1969, pp. 172–3).

4. Vol. ii, p. 415 (a few copies of the 1st edn.); 15.2 × 11.6 cm.; *Fig. 203*

Inscriptions on the base of the weather-house and around the circular medallion: see *Fig. 203*.

Scratched signature lower left beneath the base of the weather-house: *Blake d & sc*

Imprint: *Publish'd Nov⁵ 5 1802 by J Johnson Sᵗ Pauls Church Yard*

First State: known to me only through a copy of the book in the Bodleian Library and an impression (reproduced here) used to extra-illustrate a copy of Goldwin Smith, *Cowper* (London: Macmillan, 1880), in the HEH (offsets from p. 417 confirm that the print was removed from Hayley's book).

Second State (most copies of the 1st edn.). The diagonal hatching strokes representing rain right of the man upper left have been augmented and extended so that they now touch his shoulder and back. Cross-hatching has been added to the clouds above and to the right of the man, just below the roof. Reproduced in Bindman 1978, no. 399, and Essick 1980, fig. 170.

Third State (a few copies of the 1st edn. (e.g. Somerville College, Oxford)). The horizontal hatching right of the man's shoulder has been extended closer to him. A loose impression of this state in the Keynes Collection, Fitzwilliam Museum, is on paper much thinner than that used in any copy of the book I have seen, yet it bears the letterpress text recto and verso.

Fourth State (2nd edn.). The bases and upper reaches of the three trees supporting the roof of the weather-house have been darkened with short hatching strokes. More lines have been added to the roof to delineate its thatch; some of the leaves of the vine on the roof have been darkened. Dots have been added to the sun left of the woman and an additional line has been cut in the beam just below her feet. A short wavy line has been added left of the foot of the '*P*' of '*Peace*' and a second stroke has been added to the vertical of the first '*t*' of '*thought*', both in the first line of the inscription on the base of the weather-house. Lines have been added to the pendant garland, particularly just above and below the banner. More jagged lines, defining grass, have been added beneath the two lower hares. Reproduced in Wright 1929, pl. 38.

A loose impression in the Keynes Collection, Fitzwilliam Museum, represents a state intermediate between the third and fourth. It contains the additional lines defining grass beneath the hares, but not the other fourth-state additions. This impression is on paper (1802 watermark) much thinner than that used in any copy of the book I have seen; yet, like the Keynes print of the third state (see above), it bears the letterpress text recto and verso. This state may have been published in the book, but I have yet to find it in any copy.

Blake's design illustrates lines 210–14 from Book I of Cowper's *The Task*, inscribed on the base of the weather-house. The male, wearing a broad-brimmed hat, is one of Blake's typical traveller figures, generally similar to those in *The Gates of Paradise* pl. 14 and on the frontispiece to *Jerusalem*. At least some of these figures are self-representations (see Jean H. Hagstrum, 'Blake's Blake', in Heinz Bluhm (ed.), *Essays in History and Literature* (Chicago: Newberry Library, 1965), pp. 169–78). The opposition between stormy male and sunny female embodies the contrast between the sublime and the picturesque in late-eighteenth-century aesthetics. Contrary structures are also a characteristic of Blake's writings, as in *Songs of Innocence* and *Songs of Experience* and the division between male Spectre and female Emanation in his later poetry. The circular picture of Cowper's three tame hares is said by Hayley to be based on 'a drawing presented to Cowper by a friend unknown' (i. 89–90), and thus was not designed by Blake. The inscription above this medallion, 'The Peasant's Nest', also refers to *The Task* (Book I, lines

221–7), but this passage does not mention the hares. The house is 'perch'd upon the green-hill top' (line 222) in the background of the medallion. The same design is painted on a snuff box which has been in the Cowper and Newton Museum, Olney, since 1917. Wright 1929, i. 125, claims that the box was Cowper's own and attributes the painting to Romney.

5. Vol. iii, frontispiece; 20 × 14.3 cm.; *Fig. 204*

Signatures: *Francis Stone del:* [left], *W Blake. sculp* [right]

Title: *A View of St Edmund's Chapel, | in the Church of East Dereham, | Containing the Grave of William Cowper Esqre*

Imprint: *Publish'd by J Johnson St Pauls 25 March 1804*

This plate, based on an untraced drawing by Francis Stone (dates unknown), shows the monument by John Flaxman erected over Cowper's tomb. In his letter to Hayley of 13 December 1803 Blake apparently refers to this drawing, 'fetch'd' from Samuel Rose and shown to Flaxman for his suggestions (E 738, K 832). Blake's letter of 16 March 1804, however, implies that the drawing he worked from was lent by John Johnson (E 743, K 838). See comments on pl. 6 for documents concerning both plates in Hayley's vol. iii.

6. Vol. iii, variously bound after the title-page, facing p. 1, or facing p. 416; 13 × 14.5 cm.; *Fig. 205*

Inscriptions on monument: see *Fig. 205*.

Title: *A Sketch of the Monument | Erected in the Church of East Dereham in Norfolk | In Memory of William Cowper Esqre*

Signatures below title: *Etch'd by W Blake from the original Model | by John Flaxman Esqr Sculptor to his Majesty*

Imprint: as on pl. 5.

The complex development of this design can be traced through several drawings and associated documents. Flaxman's original pen-and-grey-wash sketch is in the Houghton Library, Harvard University, Cambridge, Massachusetts. The main decoration above the tablet is a lyre. With a letter of 21 February 1802 Hayley sent this drawing to Lady Hesketh and commented that he did not find Flaxman's design 'chastely *simple* enough' (Butlin 1981, p. 306). Accordingly, Hayley invented an alternative version and had Blake sketch it in his letter. This version, 8.5 × 11 cm. in pen and watercolour, is also in the Houghton Library (Butlin 1981, no. 355). It shows the Bible and Cowper's *The Task* above the tablet, as in Blake's plate, but there are two palm fronds and a wreath rests against the Bible. Hayley also notes, in his letter to Lady Hesketh, that he had sent another (untraced) drawing, presumably by Blake, of his suggested design to Flaxman for the sculptor's opinion (Bentley 1969, p. 90). Flaxman responded on 25 February (Bentley 1969, p. 91) with another version, showing a leafy branch (rather than a palm frond) and the Bible lying flat, now in the Berg Collection, New York Public Library. On the same day Hayley wrote to John Johnson (Bentley 1969, p. 90) and included a drawing by Blake showing both Flaxman's original concept and Hayley's alternative. This is probably the pen-and-watercolour drawing, 7.5 × 10 cm., now in the collection of Mary Barham Johnson (Butlin 1981, no. 356). Apparently Hayley sent another (untraced) drawing to Lady Hesketh on 7 March, showing his own version of the monument and both of Flaxman's (Bentley 1969, p. 91 and n. 3). Hayley wrote again to the Lady on 13 March (Bentley 1969, p. 91) and enclosed 'a new device of my own' for the monument, sketched by Blake. Hayley also sent Blake's drawings of this new design to Flaxman and John Johnson; the latter replied approvingly in letters of 23 March and 10 April 1802 (Bentley 1969, pp. 94–5). Two of these sketches are extant (Butlin 1981, nos. 357–8): a pen-and-watercolour drawing, 8.8 × 10.3 cm., in the Princeton University Library, Princeton, New Jersey; and a practically identical 'replica' (Butlin 1981, p. 308), 8.5 × 10 cm., in the Beinecke Library, Yale University, New Haven, Connecticut (*Fig. 206*). Both show a single palm frond and no wreath, as in Blake's plate. The Beinecke drawing is inscribed, perhaps by Blake, 'in St Nicholas Church Dereham' and 'Cowper's Monument in Dereham Church'. Blake used either one of these drawings, or yet some other version of them, as the basis for his plate, designed by Flaxman, Hayley, and Blake.

In a letter to Hayley of 2 January 1804 Flaxman commented that 'Mr. Blake's opinion that the drawing sent from Norfolk [by John Johnson for pl. 5] may be advantageously engraved for the ensuing volume [3] of Cowper's life as an agreable perspective of the Situation, seems very just, whilst the Monument itself may be represented on a larger Scale in a Vignette [pl. 6]' (Bentley 1969, pp. 137–8). By this time Blake had returned to London and was working there on both plates for Hayley's vol. iii. In a letter of 23 February 1804 Blake told Hayley that 'the plates of Cowpers Monument are both in great forwardness & you shall have Proofs in another week' (E 742, K 837). On 12 March the plates were 'almost finishd' (E 743, K 837), and four days later Blake sent unfinished proofs to

Hayley (E 743, K 838). Proofs 'with the writing' were sent on 21 March, and a dozen impressions of each plate were promised to Hayley on 31 March (E 744–5, K 839–40). In his letter to Samuel Rose of 1 April 1804 Hayley indicates that Blake had found a 'Copperplate Printer' for the two engravings (Bentley 1969, p. 151), and thus Mrs Blake was relieved of the burdensome task she had undertaken for the first two volumes.

Literature: Gilchrist 1863, i. 164–8, ii. 257, 260–1; Humphry Ward and W. Roberts, *Romney* (London: Agnew and Sons, 1904), 34–5; Russell 1912, no. 96; Walter Armstrong, *Lawrence* (London: Methuen, 1913), 180; Keynes 1921, no. 124; Thomas Wright, *The Life of William Blake* (Olney: Wright, 1929), i. 124–6; [Kenneth Povey], 'Lawrence and Cowper', *The* [London] *Times* (6 May 1930), 19; Douglas Goldring, *Regency Portrait Painter: The Life of Sir Thomas Lawrence* (London: Macdonald, 1951), 101–4; Morchard Bishop, *Blake's Hayley* (London: Gollancz, 1951), 252–4, 268–70; G. E. Bentley, jun., 'Blake, Hayley, and Lady Hesketh', *The Review of English Studies*, 7 (1956), 265–86; G. E. Bentley, jun., 'William Blake and "Johnny of Norfolk"', *Studies in Philology*, 53 (1956), 60–74; Charles Ryskamp, 'Blake's Cowperian Sketches', *The Review of English Studies*, 9 (1958), 48–9; G. E. Bentley, jun., 'Blake's Engravings and his Friendship with Flaxman', *Studies in Bibliography*, 12 (1959), 161–88; Charles Ryskamp, 'Lawrence's Portrait of Cowper', *The Princeton University Library Chronicle*, 20 (1959), 140–4; [Kenneth Garlick], *Sir Thomas Lawrence, PRA* (exhibition catalogue; London: Royal Academy, 1961), no. 48 (Fremantle drawing of pl. 3); Charles Ryskamp, 'Blake's Drawing of Cowper's Monument', *The Princeton University Library Chronicle*, 24 (1962), 27–31; Norma Russell, *A Bibliography of William Cowper to 1837* (Oxford: Clarendon Press, 1963), 250–3, 288–98; Bentley and Nurmi 1964, no. 337; Kenneth Garlick, *A Catalogue of the Paintings, Drawings and Pastels of Sir Thomas Lawrence* (Walpole Society, 39; Glasgow: Walpole Society, 1964), 22; Morton D. Paley, 'Cowper as Blake's Spectre', *Eighteenth-Century Studies*, 1 (1968), 236–52; Thomas L. Minnick, 'Blake and "Cowper's Tame Hares"', *Blake Newsletter*, 4 (1970), 11–12; Easson and Essick 1972, no. VII (pl. 4 only); Bentley 1977, no. 468; Bindman 1978, no. 399 (pl. 4 only); Irwin 1979 (see **XXXVIII**, *Literature*), p. 167; Essick 1980, pp. 168–9, 177; Robert N. Essick, 'Blake, Hayley, and Edward Garrard Marsh: "An Insect of Parnassus"', *Explorations: The Age of Enlightenment*, i (1987), 58–84.

XLV

Prince Hoare, *Academic Correspondence* (London: Robson, Payne, and Hatchard, 1804); *Fig. 207*

This pamphlet of twenty-eight pages publishes

letters and brief essays on artistic matters by the dramatist and artist Prince Hoare (1755–1834), who in 1799 became the honorary foreign secretary of the Royal Academy. The only plate is signed by Flaxman as the designer and Blake as the engraver. Flaxman recommended Blake to engrave his drawing in a letter to Hoare of 25 December 1803 (Bentley 1969, p. 136). On 4 January 1804 Hoare expressed disappointment to Flaxman that he had not yet received a 'proof of Mⸯ Blake's Etching' (Bentley 1969, p. 136); but the plate must have been completed shortly thereafter, for the pamphlet was reviewed in *The Literary Journal*, 3 (1 Feb. 1804), cols. 93–5. The reviewer, 'S.Q.', comments that 'Surely ... the Royal Academy of England might have offered an engraving worthy of the subject, and of the country' (cols. 94–5). Perhaps some of the awkwardness in Blake's plate resulted from an attempt to render the broken surfaces of the statue. Blake sent Hayley a copy of the pamphlet with his letter of 23 February 1804 (E 742, K 836).

1. Frontispiece; 16.8 × 18.5 cm.; *Fig. 207*

Scratched signatures: *J Flaxman RA. del:* [left], *W Blake. sc:* [right]
Scratched title: *Fragment of an Antique Statue of Ceres, found in the Ruins of Eleusis | and now placed in the Public Library at Cambridge*

The statue is discussed by Hoare and authors he quotes on pp. viii, 20–1, 25 (Flaxman's letter to Hoare, noting that he was including 'a slight sketch' of the statue). The scratched inscriptions are in Blake's copperplate hand and include the reverse serif on the lower-case 'g' typical of his lettering up to *c.* 1803–4. The statue, now identified as a caryatid from the Inner Propylaea at Eleusis, is in the Fitzwilliam Museum (for full description and reproductions, see Ludwig Budde and Richard Nicholls, *A Catalogue of the Greek and Roman Sculpture in the Fitzwilliam Museum, Cambridge* (Cambridge: Fitzwilliam Museum, 1964), no. 81 and pls. 24–5). Three engravings of the statue, engraved by Peltro William Tomkins after drawings by Flaxman, appear in Edward Daniel Clarke, *Greek Marbles ... Deposited in the Vestibule of the Public Library of the University of Cambridge* (Cambridge: Cambridge Univ. Press, 1809). Tomkins's plate facing p. 24 shows the statue from the side, as on the right in Blake's plate, but several differences in detail suggest that the two were not based on the same drawing.

Literature: Gilchrist 1880, i. 205; Keynes 1921, no. 126; Bentley and Nurmi 1964, no. 382; Bentley 1977, no. 473.

XLVI

The Iliad of Homer Engraved from the Compositions of John Flaxman (London: Longman, Hurst, Rees, & Orme, 1805). *The Classical Compositions of John Flaxman* (London: Bell and Daldy, 1870). *Compositions from the Iliad of Homer, Designed by John Flaxman* (London: Bell and Daldy, 1870). *Figs. 208–10*

John Flaxman's outline illustrations to *The Iliad* were first published in Rome in 1793, consisting of an engraved title-page and thirty-four plates engraved by Tommaso Piroli. For the London 1805 edition, Flaxman added five new designs. Three were engraved by Blake, and two by his former partner James Parker, in a severe outline style to match the Piroli plates they accompanied. The publisher's business records (repr. Bentley 1964, p. 35, and 1977, pp. 561–2) show that the plates were reprinted a number of times to at least 1829. A variety of wove papers was used, but it is uncertain as to how these co-ordinate with print runs. The plates were acquired by William Sotheby in 1832, but there is no record of impressions being taken from them until the 1870 *Classical Compositions* and *Compositions from the Iliad* (the latter simply a separate issue of the former). According to Ruthven Todd, 'Blake's Dante Plates', *Times Literary Supplement* (29 Aug. 1968), 928, Bell and Daldy sold the plates as scrap metal in 1917.

In a letter of 2 April 1804 Blake told William Hayley that he was engraving two of the 'additional designs' for 'a new edition of Flaxman's *Homer*' (E 746, K 841). In a letter to Hayley of 1 May 1804, Flaxman noted that 'Mⸯ Blake is to have from 5 to 6 Guineas each from Messⸯˢ Longman & Rees for the plates of the Homer according to the labor' (Bentley 1969, pp. 151–2), and three days later Blake told Hayley that 'the price I receive for engraving Flaxman's outlines of *Homer* is five guineas each' (E 749, K 844). The lesser fee was confirmed by Flaxman in 1808 and implied by Longman's cost of £26. 6*s*. for all five new plates (Bentley 1969, pp. 189, 571).

Blake's work on these three plates may have contributed to his later interest in, and criticism of, both Homer's poetry and Pope's translations. In some *Notebook* doggerel of *c*. 1808–11 Blake characterizes Hayley as a fool for having said that 'Homer is very much improvd by Pope' (E 505, K 555). But the Greek poet's writings are themselves 'Stolen' (from earlier Patriarchal works) and 'Perverted', according to the 'Preface' to Blake's *Milton* (E 95, K 480). Blake continued his attack on classicism in *On Homers Poetry* [and] *On Virgil* of *c*. 1820, but this did not prevent him from basing pictorial compositions on Homeric subjects, including *The Judgment of Paris* (Butlin 1981, no. 675) and a large pencil sketch of the *Death of Hector* from the *Iliad* (see Essick 1988).

There are a good many tracings and drawings of the *Iliad* designs nearly identical to the published images. The majority of these are copies of the prints, but a set of tracings at University College, London, may have played some role in the production process. The only imprint in the 1805 edition, dated March 1805, appears on the unsigned title-page.

Re-engraved editions of the *Iliad* designs that include those originally engraved by Blake were executed by Piroli (Rome, n.d. [*c*. 1818?], reissued 1845), Beniamino del Vecchio (no place, *c*. 1840s?), and, on a reduced scale, by Eduard Schuler (Karlsruhe, 1828), Étienne Reveil (Paris, 1836, 1844), Henry Moses (London, 1857), and J. Andrews and W. L. Ormsby (Philadelphia, 1871).

1. First design; 17 × 24.4 cm.; *Fig. 208*

Inscriptions above design: *Plate 1*. [left], HOMER INVOKING THE MUSE. [centre], *l.1* [right]
Signature right: *Blake sculp.*
Quotation below design: ACHILLES WRATH TO GREECE THE DIREFUL SPRING, | OF WOES UNNUMBERD HEAVENLY GODDESS SING! | Popes Homers Iliad.

The strong-eyed Muse (left) plays her *kithara* and sings the story of Troy to the blind bard who invokes her on his own harp. The helmet is similar to one worn by Mars elsewhere in the series; the shield with the Gorgon's head resembles those held by Achilles and Minerva. There are two preliminary drawings of the two figures alone (Fogg Art Museum and Houghton Library, Cambridge, Massachusetts). A proof before all letters is in the BMPR.

2. Second design; 16.9 × 27.3 cm.; *Fig. 209*

Inscriptions above design: *Plate 2*. [left], MINERVA REPRESSING THE FURY OF ACHILLES. [centre]
Signature right: *Blake sculp.*
Quotation below design: WHILE HALF UNSHEATH'D APPEAR'D THE GLITTERING BLADE, | MINERVA SWIFT DESCENDED FROM ABOVE. | Pope's Homers Iliad B. I. Line 260.

Achilles (second from right) has been angered by Agamemnon's threat to take Briseis from him. He is stopped from drawing his sword by Minerva, who seizes him by the hair. The seated members of the Grecian council are probably Agamemnon (far left), Chalcos, and Pelides. There are five preliminary sketches and a finished wash drawing of this design in the HEH (all but a slight verso sketch reproduced in Wark 1970, pp. 21–2, 26, 29), and one sketch in the RNE collection (reproduced in Essick and La Belle 1977, p. x). All of these works show differences from the engraving in the number and disposition of the figures; the wash drawing is probably an independent work and not part of the development of the design leading to the outline engraving. The preliminary sketches might be the 'six successive studies' noted in Colvin 1876, p. 46, then in the collection of George Wallis. The Royal Academy, London, has two drawings, one very close to the published design, and another with Minerva above Achilles and two seated figures on the left and two on the right. A drawing in the Chicago Art Institute is probably a copy after the plate. There are proofs of the plate before all letters in the Pierpont Morgan Library, New York, and the BMPR (1799 watermark).

3. Fifth design; 16.9 × 24.1 cm.; *Fig. 210*

Inscriptions above design: *Plate 5*. [left], THETIS ENTREATING JUPITER TO HONOR ACHILLES. [centre], *l. 511* [right]
Signature right: *Blake sculp.*
Quotation below design: THUS THETIS SPOKE BUT JOVE IN SILENCE HELD | THE SACRED

COUNCILS OF HIS BREAST CONCEAL'D. |
Pope's Homers Iliad B. I. Line 662.

Thetis kneels before Jupiter, seated on his throne in a
posture suggesting melancholy or contemplation. The
eagle is an emblem of his vigilance and supremacy.
The constellations in the background are (left to right)
Taurus, Leo, Gemini, Cancer, Serpens, Crater, and
Corvus (the last two from the southern hemisphere).
There are preliminary drawings in the HEH (two
figures and eagle only, reproduced in Wark 1970, p.
25) and the Royal Academy, London (as published,
but with minor variations in costumes). A pencil study,
now untraced, was sold at Sotheby's, 13 March 1969,
lot 87. A sketch at University College, London,
showing Jupiter enthroned with a kneeling figure on
the left holding a smoking torch, may be related (reproduced in Colvin 1876, pl. XIX fig. 7, and Gizzi 1986
(see **LI**, *Literature*), p. 135). Bentley 1977, p. 563, lists
a 'proof' of the plate in the BMPR, but I have not
been able to find it.

Literature: Sidney Colvin, *The Drawings of Flaxman in the
Gallery of University College London* (London: Bell and
Sons, 1876); John C. L. Sparkes, *Flaxman's Classical Out-
lines* (London: Seeley & Co., 1885), 8, 10–13; Russell 1912,
no. 100; Keynes 1921, no. 127; G. E. Bentley, jun., *The
Early Engravings of Flaxman's Classical Designs* (New
York: New York Public Library, 1964), 30–7; Bentley and
Nurmi 1964, no. 368; Robert R. Wark, *Drawings by John
Flaxman in the Huntington Collection* (San Marino: Hun-
tington Library, 1970), 19–31; Bentley 1977, no. 457;
Robert N. Essick and Jenijoy La Belle, *Flaxman's Illus-
trations to Homer* (New York: Dover, 1977); Bindman
1979, pp. 86–91, and Irwin 1979, pp. 67–85 (see
XXXVIII, *Literature*); Robert N. Essick, 'William
Blake's *The Death of Hector*', *Studies in Romanticism*, 27
(1988), 97–107.

XLVII

The Plays of William Shakspeare, ed. Alexander
Chalmers (10 and 9 vol. issues: London: F. C. and
J. Rivington, *et al.*, 1805; 9 vols.: London: J.
Nichols and Son, *et al.*, 1811); *Figs. 211–13*

Chalmers's Shakespeare contains thirty-eight
plates after designs by Fuseli, two of which are
signed by Blake as the engraver. Blake noted his
initial work on these engravings in a letter to
William Hayley of 26 October 1803, sent twenty-
two of the original parts issues of the work to
Hayley with his letter of 23 February 1804, indic-

ated that his fee was £25 for each plate in his
letter to Hayley of 22 June 1804, and commented
on the worn condition of pl. 2 in Hayley's copy
of the book on 28 December 1804 (E 738, 742,
752, 760; K 836, 848, 855). Indeed, the plates are
quite worn in the nine-volume issue of 1805, and
very worn in the 1811 edition. The proofs noted
for each plate below probably represent the state
in which the engravings left Blake's hands, just
before delivery to the writing engraver. Several
(LC and collection of Charles Ryskamp) are on
laid India paper and were probably printed for
sale to collectors. In some copies the plates are
bound at the beginning of each play, while in
others they face the passage illustrated (as
recorded below).

1. Vol. vii, facing p. 235 (1805 edn. in 10 vols.); and
vol. vi, facing p. 357 (1805 edn. in 9 vols. and 1811
edn.); 15.9 × 9.5 cm.; *Fig. 211*

Inscription above design: *Act IV.* [left], KING HENRY
VIII. [centre], *Sc. II.* [right]
Scratched signatures: *Fuseli. inv* [left], *Blake. sculp*
[right]
Title: Katharine, Griffiths & Patience. | Kath. *Spirits
of peace, where are ye? Are ye all gone?*
Imprint: *Publish'd May 12. 1804, by F & C. Rivington,
S.t Paul's Church Yard.*

The 'six Personages' of Queen Katherine's vision are
departing (top left). Her usher, Griffith (not 'Griffiths',
as in the plate), and her servant Patience sit before her.
Nothing in the text indicates that Griffith is asleep, as
he evidently is in the design. This detail contributes
indirectly to the reality of the Queen's vision, for it
explains why Griffith did not see the vision. His own
explanation is that it was only a dream. Perhaps Fuseli
even intended an allegorical interpretation of the scene:
visionary experiences require the sleep of the rational
and practical mind, not the sleep of the visionary
herself. Fuseli had illustrated this scene years before
with a more elaborate design, engraved for Thomas
Macklin's 'Poet's Gallery' in 1788 (Schiff 1973, no.
729). Fuseli's interest in this subject may have influenced Blake's four versions (Butlin 1981, nos. 247,
547.3, 448–9). The sleeping figure of Griffith in Blake's
design of 1807, repeated in a watercolour of *c.* 1825, is
clearly indebted to Fuseli's design for this edition of
Shakespeare (pointed out by Butlin 1981, p. 407).
Similar interpretive and allegorical strategies may also
pertain to Blake's two versions.

Blake prepared a pencil drawing of the design, 15.7 × 9.5 cm. and squared for transfer to the copperplate (*Fig. 212*), now in the Rosenwald Collection, National Gallery of Art, Washington (Butlin 1981, no. 561 recto). The profile in the right margin is unrelated. Proofs of the plate, with the scratched signatures but before all other letters, are in the BMPR, LC, collection of Charles Ryskamp, and a private collection, Melbourne, Australia.

2. Vol. x, facing p. 107 (1805 edn. in 10 vols.); and vol. ix, facing p. 107 (1805 edn. in 9 vols. and 1811 edn.); 17.1 × 9.2 cm.; *Fig. 213*

Inscription above design: *Act 1.* [left], ROMEO and JULIET. [centre], *Sc. 1.* [right]
Scratched signatures: *H. Fuseli. R.A. inv.* [left], *W. Blake. sc* [right]
Title: *Enter Apothecary.* | Romeo. *Come hither Man.—I see, that thou art poor;* | *Hold, there's forty ducats:—*
Imprint: *Publish'd by C & F Rivington London Jan 14. 1804.*

The design illustrates Act V, sc. i, not Act I as inscribed on the plate. Romeo calls the apothecary forward and offers him a bag of money for the sleeping potion. Fuseli has attended to Romeo's description of the apothecary's sunken face ('famine is in thy cheeks', x. 107) and his recollection of the man's 'overwhelming brows' and the 'alligator stuff'd, and other skins | Of ill-shap'd fishes' (x. 106) decorating the shop. For other comments on this design, see the Introduction. Fuseli's painting of this subject was recorded in 1843 in the collection of H. A. J. Munro, but is now untraced. Proofs of the plate, with the scratched signatures but before all other letters, are in the BMPR, HEH, LC, and the collection of Charles Ryskamp.

Literature: Gilchrist 1863, ii. 261; Russell 1912, no. 99; Keynes 1921, no. 128; Bentley and Nurmi 1964, no. 407; Schiff 1973, nos. 1285, 1295; Bentley 1977, no. 498; *The Poetical Circle: Fuseli and the British*, exhibition catalogue [by Peter Tomory] (Australia and New Zealand, 1979), no. 45 (proof of pl. 1).

outline with touches of stipple by Blake after the painting of 'Theory' personified in the Royal Academy, London, by Sir Joshua Reynolds (1723–92). Given Blake's harsh criticism in his annotations of *c.* 1808 to Reynolds's *Discourses*, he must have brought a certain detachment to this commission, particularly since Hoare (see **XLV**) praises Reynolds in this treatise.

1. Frontispiece; 8.8 × 8.5 cm.; *Fig. 214*

Title above design: *The Graphic Muse.*
Inscription on scroll: THEORY
Scratched signatures: *Sr Josh^a Reynolds pinx^t* [left], *Blake. sc.* [right]
Inscription below design: *... To explore* | *What lovelier forms in Natures boundless store* | *Are best to Art allied ...* | *Sketched from the* Picture by Sir Joshua Reynolds *on the ceiling of the Library of* | the Royal Academy.
Imprint: *Pub^d Feb,* 21, 1806, by R. Phillips, N,^{o} 6, Bridge Street, Blackfriars.

The plate does not illustrate a specific passage in the text, but rather serves as a general emblem for Hoare's aesthetic discussions. In an anonymous review of Hoare's book in *The Monthly Magazine*, 21 (25 July 1806), 607, the frontispiece is described as an 'elegant outline of the Graphic Muse'. In Reynolds's painting of 1779–80, 172.7 cm. square, the scroll reads 'Theory | is the | Knowledge | of what is truly | Nature' (reproduced in colour in Nicholas Penny, *Reynolds* (New York: Abrams, 1986), 143). In contrast, Blake wrote in his annotations to Reynolds's *Discourses* that the 'Principles' central to Blake's theories of art 'could never be found out by the Study of Nature without Con or Innate Science' (E 646, K 475).

Literature: Katharine A. McDowall, '*Theory, or the Graphic Muse* Engraved by Blake after Reynolds', *Burlington Magazine*, 11 (1907), 113–15; Russell 1912, no. 101; Keynes 1921, no. 129; Bentley and Nurmi 1964, no. 383; Bentley 1977, no. 474.

XLVIII

Prince Hoare, *An Inquiry into the Requisite Cultivation and Present State of the Arts of Design in England* (London: Richard Phillips, 1806); *Fig. 214*

The only plate is the frontispiece, engraved in

XLIX

William Hayley, *The Life of George Romney* (Chichester: T. Payne, 1809); *Figs. 215–16*

Shortly after his return from Felpham to London in the autumn of 1803, Blake began to help Hayley with his research for a biography of Romney.

Blake's letters from 13 December 1803 through to the end of the next year show that his major contribution to the project was locating Romney's works. As early as August 1803 Hayley was telling Flaxman of his plans to have Blake execute engravings for the projected work (Bentley 1969, p. 121). In a letter of 2 January 1805 to Hayley, Flaxman recommends that the biography should include several plates of Romney's more dramatic paintings, for they are 'well worth etching in a bold manner which I think Blake is likely to do with great success & perhaps at an expense that will not be burthensome—but at any rate give him one to do for a tryal' (Bentley 1969, p. 138). Blake's letter of 22 June 1804 to Hayley indicates that he was preparing a portrait plate of Romney, the progress of which can be traced through Blake's letters up to December 1804 (E 753, 758; K 846, 853). This engraved portrait, however, was not published in the book and no impression is known. Of the twelve plates in the volume, only one was engraved by Blake and seven by Caroline Watson. In a letter of 9 January 1810 Edward Garrard Marsh told Hayley that he 'never made a happier exchange than when [Hayley] employed [Watson] instead of Blake' as the engraver of the Romney plates (Bentley 1988, p. 60). This statement implies that Hayley originally intended that Blake should execute more of the plates. See the Introduction for further comments on this project and Watson's engravings.

1. Facing p. 84; 13.3 × 17.8 cm.; *Fig. 215*

Title: *Sketch of a Shipwreck after Romney.*
Signature below title: *Engraved by Blake*
Imprint: *Published April 14.th 1809 by Thomas Payne, Pall Mall.*

The plate is based on Romney's oil sketch of *c.* 1794–5, now untraced. As Hayley notes, p. 84, the scene depicts 'the horseman at the Cape of Good Hope', named Woltemad, who sacrificed himself to rescue the victims of a shipwreck in June 1772. The story is told in Karl Peter Thunberg, *Travels in Europe, Africa, and Asia* (London, 1793–5). There are two preliminary pencil sketches by Romney in the Yale Center for British Art, New Haven, Connecticut (one reproduced in Chan 1982, fig. 130). In his letter to Hayley of 22 June 1804 Blake recommends that a different engraver

be commissioned to execute each plate for the biography, and, in his list of subjects, includes 'The Shipwreck with the Man on Horseback &c which I have' (E 753, K 848). Evidently the lender of this work was the picture dealer William Saunders, who in a letter to Hayley of 16 June 1804 notes that he had 'sent' Blake 'three pictures' by Romney (Bentley 1969, p. 153). With his letter of 16 July, Blake sent Hayley 'a Sketch of the Heroic Horseman as you wishd me to do—the size the Print is to be' (E 753, K 933). This may be the pen-and-ink-drawing, 13.5 × 17.9 cm., now in the BMPR (*Fig. 216*; Butlin 1981, no. 350). The sheet has been squared, probably to facilitate the reduction of Romney's oil sketch to the size of this drawing and the plate. Since the drawing and the print have right and left in the same direction, an intervening tracing was probably counter-proofed or calked from the reverse on to the copperplate.

Blake sent Hayley unfinished proofs of the plate, each very probably in a different state, on 28 September, 23 October, and 18 December 1804 (E 755–6, 758; K 850–1, 853). In his letter of 28 December Blake indicates that his price for the engraving will be 30 Guineas (E 760, K 855). Bentley 1969, p. 152, suggests that Blake's 'suddenly startling prices' prompted Hayley to find other engravers to execute plates for the biography and enlisted Flaxman's help in the search. However, Flaxman had told Hayley on 8 June 1804 that Caroline Watson would charge '35 Guineas' per plate (Bentley 1969, p. 153), and she was in fact commissioned to prepare nine plates. Blake did not finish his single engraving until late in 1805 or early 1806, for on 11 December 1805 he told Hayley that 'a very few touches will finish the Shipwreck' (E 767, K 863). Not surprisingly, given the length of time Blake spent on the plate, it has seemed to some as over-laboured (see Russell 1912, p. 179).

In a letter of 4 May 1804 Blake thanks Hayley for sending him a copy of the 1804 edition of William Falconer's poem, *The Shipwreck*, with illustrations engraved by James Fittler after Nicholas Pocock. Blake then claims that these prints have given him 'some excellent hints in engraving; his [Fittler's] manner of working is what I shall endeavour to adopt in many points' (E 748, K 843). Although this may simply be an instance of the empty gratitude Blake addressed to Hayley, there are a few techniques in the plate after Romney, such as the execution of the waves and the general density of linear patterns, that parallel Fittler's methods. Blake's plate, however, is a good deal bolder and more rugged than Fittler's high-finish vignettes.

Whatever influence Fittler may have had on Blake's graphic style is neither dramatic nor salutary.

Literature: Gilchrist 1863, i. 178, ii. 261; Russell 1912, nos. 98 (the unused portrait plate), 102; Keynes 1921, no. 130; Bentley and Nurmi 1964, no. 378; Bentley 1977, no. 469; Jean H. Hagstrum, 'Romney and Blake: Gifts of Grace and Terror', in Robert N. Essick and Donald Pearce (eds.), *Blake in his Time* (Bloomington: Indiana Univ. Press, 1978), 201–12, substantially repeated in Hagstrum, 'Blake and British Art: The Gifts of Grace and Terror', in Karl Kroeber and William Walling (eds.), *Images of Romanticism* (New Haven: Yale Univ. Press, 1978), 61–80; Essick 1980, p. 173; Victor Chan, *Leader of my Angels: William Hayley and his Circle* (exhibition catalogue; Edmonton Art Gallery, 1982), 61.

L

Wedgwood's Catalogue of Earthenware and Porcelain (no title-page printed) (*c*. 1816–40); *Figs. 217–34*

On 29 July 1815 Josiah Wedgwood the younger wrote to Blake, returning a drawing of a 'terrine' which Blake had sent him (Bentley 1969, pp. 239–40). This letter indicates that Blake had begun to make drawings of Wedgwood creamware (also called 'Queen's ware'). On 8 September Blake sent two more drawings for approval (E 770, K 866), and the Wedgwood account books show that a good many pieces of creamware were sent to Blake in the next month and that he submitted a 'packet of Drawings' on 13 December (Bentley 1969, pp. 240–1). This copy work was not an end in itself, but a necessary stage in the production of eighteen plates, for which the Wedgwood Company paid Blake £30 on 11 November 1816 (Bentley 1969, p. 578). Although the plates are signed *Blake d & sc*, it is clear that Blake only delineated drawings as the basis for his engravings and did not design the crockery itself. Thus, the prints are properly grouped with Blake's reproductive graphics.

According to a note by Frederick Tatham on a sheet formerly kept with the proofs of pls. 6 and 7 and last recorded in the collection of W. Graham Robertson, 'Mr. Flaxman introduced Blake to Mr. Wedgwood' and 'the designs of the Pottery were made by Flaxman' (quoted from Christie's auction catalogue, 22 July 1949, lot 90; see also a proof of pl. 6, below). This introduction may have taken place as early as 1784–5, for a Wedgwood Company ledger of those years (Wedgwood Museum MS n/n, p. 123) records the payment of £3. 17*s*. to Flaxman's account for 'Blake for painting on Ceiling pictures' for Etruria Hall, the Wedgwood family estate. However, no such paintings have been traced, in spite of recent searches by curators at the Wedgwood Museum, Barleston. The claim that Flaxman designed these bowls, dishes, and other household items (repeated confidently by Hughes n.d., pp. 112–13) is unsubstantiated. Hughes 1959 argues that Mrs Blake executed the copperplates, but there is no basis for such a theory.

Blake's plates were never published and sold in a conventional manner, but were apparently used by Wedgwood and his salesmen as a pattern book without any letterpress text. As the creamware styles changed, the plates were modified over the years by unknown engravers. These changes were almost certainly not executed by Blake. The complete set of Blake's plates in the BMPR (reproduced here, with some inscriptions partly cropped) would seem to be of the first states completed by Blake with item numbers and other inscriptions. I have taken these impressions to be the equivalent of first published states in the individual catalogue entries, below. The two complete copies of the pattern book, with thirteen additional plates not by Blake, in the Keynes Collection, Cambridge University Library, and the Wedgwood Museum are mostly in states (described for each plate below) later than the BMPR set. Pls. 3–8, 10–18 in the same states as the Wedgwood Museum group are reproduced in Mankowitz 1953, nos. 15–29. Mankowitz does not identify the source of his reproductions, which do not include the pencil annotations on the Wedgwood Museum impressions. These notes relate to later changes in the creamware styles, not directly to the reworking of the copperplates.

A mixed set of eighteen impressions from twelve plates is in the Wedgwood Archive, Keele University. This group includes seven impressions of late states printed in brown ink on thin India paper (most with the top inscriptions and signatures trimmed off) and eleven early proofs before letters. Three of the proofs bear fragments of an 1816 watermark. This group may be the 'set of twelve [*sic?*] very early proofs' with 'many [actually only a few, as noted below] pencil notes and marks for correction' recorded in Keynes 1971, p. 64. Keynes 1971 also notes, p. 65, that 'eight of Blake's copper-plates have actually survived to the present day', but I have not been able to locate them. Hughes 1959, p. 196, states that the annotations on the Company (now Keele?) proofs are 'probably in the hand of Josiah Wedgwood II' and that the surviving copperplates 'all possess alterations made during a catalogue re-issue of 1838 to 1840'. Keynes 1971, p. 65, also notes printings of '1838 and 1840' with 'many alterations'. Bentley 1977, p. 631, states that 'Blake's plates were gradually replaced in successive catalogues, until the last one disappeared in the issue of *c.* 1843'.

Reilly 1989, ii. 408, locates 'three copies' of the catalogue 'in the Wedgwood archive' (at Keele?), but I have not been able to find these. He reproduces, much reduced, an unidentified copy (but presumably one of the three he mentions) in his vol. ii, pls. 626–60, that includes Blake's pls. 1, 3–17. These correspond in state to the Wedgwood Museum set described here (but see pl. 11 for one distinguishing feature).

The gradual disappearance of Blake's signature from many of the plates may be due in part to wear. In several instances, however, it is clear that purposeful scraping and burnishing removed all or part of the signatures. Thus, in the individual entries below I have recorded some differences in states on the basis of changes in the signatures.

1. 19.9 × 15.5 cm.; *Fig. 217*

Top inscriptions: WEDGWOOD [left], *P 1* [right]
Signature right: *Blake d & sc*
Item numbers: see *Fig. 217*.

Second State (Keynes Collection and Wedgwood Museum). The candlesticks have been removed, except for the one upper left, and a jug and two buttertubs have been added on the right and bottom. The signature has been removed.

2. 17.9 × 9.9 cm.; *Fig. 218*

Top inscriptions: WEDGWOOD [left], *P 2.* [right]
Signature right: *Blake. d & sc*

Item numbers: see *Fig. 218*.

A proof at Keele University lacks all letters but has item numbers added in pencil. Several details, such as the decorative finials, have been sketched only with a stipple burin. Some shading strokes are lacking. The unsigned plate in the Keynes Collection and the Wedgwood Museum, attributed to Blake and reproduced in the same state in Mankowitz 1953, no. 14, and Reilly 1989, ii, pl. 627, is a complete re-engraving with additional items. If the same copperplate was used, virtually all of Blake's work was removed from it.

3. 20.8 × 9.1 cm.; *Fig. 219*

Top inscriptions: WEDGWOOD [left], *P 3* [right]
Signature: as on pl. 1.
Item numbers: see *Fig. 219*.

Second State (Keynes Collection). Two mugs, a sauce boat, a pepper shaker, and two numbers in ovals have been added in the margins.

Third State (Wedgwood Museum). Only a ghost of the signature remains.

4. 21.4 × 16 cm.; *Fig. 220*

Top inscriptions: WEDGWOOD [left], *P 4* [right]
Signature: as on pl. 1.
Item numbers: see *Fig. 220*.

Second State (Wedgwood Museum). Signature removed.

Third State (Keele University). The single tureen at the top has been replaced by two new models (inscribed 'TAMWORTH' and 'YORK') and the bottom tureen (now labelled '*Round Etruscan*') has been shaded with fine horizontal hatching.

There are two proofs before letters in different states at Keele University. The earliest, inscribed 'corrected' in pencil, lacks many strokes, including finishing lines on decorative details and hatching lines of shading. A little more shading has been added to the centre-right tureen in the later proof, which also bears item numbers in pencil. The impression in the Keynes Collection is in the first state.

5. 22 × 16.2 cm.; *Fig. 221*

Top inscriptions: WEDGWOOD [left], *P 5* [right]
Signature: as on pl. 1 (the ampersand worn or partly burnished off in the BMPR impression).
Item numbers: see *Fig. 221*.

Second State (Wedgwood Museum). All but fragments of the signature have been removed, new tureens have replaced those numbered *1* and *113*, and three new numbers (*89, 90, 92*) have been added upper left, replacing *89*.

The impression in the Keynes Collection is in the first

state, with *90, 91* (lined through), and *92* added in pencil.

6. 21.6 × 16.2 cm.; *Fig. 222*

Top inscriptions: WEDGWOOD [left], *P 6* [right]
Signature: as on pl. 1.
Item numbers: see *Fig. 222*.

Second State (Keynes Collection). The attached saucer on the pitcher lower left has been replaced by one with an upturned rim. Below the saucer is a pencil inscription: 'is this stand right? in Bk Drawings it is dish stand'. Reproduced in Keynes 1971, pl. 21.

Third State (Wedgwood Museum). All but the first two letters of the signature have been removed.

A proof at Keele University lacks all letters, finishing lines on decorative details, and most lines of shading. A later proof state in the collection of Mrs Robert D. Chellis (reproduced in Ruthven Todd, *William Blake the Artist* (London: Studio Vista, 1971), p. 103 (wrongly attributed to the Keynes collection), and Butlin 1981, pl. 895) lacks only the WEDGWOOD inscription and a few lines of shading on the left side of the saucer lower left. This proof bears an inscription by Frederick Tatham: 'Flaxman Introduced Blake to Wedgwood. W. Blake for Wedgwood Pottery'.

7. 20.7 × 15.9 cm.; *Fig. 223*

Top inscriptions: WEDGWOOD [left], *P 7* [right]
Signature: as on pl. 1.
Item numbers: see *Fig. 223*.

Second State (Keynes Collection). The covered bowl top right has been replaced by a very different model, numbered *898*. The small ovals added in the third state are drawn in pencil.

Third State (Wedgwood Museum). Small ovals have been added above *154* (very faint) and right of *152*, and only fragments of the signature remain.

Fourth State (Keele University). The items top left and bottom right have been replaced by an '*Oval Potting Pot*' (so inscribed) and a tray.

A proof in the collection of Mrs Robert D. Chellis lacks the WEDGWOOD inscription. Hughes n.d., pl. 26, reproduces a photograph of two of the items represented on this plate, the tureen and stand, no. *146*, and the covered dish, no. *347*.

8. 20.5 × 15.5 cm.; *Fig. 224*

Top inscriptions: WEDGWOOD [left], *P. 8* [right]
Signature: as on pl. 1.
Item numbers: see *Fig. 224*.

Second State (Keynes Collection). The small egg-shaped vessels top left and right have been replaced by different models.

Third State (Wedgwood Museum). New numbers and two quadrangles have been added above item no. *198*. Only a ghost of the signature remains.

Fourth State (Keele University). Descriptive labels and many fine shading lines have been added to all bowls. The egg cup lower left has been replaced by a goblet.

A proof at Keele University lacks all three egg cups at the bottom, all letters, and some shading lines on the bowls. A later proof in the BMPR lacks only the WEDGWOOD inscription and some shading on the large bowl at the bottom (signature very faint).

9. 21.2 × 14.8 cm.; *Fig. 225*

Top inscriptions: WEDGWOOD [left], *P. 9* [right]
Signature: as on pl. 1.
Item numbers: see *Fig. 225*.

The impressions in the Keynes Collection and the Wedgwood Museum are in the same state as the BMPR print reproduced here. A proof in the BMPR, lacking all inscriptions except item numbers, has '*P 9*' added in ink top right. Item *260* is inscribed *610* corrected in ink to *260*. Items *266, 304–5,* and *309–10* lack some shading lines.

10. 20.7 × 15.4 cm.; *Fig. 226*

Top inscriptions: WEDGWOOD [left], *P 10* [right]
Signature: as on pl. 1.
Item numbers: see *Fig. 226*.

Second State (Wedgwood Museum and Keele University). Signature removed.

A proof in the HEH lacks the 'WEDGWOOD' inscription and some of the shading on the sides of the pepper shaker top left and the bottle bottom left. In the Keynes impression (first state) the bottle lower left has been crossed out in ink and 'put in 799 instead' written in ink to the left.

11. 21.1 × 15.5 cm.; *Fig. 227*

Top inscriptions: WEDGWOOD [centre], *P 11* [right]
Signature: as on pl. 1.
Item numbers: see *Fig. 227*.

Second State (Keynes Collection). The dishes at the top have been replaced by bowls. Ovals have been added in pencil where they appear in the third state.

Third State (Wedgwood Museum). Small ovals have been added right of *341* and *335*, and only the first three letters of Blake's name remain in the signature. In the Mankowitz 1953 and Reilly 1989 reproductions, the full name (but not *d & sc*) remains, and thus these impressions may represent a state intermediate between the second and third.

Fourth State (Keele University). The tureens at the bottom have been replaced by a buttertub and a bowl on stand.

Fine horizontal shading lines have been added to items *335* (centre) and *331*.

A proof at Keele University lacks all letters.

12. 21.3 × 15.6 cm.; *Fig. 228*

Top inscriptions: WEDGWOOD [left], *P 12* [right]
Signature: as on pl. 1.
Item numbers: see *Fig. 228*.

Second State (Keynes Collection and Wedgwood Museum). The deep dish lower right has been replaced by a cylindrical object, '*Oval, 916*' and '*Round, 917*' have been inscribed above the deep dish lower left, and only small fragments of the signature remain.

Third State (Keele University). Shading lines have been added to most items and names inscribed next to five of them.

A proof at Keele University lacks all letters and a few shading lines, particularly on the bowls and under-dishes centre and top. A later proof state (HEH) lacks only the 'WEDGWOOD' inscription and a few lines of shading on the under-dish, top centre.

13. 21.5 × 16 cm.; *Fig. 229*

Top inscriptions: WEDGWOOD [left], *P. 13.* [right]
Signature: as on pl. 1.
Item numbers: see *Fig. 229*.

Second State (Keynes Collection). The bowls, centre top and bottom, have been replaced by two bowls with under-dishes (bottom) and a bowl on stand with under-dish (top). Two numbers in circles, *851* and *852*, replace *851*. The signature has been removed. The numbers and circles added in the third state have been written in pencil.

Third State (Wedgwood Museum). Two numbers in circles, *854* and *855*, replace *854*.

A proof at Keele University lacks all letters and most lines of shading. The basket-bowl upper left is sketched only in stipple outline.

14. 21.4 × 15.5 cm.; *Fig. 230*

Top inscriptions: WEDGWOOD [left], *P 14* [right]
Signature: as on pl. 1.
Item numbers: see *Fig. 230*.

Second State (Wedgwood Museum). The pitcher, top centre, has been replaced by a shorter model, the shading on all four bowls has been strengthened, and '*P 14*' has been recut in thicker lines. Only the first two letters of the signature are clearly visible.

A proof at Keele University lacks all letters and a few lines of shading. Six item numbers and several notes on incorrect proportions (e.g. 'much too tall') have been added in pencil. A later proof state (BMPR) has item numbers but lacks all other inscriptions ('*P 14*'

added in ink). The Keynes impression is in the first state.

15. 21.5 × 16.2 cm.; *Fig. 231*

Top inscriptions: WEDGWOOD [left], *P 15* [right]
Signature: as on pl. 1.
Item numbers: see *Fig. 231*.

Second State (Wedgwood Museum). All but fragments of the signature have been removed. The Keynes impression is in the first state.

16. 20.5 × 14.8 cm.; *Fig. 232*

Top inscriptions: WEDGWOOD [left], *P 16* [right]
Signature: as on pl. 1.
Item numbers: see *Fig. 232*.

Second State (Keynes Collection and Wedgwood Museum). Items *1469*, *1481*, *1486*, and *1561* have been replaced by very different vessels. The cream pitcher lower left has been shaded with vertical hatching lines; only a fragment of the signature remains.

A proof at Keele University lacks all letters and many shading lines. The cream pitchers lower left and right are sketched only in outline. A later proof state (BMPR) lacks only the 'WEDGWOOD' inscription, but the signature is scratched only in very light lines.

17. 21.5 × 16 cm.; *Fig. 233*

Top inscriptions: WEDGWOOD [left], *P 17* [right]
Signature: as on pl. 1.
Item numbers: see *Fig. 233*.

Second State (Keynes Collection and Wedgwood Museum). Items *1533* and *1535* have been replaced with different covered bowls, numbered *897* and *270*. Wedgwood Museum impression reproduced in Boime 1987 (see **XXI**, *Literature*), p. 336.

Third State (Keele University). The coffee pot, no. *1429*, has been replaced by a different model; a '*French Sugar*' (so inscribed) replaces pot no. *1433*. Items *897* and *1516* have been shaded with fine horizontal hatching.

A proof at Keele University lacks all letters and most shading lines. Many items are sketched only in outline.

18. 21.1 × 15.3 cm.; *Fig. 234*

Top inscriptions: WEDGWOOD [left], *P. 18* [right]
Signature: as on pl. 1, with '*d & sc*' very faint in the BMPR impression.
Item numbers: see *Fig. 234*.

Second State (Keynes Collection). The jars lower left and right have been replaced with very different pots with new numbers. The new number above the item lower right, '*1185*', has been lined through in pencil and '*1188*' inscribed in pencil to the right of the item.

Third State (Wedgwood Museum). Items *1606*, *1609*, *1611*, and *1636* have been replaced with different models with new numbers. The number of the item lower right has been changed to '*1188*'. Only small fragments of the signature remain.

Literature: Gilchrist 1863, i. 33–4; Russell 1912, no. 106; Keynes 1921, no. 76; Wolf Mankowitz, *Wedgwood* (London: Batsford, 1953); G. Bernard Hughes, 'Blake's Work for Wedgwood', *Country Life*, 126 (3 Sept. 1959), 194–6; Hughes, *English and Scottish Earthenware, 1660–1860* (London: Abbey Fine Arts, n.d. [after 1959]), 112–14; Bentley and Nurmi 1964, no. 418; Keynes 1971, pp. 59–65; Bentley 1977, no. 511; Butlin 1981, no. 677 (the untraced drawings); Robin Reilly, *Wedgwood* (2 vols.; London: Macmillan, 1989).

LI

John Flaxman, *Compositions from the Works Days and Theogony of Hesiod* (London: Longman, Hurst, Rees, Orme & Brown, 1817). *The Classical Compositions of John Flaxman* (London: Bell and Daldy, 1870). *Compositions from the Works and Days, and Theogony of Hesiod* (London: Bell and Daldy, 1870). *Figs. 235–71*

Flaxman was contemplating a series of designs based on Hesiod, and perhaps even began sketching them (see pl. 3), in Rome in the early 1790s. A sheet of drawings by Flaxman in the collection of Christopher Powney, signed and dated July 1792, bears on its verso a list of subjects from both Homer and Hesiod, the former apparently for the series of designs first published in 1793. In 1805 Flaxman exhibited a relief plaque at the Royal Academy (no. 765, 'Mercury descending with Pandora') based on the same design as pl. 6 (three plaster versions reproduced in Panofsky and Panofsky 1965, p. 92; Margaret Whinney and Rupert Gunnis, *The Collection of Models by John Flaxman R.A. at University College London* (London: Athlone Press, 1967), pl. 5a; and Bindman 1979, no. 122). Flaxman was working on the designs in February 1807 and completed them in September 1814 (Wark 1970, p. 38), but it was not until 2 February 1816 that he entered into a contract with Longman & Co. to 'furnish a series of Drawings to illustrate Hesiod' for publication (Bentley 1977, p. 556). Blake had already been commissioned to execute all thirty-seven designs, no doubt on Flaxman's recommendation. Longman's records

(repr. Bentley 1977, pp. 557–8) show that the first plate was completed in September 1814 and the project was completed in January 1817. Blake used an unusual graphic style, for which the term 'stippled outline' seems appropriate, found nowhere else among the engravings of Flaxman's compositions. This technique creates a much softer visual effect than continuous linear outline (used for pl. 4) and may have been developed by Blake to reproduce the qualities of pencil (as distinct from ink) lines. See the Introduction for further comments on stippled outline.

Blake was paid 5 Guineas for each plate, a total of £194. 5s., plus £13. 13s. for the cost of the copperplates. The engraved cover label (used as a half-title in later issues) was cut by the writing engraver ('Jeffreys' in Longman's accounts) who executed the lettering on all the plates, probably with the exception of the stippled words within the designs on pls. 2, 9, and 21. The firm of Cox & Barnett made the first printing of 200 sets, for which they were apparently paid by February 1817 (Bentley 1977, p. 558). A copy in boards with the cover label, an 1812 watermark on pl. 35, and an 1814 watermark on a flyleaf, now in the collection of Detlef Dörrbecker, is probably from this first printing. Inserted in this copy is an announcement of the book's publication, dated February 1817, identifying the engraver as 'J. Blake'. Slightly later notices (see Bentley 1977, p. 560) repeat this error.

The copperplates were sold by Longman in 1838 to H. G. Bohn, who evidently reprinted them (Bentley 1977, p. 560). Impressions on thick, card-like paper and a rather soft, machine-made stock may be Bohn restrikes. Bell and Daldy must have acquired the copperplates for the new impressions published in the 1870 *Classical Compositions* and *Compositions from . . . Hesiod* (the latter simply a separate issue of the former). According to Ruthven Todd, 'Blake's Dante Plates', *Times Literary Supplement* (29 Aug. 1968), 928, Bell and Daldy sold the plates as scrap metal in 1917.

The lines on the plates from Hesiod's poems are quoted or paraphrased (see pl. 4) from the much-revised second (1815) edition of *The Remains of Hesiod* translated by Charles Abraham

Elton. His habit of using the Roman names of deities is followed in the notes below. The line numbers on the plates top right refer to the Greek text. The 1870 impressions are from a second state (not individually recorded below) of all plates with the imprints removed.

Flaxman's compositional method was to sketch alternative designs for each subject until he decided on an appropriate arrangement of motifs. He then must have prepared a complete set of outline drawings for the engraver. Consequently, there are a good many preliminary drawings of the Hesiod designs, but many of those nearly identical to the engravings were made after the plates by anonymous copyists. Colvin 1876, p. 46, lists drawings for the 'opening of Hesiod', never engraved, in the collection of Theodore Martin, and 'two or three Hesiod studies' in the collection of Colonel Gould Weston. The latter group may be among those listed for individual plates below.

The stippled lines of Blake's plates suggest that the final preliminary drawings from which he worked were executed by Flaxman in pencil; these may have been destroyed during transfer to the copperplates. Since the extant preliminary sketches have right and left as in the prints, the images must have been the reverse on the copperplates. This suggests that the final preliminaries were counter-proofed or calked from the reverse on to the plates. A complete, bound set of pencil, pen, and ink drawings, a few with 1809 and 1815 watermarks, is in the collection of H. D. Lyon, London (drawing of pl. 22 reproduced in the *Age of Neo-Classicism* catalogue (1972), pl. 93). These finished outlines may not have played a role in the production of the plates; they could have been prepared by Flaxman as a separate and autonomous work. It may be the set of 'the drawings from Hesiod, by Mr. Flaxman, thirty-seven in number, handsomely bound in morocco', sold at the Flaxman sale, Christie's, 1 July 1828, lot 84. The twenty-four crude wash drawings in the Metropolitan Museum of Art, New York, are no doubt copies after the plates. The 1828 auction also included, lot 38, 'a proof copy of Hesiod, 37 plates, in sheets, by J. Flaxman, the quotations by Mr. Flaxman' (now untraced). In a letter of 14 March

1827 (E 783, K 877) to Maria Denman, Flaxman's sister-in-law who retained a financial interest in the Hesiod plates, Blake offered her '15 Proofs of Hesiod' and explained that others in his possession were printed 'on both sides of the paper' or were on 'impressions from other Plates' (see pls. 13, 25, and 26 for examples). Bentley 1977, pp. 557–8, lists a complete set of proofs, many before letters and on paper with watermarks from 1811 to 1816, in the Bodleian Library. This is the same group mentioned by Keynes 1921, p. 256, then in the collection of W. E. Moss and bearing dates of receipt written from October 1814 to December 1816 by Thomas Reader, then an employee of Longman. Although Bentley tells me that he personally inspected these proofs, several searches at the Bodleian in recent years have not been able to locate them. Other drawings and proofs are listed for each plate below. It would not be surprising if further variant preliminary sketches turn up.

Four Hesiod drawings by Flaxman have washes added, principally in the backgrounds. These are unpublished designs of *Gaea and the Youthful Zeus* (BMPR; reproduced Bindman 1979, p. 129), *Rhea Consulting her Parents Uranus and Terra* (RNE; reproduced in Powney and Heim 1976, pl. 21), a variant of pl. 32 (RNE; reproduced in Bindman 1979, p. 129), and a variant of pl. 33 (German private collection; reproduced in Powney and Heim 1976, pl. 23). Since the published designs represent pure outline without tonal washes, it is unlikely that these four drawings played any role in the production of the plates. Bindman 1979, p. 129, suggests that Flaxman prepared them in contemplation of publication in some medium other than outline engraving, such as aquatint, capable of reproducing tones.

The Hesiod designs were re-engraved by Tommaso Piroli (Rome, n.d. [*c.* 1818?], reissued 1845), 'Mme Soyer' (Paris, 1821, reissued *c.* 1835), and, on a reduced scale, by Étienne Reveil (Paris, 1836, 1844). These editions were probably copied from Blake's plates rather than from Flaxman's drawings, but all are in continuous outline, not stippled lines.

1. Title-page; 15.2 × 23.9 cm.; *Fig. 235*

Inscriptions above design: PLATE I. [left], ΕΡΓΑ *656.* [right]

Title: COMPOSITIONS FROM THE|WORKS DAYS AND THEOGONY OF HESIOD.| [design]|DESIGNED BY JOHN FLAXMAN, R.A. P.S.|ENGRAVED BY WILLIAM BLAKE.

Quotation: THERE, LET ME BOAST THAT VICTOR IN THE LAY|I BORE A TRIPOD EAR'D, MY PRIZE AWAY|Works—Elton's Hesiod.

Imprint: *Published by Longman, Hurst, Rees, Orme & Brown, London, Jan. 1, 1817.*

Hesiod (left) contests successfully with blind Homer (right) for the prize from the Muse as the greatest singer of tales. Hesiod makes no mention of his adversary's name, but Flaxman has followed the commentary of Proclus (not cited in Elton's notes) that Homer was the defeated poet.

2. 17.2 × 24.1 cm.; *Fig. 236*

Inscriptions above design: 2 [left], E. *274.* [right]

Title: HESIOD ADMONISHING PERSES.| [design]|HESIODS|WORKS AND DAYS.

Quotation: DEEP LET MY WORDS OH PERSES! GRAVEN BE|HEAR JUSTICE, AND RENOUNCE THE OPPRESSOR'S PLEA| Elton's Hesiod—Works.

Imprint: as on pl. 1.

Hesiod (left) offers advice to his younger brother Perses (right). The scales are emblems of the justice recommended by Hesiod, while the shepherd's staff and spade represent his command of husbandry and agriculture. 'Graven' establishes a fortuitous reference to the engraved designs. There are two ink preliminary drawings on one sheet in the BMPR. The upper one has an oak branch between the men and 'Hesiod's Works and Days' on a tablet above; the lower sketch has the wreath and scales of the plate, but lacks the shovel and the tendrils above and on the men's seats.

3. 17.1 × 18.7 cm.; *Fig. 237*

Inscriptions above design: 3 [left], PANDORA GIFTED. [centre], E. *67.* [right]

Quotation: BADE HERMES LAST ENDUE WITH CRAFT REFINED.|l. 97 Works and Days.— Elton's Hesiod.

Imprint: *Published by Longman, Hurst, Rees, Orme & Brown, London, November 1, 1816.*

Hermes (right) gives Pandora the 'craft' of 'treacherous manners, and a shameless mind', while Minerva gives her 'the skill that sheds|A thousand colours in the gliding threads'. The goddess seems to be placing a garland on Pandora's head, but in the text this is done by 'the lovely-tressed Hours'. In a drawing for an alternative version, Pandora and two goddesses stand on the left, with Minerva on the right pointing to the fateful urn (see pls. 7 and 8). A finished wash drawing of this design is inscribed on the verso, 'given me by Mr [Guy?] Head done by Mr Flaxman December 25th 1795 Rome'. Both drawings, formerly in the collection of Christopher Powney, are reproduced in Powney and Heim 1976, pls. 18–19.

4. 17.2 × 24.4 cm.; *Fig. 238*

Inscriptions above design: 4 [left], PANDORA ATTIRED. [centre], E. *73.* [right]

Quotation: ADORED PERSUASION AND THE GRACES YOUNG|HER SLENDER LIMBS WITH GOLDEN JEWELS HUNG.|l. 103, Works and Days.—Elton's Hesiod.

Imprint: as on pl. 3.

Persuasion (far right), the three Graces, and the 'lovely-tressed Hours' (left) adorn Pandora. The second line of verse quoted on the plate has been modified from Elton's 'With chains of gold her shapely person hung' in a way that brings it closer to his first edition (1809): 'Her taper'd limbs with golden jewels hung.' A variant preliminary pen-and-pencil drawing in the BMPR shows Pandora half-clothed, a goddess on the right placing a veil over Pandora's head, and the Graces on the left. A sketch at University College, London, is much closer to the published design, with only minor differences in postures and an additional seated figure on the far right drawn over or under the standing figure (reproduced in Colvin 1876, pl. XIX, fig. 2).

5. 18.8 × 24.3 cm.; *Fig. 239*

Inscriptions above design: 5 [left], PANDORA SHEWN TO THE GODS. [centre], θ. *588.* [right]

Quotation: ON MEN AND GODS IN THAT SAME MOMENT SEIZED|THE RAVISHMENT OF WONDER WHEN THEY SAW.|l. 783, Theogony.—Elton's Hesiod.

Imprint: as on pl. 3.

Vulcan brings Pandora (both right) to the Olympian gods and goddesses. They are not named in the text, but Flaxman pictures Neptune (bottom centre), Aurora in her chariot, and seated above, left to right, Mercury with his caduceus, Jupiter, Juno, and two more goddesses. Flaxman has interpolated this scene from the *Theogony* among these illustrations to the *Works and*

Days, perhaps in order to retain the artisanal presence of Vulcan, who has no role in the *Works and Days* after he has shaped Pandora, and for narrative continuity. An ink-and-pencil preliminary drawing of the engraved version is in the BMPR (reproduced Irwin 1979, p. 92). Two very different sketches at University College, London, may picture the same event (reproduced in Colvin 1876, pl. XIX, figs. 3 and 5, and Gizzi 1986, pp. 133–4). In one, Vulcan, kneeling, presents Pandora to Jupiter and Mercury. In the other, Pandora stands meekly between two men (Vulcan and Jupiter?) holding staves.

6. 13.2 × 16.6 cm.; *Fig. 240*

Inscriptions above design: *6* [left], PANDORA BROUGHT TO EARTH. [centre], E. *85*. [right]

Quotation: HE BADE HEAVEN'S MESSENGER CONVEY THRO' AIR | TO EPEMETHEUS' HANDS | Elton's Hesiod—Works.

Imprint: as on pl. 3.

At Jupiter's command, Mercury carries Pandora to her future husband, Epimetheus, Prometheus's brother. The preliminary sketch in the Fitzwilliam Museum, Cambridge, lacks the wings on Mercury's hat and Pandora's coronet, and has many differences in the trailing drapery (Mercury's hips uncovered). This drawing may be related to the plaque, noted above. An ink sketch of the same subject in the BMPR shows the figures head-on.

7. 17 × 24.3 cm.; *Fig. 241*

inscriptions above design: *7* [left], PANDORA BROUGHT TO EPIMETHEUS. [centre], E. *84*. [right]

Quotation: BUT HE RECEIVED | Elton's Hesiod—Works.

Imprint: as on pl. 3.

Epimetheus, forgetting his brother's warning, accepts the beautiful Pandora from Mercury. The fatal 'casket' is pictured as a large covered jar, in accord with the Greek text in which the container is a *pithos*. In a preliminary sketch at University College, London, Epimetheus leans forward to receive Pandora (reproduced in Colvin 1876, pl. XIX, fig. 4). The design is reversed in a rather awkward pencil sketch in a private German collection (reproduced in David Irwin, *English Neoclassical Art* (London: Faber and Faber, 1966), pl. 73). Mercury wears his *petasus* and Epimetheus is pictured in profile but with his body turned towards us.

8. 14.1 × 21.5 cm.; *Fig. 242*

Inscriptions above design: *8* [left], PANDORA, OPENING THE VASE. [centre], E. *94*. [right]

Quotation: SHE LIFTS THE LID.—SHE SCATTERS ILLS IN AIR. | l. 132, Works and Days— Elton's Hesiod.

Imprint: as on pl. 3.

Epimetheus retreats in horror as personified 'woes innumerous' escape and begin to surround him. Hope remains seated within the (now transparent?) jar. A pencil drawing of the design, the size of the plate and perhaps copied after it, is in the Fogg Art Museum, Cambridge, Massachusetts.

9. 8.8 × 14 cm.; *Fig. 243*

Inscriptions above design: *9* [left], GOLDEN AGE. [centre], E. *112*. [right]

Quotation: AN AGE OF GOLD | LIKE GODS THEY LIVED WITH CALM UNTROUBLED MIND. | l. 151. Works and Days.—Elton's Hesiod.

Imprint: as on pl. 3.

Flaxman uses two women and a baby, not described by Hesiod, to represent the Golden Age. The 'grain-exuberant soil' of that time is indicated by the shafts of corn and vines. Hesiod does not mention the altar (right) and its fire. The BMPR has a slight pencil sketch of the figure group, two related pencil sketches on the verso of a drawing for pl. 12, and a proof of the plate lacking all letters except the Greek word ('god') within the design.

10. 15.2 × 28.6 cm.; *Fig. 244*

Inscriptions above design: *10* [left], GOOD DÆMONS. [centre], E. *123*. [right]

Quotation: EARTH-WANDERING DÆMONS THEY THEIR CHARGE BEGAN, | THE MINISTERS OF GOOD, AND GUARDS OF MAN; | l. 165. Works and Days.—Elton's Hesiod.

Imprint: as on pl. 3.

After the Golden Age, Jupiter sent winged 'ministers of good' to earth to protect the innocent from harm, here represented by a wolf. Flaxman has literalized Hesiod's 'mantle' metaphor for the night into cloaks worn by the hovering spirits. In a preliminary drawing in the BMPR, the wolf is differently configured and more prominent (reproduced in Irwin 1979, p. 95).

11. 8.4 × 14.9 cm.; *Fig. 245*

Inscriptions above design: *11* [left], SILVER AGE. [centre], E *135*. [right]

Quotation: NOR WOULD THEY SERVE THE GODS. | Elton's Hesiod—Works.

Imprint: as on pl. 3.

Flaxman represents the Silver Age with a dissolute couple engaged in 'frantic follies' and ignoring their gods and their fate. The man's sacrilege is indicated by his propping his foot on the altar.

12. 14.9 × 23.5 cm.; *Fig. 246*

Inscriptions above design: *12* [left], BRAZEN AGE. [centre], E. *l. 152*. E. [right]

Quotation: THEY BY EACH OTHER'S HANDS INGLORIOUS FELL, | IN FREEZING DARK-NESS PLUNGED, THE HOUSE OF HELL; | Works—Elton's Hesiod.

Imprint: as on pl. 1.

The men of the Brazen Age destroy each other in combat. Flaxman indicates their fall into a bestial state by picturing lions and snakes on the right, neither mentioned by Hesiod. A proof in the Pierpont Morgan Library, New York, with a proof of pl. 36 on the verso, lacks all letters. A rough pencil sketch in the HEH has fewer figures very differently arranged (reproduced in Wark 1970, p. 39). There are three preliminary versions on two sheets in the BMPR, one with additional pencil sketches in the margins. There are also three pre-liminary sketches on the verso of a BMPR drawing for pl. 20 and several small studies on the drawing for pl. 24. All vary in details from the published design.

13. 19.1 × 18.8 cm.; *Fig. 247*

Inscriptions above design: *13* [left], MODESTY AND JUSTICE RETURNING TO HEAVEN. [centre], E. *197*. [right]

Quotation: JUSTICE AND MODESTY FROM MORTALS DRIVEN | RISE TO THE IMMOR-TAL FAMILY OF HEAVEN. | Elton's Hesiod—Works.

Imprint: as on pl. 1.

Modesty, bowing meekly, and Justice stand before Jupiter, with Juno on the left, Minerva on the right, and signs of the zodiac behind. The god and goddesses are not named by Hesiod. In the Greek text the name for the second personified virtue can be translated as 'Retribution', and thus the liquid Justice pours from a vial may represent an evil descending on mankind. In Blake's Job illustrations, first executed as watercolours *c.* 1805–6 (Butlin 1981, nos. 550.5–6), Satan pours dis-eases on Job from a somewhat rounder vessel. A proof before all letters, with a proof of pl. 34 on the verso, is in the BMPR, along with two slight pencil studies. A possibly related sketch of Jupiter enthroned is on the verso of a BMPR drawing for pl. 27.

14. 14.2 × 32.2 cm.; *Fig. 248*

Inscriptions above design: *14*. [left], IRON AGE. [centre], E. *189*. [right]

Quotation: FOR SPOIL THEY WAIT | AND LAY THEIR MUTUAL CITIES DESOLATE | Elton's Hesiod—Works.

Imprint: as on pl. 1.

The 'fifth race' of mankind, here urged on by two furies with serpents and torches, descends into murder (left) and rapine while the aged 'sire' laments on the right. A pencil-and-pen preliminary drawing in the BMPR is inscribed 'Iron Age'. It is close to the published design, except that the man second from the right looks back to the left.

15. 15 × 21.4 cm.; *Fig. 249*

Inscriptions above design: *15*. [left], THE EVIL RACE. [centre], E. *224*. [right]

Quotation: THEY THRUST PALE JUSTICE FROM THEIR HAUGHTY GATES. | Elton's Hesiod—Works.

Imprint: as on pl. 1.

Justice (see pl. 13), holding her scales, departs from an unjust world. The 'gates' are represented by only two lines, top left. The preliminary pen-over-pencil drawing in the BMPR is close to the published design.

16. 11.7 × 22.6 cm.; *Fig. 250*

Inscriptions above design: *16* [left], THE EVIL RACE. [centre], E. *243* [right]

Quotation: THE GOD SENDS DOWN HIS ANGRY PLAGUES FROM HIGH | FAMINE AND PESTILENCE; IN HEAPS THEY DIE | Elton's Hesiod—Works.

Imprint: as on pl. 1.

A spirit on the left, with a surprisingly sympathetic expression on her face, pours pestilence and famine from two vials (see Justice's vials, pl. 13). Justice (not mentioned by Hesiod) with her scales and a per-sonification of Jupiter's 'wrath' follow. Two drawings of 'The Angel of Pestilence' at University College, London, may be variant designs of the same subject. Both show a single large figure in the sky, head on the right, and suffering figures below (reproduced in Colvin 1876, pls. VII, fig. 1, and XI, fig. 9). A similar sketch is in the HEH (reproduced in Wark 1970, p. 40). A slight pencil-and-pen sketch close to the published version, but with the head of the top right figure perhaps turned to the right, is in the BMPR (same sheet as the drawing for pl. 17).

17. 14.4 × 29.2 cm.; *Fig. 251*

Inscriptions above design: *17* [left], THE GOOD RACE [centre], E. *227.* [right]

Quotation: GENIAL PEACE | DWELLS IN THEIR BORDERS, AND THEIR YOUTH INCREASE | Elton's Hesiod.—Works.

Imprint: as on pl. 1.

Flaxman returns to a slightly earlier passage than the one illustrated in pl. 16. Family groups with babes, shafts of corn, and vines represent this just world (note the scales, top centre) where all is fruitful. Three female spirits bring blessings to mankind, whose harmony is intimated by the musician on the right. A pen drawing in the BMPR varies from the published version only in minor details (reproduced in Constable 1927, pl. VII). A preliminary drawing, formerly owned by Christopher Powney, is now in a private collection.

18. 12.9 × 23.4 cm.; *Fig. 252*

Inscriptions above design: *18* [left], PLEIADES. [centre], E. *383.* [right]

Quotation: WHEN, ATLAS BORN, THE PLEIAD STARS ARISE | Elton's Hesiod—Works.

Imprint: as on pl. 1.

The Pleiades, represented both as stars and as the seven daughters of Atlas after whom they are named, rise in the autumn sky as the harvest begins. The lowest Pleiad may be Merope, ashamed to show her face because she wed a mortal. The BMPR has a pen-over-pencil preliminary drawing close to the published version and, on the same sheet bearing the drawing for pl. 37, two slight pencil sketches of the Pleiades, one without the harvesters and one with the men on the left. A pen drawing in the Princeton University Art Gallery, Princeton, New Jersey, is probably a copy after the print. A pencil, pen, and grey-ink sketch, on paper with an 1809 watermark, of the female figures and stars, showing slight variations in the positions of the women's heads top centre, is in the collection of Jenijoy La Belle (reproduced in *Blake: An Illustrated Quarterly*, 24 (summer 1990), 237).

19. 12.8 × 23.5 cm.; *Fig. 253*

Inscriptions above design: *19* [left], PLEIADES. [centre], E. *384* [right]

Quotation: AND WHEN THEY SINK BELOW | THE MORN-ILLUMINED WEST, TIS TIME TO PLOUGH | Elton's Hesiod. Works.

Imprint: as on pl. 1.

The Pleiades (see pl. 18) descend in the spring sky. A pen-over-pencil preliminary drawing close to the

published version and a rough sketch on another sheet are in the BMPR.

20. Early copies (first printing?) of the 1817 edn. (e.g. BL, Detlef Dörrbecker, RNE, Royal Academy, London); 15.3 × 23.9 cm.; *Fig. 254*

Inscriptions above design: *37* [left], THE HAPPY MAN. [centre], E. *l. 827* [right]

Quotation: HE TO WHOSE NOTE THE AUGURIES ARE GIVEN | NO RITE TRANSGRESS'D, AND VOID OF BLAME TO HEAVEN. | Days— Elton's Hesiod.

Imprint: as on pl. 1.

Second State (later copies of the 1817 edn.). The number top left has been corrected to '*20*'. Bentley 1977, p. 559, suggests that this change was one of those for which Longman paid the writing engraver, Jeffreys, for alterations to eleven plates. The Longman accounts record payments for this work on 10 December 1816 and 28 January 1817 (Bentley 1977, p. 557). These dates suggest that these alterations may have been made prior to the first printing of 200 sets which very probably contained the first state.

The prosperity of the good and happy farmer, leaning on his plough, is indicated by the sturdy oxen. His attention to the gods is signified by the altar, right. Jupiter, a goddess (Juno?), and Apollo attend in the sky. The scales of Justice rest in perfect balance upper left; birds soar into the sky as a good augury on the right. A pen-over-pencil preliminary drawing in the BMPR also bears two slight pencil sketches of the design. All three are close to the engraved version. A pencil drawing of Apollo and Jupiter only, with their positions reversed, is in the Princeton University Art Gallery, Princeton, New Jersey.

21. Title-page for the *Theogony*; 13.4 × 24.3 cm.; *Fig. 255*

Inscriptions above design: *21* [left], *l. 22. θ* [right]

Title: THEOGONY

Quotation: THEY TO HESIOD ERST | HAVE TAUGHT THEIR STATELY SONG: | Elton's Hesiod—Theogony 2.ᵈ Edition.

Imprint: as on pl. 1.

The muse instructs the pastoral poet. Jupiter's altars stand right and left; Hesiod's flock grazes on Helicon. Both the sun (setting in the west) and the moon are named in the text as among Hesiod's many instructors. The dog is not mentioned. A pen-over-pencil preliminary drawing in the BMPR lacks the sun and moon but has more sheep and fire pots on both altars. Another sketch in the same collection shows the muse, Hesiod, and a third figure above holding a pot, but lacks the other motifs in the published version.

22.   17.2 × 28.8 cm.; *Fig. 256*

Inscriptions above design: *22* [left], HESIOD AND THE MUSES. [centre], *θEOTONIA 30.* [right]
Quotation: AND GAVE UNTO MY HAND | A ROD OF MARVELLOUS GROWTH A LAUREL BOUGH | Elton's Hesiod—Theogony.
Imprint: as on pl. 3.

One of nine muses presents the poet with the emblem of victory. The muse far left leans on a bust of Jupiter, the father of them all. There are two pen-over-pencil preliminary drawings in the BMPR, one of the published design, the other with Hesiod standing upright, only four muses, all standing, and a dog next to Hesiod. A pencil drawing of the seven muses on the left in the Princeton University Art Gallery, Princeton, New Jersey, may be a copy after the plate.

23.   10.5 × 25.7 cm.; *Fig. 257*

Inscriptions above design: *23* [left], JUPITER AND THE MUSES. [centre], *θ. 36.* [right]
Quotation: THEY THE GREAT SPIRIT OF THEIR FATHER JOVE | DELIGHT IN HEA-VEN; | Elton's Hesiod—Theogony.
Imprint: as on pl. 3.

Five muses sing or play music for Jupiter, who holds stylized shafts of lightning. There are two preliminary drawings in the BMPR, one lacking Jupiter and with the muse on the right resting her chin in her hand. The other drawing is very close to the published version; a sketch on the same sheet shows five muses very differently arranged in a vertical format.

24.   16.7 × 15.1 cm.; *Fig. 258*

Inscriptions above design: *24* [left], NIGHT LOVE EREBUS CHAOS [centre], *θ. 116.* [right]
Quotation: THEN LOVE MOST BEAUTEOUS OF IMMORTALS ROSE | Elton's Hesiod—Theogony.
Imprint: as on pl. 1.

Winged and radiant Love rises in victory over the figures sprawled at the bottom: Chaos (right) and his offspring Erebus (centre) and Night shrouded in a cloak. The plate is bound as the general frontispiece in both 1870 issues. There is a small ink preliminary sketch in the BMPR, close to the published design.

25.   9 × 18.9 cm.; *Fig. 259*

Inscriptions above design: *25* [left], VENUS. [centre], *θ 192.* [right]

Quotation: THE WAFTING WAVES | FIRST BORE HER TO CYTHERA'S HEAVENLY COAST | Theogony, Elton's Hesiod, l. 265.
Imprint: as on pl. 3.

The waves, two dolphins, a Triton, and two putti bear Venus Anadyomene towards Cythera. None of the attendants is mentioned by Hesiod. A proof before all letters, with pl. 7 from Rees's *Cyclopaedia* (**LII**) on the verso, is in the Pierpont Morgan Library, New York. There is a pen-over-pencil preliminary drawing in the BMPR close to the published design, and another with many more figures and Venus raised higher on the dolphin's back and looking to the right.

26.   9.4 × 21.1 cm.; *Fig. 260*

Inscriptions above design: *26* [left], VENUS. [centre], *θ—195.* [right]
Quotation: HER APHRODITE GODS AND MORTALS NAME | THE FOAM BORN GOD-DESS. | Elton's Hesiod.—Theogony.
Imprint: as on pl. 3.

The goddess steps forward to land on Cyprus, attended by two putti and two Tritons. A proof before all letters, with pl. 6 from Rees's *Cyclopaedia* (**LII**) on the verso, is in the BMPR. The same collection has two sheets bearing preliminary sketches. In one, Venus raises her hands above her head. Another, on the same sheet as a drawing for pl. 25, is close to the published design.

27.   15.8 × 20.8 cm.; *Fig. 261*

Inscriptions above design: *27* [left], VENUS. [centre], *θ—203.* [right]
Quotation: HER HONORS THESE | FROM THE BEGINNING. | l.   278.   Theogony.—Elton's Hesiod.
Imprint: as on pl. 3.

Venus presents a winged personification of love to Jupiter and Juno. The three Graces embrace in their traditional circular arrangement on the right. Three zodiacal constellations (left to right, Gemini, Leo, and Virgo) and other stars indicate the heavenly setting. None of these motifs is mentioned by Hesiod. The BMPR has a pen-over-pencil preliminary drawing lacking the stars and constellations. Another sheet in the same collection bears two smaller sketches, one with stars.

28.   8.2 × 31.6 cm.; *Fig. 262*

Inscriptions above design: *28* [left], SEA DIVIN-ITIES. [centre], *θ. 240* [right]
Quotation: FROM NEREUS AND THE FAIR

HAIRED DORIS, NYMPH|OF OCEAN'S PERFECT STREAM, THE LOVELY RACE|OF GODDESS NEREIDS ROSE|Elton's Hesiod—Theogony.
Imprint: as on pl. 1.

Two dolphins and ten of the fifty Nereids disport on each side of Nereus and Doris (centre). There are three sheets of pen-and-pencil preliminary drawings in the BMPR, including one with studies for pl. 31 on the verso, one with a sketch perhaps related to pl. 35, and one with a list of subjects from Hesiod and a variant design for this plate in which there are more women differently arranged and Nereus looks to the left. A drawing at University College, London, of river or sea gods may be related to this subject (reproduced in Colvin 1876, pl. XXVII, fig. 1). A small sketch in the Victoria and Albert Museum, London, is close to the published version.

29. 11.8 × 28 cm.; *Fig. 263*

Inscriptions above design: *29* [left], TYPHAON ECHIDNA GERYON. [centre], *304. θ* [right]
Quotation: ECHIDNA THE UNTAMEABLE OF SOUL|ABOVE A NYMPH WITH BEAUTY BLOOMING CHEEKS|Elton's Hesiod.—Theogony.
Imprint: as on pl. 1.

Echidna, half-woman and half-serpent, receives the attention of Typhon (left). Her monster offspring flesh out the scene: the Sphinx (left), the triple-headed Geryon, two heads (goat and lion) of the Chimaera, and the Lernean Hydra. There are two preliminary pencil sketches in the Fogg Art Museum, Cambridge, Massachusetts, one picturing only the three titular characters.

30. 18.9 × 18.9 cm.; *Fig. 264*

Inscriptions above design: *30*. [left], ASTRÆUS AND AURORA. [centre], *θ. 376.* [right]
Quotation: THE MORNING TO ASTRÆUS BARE THE WINDS|OF SPIRIT UNTAMED, WEST SOUTH AND NORTH|Elton's Hesiod—Theogony.
Imprint: as on pl. 1.

Aurora is greeted by the Titan Astraeus. Three of their four children hover below: Boreas, the north wind, with clenched fists; Zephyrus, the west wind, emptying rain from a bowl; and mild Notus, the south wind, bearing flowers. At the top shines Lucifer, the morning star. There are three pen-and-pencil preliminary drawings in the BMPR on one sheet, including one very close to the published version, a variant with Astraeus and Aurora seated, and a very small sketch of the two central figures only.

31. 8.8 × 16.5 cm.; *Fig. 265*

Inscriptions above design: *31.* [left], SATURN AND HIS CHILDREN. [centre], *θ 459.* [right]
Quotation: DID SATURN HUGE|DEVOUR|Elton's Hesiod Theogony
Imprint: as on pl. 1.

Saturn reaches for a second child, still held by Rhea. Flaxman has added two ameliorative spirits to the ghastly scene, but they seem to be plucking fruits or flowers, much as Saturn harvests his offspring. The verso of a drawing for pl. 28 in the BMPR bears several studies of the design with slight variations.

32. 12.5 × 13.9 cm.; *Fig. 266*

Inscriptions above design: *32.* [left], INFANT JUPITER. [centre], *θ. 479.* [right]
Quotation: VAST EARTH|TOOK TO HERSELF THE MIGHTY BABE|Elton's Hesiod—Theogony.
Imprint: as on pl. 1.

Rhea, to save her son Jupiter from Saturn, gives the child to her mother, Earth (Gaea). Rhea's father, Heaven (Uranus), looks down upon the scene. Hesiod does not mention the lion, lower right. The pen-and-pencil preliminary drawing in the BMPR is a variant design, with Rhea floating in the sky, Saturn trying to snatch the babe, and Earth rising on one knee to receive Jupiter. An ink sketch in the BMPR, with a large bearded figure above and to the left of two women with a child and a drawing for pl. 33 on the same sheet, may be related. A pen-over-pencil sketch at University College, London, is close to the published design (reproduced in Gizzi 1986, p. 135).

33. 17.6 × 13.3 cm.; *Fig. 267*

Inscriptions above design: *33.* [left], THE BRETHREN OF SATURN DELIVERED. [centre], *θ. 501.* [right]
Quotation: THE BRETHREN OF HIS FATHER TOO HE LOOSED.|Elton's Hesiod—Theogony.
Imprint: as on pl. 1.

Jupiter (second from left) releases Saturn's brothers from captivity. The defeated Titan looks on, bottom left, while the sun of a new era arises. Or is it the setting sun of the old order? A pen-and-pencil preliminary drawing in the BMPR, on the same sheet as the drawing for pl. 32, contains only the three brethren.

34. 19.1 × 20.3 cm.; *Fig. 268*

Inscriptions above design: *34* [left], GODS AND
    TITANS. [centre], *386. θ* [right]
Quotation: NOR LONGER THEN DID JOVE |
    WITHHOLD HIS FORCE | Elton's Hesiod.
    Theogony.
Imprint: as on pl. 1.

The line reference (top right) to the Greek text should
read *686*. Jupiter, hurling thunderbolts, and five other
Olympian gods (from left to right, Mercury, Minerva,
Neptune, Mars, and Apollo) in the sky attack seven
Titans below. A proof before all letters in the BMPR,
with a proof of pl. 13 on the verso, lacks some of the
scales on the serpent tails and a few lines on the face,
lower right. The BMPR also has several preliminary
drawings: a pen-over-pencil drawing close to the published design (reproduced in Irwin 1979, p. 93), another
with Jupiter turned towards the viewer, three pencil
sketches on a sheet with a drawing for pl. 27, a drawing
close to the published version on a sheet with a drawing
for pl. 35, and one of Jupiter on the verso of a drawing
for pl. 27. See also pl. 35. An ink drawing in the
Princeton University Art Gallery, Princeton, New
Jersey, of the Titan being speared by an Olympian may
be a copy after the engraving.

35. 19.3 × 19 cm.; *Fig. 269*

Inscriptions above design: *35* [left], GIANTS AND
    TITANS. [centre], *713. θ* [right]
Quotation: THE WAR UNSATED GYGES,
    BRIAREUS | AND COTTUS BITTEREST
    CONFLICT WAGED | Elton's Hesiod. Theogony.
Imprint: as on pl. 1.

The three named Giants hurl great rocks at the falling
Titans. Two pen-over-pencil preliminary drawings in
the BMPR vary slightly from the published version.
The same sheet also bears several small sketches, one
of which (lower right) is probably an alternative version
of pl. 34 (full sheet reproduced in Bindman 1979, p.
128). The BMPR also has a sheet with two pen-over-
pencil studies and another with Flaxman's list of subjects for illustrating Hesiod. The verso of a BMPR
drawing for pl. 28 bears a pencil sketch that may be
related. The small preliminary sketch in the Victoria
and Albert Museum, London, shows only slight variations in the positions of the lower figures.

36. 11.6 × 27.4 cm.; *Fig. 270*

Inscriptions above design: *36* [left], FURIES CERB-
    ERUS PLUTO RROSERPINE [*sic*] HARPIES
    DEATH [centre], *θ. 768.* [right]

Quotation: THE HOLLOW SOUNDING PAL-
    ACES | OF PLUTO STRONG THE SUB-
    TERRANEAN GOD | Elton's Hesiod—Theogony.
Imprint: as on pl. 1.

The god of the underworld and his attendants are
identified in the inscription above the design. In the
passage illustrated, only Pluto, Proserpine, and Cerberus are mentioned. A proof lacking all letters is in the
Pierpont Morgan Library, New York. The pen-over-
pencil preliminary drawing in the BMPR is close to
the published design.

37. 16.4 × 13.1 cm.; *Fig. 271*

Inscriptions above design: *37* [left], IRIS. [centre],
    784. θ [right]
Quotation: JOVE SENDS IRIS DOWN | TO BRING
    THE GREAT OATH IN A GOLDEN EWER |
    Elton's Hesiod.—Theogony.
Imprint: as on pl. 1.

The goddess of the rainbow (pictured in the background) fills her ewer with the waters named by Hesiod
as 'the great oath' of the gods, three of whom look on.
The pen-and-pencil preliminary drawing in the BMPR
is close to the published version.

Literature: Gilchrist 1863, i. 247–8 (criticizing the engravings
    as 'deficient in force'), ii. 261; Colvin 1876, and Sparkes
    1885, pp. 18–20 (see **XLVI**, *Literature*); Laurence Binyon,
    *Catalogue of Drawings by British Artists ... in the British
    Museum* (London: British Museum, 1900), ii. 141–5;
    Russell 1912, no. 107; Keynes 1921, no. 131; Constable
    1927, p. 49 (see **XXXVIII**, *Literature*); Bentley 1964, pp.
    53–7 (see **XLVI**, *Literature*); Bentley and Nurmi 1964,
    no. 367; G. E. Bentley, jun., 'Blake's Hesiod', *The Library*,
    20 (1965), 315–20; Dora Panofsky and Irwin Panofsky,
    Pandora's Box: The Changing Aspects of a Mythical Symbol
    (New York: Harper and Row, 1965), 92–102; Wark 1970,
    pp. 38–40 (see **XLVI**, *Literature*); *The Age of Neo-Classi-
    cism* (1972), 339–40 (see **XXXVIII**, *Literature*); Chris-
    topher Powney and Heim Gallery, *John Flaxman* (sale
    catalogue; 1976); Bentley 1977, no. 456; Bindman 1979,
    pp. 155–6, and Irwin 1979, pp. 90–1 (see **XXXVIII**,
    Literature); Essick 1980, p. 177; Corrado Gizzi, *Flaxman
    e Dante* (Milan: Mazzotta, 1986), 133–4, 208.

LII

Abraham Rees, *The Cyclopaedia; or, Universal
Dictionary of Arts, Sciences, and Literature* (39 text
vols., 6 plates vols.; London: Longman, Hurst,
Rees, Orme, & Brown, *et al.*, 1820); *Figs. 272–80*

The *Cyclopaedia*, originally issued in fascicles

between 1802 and 1820, contains five plates signed by Blake as the engraver, one signed by him as both the engraver and delineator (of the preliminary drawings, not the objects represented), and one signed by Blake and Wilson Lowry (1762–1824). The jointly engraved design was printed from two different copperplates—see pls. 3A–B, below. The 'Sculpture' plates (4–7) are engraved in stippled lines, like the Hesiod illustrations (LI), but with stipple shading added to create a sense of volume.

John Flaxman was probably instrumental in securing the commission for Blake. According to an anonymous notice in *The Philosophical Magazine and Journal*, 56 (1820), 218–24, Flaxman co-authored the essay on sculpture (with John Bacon and Prince Hoare), and Charles Koenig wrote the article on gem engraving. Flaxman is named as the author of the articles on armour, basso-relievo, and several others in *The Annual Biography and Obituary for the Year 1828*, 12 (1828), 24–5 (see also Bentley 1969, pp. 138, 238). Blake may have become involved in the project as early as 1803, for Flaxman wrote to William Hayley on 2 January 1804 that he was sending, via Blake, his essay on 'Basso Relievo, with one of the prints referred to at the end of the article, the rest are not yet engraven' (Bentley 1969, p. 138). This print was probably of 'PLATE III' engraved by James Parker, the only 'Basso Relievo' illustration with an 1804 imprint.

According to a fragmentary ledger still in Longman's archives, Blake was paid £10. 10s. 'for a plate of Sculpture' on 19 August 1815 (Bentley 1988, pp. 71–2). This fee may have been for pl. 6, for it bears an imprint date closest to the time of payment. For Blake's possible participation on other plates in the *Cyclopaedia*, see comments on the drawing for pl. 2. The catalogue of the *Exhibition of Books, Water Colors, Engravings, Etc. by William Blake* (Museum of Fine Arts, Boston, 1891) includes in no. 114 proofs before letters of pl. 1 and 'a plate representing antique sculptures', both from the collection of Edwin W. Hooper (now untraced).

The compiler of the *Cyclopaedia*, Abraham Rees (1743–1825), was a Presbyterian minister active in dissenting circles in London. He re-edited the encyclopaedia of Ephraim Chambers in 1778, and shortly thereafter launched the far larger and more comprehensive project under his own name.

1. Vol. i of the plates, 'Armour', composite pls. 4 and 5 (first published in fascicle 78, Sept. 1819); 24 × 17.4 cm.; *Fig. 272*

Inscriptions above design: ARMOUR. [centre], *PLATE IV & V.* [right]
Inscriptions around images: see *Fig. 272*.
Signature right: *Blake sc*
Imprint: *Published as the Act directs, Dec.ᵗ 10, 1818, by Longman, Hurst, Rees, Orme & Brown, Paternoster Row.*

In the article on 'Armor' (vol. ii, fos. 5B₂ᵛ–5B₄ᵛ), the individual figures in this engraving are briefly described. Figs. 3 and 4 (top right) represent Danish armour in the time of King Canute. Pl. IV, fig. 6 (bottom centre), is based on the monument for the Earl of Warwick, 1370. A suit of armour made for the young Henry VIII is pictured bottom right. Pl. V, fig. 2 (centre right), is a piece of horse armour.

2. Vol. ii of the plates, 'Basso Relievo', pl. 4 (first published in fascicle F, Sept. 1819); 24.4 × 18 cm.; *Fig. 273*

Inscriptions above design: Basso Relievo. [centre], *PLATE IV.* [right] | *PAGAN ALTARS*.
Inscriptions below reliefs: *Fig. 1.—Basso-relievo round a Capital in the Cathedral of Carrara.* [upper centre] | *Fig. 2.—Basso-relievo of Zethus, Antiope & Amphion.* [bottom left]
Other inscriptions: see *Fig. 273*.
Signature right: *Blake sc*.
Imprint: *Published by Longman, Hurst, Rees, Orme & Brown, London, Novem.ᵗ 11ᵗʰ 1818.* [not reproduced]

Flaxman's article on basso-relievo, vol. iii, fos. 5Dᵛ–5Eᵛ, ends with captions for two of the images on this plate: '1. A capital of a column in the west door of the cathedral of Carrara, representing part of the history of Abraham; a work of the twelfth century. 2. A beautiful Greek basso-relievo, near the time of Phidias, of Zethus am [*sic*] Amphion comforting their mother Antiope; from the Villa Albani.' The five pagan altars illustrate a completely separate article on 'altars', vol. i, fos. 5F₃ʳ–5F₄ᵛ. This essay refers the reader to 'Miscellany, *Plate I*', but the captions that follow clearly describe the altars on this plate:

Nº 1, represents an alter dedicated to Neptune. ... Nº 2, is a four-square altar, dedicated to the nymphs. ... Nº 3, exhibits a Bacchanal with a thyrsus in his hand. ... Nº 4, which was triangular, exhibited a genius, one of whom is seen carrying an oar upon his neck, which seems to indicate that it belonged to Neptune. Nº 5, with the inscription 'ara Neptuni', is of a round figure; the god [Neptune] is represented wholly naked, preserving the pallium on his shoulder, and holding in his left hand a trident, and in his right a dolphin.

Blake's pencil drawing for '*Fig. 2*' (lower left) is presently in the estate of the late Albert S. Roe, Ithaca, New York (Butlin 1981, no. 678). The sheet, 31.7 × 28.3 cm., also bears pencil sketches for 'Hercules and Apollo contending for the Tripod from the Villa Albani', engraved by William Bond on 'Basso Relievo' pl. II; and 'An Egyptian Hieroglyphical Sphinx' and 'Jupiter with the thunder and trident, a Greek gem of the oldest style', reproduced in 'Basso Relievo', pl. I. In Essick 1982, pp. 54–5, I suggest some reasons for attributing this last, unsigned, plate to Blake. The evidence, however, is not sufficient for including 'Basso Relievo', pl. I, in this catalogue, particularly since the same sheet of preliminary drawings indicates that Blake drew designs for at least one plate (II) engraved by another craftsman.

3A. A few copies of vol. iii of the plates, 'Miscellany', pl. 18 (first published in fascicle F, Sept. 1819); 21 × 17.1 cm.

Inscriptions above design: MISCELLANY. [centre], *PLATE XVIII.* [right] | *GEM Engraving.*
Other inscriptions: see *Fig. 274* (pl. 3B).
Signatures: *Drawn by Farey.* [left], *Engraved by W. Blake & W. Lowry.* [right]
Imprint: *Published as the Act directs, 1819, by Longman, Hurst, Rees, Orme & Brown, Paternoster Row.*

The individual figures on this plate are described at the conclusion of the article on 'Gems', vol. xv, fos. 5B$_1$^{r}–5D$_4$^{r}. The method of cutting the bust of Jupiter Serapis, shown in three views on this plate, is recorded in some detail. A proof of the plate in the Pierpont Morgan Library, New York, shows only the three views of the bust and lacks all letters and the wavy lines defining the dark background of the gem. Another impression of the same proof state is on the verso. These three images are no doubt the only parts of the plate executed by Blake. The tools at the top, engraved in a very different manner, were cut by Lowry, and

the letters either by Lowry or an anonymous writing engraver. Ryskamp 1977, p. 40, notes that the version of the plate represented by the Morgan proof was 'not used', but I have found finished impressions of this copperplate in copies of Rees in the HEH and Princeton University Library, Princeton, New Jersey (see Essick 1983, no. LXXII). For a portrait of Wilson Lowry engraved by Blake and John Linnell after Linnell's painting, see Essick 1983, no. XLIII. I can find no information about the draughtsman, 'Farey'.

3B. Most copies of vol. iii of the plates; *Fig. 274*
Inscriptions and size: as for pl. 3A.

The plate is very similar to 3A, but the relative proportions and placement of images indicate that 3A and 3B are two distinct copperplates. Two small features can be used to distinguish them easily. In pl. 3B the horizontal hatching lines in the background of the gem on the left extend into the thin border defining its outer rim, whereas in pl. 3A this border is free of all hatching. The tube-like fold of cloth on the left shoulder of the bust on the right has its opening defined by two parallel circular lines in pl. 3A. In 3B a single line delineates this circle. The simplest explanation for the existence of two nearly identical copperplates of this design is that one (probably the rarer 3A) was damaged in the course of printing or lost and the other prepared as a substitute. For other gem engravings and Blake's comments on them, see **XLI**.

4. Vol. iv of the plates, 'Sculpture', pl. 1 (first published in fascicle 67, Oct. 1816); 23.7 × 18 cm.; *Fig. 275*
Inscriptions above design: SCULPTURE. [centre], *PLATE I.* [right]
Inscriptions below images: *Hercules of Dædalus, | from a small Bronze.* [top left], *Cupid of Praxiteles. | British Museum &c.* [top centre], *Minerva of Dipænus & Scyllis, | in the Villa Albani.* [top right], *Venus of Praxiteles, | Perriers Statues.* [bottom left], *Jupiter Olympius. See Pausanius, Ancient | Statues, Coins & Gems.* [bottom centre], *Minerva of the Acropolis in Athens. | See Hunters Coins.* [bottom right]
Signature right: *Blake sc.*
Imprint: *London, Published as the Act directs, Feb.ʸ 1, 1816, by Longman, Hurst, Rees, Orme, & Brown, Paternoster Row.*

Flaxman's article on 'Sculpture', vol. 32, fos. H$_3$^{v}–N$_2$^{v}, concludes by referring the reader to all 'the engravings which are distinguished by the word *Sculpture*', but offers no elaboration of the captions on pls. 4–7. There are, however, at least passing references to most of the illustrated sculptures in Flaxman's long essay. Pausanias's descriptions of the statues of Jupiter and Minerva are summarized on fos. K^v–K$_2$^{v}. The figures on the plinth supporting Jupiter are, from left to right, Apollo, Cupid, Venus, Persuasion, Juno, Jupiter, the three Graces with Neptune below, Hermes, Vesta, and Diana. The plate closely follows Blake's pencil, pen, and wash preliminary drawing, 27.4 × 21.8 cm., now in the LC (*Fig. 276*; Butlin 1981, no. 678A). On the verso is a rough pencil sketch, 9.5 × 4.5 cm., of 'Persian Sculpture, at Persepolis', engraved lower left on pl. 7. The ink inscription at the bottom of the recto is by Frederick Tatham.

In his *Descriptive Catalogue* of 1809 Blake states that 'the Venus, the Minerva, the Jupiter, the Apollo [see pl. 6] … are all of them representations of spiritual existences of God's immortal' (E 541, K 576). However, in the same work he also states that the 'Hercules, Farnese [pl. 5], Venus of Medicis [pl. 6], Apollo Belvidere [pl. 6], and all the grand works of ancient art' were 'copied' by 'the Greeks and Hetrurians' after 'those wonderful originals called in the Sacred Scriptures the Cherubim' (E 531, K 565). About eleven years later Blake wrote in his 'Laocoön' inscriptions that 'The Gods of Greece & Egypt were Mathematical Diagrams' (E 274, K 776). These comments epitomize Blake's ambivalent attitude towards classical art and his attempt to preserve the beauties of classical sculpture through an historical myth that granted them biblical meanings.

5. Vol. iv of the plates, 'Sculpture', pl. 2 (first published in fascicle 68, Oct. 1816); 24.9 × 14.9 cm.; *Fig. 277*

Inscriptions above design: SCULPTURE. [centre], *PLATE II.* [right]

Inscriptions above and below images: *Hercules Farnese* [top left], *Phocion* [top right], *Dirce* [above lower image]

Signature: *Blake, sculp.* [below lower-right corner of bottom image]

Imprint: *Published as the Act directs, Jany 1, 1816, by Longman, Hurst, Rees, Orme & Brown, Paternoster Row.*

The statue of Dirce being tied to a bull is a re-creation of a work Flaxman attributes to Apollonius and Tauriscus of Rhodes (vol. xxxii, fo. K$_2$^{v}). The statue of the Athenian statesman Phocion is not described. In his *Descriptive Catalogue* of 1809 Blake compares Chaucer's Miller and Ploughman to 'Hercules' and quotes an unnamed person as proposing 'the Apollo [pl. 6] for

the model of your beautiful Man and the Hercules for your strong Man' (E 536, 544; K 571, 579). Blake's portrayal of Giant Despair in *Christian and Hopeful Escape from Doubting Castle* among his illustrations of *c.* 1824–7 to Bunyan's *Pilgrim's Progress* is based closely on the Hercules Farnese (first pointed out in Stephen A. Larrabee, *English Bards and Grecian Marbles* (New York: Columbia Univ. Press, 1943), 100). According to Benjamin Heath Malkin, writing in 1806, Blake's father bought his young son 'casts in plaster of the various antiques', including 'the Venus of Medicis' (see pl. 6) and 'the Hercules' (Bentley 1969, p. 422). See also comments on pl. 4.

6. Vol. iv of the plates, 'Sculpture', pl. 3 (first published in fascicle 66, July 1816); 25 × 14.9 cm.; *Fig. 278*

Inscriptions above design: SCULPTURE. [centre], *PLATE III.* [right]

Inscriptions above or below images: *Venus de Medicis.* [top left], *Apollo Belvedere.* [top right], *Laocoon.* [above lower image]

Signature right: *Blake del et sc.*

Imprint: *Published as the Act directs, Octr 1, 1815, by Longman, Hurst, Rees, Orme & Brown, Paternoster Row.*

See comments on pls. 4 and 5. A proof of pl. 6, lacking all letters and with a proof of pl. 26 of the Hesiod illustrations (LI) on the verso, is in the BMPR. It is inscribed in pencil by Frederick Tatham, 'Blake went to the Royal Academy and made an original drawing of which this is a print' (see also Bentley 1969, p. 238). This 'original drawing' is probably the detailed pencil sketch, 19 × 15 cm., of the 'Laocoön' only, now in the Yale Center for British Art, New Haven, Connecticut (*Fig. 279*; Butlin 1981, no. 679). In his inscription on this drawing, Tatham notes that it 'was made by Mr Blake in the Royal Academy Somerset House for a small plate he made of the Laocoon for the Article in the Encyclopedia'. Blake must have based his drawing on the cast of the sculpture group in the Royal Academy (reproduced in Keynes 1976, p. 26). In its present condition, this cast shows the son on the left extending his right arm vertically, whereas his arm bends to the right over his head in Blake's drawing and engraving. This alteration accords with modern reconstructions of the original statue in the Vatican. Blake appears to have made as well a pen drawing of the Laocoön, untraced since 1885 (Butlin 1981, no. 680).

Work on this *Cyclopaedia* plate probably provided the direct stimulus for Blake's execution, *c.* 1820, of a separate plate of the Laocoön surrounded with his own aphoristic comments (Essick 1983, no. XIX; text in E 273–5, K 775–7). In his inscriptions Blake notes that the sculpture was 'copied from the Cherubim of Solomons Temple by three Rhodians'. This theory (see also pl. 4) may have been suggested in part by Flaxman's statement in his article on sculpture (vol. xxxii, fo. K_2^v) that 'the style of this work, as well as the manner in which Pliny introduces it into his history, gives us reason to believe it was not ancient in his time'. If it is a work of late antiquity, then there may have been earlier models for it, as Blake speculates. In about 1825 he also drew a large *Free Version of the Laocoön* showing the priest gowned (Butlin 1981, no. 681). Blake used a slightly more closed version of Laocoön's stance, reversed, for the figure in *Christian Fears the Fire from the Mountain*, one of the illustrations of *c.* 1824–7 to Bunyan's *Pilgrim's Progress* (Butlin 1981, no. 829.8). Blake based his portrayal of Cambel on pl. 81 of *Jerusalem* on the Medici Venus. His study of the Royal Academy cast of the Apollo Belvedere in preparation for this plate may have influenced Blake's later (*c.* 1815) version of *The Overthrow of Apollo and the Pagan Gods* (Butlin 1981, no. 542.4) among his watercolour illustrations to Milton's 'On the Morning of Christ's Nativity'. In the version of 1809 (Butlin 1981, no. 538.4) Apollo holds the serpent and has no cloak.

7. Vol. iv of the plates, 'Sculpture', pl. 4 (first published in fascicle 69, Feb. 1817); 21.6 × 17.7 cm.; *Fig. 280*

Inscriptions above design: SCULPTURE. [centre], *PLATE IV*. [right]

Inscriptions under images: *Durga Slaying Mahishasura, a Hendee group.* [top left], *An Etruscan Patera, in the British Museum.* [top centre], *A Colossal Statue, at Thebes.* [top right], *Persian Sculpture, at Persepolis.* [bottom left], *A Chinese Statue.* [bottom centre], *Persian Sculpture, at Persepolis.* [bottom right]

Signature right: *Blake sculp.*

Imprint: *Published as the Act directs, March 1, 1816, by Longman, Hurst, Rees, Orme & Brown, Paternoster Row.*

See comments on pl. 4 for textual context and a sketch of the sculpture bottom left. A proof of pl. 7, lacking all letters and with a proof of pl. 25 of the Hesiod illustrations (LI) on the verso, is in the Pierpont Morgan Library, New York (sheet watermarked 1811).

Literature: Gilchrist 1863, i. 248, ii. 261 (pls. 1, 4–7 only); Russell 1912, no. 105; Keynes 1921, no. 132; Bentley and Nurmi 1964, no. 399; Roe 1969, pp. 192–4 (on pl. 7; see XXI, *Literature*); Geoffrey Keynes, *William Blake's Laocoön: A Last Testament* (London: Trianon Press, 1976); Bentley 1977, no. 489; Charles Ryskamp [actually Thomas V. Lange], 'A Blake Discovery', *Times Literary Supplement* (14 Jan. 1977), 40–1 (on the proof of pl. 3A); Morton D. Paley, '"Wonderful Originals"—Blake and Ancient Sculpture', in Robert N. Essick and Donald Pearce (eds.), *Blake in his Time* (Bloomington: Indiana Univ. Press, 1978), 182–4, 190–2; Essick 1980, p. 195; James Bogan, 'Blake's Jupiter Olympius in Rees' *Cyclopaedia* [pl. 4]', *Blake: An Illustrated Quarterly*, 15 (1982), 156–63; Robert N. Essick, review of Butlin 1981, *Blake: An Illustrated Quarterly*, 16 (1982), 54–5; Gott 1989 (see XXVII, *Literature*), pp. 128–33; Irene H. Chayes, 'Blake's Ways with Art Sources II: Some Versions of the Antique', *Colby Quarterly*, 26 (1990), 28–58.

LIII

The Pastorals of Virgil, with a Course of English Reading, Adapted for Schools ... by Robert John Thornton (2 vols., 3rd edn., London: F. C. & J. Rivingtons, *et al.*, 1821); *Figs. 281–6*

Thornton's modest school text of Virgil and associated imitations in English is now a book famous in the history of the graphic arts because it includes seventeen small wood engravings designed and executed by Blake (Easson and Essick 1972, no. X; Bindman 1978, nos. 602–18). These innovative and influential works have overshadowed Blake's humbler contributions to the volumes: four wood engravings designed by Blake but cut by an anonymous journeyman, a reduced drawing of Nicolas Poussin's *Polyphemus* engraved in wood by John Byfield, and six intaglio line-and-stipple engravings of busts and coins signed by Blake as the delineator and engraver. This last group falls into the category covered by this catalogue, for, although the signatures indicate that Blake made the preliminary drawings (untraced), he did not, of course, design the objects pictured.

Robert Thornton (1768?–1837) was the physician for the family of John Linnell, Blake's great patron in the last nine years of his life. Blake met Thornton at Linnell's home by September 1818 (Bentley 1969, p. 285), and their host was probably instrumental in acquiring the commission to illustrate the third edition of Thornton's Virgil. With a letter to Linnell of 15 September 1820, Thornton sent an impression of 'Blake's Augustus' (pl. 3) and comments on 'How much better will be the Stone'—that is, a lithograph (Bentley 1969, p. 266). Linnell noted in his journal for 2 October 1820 that he went 'with Dr Thornton Dartmouth St Westminster to the Lithography Press to prove a head of Virgil' (Bentley 1969, p. 267). This may have been a lithograph of pl. 2, but all the plates catalogued here were printed from intaglio copperplates. Vol. i contains two maps 'On Stone by J. Wyld' and printed at 'The Lithographic Press 6 Dartmouth St. West!', but these are clearly distinct in ink texture from Blake's plates. Perhaps the poor quality of Wyld's work discouraged Thornton from proceeding with his evident plans to have Blake's plates converted to lithographs. Indeed, it seems odd to commission intaglio engravings in the first place if lithography was intended as the final printing medium.

Work on Thornton's volumes was probably one of the immediate stimuli for Blake's composition, *c.* 1820, of his brief tract, *On Homers Poetry* [and] *On Virgil*. The Roman poet's praise of the two Caesars (pls. 3 and 5) must have represented for Blake the submission of art to 'War & Dominion' (E 270, K 778). In the harshly critical annotations he wrote in the last months of his life to Thornton's *New Translation of the Lord's Prayer*, Blake concludes by calling Augustus 'Caesar Virgils Only God [—] See Eclogue i' (E 670, K 789).

1. Vol. i, facing p. 3; 10 × 7.2 cm.; *Fig. 281*

Signature right: *Blake, del. et Sculp.*

Title: *Theocritus,* | *A Grecian Poet, of Sicily Flourished 273 years* | *before the Birth of Christ, and quitting his* | *native country, governed by Hiero, King of* | *Syracuse, went over to King Ptolemy in Egypt,* | *by whom he was greatly patronized.* | *Vide Idyllium, 17.*

Imprint: *London, Published by Dr Thornton, 1821.*

Pls. 1 and 2 are bound in and illustrate 'A Discourse on Pastoral Poetry, by Alexander Pope', i. 1–4. There are no specific textual references to these busts.

2. Vol. i, facing p. 4; 10.2 × 6.9 cm.; *Fig. 282*

Signature right: *Blake, del. et Sculp.*

Title: *Publius Virgilius Maro.* | *Poetarum Latinorum*

Princeps. | *Born 69 years before the Birth of Christ; was 7 years older* | *than Augustus; lost his Estate, at 30; recovering it was nearly killed* | *by Arius, the Centurion; some think he began his Eclogues, at 31;* | *which took him 3 years. Commenced his Georgies [sic], at 34, which* | *occupied him 7 years; and at 41 began his Æneid, which employed* | *him 11 years; at 52, Virgil died, 19 years before the Christian Æra.*

Imprint: as on pl. 1.

See comments on pl. 1. A proof in the BMPR lacks all letters, some of the lines defining hair, and some of the shading on the face.

3. Vol. i, following pl. 2; 12.5 × 8.5 cm.; *Fig. 283*

Signature right: *Blake, del. et Sculp.*

Title: *Octavius Augustus Cæsar.* | *Was Nephew to Julius Cæsar, and 18 years old when Cæsar was assassinated;* | *joins Antony, and Lepidus, and defeats Brutus and Cassius, at the* | *Battle of Phillippi, 41 years B.C.—Antony marries Octavia, Sister* | *to Augustus, whom he deserts for Cleopatria [sic], Queen of Egypt, whom* | *Cæsar defeats in a naval battle at Actium, 31 years before Christ,* | *—Shuts the Temple of Janus, the world having been created 3948* | *years, when a new Æra commences, the Birth of Christ;—dies,* | *14 years after that period, at 76, having reigned 44 years.*

Imprint: as on pl. 1.

Although the plate is bound in Pope's essay, Augustus is not mentioned therein. This bust of Virgil's patron would seem to have its closest point of textual contact with Virgil's Eclogue I, beginning on i. 5 and expressing the poet's gratitude to Augustus. The H. Buxton Forman auction catalogue, Anderson Galleries, New York, 26 April 1920, includes in lot 63 a 'proof before letters' of 'Prince Octavius'—perhaps a reference to this plate.

4. Vol. i, facing pl. 3; 13.2 × 8.3 cm.; *Fig. 284*

Inscription above design: *From Antique Coins.*

Inscriptions above or below images: Pollio [top left], Gallus [top right], Agrippa [centre], Varus [bottom left], Mecænas [bottom right]

Signature right: *Blake del et Sculp.*

Title: *Pollio was a Poet, a General, & a great favourite to Augustus, & was twice Consul.* | *Gallus was made Præfect of Egypt, a Poet, who slew himself having ruled Tyrannically.* | *Agrippa a famous General to Augustus, commanded in all his battles, & was married to Julia daughter to Augustus.* | *Varus was of noble extraction, Father to Maia, Virgil's wife, was also a Poet, & Governor of Gisalpine Gaul.* | *Mecænas was*

prime Minister to Augustus, & died 7 Years after the birth of Christ.
Imprint: as on pl. 1.

There is no clear textual reference for this plate, the portraits of which add to the histories of Virgil and Augustus begun on pls. 2–3. A proof in the BMPR lacks all letters, the lines of radiance around the central image, and the stipple shading defining the backgrounds around the heads.

5. Vol. ii, facing p. 229; 12.5 × 8.4 cm.; *Fig. 285*
Signature right: *Blake, del. et Sculp.*
Title: *Caius Julius Cæsar, | Assassinated 44 years before the Christian Æra. | Virgil: æt. 26.*
Imprint: as on pl. 1.

The portrait illustrates the 'Fifth Pastoral, Named Julius Caesar', ii. 215–356, and a supplementary quotation from Lucan's *Pharsalia* (ii. 228–9) describing Caesar's character.

6. Vol. ii, facing p. 360; 10.3 × 7.1 cm.; *Fig. 286*
Signature right: *Blake, del. et Sculp.*
Title: *Epicurus. | A Grecian Philosopher, Flourished 264 years before | Christ, His philosophy was transfused into Latin, | by the great Roman Poet Lucretius, who | flourished 105 years before Christ, and wrote | his "De Rerum Naturâ" on the Nature of | Things. He placed the summum bonum on | Tranquility of Mind, arising from Virtue, and | the Contemplation of Nature. | He is said to have been born 342 B.C. Died 270 B.C. æ: 72.*
Imprint: as on pl. 1.

The portrait illustrates the 'Sixth Pastoral, the Epicurean Philosophy' (ii. 357–452), and a supplementary quotation from Lucretius (ii. 360–2) praising Epicurus.

Literature: (omitting works on the original woodcuts only): Gilchrist 1863, i. 275; Russell 1912, no. 30; Keynes 1921, no. 77; Bentley and Nurmi 1964, no. 411; Bentley 1977, no. 504.

Appendix i

Blake's Apprentice Engravings

In August 1772, when not quite fifteen years old, Blake was apprenticed by his father to the engraver James Basire (1730–1802) for the usual term of seven years (Bentley 1969, p. 9). During that period Blake must have assisted in the production of a great many book illustrations. His labours probably ranged from such subsidiary tasks as burnishing plates and laying etching grounds to creating most of a graphic image. All evidence indicates that it was standard practice for plates produced in an engraver's shop to be signed by the master, as a sign of his approval even if not the work of his own hands, and thus we should expect even plates wholly executed by Blake the apprentice to appear above Basire's name. As a result, the identification of Blake's apprentice book illustrations must rely on extrinsic documentation or stylistic evidence.

At some time after about 1810 Blake reworked an early separate plate into 'Joseph of Arimathea among the Rocks of Albion' and added an inscription, 'Engraved by W Blake 1773 from an old Italian Drawing' (Essick 1983, no. I). If we can trust this date, then the unique first-state impression of this etching/engraving reveals a remarkable level of technical proficiency for a youth in only his second year of apprenticeship. Unfortunately, the print is not a good touchstone for the identification of other apprentice work. Its complexity and density of linear patterns are very different from Basire's book illustrations, including those that have been attributed to Blake's hand. Further, the first state of 'Joseph of Arimathea' shows nothing in its graphic style to distinguish it from the work of several other engravers of the period. For published engravings, we can hardly expect the work of an apprentice to diverge in any clear way from the house style taught by his master. Nor do comparisons between possible apprentice plates and Blake's later engravings offer much help in making attributions. Similarities may simply reveal what the apprentice learnt from the master and continued to use throughout his career. I have found stylistic considerations useful in only one instance (see **F**, below).

In his essay on Blake in *A Father's Memoirs of his Child* (1806), Benjamin Heath Malkin comments that, during his apprenticeship, Blake was 'employed in making drawings from old buildings and monuments, and occasionally, especially in winter, in engraving from those drawings' (Bentley 1969, p. 422). The examples Malkin provides are all from Gough's *Sepulchral Monuments* (**F**). Since the most likely source of this information is Blake himself, Malkin's comments carry considerable authority. He emphasizes Blake's authorship of the drawings, and makes no further statement about engravings. It seems reasonable to assume, however, that an apprentice who made drawings for engravings would have a greater probability of participating in their execution in copper than would pertain to other plates produced by his master's shop. The same line of reasoning leads to the inclusion of Ayloffe's essay (**E**) in this appendix, although the attribution of the Ayloffe drawings to Blake is not as directly supported by documentary evidence as are the Gough drawings.

The next best authority, after Malkin, on Blake's earliest engravings is Gilchrist 1863: 'The 'prentice work as assistant to Basire of these years (1773–78) may be traced under Basire's name in the *Archaeologia*, in some of the engravings of coins, &c., to the *Memoirs of Hollis* (1780), and in Gough's *Sepulchral Monuments*, not published till 1786 and 1796' (i. 19). As usual, Gilchrist does not give his source for this information, but it may have come from someone, such as Tatham or Linnell, who knew Blake. Unfortunately, Gilchrist does not specify whether the plates in the works he names were engraved by Blake or only based on his drawings. For one specific plate, however, he does claim Blake as the engraver and hints at others from his hand: 'In the *Sepulchral Monuments, vol.* 1, *pt.* 2 (1796), occurs a capital engraving as to drawing and feeling, "Portrait of Queen Philippa from her Monument" [F, pl. 3], with the inscription *Basire delineavit et sculpsit*; for which, as in many other cases, we may safely read "W. Blake"' (i. 20).

The evidence and types of arguments cited above have been used to compile the following list of Blake's possible apprentice engravings of book illustrations. More specific reasons for inclusion, and the degree of certainty of the attributions, are indicated under each entry. See also Appendix ii, no. 1.

A. *Archaeologia: or Miscellaneous Tracts Relating to Antiquity. Published by The Society of Antiquaries of London*, vols. ii–v (1773–9)

At its meeting on 8 March 1759 the Society of Antiquaries elected James Basire Engraver to the Society (Evans 1956, p. 129). He continued in that capacity until his death in 1802. During this tenure Basire's shop produced hundreds of book illustrations for the Society, including those in its collections of miscellaneous papers published as small quarto volumes at approximately two-year intervals under the title *Archaeologia*. Many of the plates are signed by Basire as the engraver, and even those lacking a signature are very probably the work of his shop. The essays illustrated range widely through many fields of archaeological discovery and speculation, but most are concerned with single items from classical or early British antiquity. Plate sizes range from folding plates as large as 23×40 cm. to small vignettes. As Gilchrist 1863 notes, Blake's apprentice work 'may be traced under Basire's name' in this publication (i. 19). Yet I know of no way to determine the extent of Blake's work or which plates he had a hand in producing. He is most likely to have participated in the engraving of plates for the following issues:

Vol. ii (1773): four folding plates, seventeen full page, two half page, and one vignette. One plate includes an illustration of a 'Druid' trilithon, a motif Blake frequently used in his later art (e.g. *Milton* pls. a and 4, *Jerusalem* pls. 70 and 100, and pls. 5 and 7 among the Job illustrations).

Vol. iii (1775; some copies dated 1776): five folding plates, fifteen full page, seven vignettes. This volume includes Sir Joseph Ayloffe, 'An Account of the Body of King Edward the First, as it appeared on opening his Tomb in the Year 1774',

pp. 376–413 (also published as a separate pamphlet in the same year). Blake probably witnessed this event and drew two pictures of the open coffin (Butlin 1981, nos. 1–2), but Ayloffe's essay is not illustrated.

Vol. iv (1777): four folding plates, twenty-one full page, and three vignettes.

Vol. v (1779): five folding plates, twenty-six full page, three half page, and five vignettes. The next volume did not appear until 1782.

Literature: Gilchrist 1863, i. 19; Russell 1912, no. 115; Joan Evans, *A History of the Society of Antiquaries* (Oxford: Society of Antiquaries, 1956), 129, 134–47 (history of the *Archaeologia* without reference to Blake).

B. *Philosophical Transactions of the Royal Society of London*, vols. 63–9 (1773–9)

Basire was appointed official engraver to the Royal Society in 1770 (*Bryan's Dictionary of Painters and Engravers*, ed. George C. Williamson (London: Bell and Sons, 1918), i. 93). During Blake's term of apprenticeship Basire produced well over one hundred plates for the Society's annual volume of miscellaneous essays on scientific subjects, the *Philosophical Transactions*. The extent of Blake's involvement with these plates cannot be determined, but the volumes listed above are those most likely to contain his work. Contact with this publication, however minor, may have provided the young Blake with an introduction to eighteenth-century scientific investigations and the habits of thought they exhibit, a subject on which the mature Blake had much to say. For a list of the plates signed by Basire, 1772–8, arranged into subject groups, see William S. Doxey, 'William Blake, James Basire, and the *Philosophical Transactions*: An Unexplored Source of Blake's Scientific Thought?', *Bulletin of the New York Public Library*, 72 (1968), 252–60.

C. Jacob Bryant, *A New System, or, an Analysis of Ancient Mythology* (3 vols.; London: T. Payne, P. Elmsly, B. White, and J. Walter, 1774–6; 2nd edn., 1775–6); *Figs. 287–8*

Bryant's study of Near Eastern and classical mythology includes twenty-five plates signed by Basire as the engraver and three unsigned plates very probably by his shop. Blake's familiarity with the book is certain, for he refers to what 'Jacob Bryant, and all antiquaries have proved' in *A Descriptive Catalogue* of 1809 (E 543, K 578). Many of Blake's excursions into syncretic mythology may have been influenced by Bryant's theories and several of Blake's designs were very probably influenced by the illustrations in the book. For example, Basire's plate of a moon ark (iii. 601; see *Fig. 287*) is a likely source for similar vessels in *Jerusalem*, pls. 24 and 44, while Bryant's illustrations of winged circles (i, facing p. 488; see *Fig. 288*) surely influenced the same device on *Jerusalem* pl. 37. The row of figures with raised and overlapping arms on a frieze illustrated in Bryant (ii, facing p. 124) has the same configuration as one of Blake's watercolour illustrations of *c.*1795–7 to Edward Young's *Night Thoughts* (Butlin 1981, no. 330.437) and several later designs, including pl. 14 of the Job engravings. Such close parallels, however, do not offer a very solid basis for attribution, since Blake is as capable of borrowing from the work of another copy engraver as his own. Russell 1912, p. 191, was the first to suggest that some of the plates in Bryant's book 'are evidently either wholly or at least in part from the hand of Blake'. Further, 'it is possible that the design, as well as the engraving', of the moon ark 'is Blake's' because of the similarities in the treatment of waves between this plate and Blake's 'Joseph of Arimathea among the Rocks of Albion' (Essick 1983, no. I). This specific attribution is supported enthusiastically by Todd 1946, p. 38, and Keynes 1971, p. 26. The crucial stylistic evidence, however, is not compelling, for Basire used the same technique for representing short, choppy waves—see, for example, his 'View of the Antient Royal Palace called Placentia', published by the Society of Antiquaries in 1767.

There is a good possibility that Blake worked on the plates for Bryant's volumes. I am not able, however, to determine the extent of his involvement, nor to attribute individual plates to his hand, with any degree of certainty. The octavo edition of 1807 has reduced plates engraved by others.

Literature: Russell 1912, no. 110; Ruthven Todd, *Tracks in the Snow* (London: Grey Walls Press, 1946), 37–8; Bentley and Nurmi 1964, no. 355; Keynes 1971, p. 26; Bentley 1977, no. 439; Easson and Essick 1979, no. XII (with reproductions of all plates signed by, or ascribable to, Basire); Essick 1980, pp. 30–1.

D. *Memoirs of Thomas Hollis* [ed. Francis Blackburne] (London: privately printed, 1780)

The *Memoirs* of the republican, antiquarian, and bibliophile Thomas Hollis (1720–74) contains nine full-page plates and one small vignette signed by Basire as the engraver. The main reason for associating these plates with Blake is Gilchrist's inclusion of the book in his list of Blake's apprentice work, quoted above. There is, however, one other slight possibility. The book contains five portraits of John Milton, all engraved by John Baptist Cipriani in 1760 (four) and 1767 (one). In a letter of March 1879 by Samuel Palmer to George Richmond, known only through a transcription by Ruthven Todd, Palmer notes that Blake believed that one of these Milton portraits was 'indicative of his greatness'. Palmer believes that this was the plate based on 'a plaster cast or bust', a description that fits only the portrait of blind Milton facing p. 513, based on a crayon drawing by William Faithorne. Palmer then argues that the face (but not the torso, background, or framing wreath) in this plate is executed in a style different from that of Cipriani's other portraits, and that the engraving of the face is attributable to Blake. Palmer's claim that Blake knew and approved of these portraits is confirmed by Blake's conversation about them with Henry Crabb Robinson in 1825 (Bentley 1969, pp. 317 n. 1, 543). The specific plate discussed by Palmer may have influenced Blake's portrait of Milton among the 'Heads of the Poets' of *c.*1800–3 (Butlin 1981, no. 343.11). That tempera painting is based on William Faithorne's engraving, but Blake has changed his sighted visage of Milton to a blind one, as in the Hollis plate.

It is of course possible that Cipriani's plate of 1770 was reworked in Basire's shop for publication in Hollis's *Memoirs*. However, neither the evidence of Blake's interest in the plate, nor the stylistic speculation offered by Palmer, makes a convincing case for attributing the engraving to Basire, much less Blake. The stipple work on the face is a bit finer and denser than in Cipriani's other portrait plates; but low-power magnification reveals that the technique, including the integration of stipple with line-and-flick work, is the same on all the plates. There is nothing in the execution of the plate facing p. 513 to suggest the graver of Blake or his master.

Literature: Russell 1912, no. 112 (singles out a plate of a sculpted monument with a winged head for its 'Blake-like qualities'); G. E. Bentley, jun., 'A Portrait of Milton Engraved by William Blake "When Three years of Age"? A Speculation by Samuel Palmer', *University of Toronto Quarterly*, 51 (1981), 28–35 (discussion of Palmer's letter and the plate in question).

E. Joseph Ayloffe, *An Account of Some Ancient Monuments in Westminster Abbey* (London: Society of Antiquaries, 1780); reissued as part of the Society's *Vetusta Monumenta*, vol. ii (London, *c.*1789)

Ayloffe's essay is accompanied by seven large engravings, about 46.5 × 29 cm., picturing the monuments of Aveline, Countess of Lancaster, King Sebert (including a figure of Henry III), and Anne of Cleves. All are signed *Basire del. et Sc.*, indicating not only that Basire's shop engraved the plates, but that the drawings of the monuments were 'taken under the inspection of Mr. Basire' when the 'wainscot and tapestry hangings' covering the monuments were removed 'in the summer of the year 1775' (as Ayloffe states, pp. 1, 4). Malkin's account of Blake's apprentice activities in Westminster Abbey (see introduction to this Appendix) includes the statement that he made drawings of 'all the old monuments in Westminster Abbey' (Bentley 1969, p. 423). Since we have good evidence that Blake was making drawings for Gough's book *c.*1774–9 (see **F**), it would have made sense for Basire to have Blake make the Ayloffe drawings rather than hiring a third party. This circumstantial evidence, plus stylistic considerations, led Martin Butlin to attribute to Blake the nine finished preliminary drawings now in the Society of Antiquaries, London (Butlin 1981, nos. 3–11). Basire's name on these drawings may have been added some years after the production of the drawings themselves. Replicas of these drawings, also attributed to Blake, are in the Bodleian Library, Oxford (Butlin 1981, nos. 12–18).

Given the probability of Blake's authorship of the preliminary drawings for all seven plates, it seems likely that he also had some hand in engraving them. That possibility, however, is somewhat diminished by the fact that, according to the minutes of the Society of Antiquaries, proofs of the Ayloffe plates were not pre-sented until 14 March 1780 (Miner 1963, p. 642 n. 11), six and a half months after the end of Blake's term of apprenticeship with Basire.

Literature: W. R. Lethaby, *Westminster Abbey and the Kings' Craftsmen* (London: Duckworth, 1906), 371; Russell 1912, nos. 113 (Blake is 'likely ... to have assisted his master, Basire, in the work of engraving' the plates), 114; Wright 1929 (see **XLIV**, *Literature*), i. 5–6 (the plates 'were doubtless partly, and probably largely, Blake's work'); Blunt 1959 (see **XXI**, *Literature*), p. 3 n. 3 (the plates are 'clearly by Blake'); Paul Miner, 'The Apprentice of Great Queen Street', *Bulletin of the New York Public Library*, 67 (1963), 639–42; Keynes 1971, p. 17; Bentley 1977, no. 503; Easson and Essick 1979, no. XVI (with reproductions of all seven plates); Essick 1983, no. LIX (separate sale of the plates).

F. Richard Gough, *Sepulchral Monuments in Great Britain*, Part I (sometimes divided into 2 vols., and so indicated on the title-pages) (London: For the Author, and sold by T. Payne, 1786; vol. i of Part II, 1796); *Figs. 289–94*

Gough's study includes twenty-three plates, signed by Basire, of monuments in Westminster Abbey. Malkin's comments on these, quoted in part in the introduction to this Appendix, are the best authority for attributing some of the drawings for these plates to Blake. This documentary evidence, coupled with stylistic considerations, led Martin Butlin to attribute to Blake twenty-nine preliminary drawings for Gough, now in the Bodleian Library (Butlin 1981, nos. 19–47). Malkin's general statement that Blake engraved his drawings of 'old buildings and monuments' lends some support to the supposition that Blake probably had a hand in producing plates based on his own drawings. The Bodleian also houses the original copperplates for Gough, as well as a large collection of proofs before letters and impressions in published states.

Among the Gough plates signed by Basire, six large oval portraits demand particular notice. Malkin singles out the monuments of 'King Henry the Third, the beautiful monument and figure of Queen Elinor, Queen Philippa, King Edward the Third, King Richard the Second and his Queen [Anne]' and states that the 'heads' of these monarchs were 'considered as portraits' by Blake (Bentley 1969, p. 422). The drawings for these plates are in pencil, whereas all the other preliminaries are in pen and wash. In accord with these different media, the engravings of the heads are in a style clearly distinct from the typical Basire shop-techniques that lend anonymity to their companion plates. All six portraits are developed with bold and extremely simple patterns of hatching and cross-hatching—just what we might expect from an apprentice. Yet this simplicity suggests the innovator as much as the amateur, and the visibility of the hatching patterns gives them something of the graphic self-reflexivity distinguishing Blake's later work. Among all of Blake's possible apprentice plates, these six have the greatest likelihood of being in large part his own productions. Accordingly, they are reproduced herein and individually catalogued below. In the BL copy of Gough, pls. 3–6 are bound in 'Vol. I. Part II', dated 1796 on the title-page. In other copies, all the plates described here are bound in Part I of 1786.

Blake's work for Basire in Westminster Abbey had a profound effect upon his interest in ancient England and his idealization of a medieval aesthetic in his nineteenth-century writings on the arts. Blake's early interest in the old kings and queens of England is also evinced by the dramatic fragment, 'King Edward the Third' (see pls. 3 and 4) printed in *Poetical Sketches*, 1783.

1. Facing p. 57; 35.8 × 27.1 cm.; *Fig. 289*

Inscription top right: *Pl. XXII. p. 57.*
Title: *Portrait of Henry III. from his Monument.*
Stipple signature right: *Basire del & Sc.*

For the drawing of Henry III (d. 1272), see Butlin 1981, no. 22. The effigy was sculpted by Pietro Odersi c.1280. There are four proofs in the Bodleian Library: one lacking all letters, two inscribed 'Henry II. Pl. XXX' (one corrected with pen and ink) and the signature in line rather than stipple, and one with the signature in line, faint and partly erased (in preparation for re-engraving in stipple?).

2. Facing p. 63; 33.4 × 27.3 cm.; *Fig. 290*

Inscription top right: *Pl. XXIII*. p. 63.*
Title: *Portrait of Queen Eleanor from her Monument.*
Signature right: *Basire del. & sc.*

For the drawing of this head, see Butlin 1981, no. 25. A proof before all letters, and six impressions of the published state (one with the signature not inked), are in the Bodleian Library. Blake's continued interest in Eleanor of Castille (d. 1290) and her husband, King Edward I, is indicated by his separate plate of 1793, 'Edward & Elenor' (Essick 1983, no. IV). The 'Visionary Head' (c.1819–20) of *Queen Eleanor* may also represent this woman, although several other queens have the same name (Butlin 1981, no. 726; see also nos. 335.62, 655). A photograph of the head of the effigy (by William Torel, 1291) is reproduced in Pevsner 1957, pl. 11, and in Miner 1963, following p. 642.

3. Facing p. 125; 32.9 × 26.8 cm.; *Fig. 291*

Inscription top right: *Pl. XLIX. p. 125.*

Title: *Portrait of Queen Philippa from her Monument.*
Signature right: *Basire del. & sc.*

The tomb effigy of Philippa of Hainault (d. 1369), wife of Edward III, was carved in marble by Hennequin de Liége. For the preliminary drawing, see Butlin 1981, no. 40. There are three proofs in the Bodleian Library, two lacking all letters and many of the lines throughout the image, and one without letters lacking only some of the shading strokes on the face and neck. A proof in the collection of Raymond Lister lacks all letters but bears the title inscription in pen and ink and a pencil note (by Gough?) objecting to the spelling of 'Philippa'. According to J. T. Smith, in his life of Blake published in 1828, Thomas Stothard stated that Blake drew 'the head of Queen Philippa' (Butlin 1981, no. 40), but referred to the plate as having been 'engraved by Basire' (Bentley 1969, p. 466). This last comment may only be a reference to the signature on the plate and not a specific attribution. For Gilchrist's attribution of this plate to Blake, see the introduction to this Appendix. A photograph of the head of the effigy is poorly reproduced in Miner 1963, following p. 642.

4. Facing p. 139; 35.3 × 26.8 cm.; *Fig. 292*

Inscription top right: *Pl. LV. p. 139.*
Stipple and line signature, centre: *Basire del et Sc.*
Title: *Portrait of Edward III. from his Monument.*

The effigy of Edward III (d. 1377) was probably carved by John Orchard. For the preliminary drawing, see Butlin 1981, no. 43. There is also a related drawing, 9.5 × 7.8 cm., of the head and upper torso of Edward III in the Victoria Library, London (for description and reproduction, see Butlin 1988). There are two proofs lacking all letters in the Bodleian Library. A photograph of the head of the effigy is reproduced in Miner 1963, facing p. 642.

5. Facing p. 165; 35.2 × 26.9 cm.; *Fig. 293*

Inscription top right: *Pl. LXIII. p. 165.*
Stipple and line signature, centre: *Basire del et Sc.*
Title: *Portrait of Richard II. from his Monument.*

For the drawing of Richard II (d. 1400), see Butlin 1981, no. 46. One proof in the Bodleian Library lacks all letters; another lacks only the signature. A photograph of the head of the bronze effigy (by Nicholas Broker and Geoffrey Prest) is reproduced in Pevsner 1957, pl. 15, and in Miner 1963, facing p. 643.

6. Facing p. 167; 34.5 × 26.9 cm.; *Fig. 294*

Inscription top right: *Pl. LXIV. p. 167.*
Stipple and line signature, centre: *Basire del. et Sc.*
Title: *Portrait of Anne Queen of Richard II. from her Monument.*

The effigy of Richard's first queen, Anne of Bohemia (d. 1394), was also sculpted by Broker and Prest (see pl. 5). For the preliminary drawing, see Butlin 1981, no. 47. One proof in the Bodleian Library lacks all letters and the cross-hatching on the figure's right shoulder immediately above the floral clasp; another proof lacks only the signature and the final digit, top right.

Literature: Gilchrist 1863, i. 17–20, ii. 259; Russell 1912, no. 117 (Blake was 'probably … the engraver of some of' the plates); Keynes 1921, no. 67 (the engraving of the 'Portraits is characteristic and may with certainty be attributed to Blake'); Laurence Binyon, *The Engraved Designs of William Blake* (London: Ernest Benn, 1926), nos. 2–7 ('it is probable that' pl. 3 'and other heads in a similar style were engraved as well as drawn by Blake'); Nikolaus Pevsner, *London: I, The Cities of London and Westminster* (London: Penguin, 1957); Blunt 1959 (see **XXI**, *Literature*), p. 3 (Blake engraved 'some' of the plates, singling out pls. 3 and 4); Miner 1963 (see **E**, *Literature*); Bentley and Nurmi 1964, no. 372; Keynes 1971, pp. 14–18 ('there are strong reasons for believing that many of the plates … were done by' Blake, singling out pls. 1–6 plus twelve others); Bentley 1977, no. 461 ('it seems likely that Blake engraved some of' the plates); Easson and Essick 1979, no. XXXI (with reproductions of all twenty-three plates of monuments in Westminster Abbey signed by Basire, including one (Easson and Essick pl. 19) based on a drawing not attributed to Blake in Butlin 1981); Essick 1980, pp. 31–2; Martin Butlin, 'A New Blake from his Apprentice Years?', *Blake: An Illustrated Quarterly*, 21 (1988), 143.

Appendix ii
False and Conjectural Attributions

OVER the years, a good many questionable and unsubstantiated attributions of book illustrations have gathered around the name of Blake. The very anonymity of so much copy engraving, along with Blake's own practice of conventional house styles in his early years, has contributed to the ease with which one can say that Blake 'might' have been the engraver of a great many unsigned plates. In at least two instances (see nos. **16** and **35**, below), plates bearing 'Blake' signatures are probably the work of some other, lesser craftsman of the same name. A few doubtful attributions were initiated by nineteenth-century booksellers whose optimism may have been prompted by financial considerations. Even when denied by disinterested scholars, some of these ascriptions have been perpetuated innocently by later dealers and curators.

No list of false and conjectural attributions has been published since Russell 1912. A good deal of information has come to light since then, and further questionable ascriptions have been proposed. The following accounting includes engraved book illustrations that have been attributed to Blake, or suggested as possibly by him, with what I believe to be insufficient evidence. In all such cases I assume that the burden of proof rests on those making attributions. In a few cases, such as no. **17**, informed opinions may differ and evidence as yet undiscovered could justify the ascriptions to Blake. I am very grateful to G. E. Bentley, jun., for pointing out to me many of these questionable attributions.

1. James Cook, *A Voyage towards the South Pole, and Round the World* (2 vols.; London: W. Strahan and T. Cadell, 1777)

Smith 1985 (see **XXVII**, *Literature*), p. 174, reproduces two plates from this work signed by William Hodges as the designer and James Basire as the engraver, 'Man of the Island of Tanna' and 'Woman of the Island of Tanna' (ii, facing pp. 78, 80), and comments that 'it is not too fanciful to glimpse, in their wiry linearity and characteristic intensity, the presence of Blake's own hand'. The same attribution is suggested, with particular attention to the supposedly Blakean qualities of the curly-headed child in the second plate, in Rüdiger Joppien and Bernard Smith, *The Art of Captain Cook's Voyages* (New Haven: Yale Univ. Press, 1985), ii. 110, with the two plates and Hodges's drawing for the second reproduced. I see no more reason to attribute these engravings to Blake than a host of other plates by Basire datable to the period of Blake's apprenticeship (see Appendix i).

2. *Etchings of Coade's Artificial Stone Manufacture* (London: privately printed, *c.*1777–9), often bound as a companion to [Eleanor] Coade, *A Descriptive Catalogue of Coade's Artificial Stone Manufactory* (London: to be had at the Manufactory, and of J. Strahan, 1784)

According to S. B. Hamilton, 'Coade Stone', *Architectural Review*, 116 (1954), 295–301, the first plate in this group of trade-catalogue illustrations was 'etched by William Blake' (p. 297). This unsupported attribution is quoted and discussed in catalogue 6 issued by the Bath bookdealer James Burmester in April 1987, item A. The unsigned plate in question, showing a statue of a 'River God, with an Urn' (item 1 in the 1784 catalogue), is etched in a free style similar to the one used by John Hamilton Mortimer and other etchers of his designs. In 1790 Blake used a modified version of this style for two plates after Fuseli (Essick 1983, nos. XXXIII and XXXIV), but this slight parallel is insufficient to support an attribution of the river-god plate to Blake (reproduced Hamilton, p. 296). Further,

Blake was still an apprentice during most of the period when the plate was probably executed (according to Burmester). An impression of the plate, acquired by the BMPR in 1873, is inscribed 'by Blake' in pencil, but has long been housed in a folder marked 'Doubtful'.

3. *The Lady's Magazine* (London: G. Robinson or G. G. J. and J. Robinson, 1779–1818)

Gilchrist 1863, i. 32, states that, 'during the years 1779 to 1782 and onwards, one of two booksellers gave him [Blake] employment in engraving from afterwards better known fellow designers. Harrison of Paternoster Row employed him for his *Novelists' [sic] Magazine* [XI], or collection of approved novels; for his *Ladies' Magazine* [sic], and perhaps other serials.' One of the 'better known ... designers' to whom Gilchrist alludes was probably Stothard, who designed all the plates Blake engraved for *The Novelist's Magazine* and may have designed as many as ninety plates for *The Lady's Magazine* between 1780 and 1797, although none bears his name. Nor do any of the plates bear an engraver's signature, although it is possible for Blake to have executed some of them, *c*.1779–90, when he was using graphic techniques indistinguishable from those employed by several other craftsmen. A few of these plates are engraved in a style similar to what we see in *The Novelist's Magazine*, while others look nothing like Blake's work. The fact that Robinson published *The Lady's Magazine*, rather than Harrison, for whom Blake engraved numerous plates, slightly lessens the viability of this attribution.

See Essick 1983, no. LIV, for a plate signed 'Blake Sc.', known only through separate impressions, which Coxhead 1906, p. 46, associates with *The Lady's Magazine*. The presence of a J. Johnson imprint on the second state of this plate, 'The Morning Amusements of her Royal Highness [and] A Lady in the full Dress', considerably reduces the possibility that it was intended for a magazine published by Robinson.

Literature: A. C. Coxhead, *Thomas Stothard* (London: A. H. Bullen, 1906), 42–9 (a list of illustrations in the magazine possibly by Stothard); Russell 1912, no. 111 (Blake 'may well have' engraved 'some' of the plates).

4. Henry Emlyn, *A Proposition for a New Order in Architecture* (1781, 1784, 1797)

For the attribution of an unsigned plate in this volume to Blake, see **IV**.

5. *The Lady's Poetical Magazine, or Beauties of British Poetry* (4 vols.; London: Harrison and Co., 1781–2)

John Thomas Smith, *Nollekens and his Times* (London: Henry Colburn, 1828), ii. 471, includes the following statement in a footnote: 'The collectors of Stothard's numerous and elegant designs, will recollect the name of Blake as the engraver of several plates in the Novelist's Magazine [XI], the Poetical Magazine, and also others for a work entitled the Wit's Magazine [XVI], from drawings produced by the same artist' (repr. in Bentley 1969, p. 466). There are several difficulties with this statement. The two works Smith names with known Blake engravings were published in 1782–4, but there is no 'Poetical Magazine' until 1804 and Stothard is not known to have designed illustrations for any publication of that title. Smith was probably referring to *The Lady's Poetical Magazine*, a work issued by the same company that published the two other works he mentions. Stothard designed twenty-nine full-page illustrations and five vignettes for *The Lady's Poetical Magazine*, but all are signed by engravers other than Blake. The attribution is noted, without comment, in Russell 1912, no. 135. Stothard's full-page plates are listed in Coxhead 1906 (see **3**, *Literature*), pp. 33–7.

6. William Frederick Martyn, *The Geographical Magazine, or, New System of Geography* (2 vols.; London: Harrison and Co., 1782)

Coxhead 1906 (see **3**, *Literature*), pp. 168–9, states that the frontispieces to these two volumes, designed by Stothard and dated 1782 and 1784 in their imprints, were 'engraved by Blake'. As Russell 1912, No. 116, points out, both plates are clearly signed by James Heath as the engraver. Coxhead may simply have confused this work with **XVII**.

7. Daniel Fenning and Joseph Collyer, *A New System of Geography* (1785–6)

For the conjectural attribution to Blake of the frontispiece to vol. i, see **XVII**, pl. 1.

8. *Little Thumb and the Ogre* (1788)

Blake 'contributed some metal-engravings' to this book, according to David Bland, *The Illustration of Books* (London: Faber and Faber, 1951), 96. The claim is repeated in the second edition (1953), p. 96, and in the third (1962), p. 128. I have not been able to locate a copy of this work or any other reference to it. It is unlikely that its illustrations were engraved by Blake.

9. Joachim Heinrich Campe, *Elementary Dialogues, for the Improvement of Youth*, trans. Mr Seymour (London: Hookham and Carpenter, 1792)

For Quaritch's attribution of the sixteen unsigned plates to Blake in a '1791' edition (no copy or other listing located), see **17**, below. Like Russell 1912, no. 121 (citing a 1798 edition), I can find no reason to attribute these poorly executed plates to Blake. They resemble in design the illustrations in Salzmann's *Elements of Morality* (**XXIII**), and may also be based on originals by Chodowiecki, but the graphic style of the Campe plates is very different from Blake's.

10. [Elizabeth Pinchard], *Dramatic Dialogues, for the Use of Young Persons. By the Author of The Blind Child* (London: E. Newbery, 1792)

A copy of this work in the Pierpont Morgan Library, New York, bears the following pencil note on the verso of the front free endpaper: 'Wm Blake|Early work of | Excessively scarce'. I can find no basis for attributing the three unsigned plates to Blake.

The frontispiece, designed and engraved by Blake, for *The Prologue and Characters of Chaucer's Pilgrims* (London: Harris, 1812), bears an imprint recording 'Newberry' of St Paul's Church Yard as its publisher (Bentley 1977, no. 443). This indicates that Blake had dealings with Elizabeth Newbery in the nineteenth century, and thus may have worked for her as a copy engraver in earlier years. No such plates, however, have come to light. See also **13** and **14**, below.

11. *The Fables of Aesop* (2 vols.; London: John Stockdale, 1793)

An advertisement bound at the end of some copies of Gay's *Fables*, published by Stockdale in 1793 (see **XXVI**), states that his edition of 'Barlow's Aesop's Fables' includes 'Barlow's Designs . . . engraved by . . . Blake' and others. Of the 112 plates in this work, 108 are signed by engravers other than Blake. Only one among the four unsigned plates (ii, facing p. 35) bears any clear resemblance to Blake's work, but the similarities are far from sufficient to be the basis for an attribution.

12. John Flaxman, *The Odyssey of Homer Engraved by Thomas Piroli from the Compositions of John Flaxman Sculptor* (Rome, 1793)

Gilchrist 1863, i. 114, states that the 'first set of plates' of Flaxman's classical outlines, 'those to the *Odyssey*,— were lost in the voyage to England, and Blake was obtained to make engravings in their stead, although Piroli's name still remained on the general title-page (dated 1793); probably as being likelier credentials with the public'. As usual, Gilchrist offers no source for this information. There is independent authority for Piroli's copperplates having been seized by the French in their journey from Italy to England (Bentley 1964, pp. 19–20), but it seems highly unlikely that Blake had anything to do with engraving another group of plates. There are two 1793 printings of the *Odyssey* illustrations from two different sets of copperplates, but the very slight graphic differences between them are insufficient indications of two different engravers. Both printings are on paper of continental manufacture, and this would seem unlikely if one set of plates had been produced in England, particularly in light of the political situation that prevented delivery of the original set of coppers and blocked most commerce between England and the Continent. Just as Piroli seems to have made more than one set of plates of Flaxman's *Iliad* and Aeschylus designs, he probably executed the replacement set of the *Odyssey* copperplates. The plates in the London 1805 edition of the *Odyssey* illustrations are signed by James Parker and John Neagle as their engravers.

Literature: Gilchrist 1863, ii. 260; Russell 1912, no. 122 (denying the attribution); Edward Croft-Murray, 'An Account-Book of John Flaxman', in *The Twenty-Eighth Volume of the Walpole Society* (Oxford: Univ. Press, 1940), 54 (attributing the *Odyssey* plates to Blake without explanation); Bentley 1964 (see **XLVI**, *Literature*), pp. 16–21 (a full and convincing discussion).

13. [H. S.], *Anecdotes of Mary; or, The Good Governess. By the Author of the History of the Davenport Family* (London: E. Newbery, 1795)

Russell 1912, no. 81, and Keynes 1921, no. 107, state that the unsigned frontispiece is 'probably engraved by Blake'. This attribution has not been accepted by later scholars. I can find no convincing evidence for the ascription to Blake, although the plate has some general similarities in technique to his work in Salzmann's *Elements of Morality* (**XXIII**). For Blake's later contact with the publisher Newbery, see **10**, above.

14. [Richard Johnson?], *Moral Sketches for Young Minds* (London: E. Newbery, 1797)

According to Joyce Irene Whalley and Tessa Rose Chester, *A History of Children's Book Illustration* (London: John Murray, 1988), 30, it 'has been suggested' that Blake 'had a hand in the illustrations' appearing in '*Moral Sketches for Young Minds* (1797)'. The authors offer no evidence for this claim, nor do they indicate who has made such a suggestion. I see no reason to attribute these six unsigned plates to Blake. For Blake's later contact with the publisher Newbery, see **10**, above.

15. Mrs [Sarah] Trimmer, *Series of Prints from the Old Testament. Designed to Accompany a Book Intitled, Scripture Lessons* (London: John Marshall, n.d. [pl. 1 dated 1797]. *A Series of Prints Taken from the Old Testament; Designed to Illustrate Mrs. Trimmer's Scripture Lessons* (London: Baldwin, Cradock, and Joy, *et al.*, 1817, 1825, 1829)

In his 1885 flyer (see **17**, below), Quaritch attributes to Blake the sixty-four plates in a work entitled 'Scripture Lessons, illustrated by a Series of (64) Prints, 2 vols., 24mo, 1816–17'. Like Russell 1912, no. 132 (where the title is given as *A Series of Prints Taken from the Old Testament, Designed to Illustrate Mrs. Trimmer's Scripture Lessons*, 1797), I find no reason to attribute these crude, unsigned plates to Blake. A different and slightly more skilful set of twenty-four unsigned plates, based on different designs, appears in *A New Series of Prints, Accompanied by Easy Lessons: Being an Improved Edition of the First Set of Scripture Prints, from the Old Testament* (London: J. Harris, J. Hatchard, B. Tabart, 1803; repr. 1808, 1816, 1822). Yet a third different set of thirty-one exceedingly crude and unsigned plates appears in *A Series of Prints, Designed to Illustrate the Scripture History of Mrs. Trimmer* (London: Baldwin and Cradock, N. Hailes, John Marshall, 1828). There is no basis for ascribing any of these plates to Blake, nor those in various editions of illustrations to Trimmer's *Scripture Lessons* on the New Testament.

16. *The Poetry of Various Glees, Songs, &c., as Performed at the Harmonists* [ed. George Fryer?] (London: Printed at the Philanthropic Reform, 1798)

The frontispiece to this work is signed 'Blake sc. Change Alley' in some copies but unsigned in others.

Russell 1912, no. 90, attributes this plate to Blake; Keynes 1921, no. 117, includes the book but expresses doubts. We now know that the Blake who worked at 'Change' (i.e. Exchange) Alley was the writing engraver William Staden Blake (*c.*1746–1817). For information on W. S. Blake, see G. E. Bentley, jun., 'A Collection of Prosaic William Blakes', *Notes and Queries*, 12 (1965), 174–6; Keynes 1971, pp. 46–9.

17. Christian Gotthilf Salzmann, *Gymnastics for Youth* (London: J. Johnson, 1800), *Fig. 295*

The first to attribute the ten unsigned plates in this volume to Blake was the London bookseller Bernard Quaritch. In an advertising flyer entitled 'William Blake's Original Drawings' and dated May 1885, Quaritch offers as a single lot for £28 eleven books 'illustrated with Blake's Plates, or with designs engraved by him' (p. 2). The group contains five works with plates signed by Blake, plus Salzmann's *Elements of Morality* (**XXIII**), his *Gymnastics for Youth*, and four titles also included in this appendix (**9, 15, 21, 26**). The flyer was reissued in November 1886 (and, according to Keynes 1921, p. 295, again in May 1887), and the same group of volumes was offered as lot 10258 in Quaritch's massive *General Catalogue* of 1887. The collection did not sell, and was offered in several later catalogues, including those of February 1891 (lot 106, £25) and January 1895 ('Rough List' no. 147, pp. 47–8, £15).

Quaritch's attribution of the plates in Salzmann's *Gymnastics* is rejected by Ralph Thomas (*Notes and Queries*, 11 (1897), 302–3) and by Russell 1912, no. 123, but accepted by Keynes 1921, no. 121, for unexplained stylistic reasons. Bentley and Nurmi 1964, no. 403, and Bentley 1977, no. 493, accept the plates as Blake's work, 'though not happily'. The graphic technique shows some similarity to the plates in Salzmann's *Elements of Morality*, and this alone may have prompted Quaritch's original ascription. But this parallel is only superficial. The deviations from conventional norms in the *Elements* illustrations result in large part from the exaggeration and simplification of standard techniques. The crudities in the *Gymnastics* plates do not seem the result of such purposeful (if not always successful) innovations, but simply the product of an unskilled execution of conventional hatching and cross-hatching patterns. In comparison to plates engraved by Blake for Johnson at about the same time, such as those for Allen's two books (**XXXVI, XXXVII**), the *Gymnastics* plates exhibit nothing of the characteristic style

Blake had developed by the late 1790s. One cannot absolutely exclude the possibility that Blake produced the *Gymnastics* plates as mere hack work, but the evidence for his involvement is insufficient to support Quaritch's attribution. I reproduce one plate, facing p. 237 in the *Gymnastics*, as an example (*Fig. 295*).

18. *An Authentic Narrative of the Life of J. W.* [Joseph Wall] (London: J. Roach, 1802)

This book is said to have a 'frontispiece perhaps by Blake' in the Sotheby auction catalogue of the collection of W. E. Moss, 2 March 1937, lot 226 (with sixteen other works, £1. 10s. to 'Last'). The only copy I have been able to locate (BL) is of the 'Second Edition' (n.d.) and contains no plates. It is unlikely that the apparently unsigned plate reported in the Sotheby catalogue is by Blake.

19. *Short Stories in Words of One Syllable* (1803)

See **27**, below.

20. William Enfield, *Exercises in Elocution* (a new edn., London: J. Johnson, 1804)

G. E. Bentley, jun., tells me that a copy of this work belonging to Wilmarth S. Lewis contains a pencil note stating that the unsigned frontispiece, 'The Choice of Hercules', is perhaps by Blake. I can find no reason for attributing this or the three other unsigned plates to Blake. All appear to be crude copies (or perhaps greatly reworked states) of the plates appearing in some earlier editions (e.g. 1795, 1798, 1801), signed by James Heath as their engraver. The plates in the 1804 edition repeat the 1782 imprint dates on Heath's plates.

21. Edward Baldwin [pseudonym of William Godwin], *Fables Ancient and Modern* (2 vols.; London: Thomas Hodgkins, 1805)

For Quaritch's attribution of the '73' (actually seventy-two) unsigned plates to Blake, see **17**, above. Like Russell 1912, no. 124, I find no basis for ascribing these crude, but charmingly picturesque, plates to Blake. The designer was 'probably' Mulready (see **26**, below), according to F. G. Stephens, *Memorials of William Mulready* (London: Bell and Daldy, 1867), 27.

22. *The Book of Trades, or Library of the Useful Arts,* Part III (London: Tabart and Co., 1805)

According to the card catalogue at the Liverpool University Library, its two copies of this work contain plates by Blake. I can find no basis for attributing these twenty crude, unsigned prints to Blake, dated 1804 or 1805 in their imprints.

23. Edward Baldwin [pseudonym of William Godwin], *The Pantheon: or Ancient History of the Gods of Greece and Rome* (London: Thomas Hodgkins, 1806)

Russell 1912, no. 126, states that the twelve unsigned plates in this work are 'commonly ascribed to Blake', but I have not been able to find such an assertion in print prior to 1912. Like Russell, I find no basis for attributing these loosely etched plates to Blake, although bookdealers have claimed as much as late as the 1970s. See also **21**, above.

24. David Hume, *The History of England* (5 vols. (sometimes bound in 10); London: R. Bowyer, 1806)

'W. Blake' is named as one of the 'eminent Engravers' commissioned to execute plates for this work in Robert Bowyer's prospectus of 'January, 1792' in the John Johnson Collection, Bodleian Library. Another prospectus in the same collection, probably issued in the next month, states that the same engravers 'are actually engaged' in preparing the illustrations (Bentley 1969, p. 46). However, all 195 plates in Bowyer's edition are signed by engravers other than Blake.

25. François Fénelon, *The Adventures* [*History* on the printed wrapper] *of Telemachus* (London: B. Tabart, 1807)

Russell 1912, no. 127 (citing the '*History of Telemachus*'), states that the four unsigned and hand-coloured plates in this work 'are attributed to Blake', but does not give the source or reason for such an ascription, nor his own opinion of it. I can find no reason to attribute these simple engravings to Blake.

26. Charles [and Mary] Lamb, *Tales from Shakespeare Designed for the Use of Young Persons* (2 vols.; London: Thomas Hodgkins, 1807; M. J. Godwin & Co., 1810, 1816, 1822)

Twenty unsigned plates, said to be 'by Wm. Blake' in William Thomas Lowndes, *The Bibliographer's Manual*, rev. Henry G. Bohn (London: Bohn, 1858), ii. 1300. For Quaritch's repetition of this attribution, see **17**, above. The illustrations were designed by William Mulready (1786–1863), a close friend of John Varley, who knew Blake (but probably not before 1818 (see Bentley 1969, p. 257)). Luther S. Livingston, *A Bibliography of . . . Charles and Mary Lamb* (New York: J. A. Spoor, 1903), 64, notes that 'the plates were engraved by William Blake', while Ralph Thomas, *Notes and Queries*, 5 (1906), 86, states that 'there is every probability that [Blake] engraved Mulready's drawings'. Like Russell 1912, no. 128, Keynes 1921, p. 195, and Kathryn Moore Heleniak, *William Mulready* (New Haven: Yale Univ. Press, 1980), 233 n. 87, I can find no basis for such an attribution, most recently repeated in Marcia Pointon, *Mulready* (London: Victoria and Albert Museum, 1986), no. 123.

27. *Stories of Old Daniel: or Tales of Wonder and Delight* (London: Juvenile Library, 1808)

A copy in the BL is inscribed on the inside front cover in pencil, 'W. Blake's frontispieces', and on the front free endpaper, 'the frontispiece is by W. Blake'. The first inscription apparently refers to the unsigned frontispieces in *Stories of Old Daniel* and in the work bound with it: *Short Stories in Words of One Syllable by the Author of Summer Rambles* (London: E. Lloyd, 1803). I see no reason to attribute either plate to Blake. The BL inscription may be the basis for Stephanie Hutcheson's claim, in the Preface (p. xxi) to a facsimile of the 1810 edition of *Stories of Old Daniel* (New York: Johnson Reprints, 1969), that the frontispiece in one of two 1810 editions 'has been attributed to William Blake'. A copy of the 1810 edition at the BL contains the unsigned plate, but other copies of both 1808 (HEH and Osborne Collection, Toronto Public Library) and 1810 (Osborne Collection, reproduced in the 1969 facsimile) contain a different plate of the same basic image, signed by Henry Corbould as the designer and 'Springsguth' as the engraver. *Stories of Old Daniel* has frequently been attributed to Charles Lamb, but the 1969 facsimile attributes it to Margaret Jane (King) Moore, Countess of Mount Cashell.

28. Tom Tit, *The Eagle's Masque* (London: J. Mawman, 1808)

Russell 1912, no. 198, states that the six crude, unsigned plates are 'sometimes stated to be engraved by Blake', but gives no examples of such statements. Like Russell, I find no reason for this attribution, nor can I find any confirmation of Russell's note that William Mulready is the book's author (see also **26**, above). The plates in the copy now in the BL are stated to be 'attributed to William Blake' in Thomas James Wise, *The Ashley Library: A Catalogue* (London: privately printed, 1922), i. 35.

29. Samuel Johnson, Oliver Goldsmith, *et al.*, *Moral Tales, Eastern Tales, &c.* (4 vols.; 1809)

Russell 1912, no. 130, states that 'several of the plates in these volumes are commonly ascribed to Blake' but is 'unable to state whether or no this is the case'. I have not been able to find a copy of this work or any other listing of it.

30. William Frederic Mylius, *The Junior Class-Book; or, Reading Lessons for Every Day in the Year* (London, 1809)

According to the auction catalogue of the H. Buxton Forman collection, Anderson Galleries, New York, 26 April 1920, lot 53, this book is 'illustrated with six plates by Blake'. I have not been able to locate a copy, but suspect that this attribution has no merit.

31. *The Minor's Pocket Book* (1814)

According to its acquisition records, the BMPR purchased from 'Messʳˢ Evans' on 9 July 1859, no. 748, 'an illustration' attributed to Blake (but perhaps as the designer and not the engraver): ' "The World before the Flood. Canto 7. page 136" being the Frontispiece to The Minor's Pocket Book. 1814'. I have not been able to find such a print at the BMPR or any copy or other listing of the book. For a discussion of this acquisition record, see G. E. Bentley, jun., 'A Fugitive or Apocryphal Blake Engraving', *Blake Newsletter*, 2 (1969), 74.

32. Arthur Crichton, *The Festival of Flora* (2nd edn., London: N. Hailes, 1818; engraved title-page and plates dated 1819)

G. E. Bentley, jun., tells me that a Puttick & Simpson

auction catalogue of 30 June 1899 (no copy located) claims that the eight plates in this work are by Blake. I can find no reason to attribute these crude, unsigned engravings to his hand. The first edition (1815) is not illustrated.

33. Abraham Rees, *The Cyclopaedia* (1820)

For evidence that Blake may have been involved in the production of an additional engraving ('Basso Relievo' pl. I) in this work, see LII, pl. 2.

34. *Plutarch's Lives, Abridged, Selected and Adapted for Youth by J. Faucit Savill* (London, 1823)

According to the auction catalogue of the H. Buxton Forman collection, Anderson Galleries, New York, 26 April 1920, lot 55, this work contains 'a brilliant woodcut frontispiece by Blake'. I have not been able to locate a copy, but suspect that this attribution is without merit.

35. *The Seaman's Recorder*, vol. i (London: J. Eedes, 1824); vol ii (London: J. Gifford, 1825); vol. i repr. (London: Jacques & Wright, 1827)

Bentley 1970, pp. 31–6, attributes to Blake six engravings in this work, all signed 'Blake sc' or 'Blake del et sc.'. In spite of this prima-facie evidence, Keynes 1972, p. 60, sharply rejects the attribution and comments that the plates had 'obviously been executed by an incompetent craftsman whose name happened to be Blake'. William Blake might have been capable of such crude work in his early years, but it is totally out of character with his great skill and highly individual style

of the 1820s. Heppner 1978 has demonstrated that the signatures on the *Seaman's* plates are very similar to the 'Blake' and 'E. Blake' signatures on some engravings of theatrical characters published by W. West in 1825 (see Russell 1912, no. 131, and Essick 1983, no. LXXIV). I am confident that the *Seaman's* plates are not the work of William Blake; they are probably by E. Blake, about whom nothing further is known.

Literature: G. E. Bentley, jun., 'Byron, Shelley, Wordsworth, Blake and *The Seaman's Recorder', Studies in Romanticism*, 9 (1970), 21–36 (all six 'Blake' plates reproduced); Keynes 1972 (see XXVI, *Literature*); Bentley 1977, no. 496; Christopher Heppner, 'Blake and *The Seaman's Recorder*: The Letter and the Spirit in a Problem of Attribution', *Blake: An Illustrated Quarterly*, 12 (1978), 15–17 (with enlarged reproductions of the signatures).

36. Joseph Grego, *Mrs. Q—and 'Windsor Castle'* (London: Kegan Paul, Trench, Trubner & Co., 1906)

One of the two plates in this book is stated (or at least implied) to be an impression of 'M^{rs} Q', a separate plate engraved by Blake and first published in 1820, in Geoffrey Keynes, *Engravings by William Blake: The Separate Plates* (Dublin: Emery Walker, 1956), p. 84, and in Bentley 1977, no. 462. The illustration is in fact a lithographic reproduction of Blake's plate—see Essick 1983, pp. 199–200.

37. 'Etchings. Subjects from Shakespeare.' (n.d.)

Gilchrist 1863, ii. 258, includes these prints in a list of 'works designed as well as engraved by Blake' and refers to their presence in 'T. H. Burke's Sale, Christie's, June 21st, 1852'. The auction catalogue, lot 216, lists 'Subjects from Shakespeare, &c., etched' by Blake, plus fourteen unrelated items (11s. to 'Lilly'). These plates were probably loose impressions from XLII, XLVII, or 26 (above) and not an independent work.

Index

Main entries for books with Blake's plates are printed in **bold-face type**.

FIGURES

2. Olivier, *Fencing Familiarized* (1780)

1. Enfield, *The Speaker* (1780)

JONAH
Chap. 3. Ver. 4.

To the Reverend Thoˢ Lloyd, D.D.
Dean of Bangor;
This PLATE is most humbly Inscribed,
By his most Obedᵗ Servant Jnᵒ Herries

Published Octoʳ 13, 1781 by J. Fielding, Paternoster Row, London.

4.

JUDITH,
Chap. 13, Ver. 10

Blake. ſc.

To the Reverend Joſ Dickson, A.M.
Dean of Down,
This PLATE is most humbly Inscribed
By his most Obedt Servt Jnº Herries.

Published Decr 22, 1781, by J. Fielding, Paternoster Row.

5.

MATTHEW,
Chap. 3. Ver. 13

To the Honble *and* *Rev.* *Jn.*^o *Harley,* D.D.
Dean of *Windsor*
This PLATE *is most* *humbly Inscribed*
By his most Obed.^t *Servant,* *Jn.*^o *Herries.*
Published Augt 18, 1781, by J. Fielding, Paternoster Row, London

REVELATIONS,
Chap. 1 Ver. 12 & 13

To the Reverend Rich.? Dobbs, A.M.
Dean of Connor,
This PLATE is most humbly Inscribed,
By his most Obedient Servant Jn.º Herries

Published Feb.? 23 1782 by J. Fielding, Paternoster Row

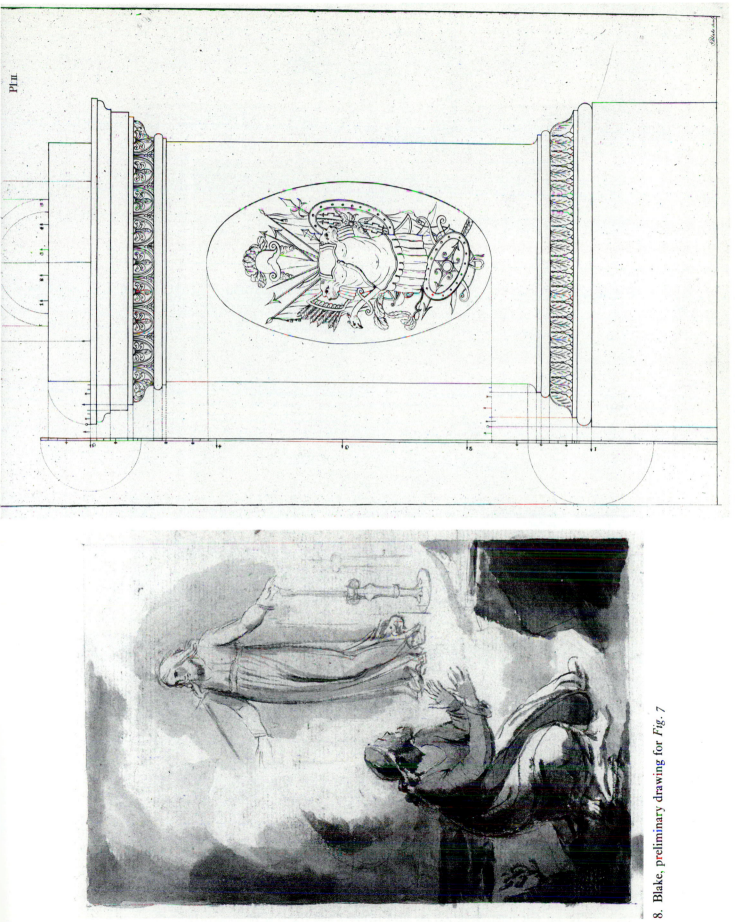

9. Emlyn, *New Order in Architecture* (1781)

8. Blake, preliminary drawing for *Fig. 7*

12. Unpublished version of *Fig. 11*

13. Stothard, preliminary drawing for *Figs. 11–12*

Engraved for *Kimpton's History of the Bible*.

JUDGES IX—46.

THE FUGITIVE SHECHEMITES

Burnt and Suffocated in the Holds of their Idol Berith, by order of King Abimelech.

GENESIS.
XVIII . 2.

Abraham & the Three Angels.

Gen:
XIX. 26.

Lots Escape.

15.

16.

15–19. *Protestant's Family Bible* (*c.*1781)

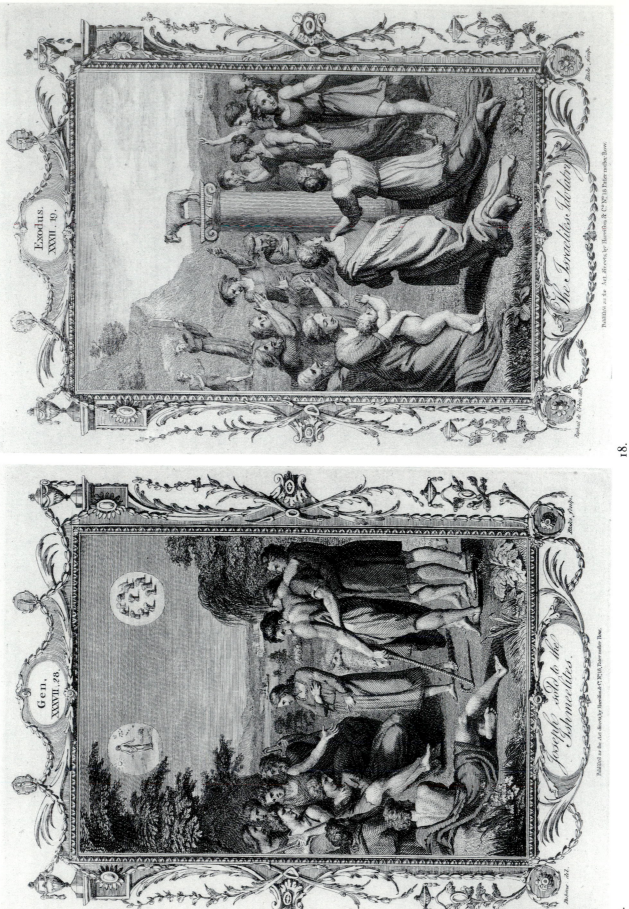

20. Bonnycastle, *Introduction to Mensuration* (1782)

21. Nicholson, *Introduction to Natural Philosophy* (1782)

19.

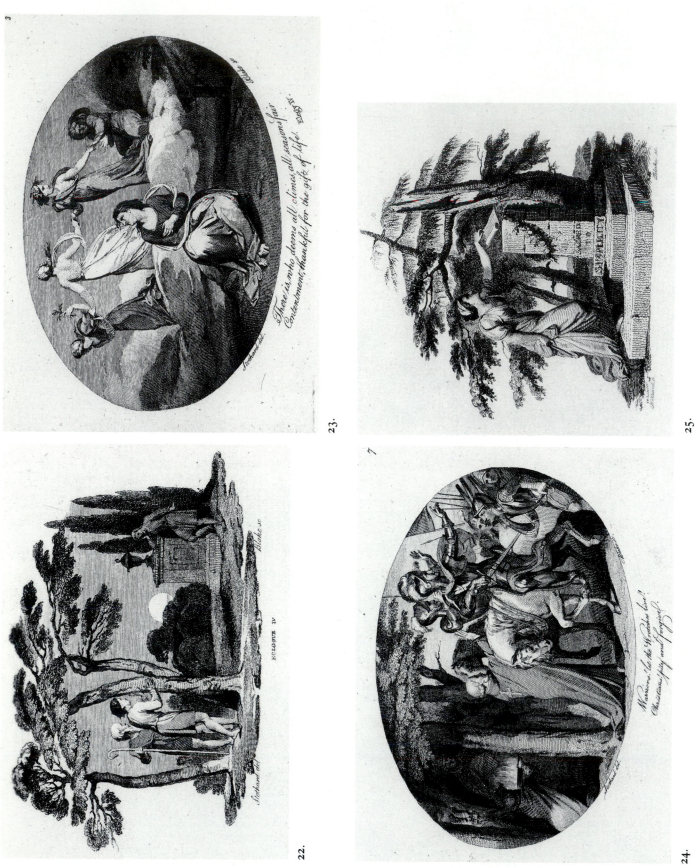

22–5. Scott, *Poetical Works* (1782)

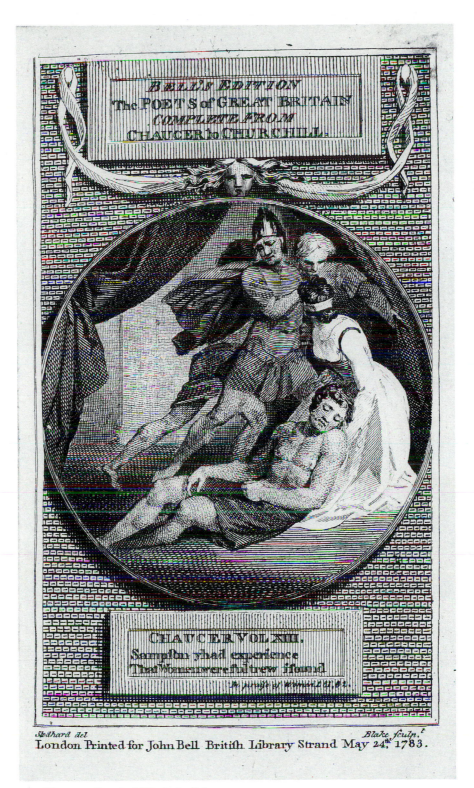

26. Chaucer, *Poetical Works* (1782)

Shepherd del.   Plate XII.   Published as the Act directs by Harrison and Co. Jan. 18, 1783.   Blake sculp.

GRANDISON

Statham del.   Plate VI.   Published as the Act directs, by Harrison & Co. Dec. 7, 1782.   Blake sculp.

GRANDISON

36. Stothard, preliminary drawing for *Fig. 35*

Stothard del.

THE TEMPLE OF MIRTH.

Published as the Act directs, by Harrison & Co. Feb.ʳ 1784.

Blake sculp.

Stothard del.

Bose sculp.

THE TEMPLE OF MIRTH.

Published as the Act directs by Harrison & Co. Feby. 1. 1784.

Collings del.

Blake sculp.

TYTHE IN KIND; OR THE SÓW'S REVENGE.

Publiſhed as the Act directs, by Harriſon & Cº. March 1. 1784.

THE DISCOMFITED DUELLISTS.

Published as the Act directs, by Harrison & Cᵒ April 1, 1784.

Collings del.   Blake sculp.

THE BLIND BEGGARS HATS.

Published as the Act directs, by Harrison & Cº May 1.1784.

Collings del.

MAY-DAY IN LONDON.

Blake sculp.

Publish'd as the Act directs, by Harrison & Cº June 1.1784.

57-8. Fenning and Collyer, *New System of Geography* (1785-6)

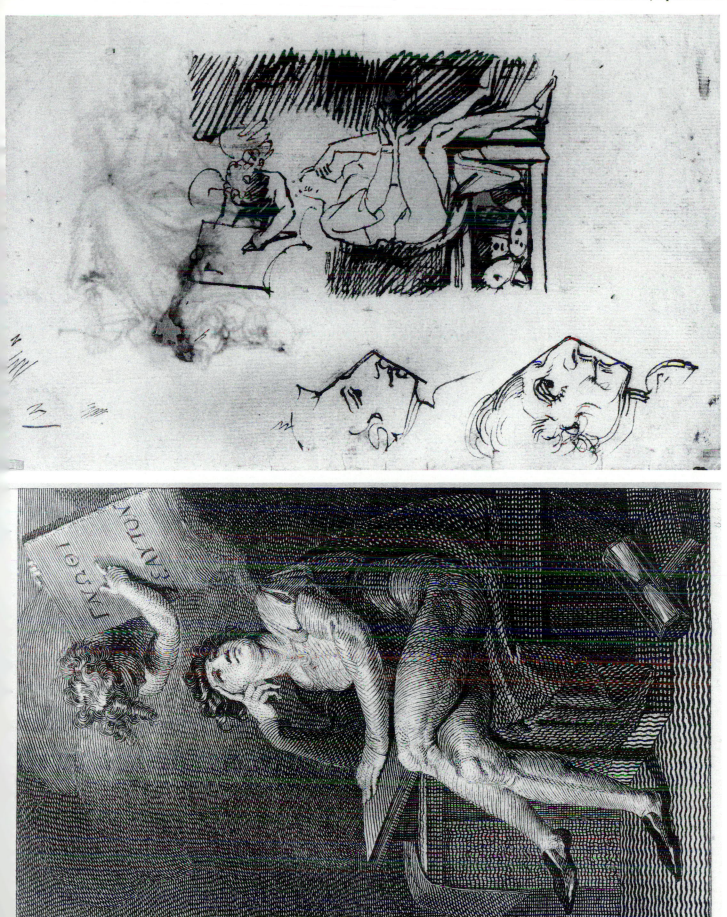

59.

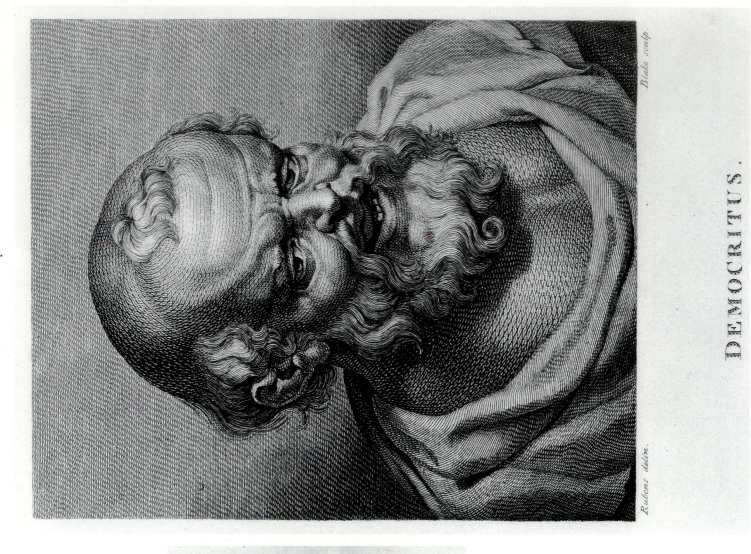

Rubens delin.

Blake sculp.

DEMOCRITUS.

61.

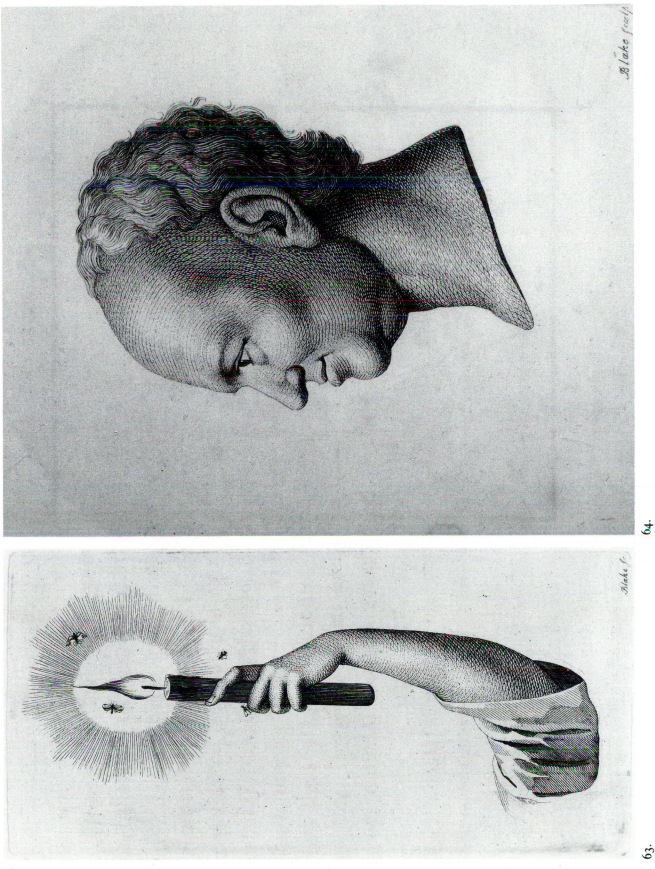

Painted by W.ᵐ Hogarth.

Engraved by W. Blake.

BEGGAR'S OPERA, Act III.

"When my hero in Court appears, &c."

From the Original Picture, in the Collection of his Grace the Duke of Leeds.

Published June 1790, by Col.ᵒ Ralph Humphries, in the Prologue Gallery, Pall Mall, London.

66. Proof of *Fig. 65*

Fertilization of Egypt.

London, Publish'd Decr 1.st 1791. by J. Johnson St Pauls Church Yard.

67.   67–74. Darwin, *Botanic Garden* (1791) and *Poetical Works* (1806)

Sketched by Fuseli for Blake to engrave from

68. Fuseli, preliminary sketch for *Fig. 67*

69. Blake, preliminary drawing for *Fig. 67*

The Portland Vase.

1. London, Published Decr 1.st 1791, by J. Johnson, St Paul's Church Yard.

The first Compartment.

London, Published Dec.r 1.st 1791. by J. Johnson, St. Paul's Church Yard.

The second Compartment.

72.

The Handles & Bottom of the Vase.

73.

H Fuseli R.A. inv.   W Blake sc.

Tornado.

London. Published Aug.t 1.st 1795. by J. Johnson. St Paul's Church Yard.

Blake. sc.

David Hartley, M.A.

From a Painting, by Shackelton.

Published by J. Johnson, in St Pauls Church-yard, March 1st 1791.

75. Hartley, *Observations on Man* (1791)

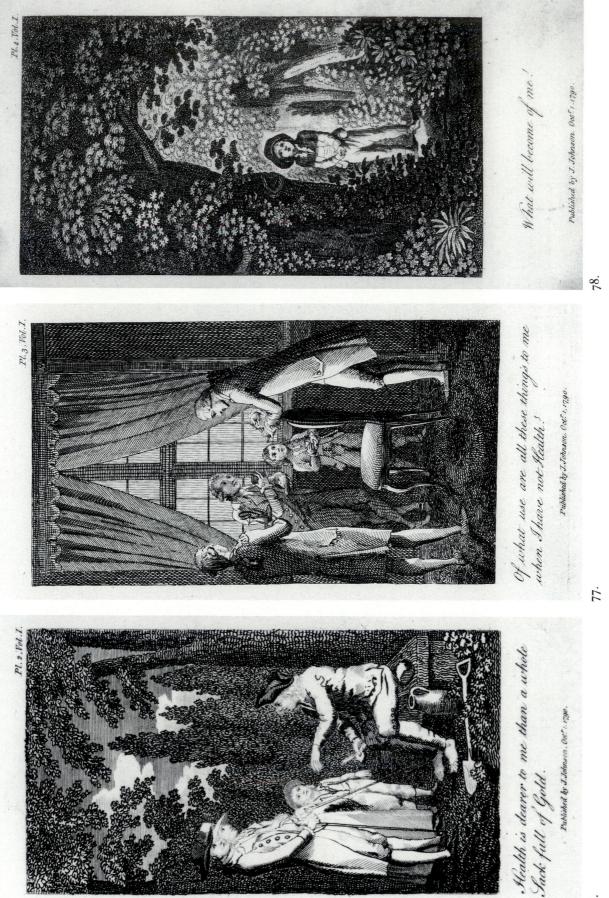

78.

77.

76.

76–120. Salzmann, *Elements of Morality* (1791)

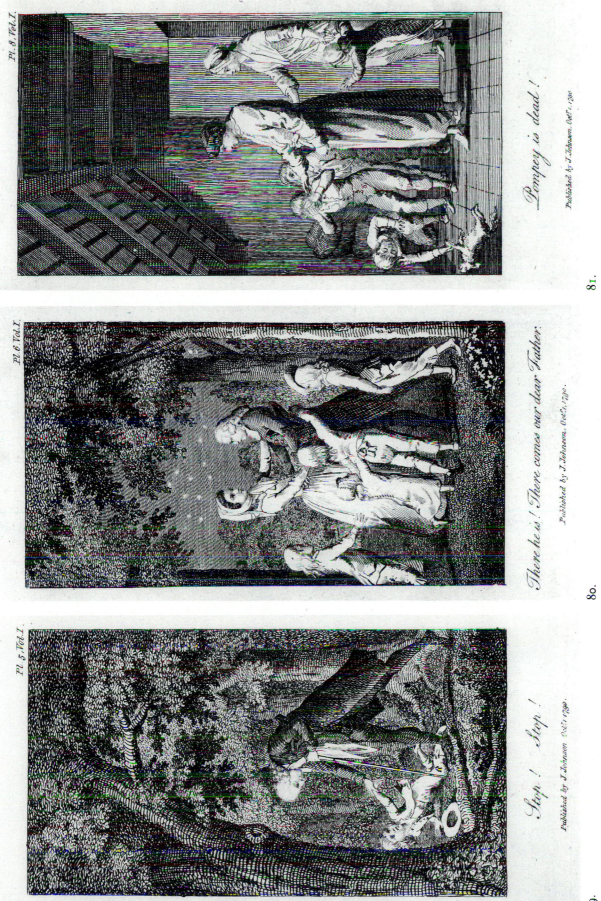

Pl. 8. Vol. I.

Pompey is dead!

Published by J. Johnson. Oct.r 1790.

81.

Pl. 6. Vol. I.

There he is! There comes our dear Father.

Published by J. Johnson. Oct.r 1790.

80.

Pl. 5. Vol. I.

Stop! Stop!

Published by J. Johnson. Oct.r 1790.

79.

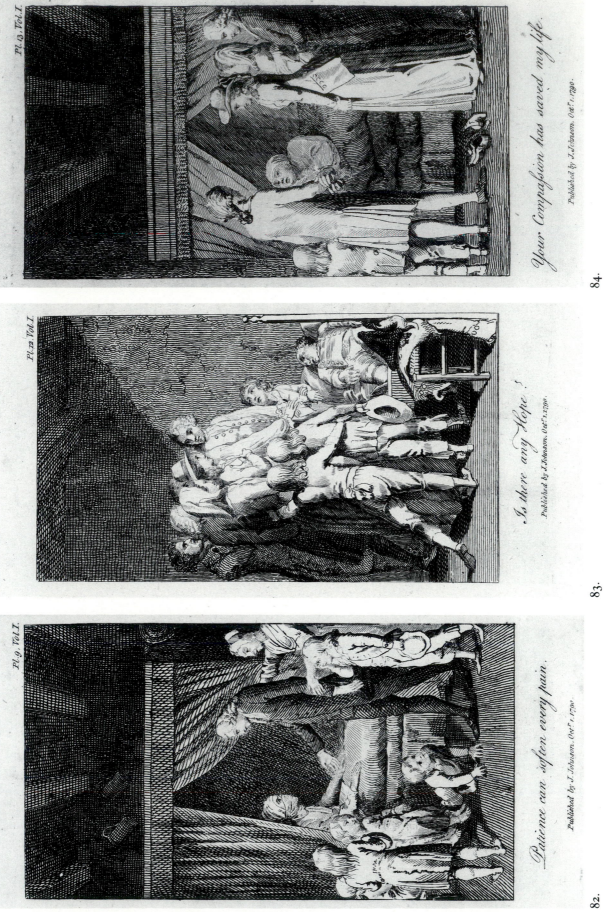

Pl. 13. Vol. I.

Your Compassion has saved my life.

Published by J. Johnson. Oct.r 1. 1790.

84.

Pl. 12. Vol. I.

Is there any Hope?

Published by J. Johnson. Oct.r 1. 1790.

83.

Pl. 9. Vol. I.

Patience can soften every pain.

Published by J. Johnson. Oct.r 1. 1790.

82.

Pl.16.Vol.II.

An Idle Man will never be Content.

Published by J.Johnson. Oct.1.1790.

87.

Pl.15. Vol.I.

If we love others, they will love us in return.

Published by J.Johnson. Oct.1.1790.

86.

Pl.14.Vol.I.

I hate you!

Published by J.Johnson. Oct.1.1790.

85.

Pl. 19. Vol. II.

Now I see that you love Truth, I shall always in future believe you.

Published by J. Johnson. Jany 1. 1791.

90.

Pl. 18. Vol. II.

Prodigality has made me poor.

Published by J. Johnson. Jany 1. 1791.

89.

Pl. 17. Vol. II

While I live I never will disobey you.

Published by J. Johnson. Jany 1. 1791.

88.

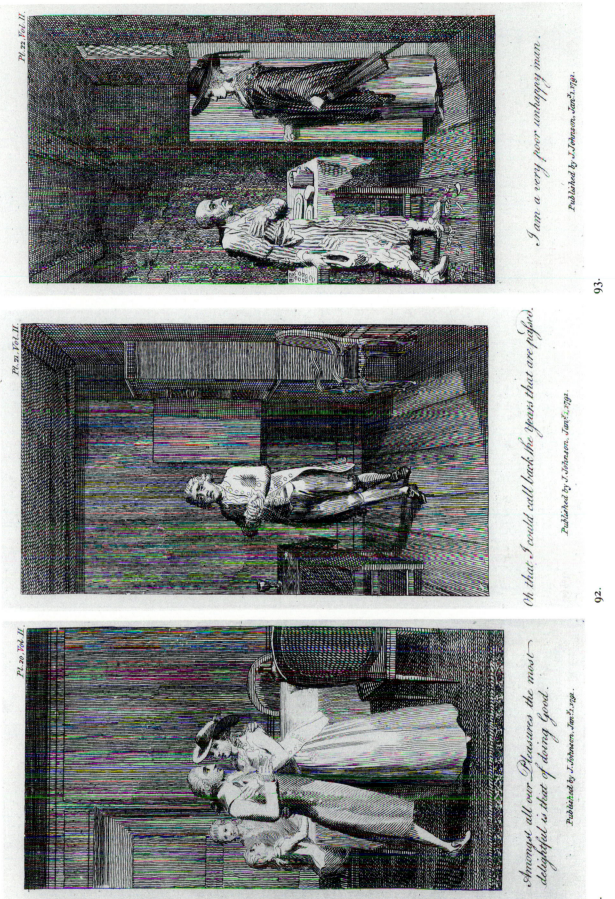

Pl. 22. Vol. II.

I am a very poor unhappy man.

Published by J. Johnson. Jan.ʳ1.1791.

93.

Pl. 21. Vol. II.

Oh that I could call back the years that are passed.

Published by J. Johnson. Jan.ʳ1.1791.

92.

Pl. 20. Vol. II.

Amongst all our Pleasures the most delightful is that of doing Good.

Published by J. Johnson. Jan.ʳ1.1791.

91.

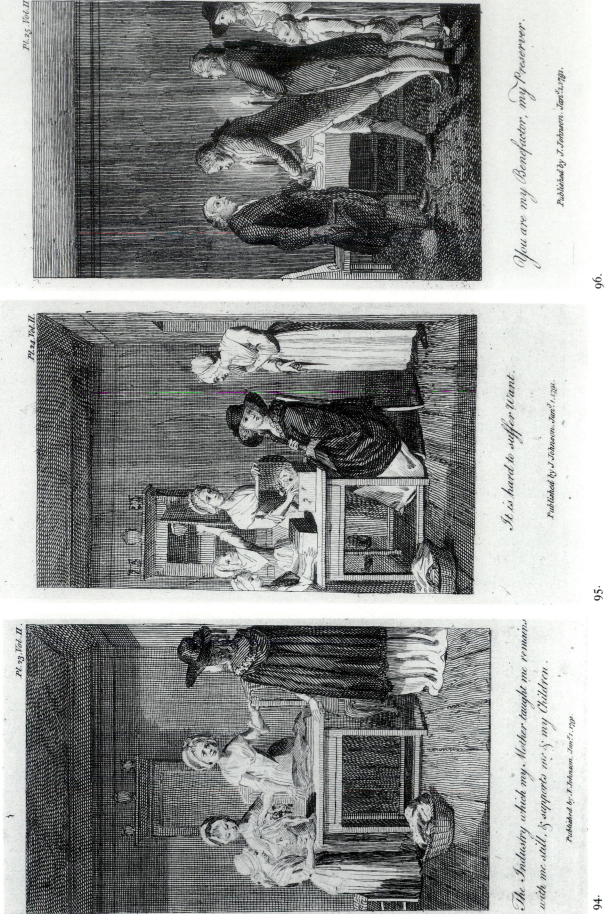

You are my Benefactor, my Preserver.

Published by J. Johnson. Jan. 2, 1791.

96.

It is hard to suffer Want.

Published by J. Johnson. Jan. 1, 1791.

95.

*The Industry which my Mother taught me remains
with me still, & supports me & my Children.*

Published by J. Johnson. Jan. 1, 1791.

94.

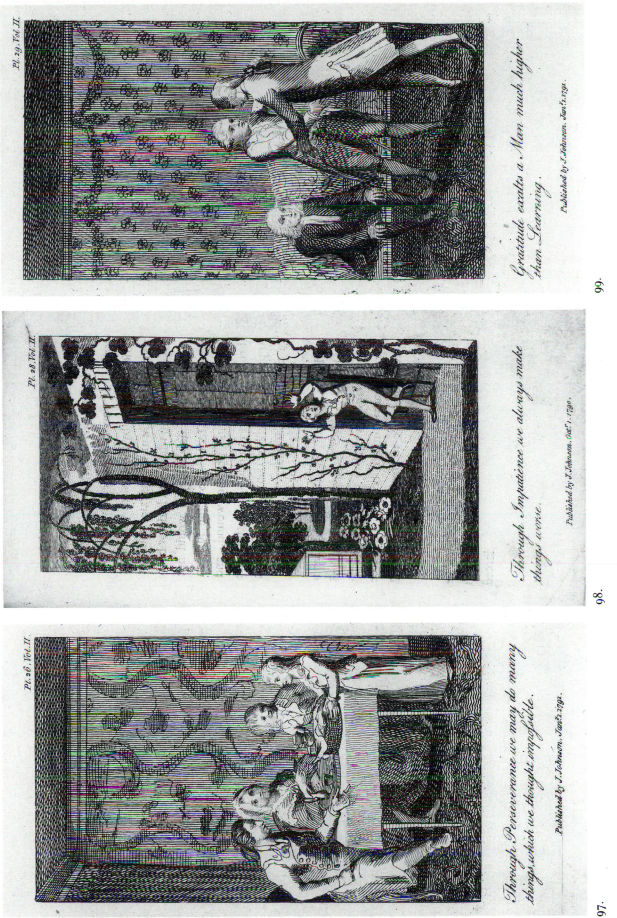

Pl. 29. Vol. II.

Gratitude exalts a Man much higher than Learning.

Published by J. Johnson. Jan.ᵗ 1. 1791.

99.

Pl. 28. Vol. II.

Through Impatience we always make things worse.

Published by J. Johnson. Oct.ʳ 1. 1790.

98.

Pl. 26. Vol. II.

Through Perseverance we may do many things, which we thought impossible.

Published by J. Johnson. Jan.ʳ 1. 1791.

97.

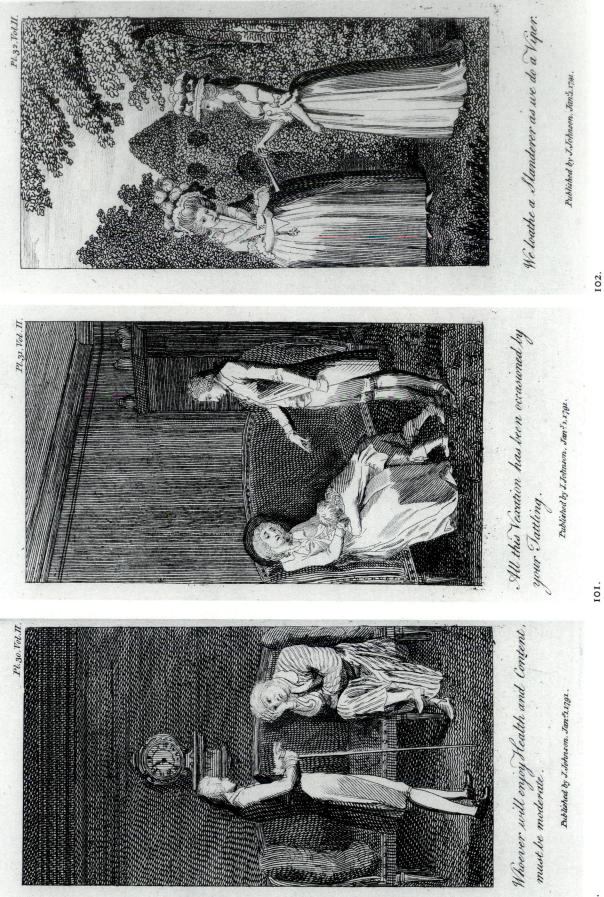

Pl.32.Vol.II.

We loathe a Slanderer as we do a Viper.

Published by J.Johnson. Jan.ˢᵗ,1791.

102.

Pl.31.Vol.II.

All this Vexation has been occasioned by your Tattling.

Published by J.Johnson. Jan.ˢᵗ,1791.

101.

Pl.30.Vol.II.

Whoever will enjoy Health and Content, must be moderate.

Published by J.Johnson. Jan.ˢᵗ,1791.

100.

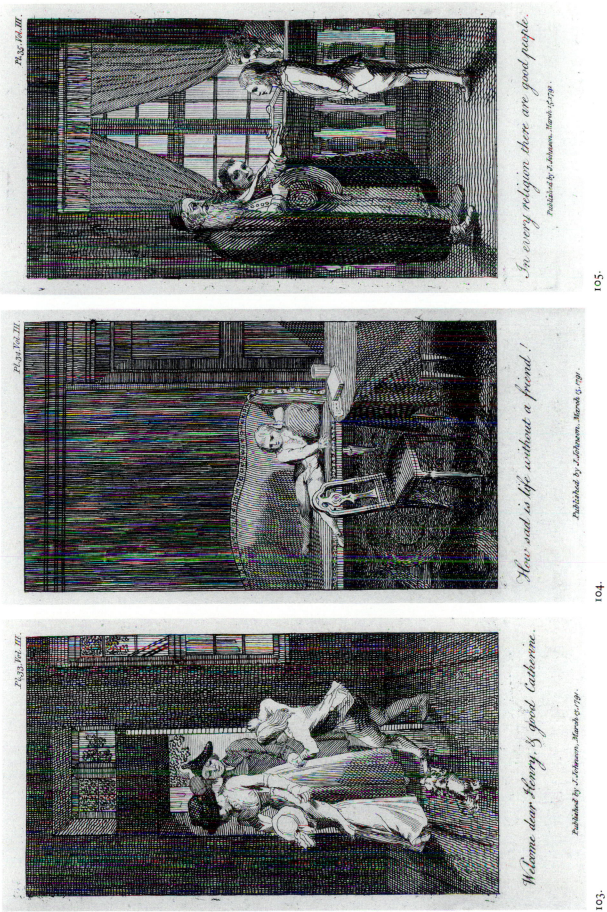

Pl.35.Vol.III.

In every religion there are good people.

Published by J.Johnson. March 5. 1791.

105.

Pl.34.Vol.III.

How sad is life without a friend!

Published by J.Johnson. March 5. 1791.

104.

Pl.33.Vol.III.

Welcome dear Henry, & good Catherine.

Published by J.Johnson. March 5. 1791.

103.

Pl.38.Vol.III.

*What wicked children must they be,
who can vex their parents.*

Published by J.Johnson. March 15.1791.

108.

Pl.37. Vol.III.

*A wicked man is more to be pitied
than a cripple.*

Published by J.Johnson. March 15.1791.

107.

Pl.36. Vol.III.

*He who can torment a little helpless
animal, has certainly a bad heart.*

Published by J.Johnson. March 15.1791.

106.

Pl. 41. Vol. III.

How happy it is that there are rich men in the world.

Published by J. Johnson. March 15. 1791.

III.

Pl. 40. Vol. III.

Her honesty has gained my entire confidence.

Published by J. Johnson. March 15. 1791.

110.

Pl. 39. Vol. III.

See how much good a single man can do!

Published by J. Johnson. March 15. 1791.

109.

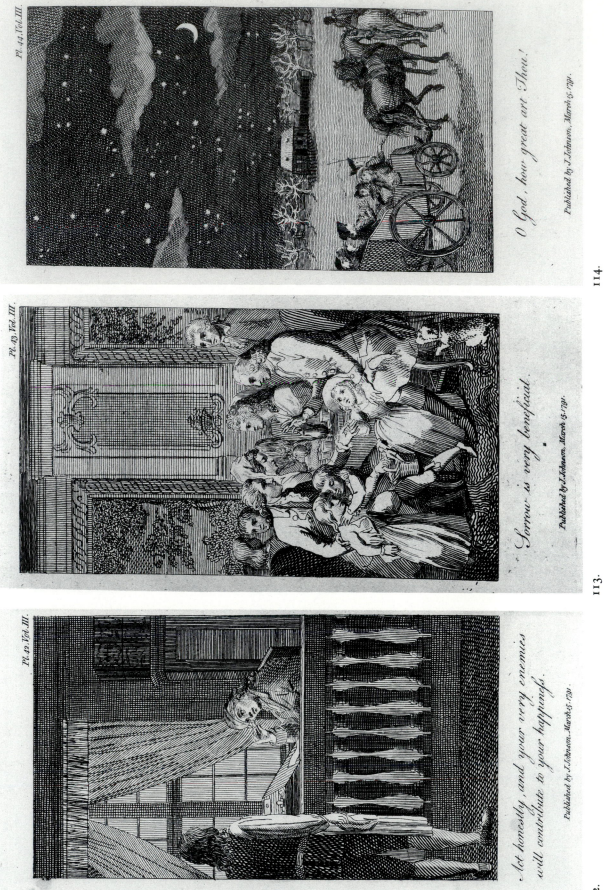

Pl. 44. Vol. III.

O God, how great art Thou!

Published by J.Johnson, March 5. 1791.

114.

Pl. 43. Vol. III.

Sorrow is very beneficial.

Published by J.Johnson, March 5. 1791.

113.

Pl. 42. Vol. III.

Act honestly, and your very enemies will contribute to your happiness.

Published by J.Johnson. March 5. 1791.

112.

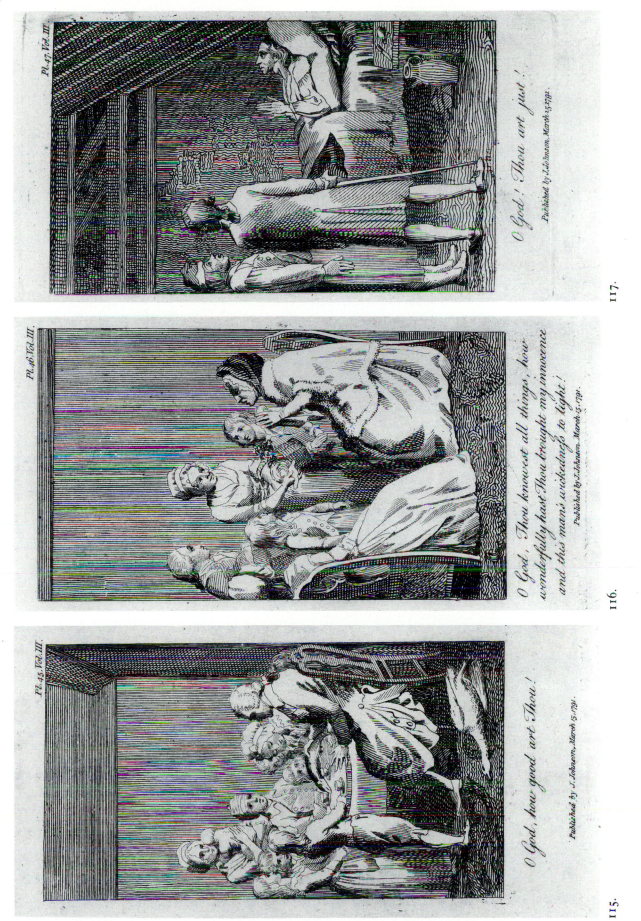

Pl. 47. Vol. III.

O God! Thou art just!

Published by J. Johnson, March 15.1791.

117.

Pl. 46. Vol. III.

O God, Thou knowest all things, how wonderfully hast Thou brought my innocence and this man's wickedness to light!

Published by J. Johnson, March 15. 1791.

116.

Pl. 45. Vol. III.

O God, how good art Thou!

Published by J. Johnson, March 15. 1791.

115.

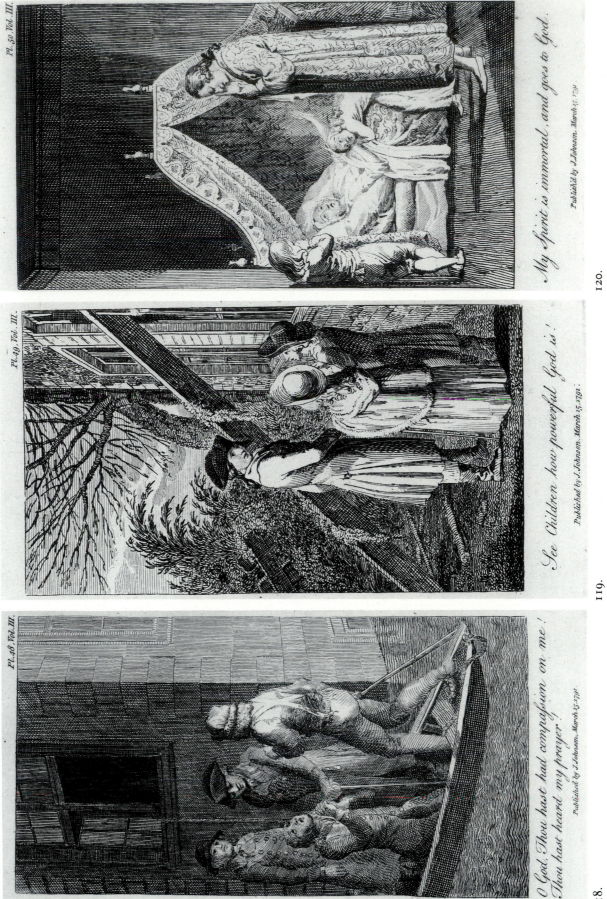

Pl. 50. Vol. III.

My Spirit is immortal, and goes to God.

Published by J. Johnson. March 15, 1791.

120.

Pl. 49. Vol. III.

See Children how powerful God is!

Published by J. Johnson. March 15, 1791.

119.

Pl. 48. Vol. III.

O God, Thou hast had compassion on me!
Thou hast heard my prayer.

Published by J. Johnson. March 15, 1791.

118.

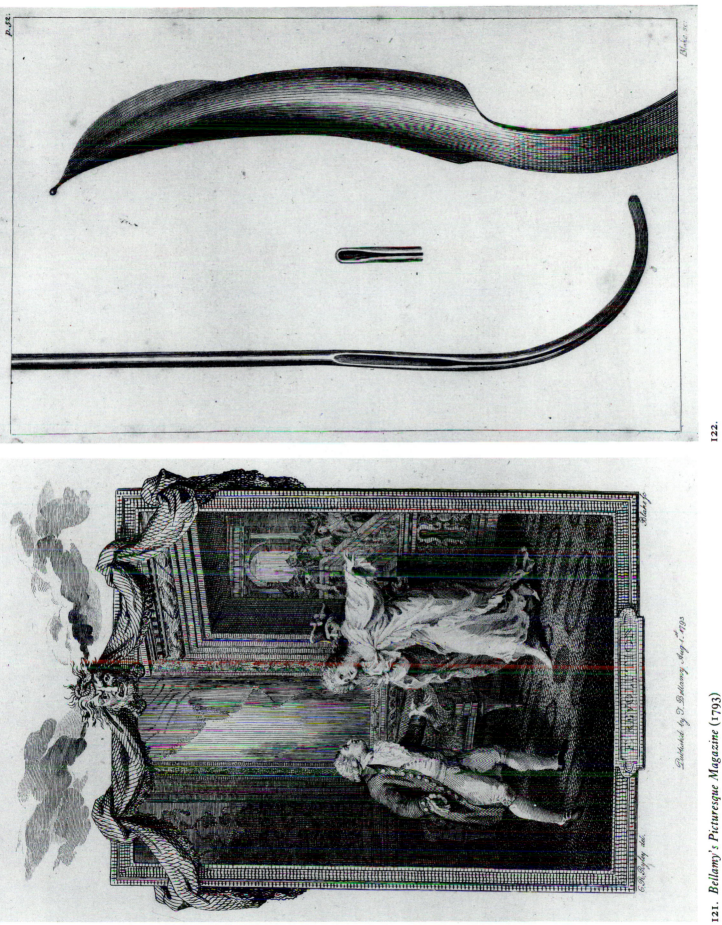

122–4. Earle, *Operation for the Stone* (1793)

122.

121. *Bellamy's Picturesque Magazine* (1793)

123.

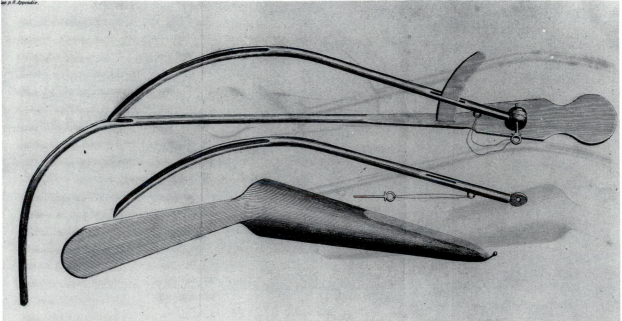

124.

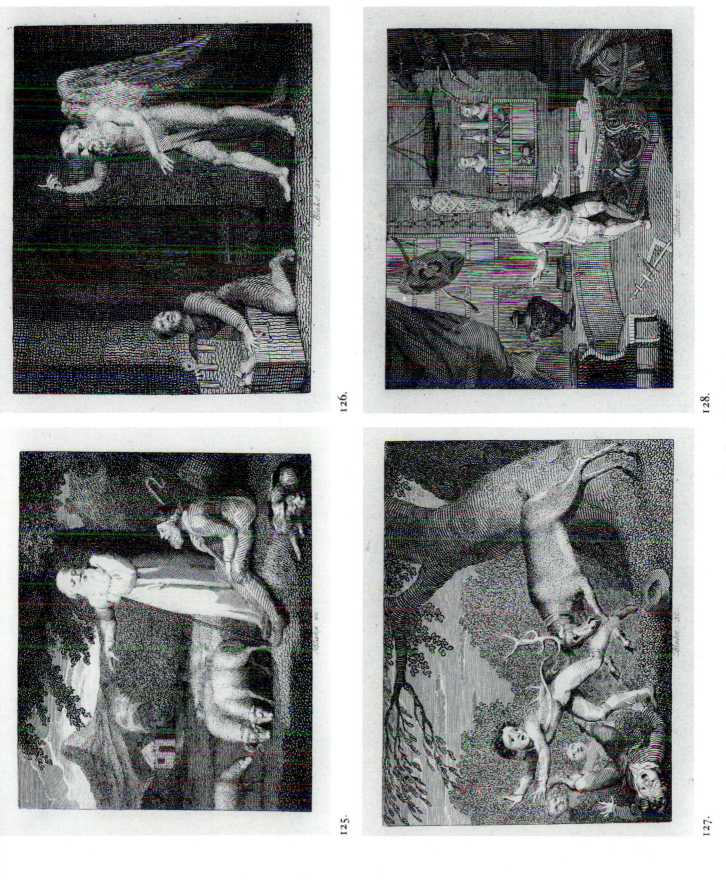

130.

132.

129.

131.

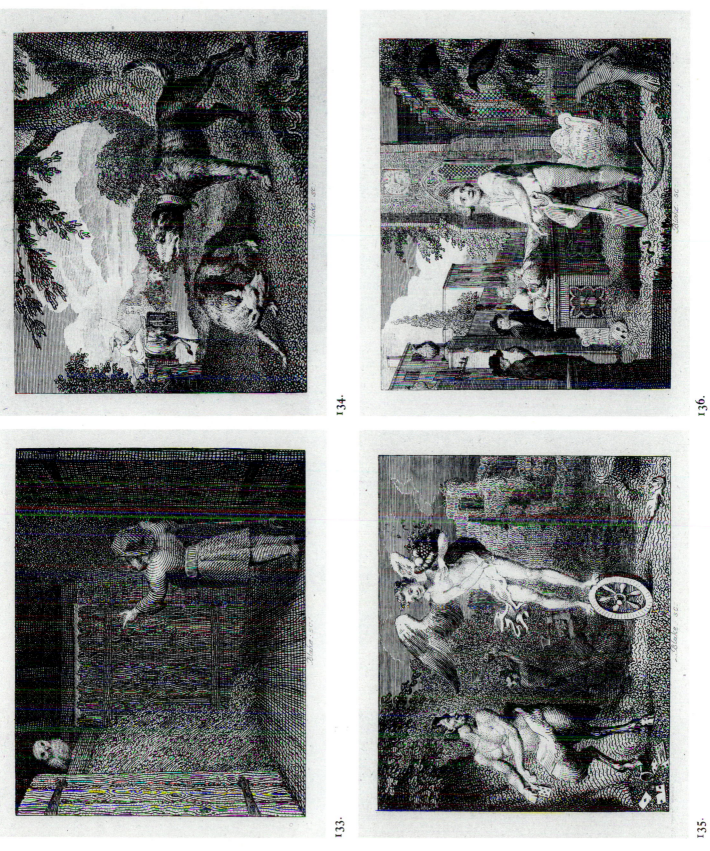

134.

136.

133.

135.

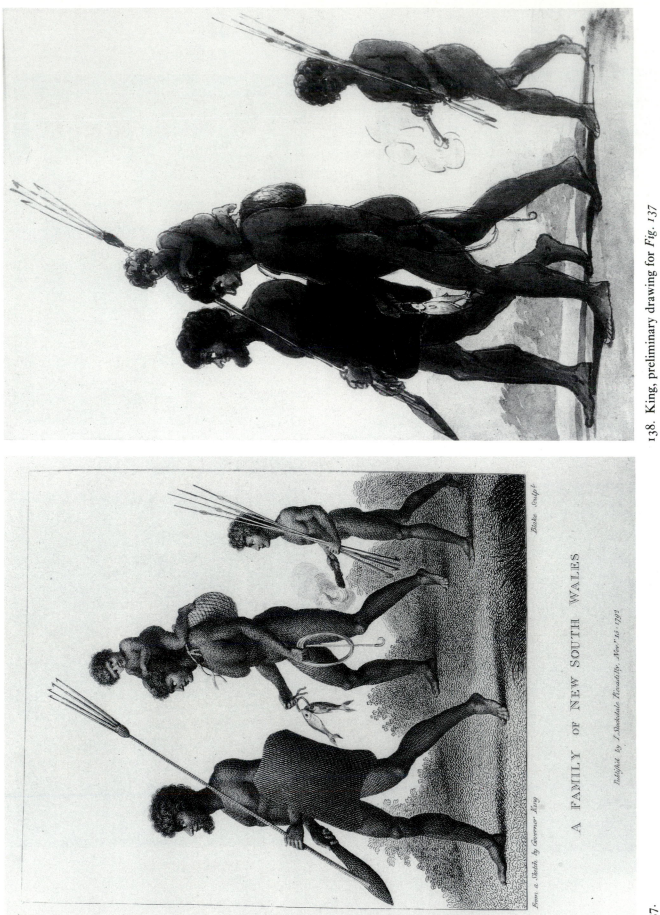

138. King, preliminary drawing for *Fig. 137*

137–8. Hunter, *Historical Journal* (1793)

139.

40.

139–42. Stuart and Revett, *Antiquities of Athens* (1794)

143. Brown, *Elements of Medicine* (1795)

144.

145.

144–5. *Poems of Catullus* (1795)

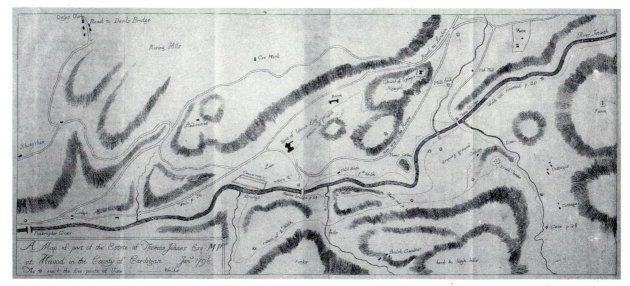

146. Cumberland, *Attempt to Describe Hafod* (1796)

147.

148.

147–54. Cumberland, *Thoughts on Outline* (1796), and *Outlines from the Antients* (1829)
(*Figs. 149–50, 153–4* only)

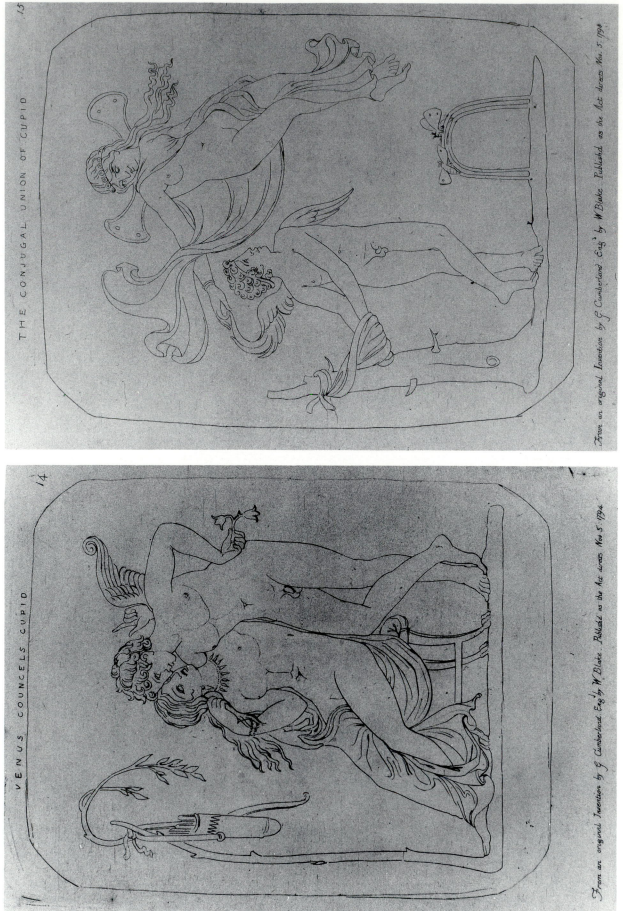

150.

149.

CUPID & PSYCHE

From an original Invention by G. Cumberland. Eng: by W. Blake. Publish'd as the Act directs Nov. 5. 1794

151.

IRON AGE

Then cursed steel & more accursed gold
Gave mischief birth & made that mischief bold.
Ovid. Iron Age.

From an original Invention by G. Cumberland. Eng: by W. Blake. Publish'd as the Act directs Nov. 5. 1794.

152.

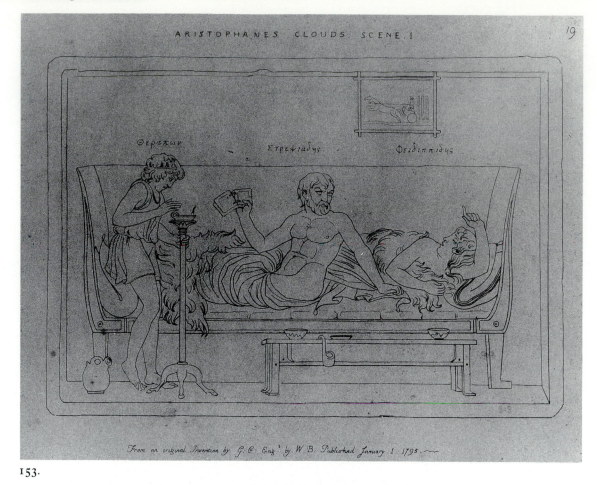

153.

154.

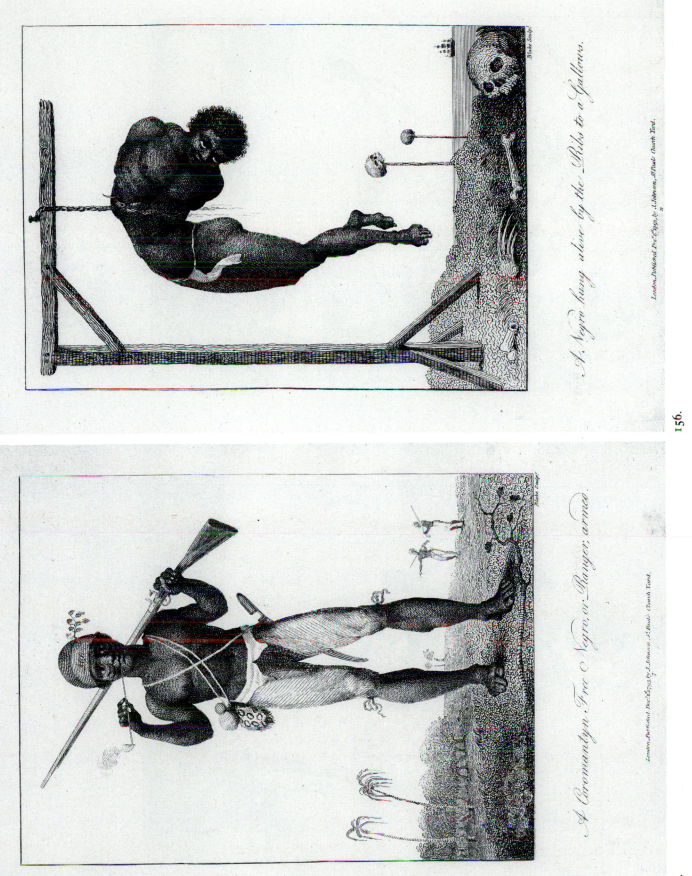

A Negro hung alive by the Ribs to a Gallows.

London, Published Dec.r 1.st 1793, by J. Johnson, S.t Paul's Church Yard.

156.

A Coromantyn Free Negro, or Ranger, armed.

London, Published Dec.r 2.d 1793, by J. Johnson, S.t Paul's Church Yard.

155.

155–70. Stedman, *Narrative of Surinam* (1796)

The Mecoo & Kishee Kishee Monkeys.

A private Marine of Col. Fourgeoud's Corps.

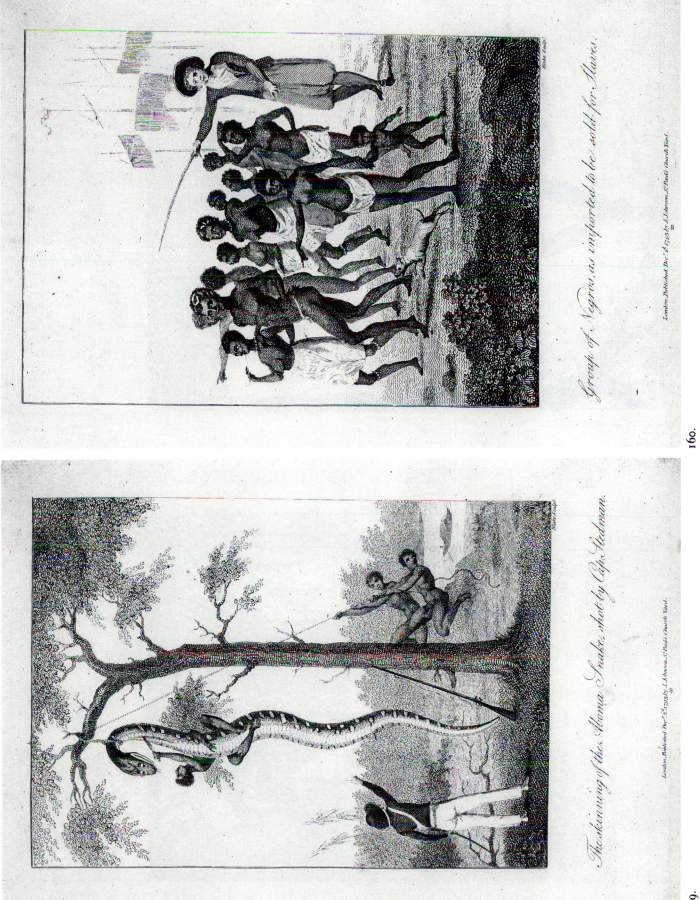

Group of Negroes, as imported to be sold for Slaves.

London, Published Dec.r 2.d 1793, by J. Johnson, St. Paul's Church Yard.

The skinning of the Aboma Snake, shot by Cap.t Stedman.

London, Published Dec.r 2.d 1793, by J. Johnson, St. Paul's Church Yard.

160.

159.

The Execution of Breaking on the Rack.

London, Published Dec'r 2d 1793, by J. Johnson, St Paul's Church Yard.

168.

Family of Negro Slaves from Loango.

Blake Sculp.

London, Published Dec'r 1st 1793, by J. Johnson, St Paul's Church Yard.

167.

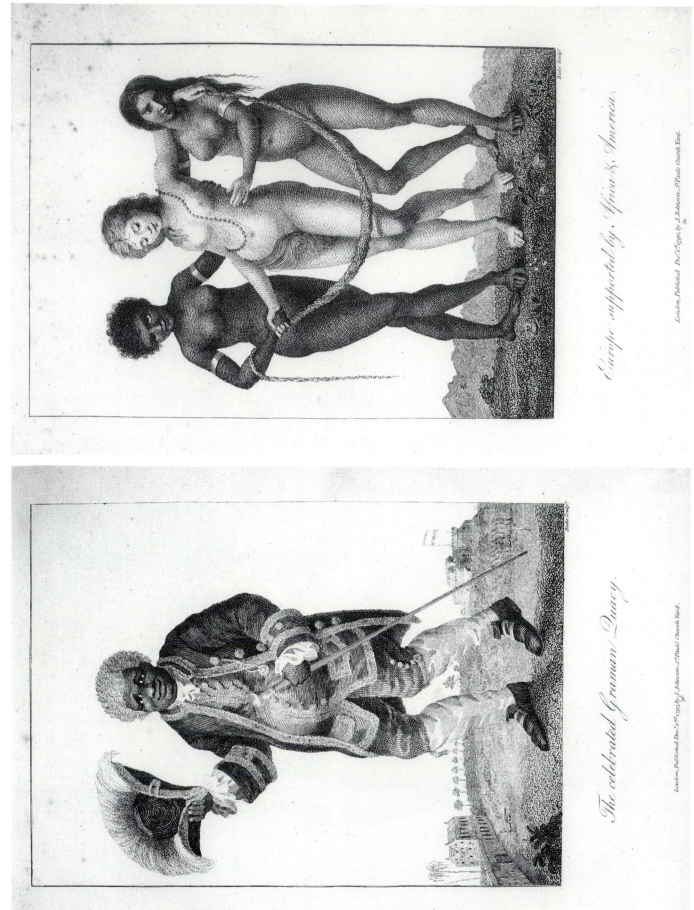

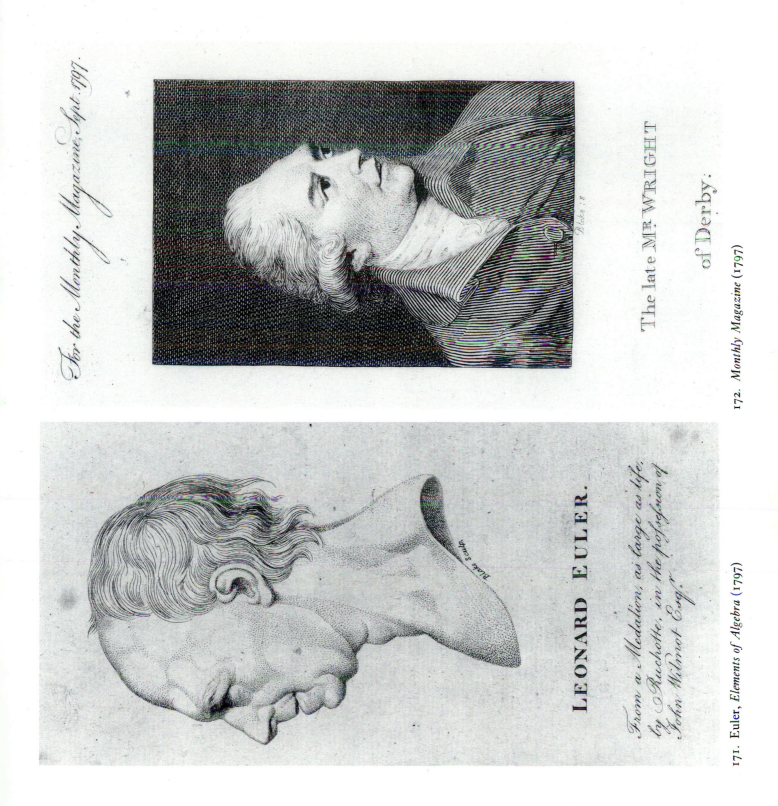

For the Monthly Magazine, Sept. 1797.

Blake : s

The late MR WRIGHT

of Derby.

172. *Monthly Magazine* (1797)

LEONARD EULER.

From a Medalion, as large as life,
by Ruchotte, in the possession of
John Wilmot Esqr

171. Euler, *Elements of Algebra* (1797)

P. 15.

Blake: s

Alfred and the Neat-herd's Wife.

London, Published Dec.ʳ 1. 1797 by J. Johnson, Sᵗ Paul's Church Yard.

173.

P. 78.

Blake: sc

King John absolved by Pandulph.

London, Published Dec.ʳ 1. 1797 by J. Johnson, Sᵗ Paul's Church Yard.

174.

173–6. Allen, *History of England* (1798)

175.

176.

177.

178.

177–80. Allen, *Roman History* (1798)

P. 171

P. 202

Blake: sc

Blake: s

C. Marius at Minturnum.

The Death of Cleopatra.

London, Published Dec.r 1, 1797, by Johnson, St Pauls Church Yard.

London, Published Dec.r 1, 1797, by J. Johnson, St Pauls Church Yard.

179.

180.

182. Flaxman, preliminary drawing for *Fig. 181*

181–4. Flaxman, *Letter . . . for Raising the Naval Pillar* (1799)

181.

Plate 2

1 Obelisk   2 Column   3 Meta

4 Arch   5 Pharos   6 Temple

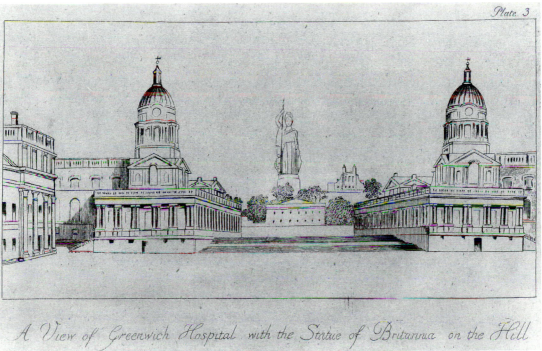

Plate 3

A View of Greenwich Hospital with the Statue of Britannia on the Hill

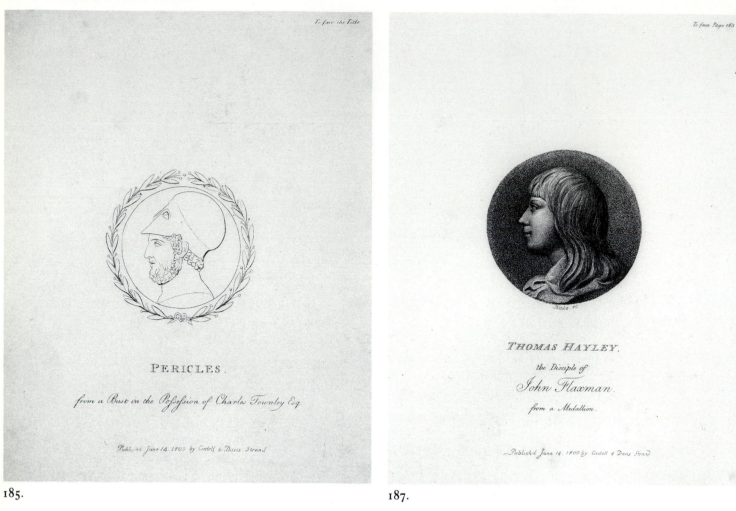

185.

187.

186.   185–7. Hayley, *Essay on Sculpture* (1800)

189. Fuseli and Blake, preliminary sketch for *Fig. 188*

188–9. Fuseli, *Lectures on Painting* (1801)

188.

From an Antique Gem
Publish'd June 1 1802 by W Blake Felpham

190.

From an Antique
Publish'd Aug.ˢᵗ 5 1802 by WBlake Felpham

191.   *190–1. Designs to . . . Ballads . . . by Hayley* (1802)

Painted by J. Opie.

Variation

Engrav'd by W. Blake.

SHAKSPEARE.
Romeo and Juliet,
ACT IV. SCENE V.

Pub.d March 28 1799, by John & Josiah Boydell, at the Shakspeare Gallery, Pall, Mall, & N.o. 90, Cheapside.

192. *Dramatic Works of Shakspeare* (1802), and *Boydell's Graphic Illustrations . . . of Shakspeare* (c.1803)

193.

194.

193–8. Hayley, *Triumphs of Temper* (1803)

Canto. III.   Verse. 201

Maria Flaxman inv & del: W. Blake. sc

Publish'd May 1 1803 by Cadell & Davies. Strand

Canto. IV.   Verse 328

Maria Flaxman inv & del   W. Blake. sculp.

Publish'd May 1. 1803. by Cadell & Davies. Strand

Canto V. Verse 43

Maria Flaxman inv & del   W Blake sculp

Publishd May 1 1803 by Cadell & Davies Strand

197.

Canto. VI. Verse 294.

Maria Flaxman inv & del   W Blake sculp

- Publishd May 1 1803 by Cadell & Davies Strand

198.

From a Portrait in Crayons Drawn from the Life by Romney in 1792   Engrav'd by W Blake 1802

WILLIAM · COWPER

Carmine Nobilem
Hor.

Publish'd Novemb.ʳ 5, 1802, by J Johnson S.ᵗ Pauls Church Yard

William Cowper Esqr.

Given by the Poet; to his friend Hayley

200. Blake, preliminary drawing for *Fig. 199*

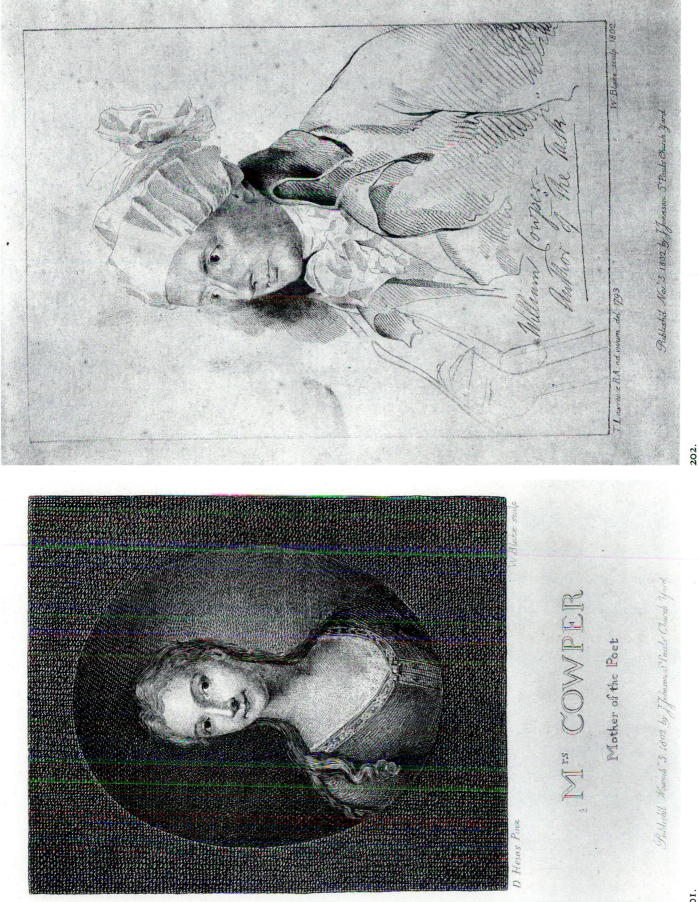

202.

201.

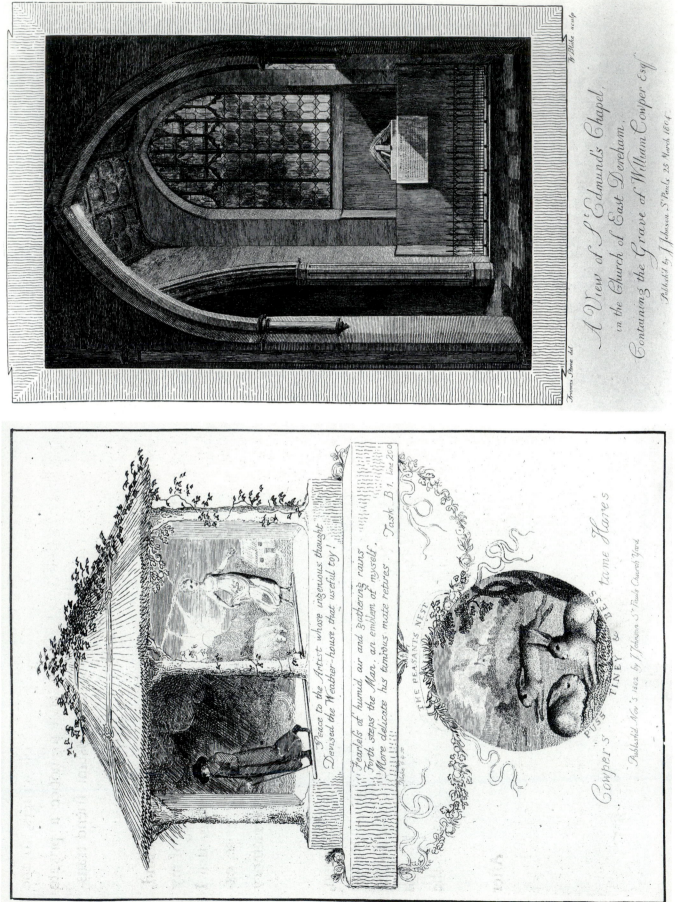

A View of S.t Edmunds Chapel,
in the Church of East Dereham.
Containing the Grave of William Cowper Esq.r

Published by J Johnson S.t Pauls 25 March 1804.

Frances Stone del.

W Blake sculp

204.

"Peace to the Artist whose ingenuous thought
Devised the Weather-house, that useful toy!

"Fearless of humid air and gathering rains
Forth steps the Man, an emblem of myself,
More delicate his timrous mate retires."

Task. B.1. line 200.

THE PEASANTS NEST

Cowper's
PUSS TINEY & BESS tame Hares

Published Nov.r 5 1802 by J Johnson S.t Pauls Church Yard.

203.

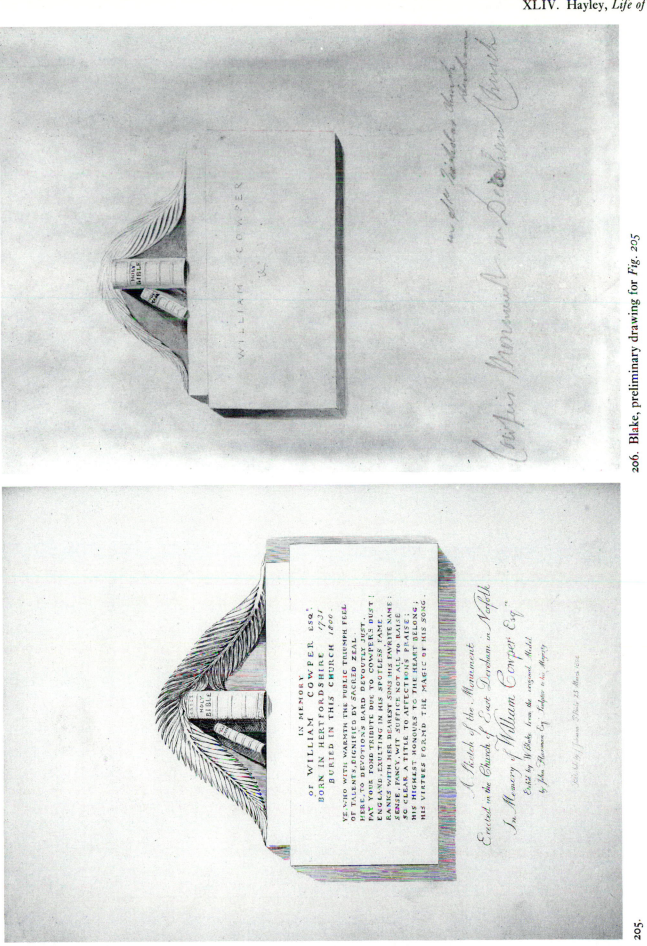

Fragment of an Antique Statue of *Ceres*, found in the Ruins of *Eleusis* and now placed in the Public Library at *Cambridge*

207. Hoare, *Academic Correspondence* (1804)

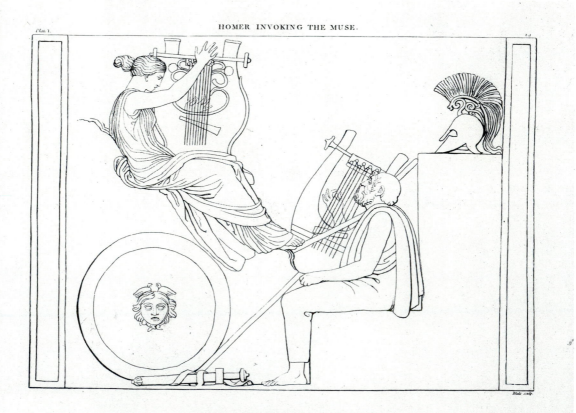

HOMER INVOKING THE MUSE.

ACHILLES WRATH TO GREECE THE DIREFUL SPRING,
OF WOES UNNUMBERD HEAVENLY GODDESS SING!

208.

208–10. Flaxman, *Iliad Compositions* (1805), *Compositions of Flaxman* (1870), and *Compositions from the Iliad* (1870)

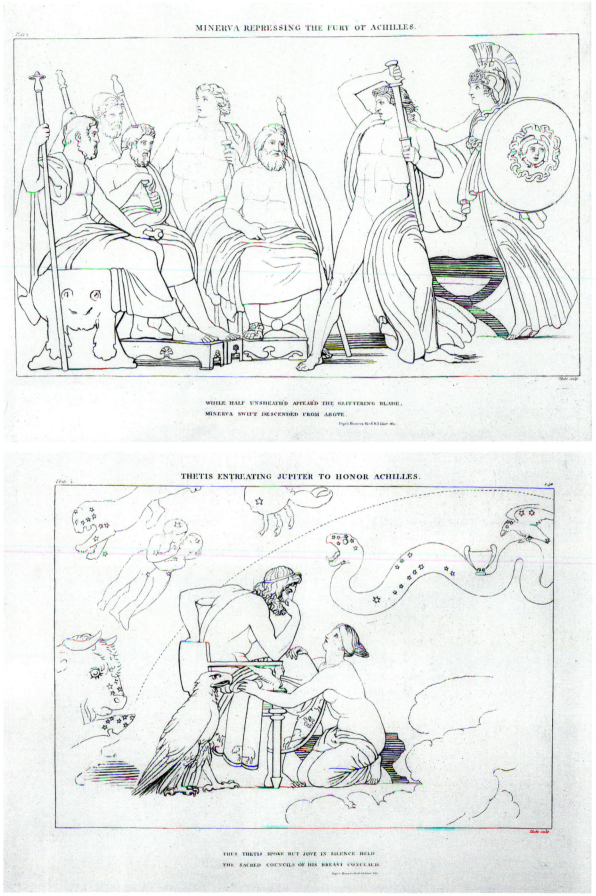

MINERVA REPRESSING THE FURY OF ACHILLES.

WHILE HALF UNSHEATH'D APPEAR'D THE GLITTERING BLADE,
MINERVA SWIFT DESCENDED FROM ABOVE.

Pope's Homer's Iliad B.I Line 280.

209.

THETIS ENTREATING JUPITER TO HONOR ACHILLES.

THUS THETIS SPOKE BUT JOVE IN SILENCE HELD
THE SACRED COUNCILS OF HIS BREAST CONCEAL'D.

Pope's Homer's Iliad B.I Line 645.

210.

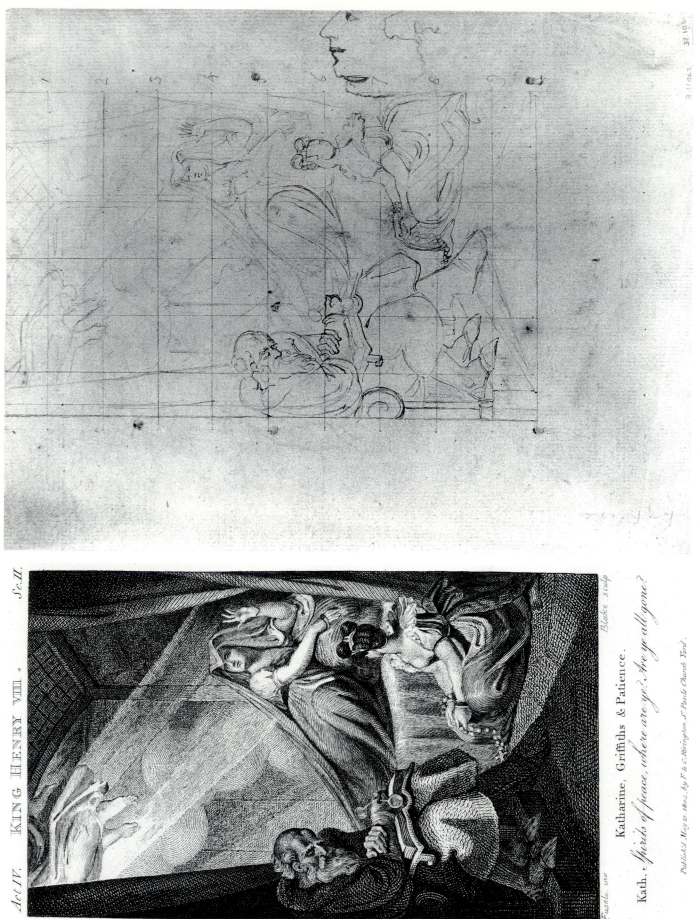

Fuseli. inv   *Blake. sculp*

KING HENRY VIII.   *Sc. II.*

Act IV.

Katharine, Griffiths & Patience.

Kath. *Spirits of peace, where are ye? Are ye all gone?*

Publish'd May 22. 1804. by F. & C. Rivington, S.t Paul's Church Yard.

211.

212. Blake, squared drawing for *Fig. 211*

211–13. *Plays of Shakspeare* (1805)

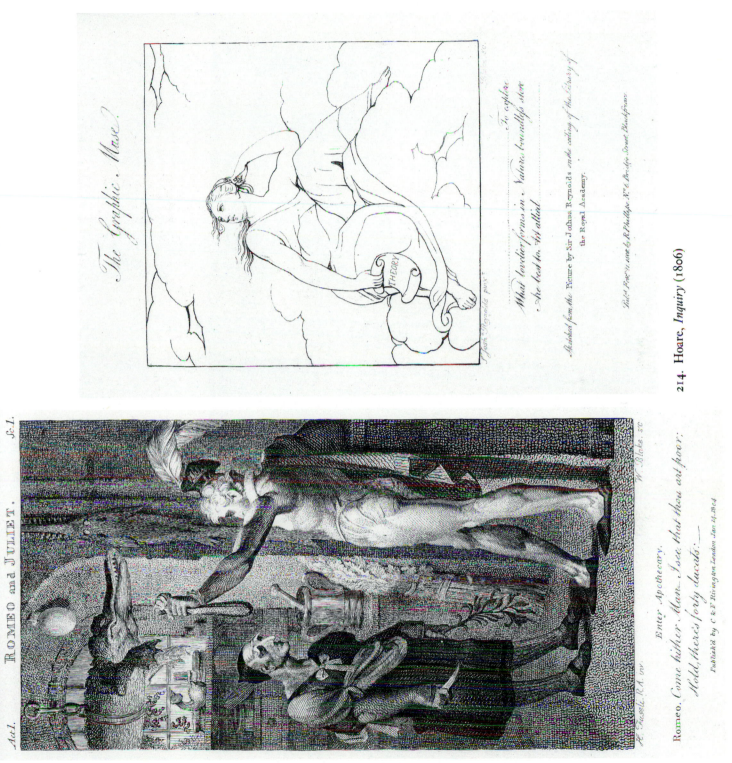

The Graphic Muse.

J. Josh. Reynolds pinxt.

To explore
What lovelier forms in Nature's boundless store
She best to Art allied.

Sketched from the Picture by Sir Joshua Reynolds on the ceiling of the Library of the Royal Academy.

Pub.d Feb.y 14, 1806 by R. Phillips N.o 6 Bridge Street Blackfriars.

214. Hoare, *Inquiry* (1806)

Act I. ROMEO and JULIET. *Sc. I.*

Enter Apothecary.

Romeo. *Come hither Man. I see that thou art poor;*
Hold, there's forty ducats:—

H. Fuseli. R.A. inv.   *W. Blake. sc*

Publish'd by C & F. Rivington London. Jan 14, 1804.

213.

Sketch of a Shipwreck after Romney.

Engraved by Blake

Published April 11th 1809 by Thomas Payne, Pall Mall.

216. Blake, squared drawing for *Fig. 215*

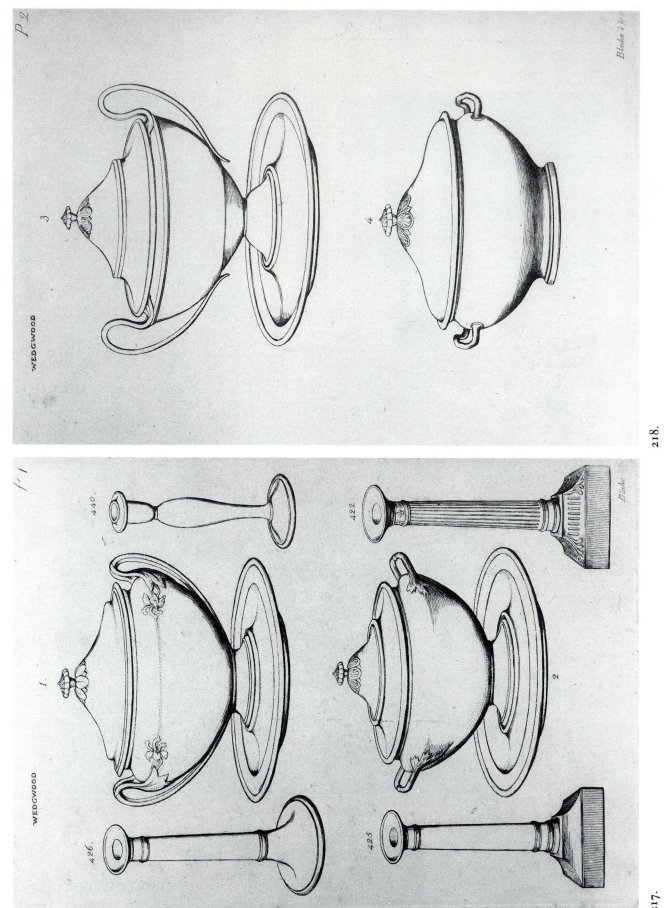

217–34. Wedgwood's Catalogue (c.1816)

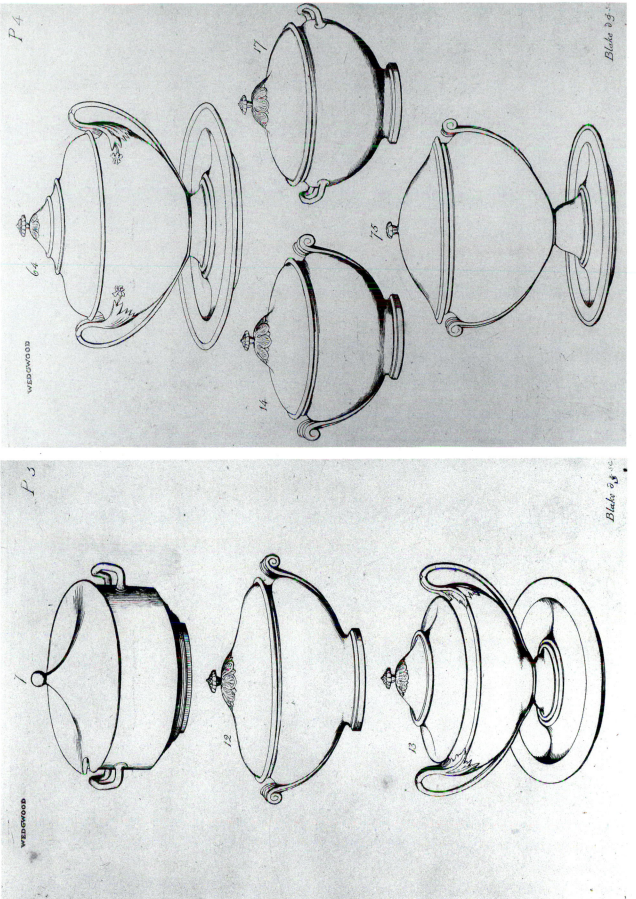

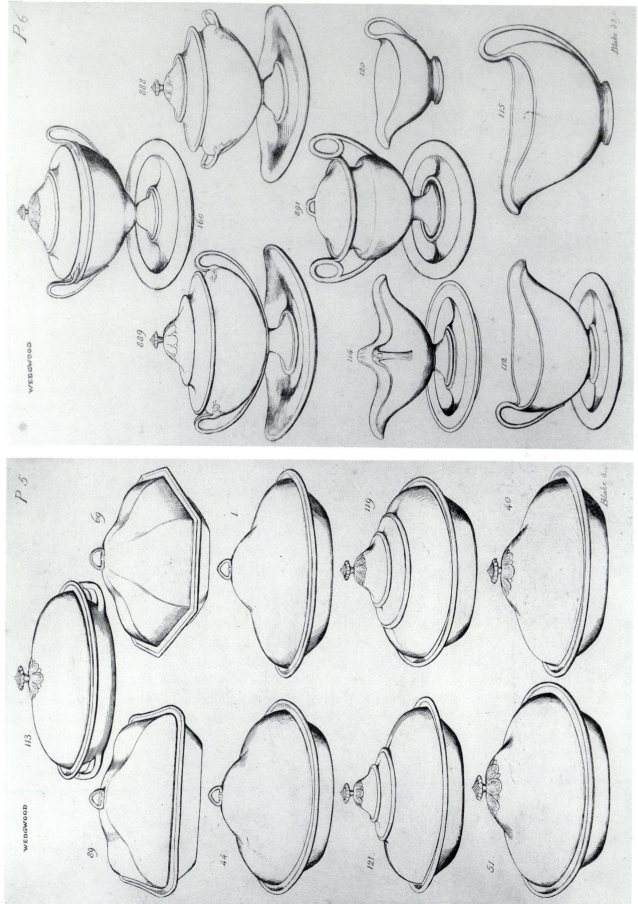

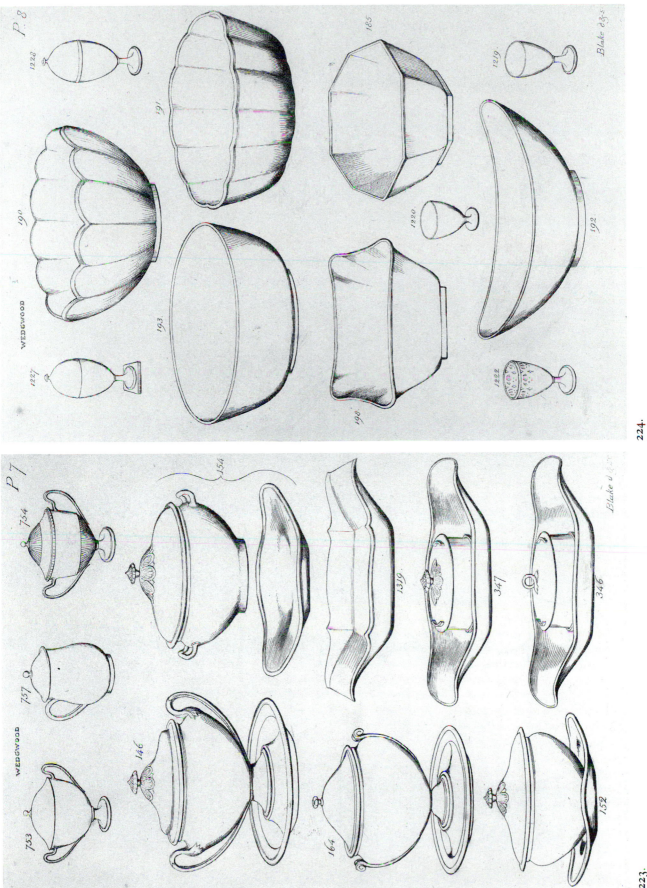

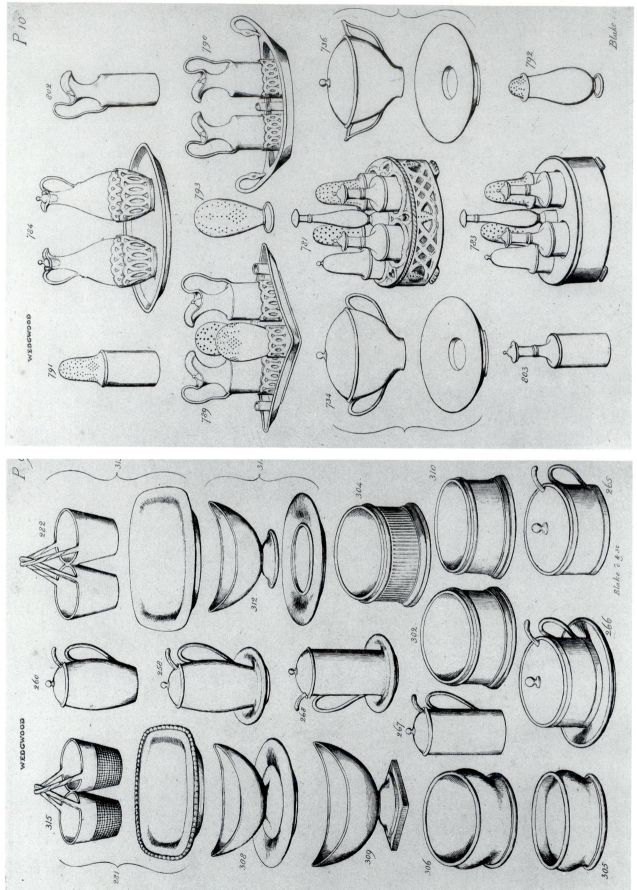

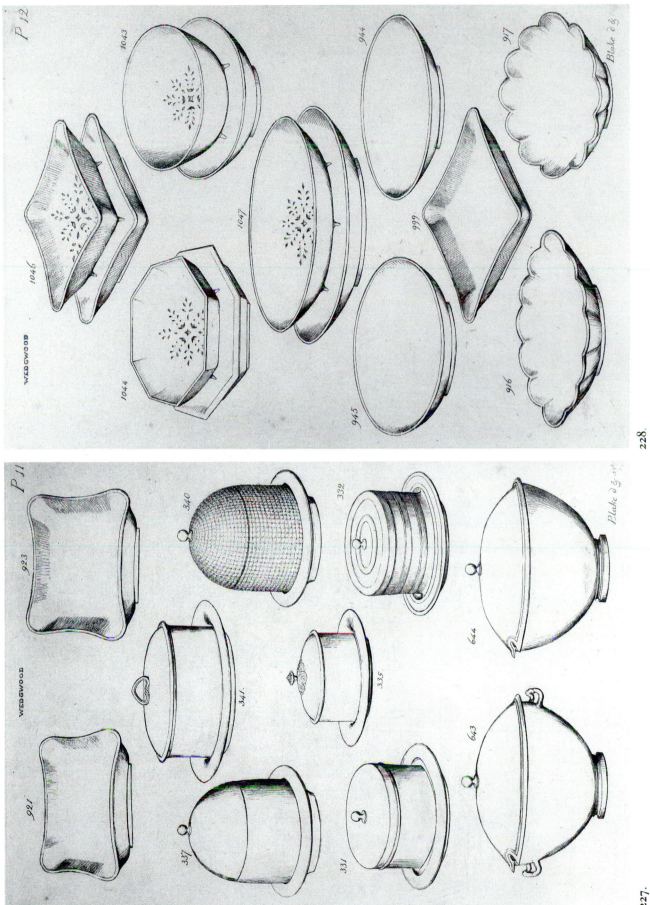

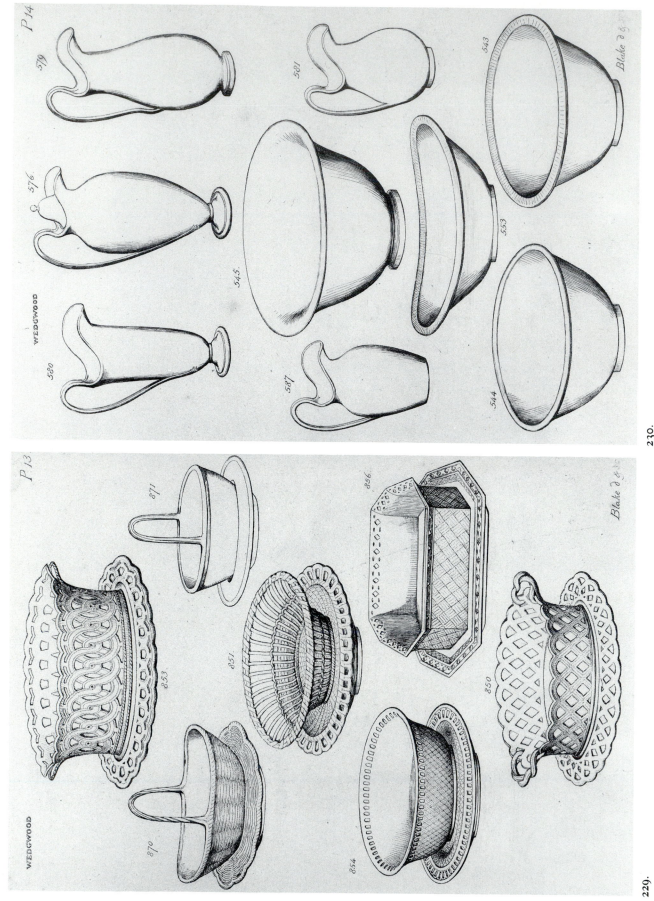

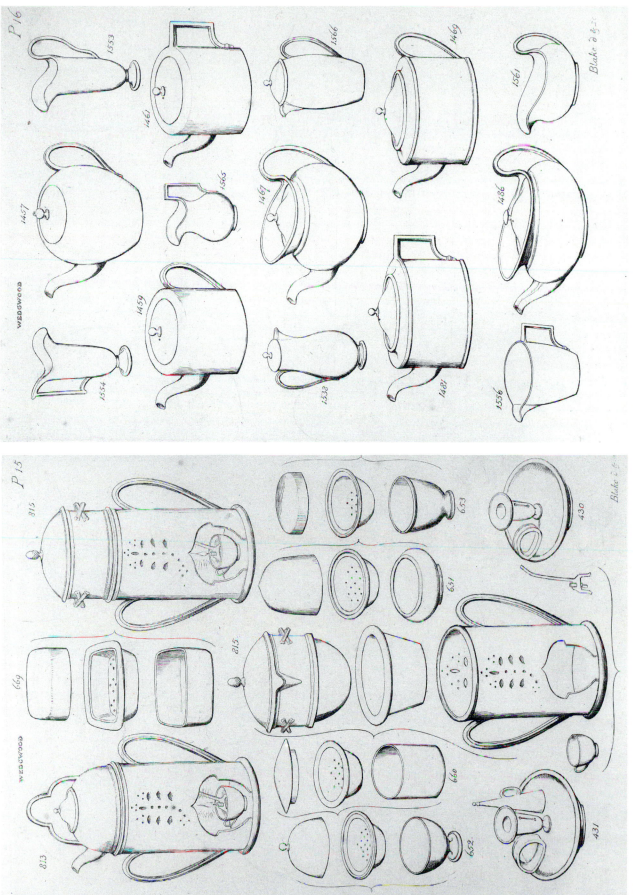

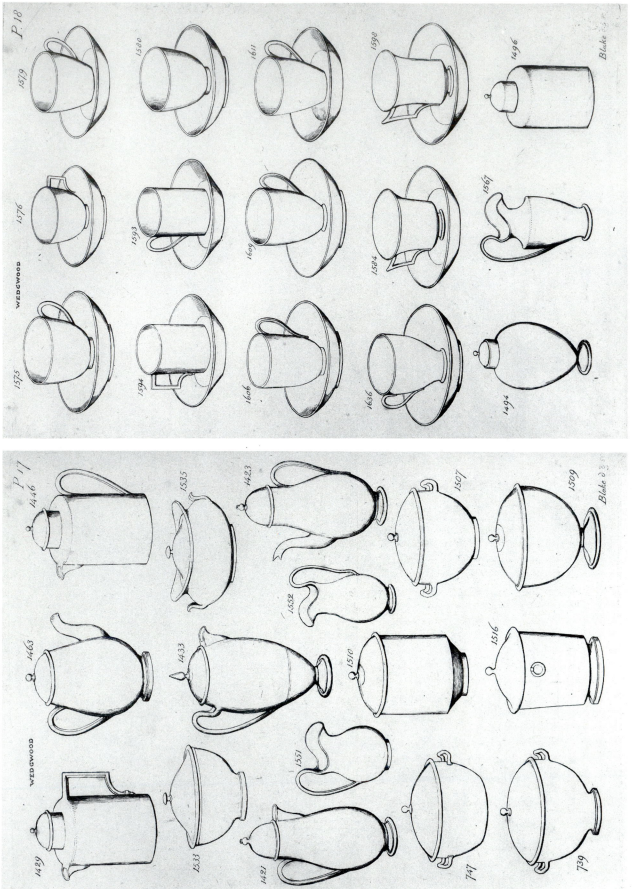

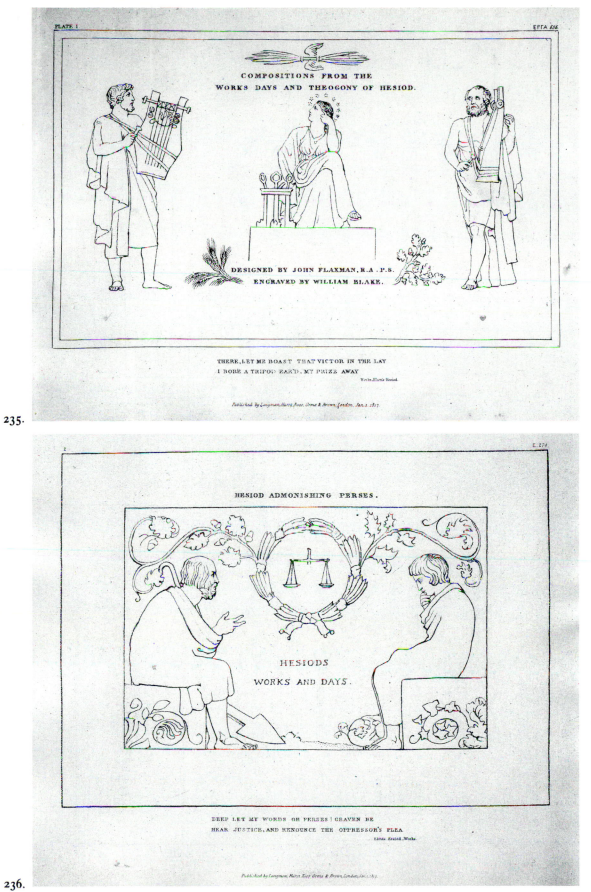

235–71. Flaxman, *Compositions from Hesiod* (1817), *Compositions of Flaxman* (1870), and *Compositions from Hesiod* (1870)

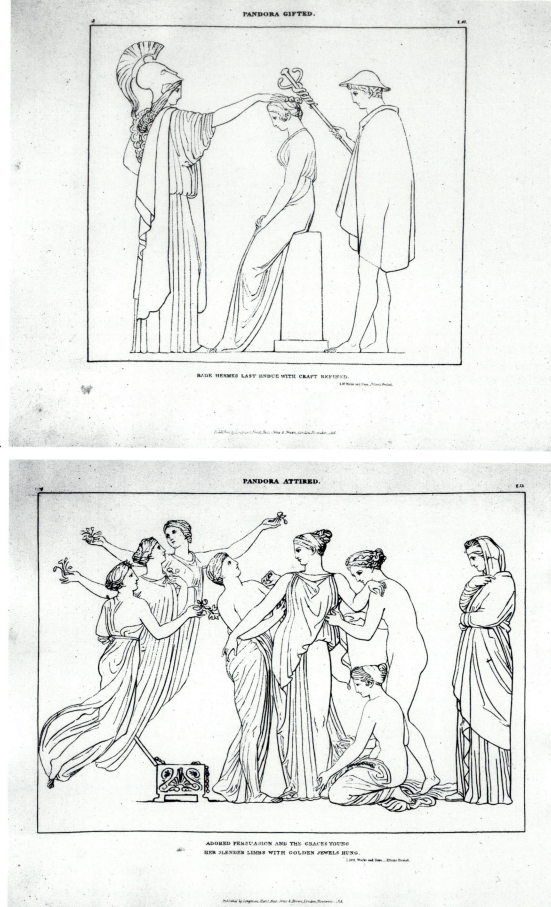

PANDORA GIFTED.

BADE HERMES LAST ENDUE WITH CRAFT REFINED.

237.

PANDORA ATTIRED.

ADORED PERSUASION AND THE GRACES YOUNG
HER SLENDER LIMBS WITH GOLDEN JEWELS HUNG.

238.

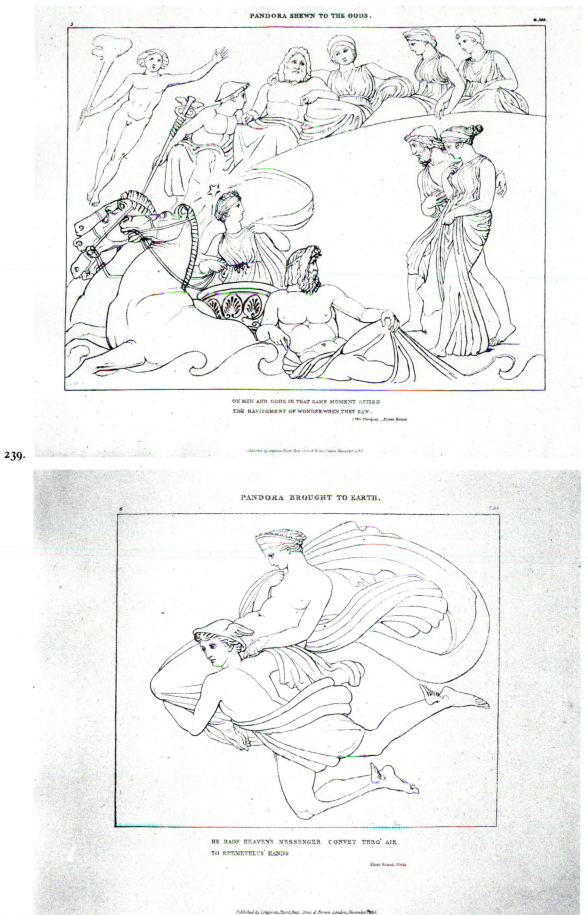

PANDORA SHEWN TO THE GODS.

ON MEN AND GODS IN THAT SAME MOMENT SEIZED
THE RAVISHMENT OF WONDER WHEN THEY SAW.

239.

PANDORA BROUGHT TO EARTH.

HE BADE HEAVEN'S MESSENGER CONVEY THRO' AIR
TO EPEMETHEUS' HANDS

240.

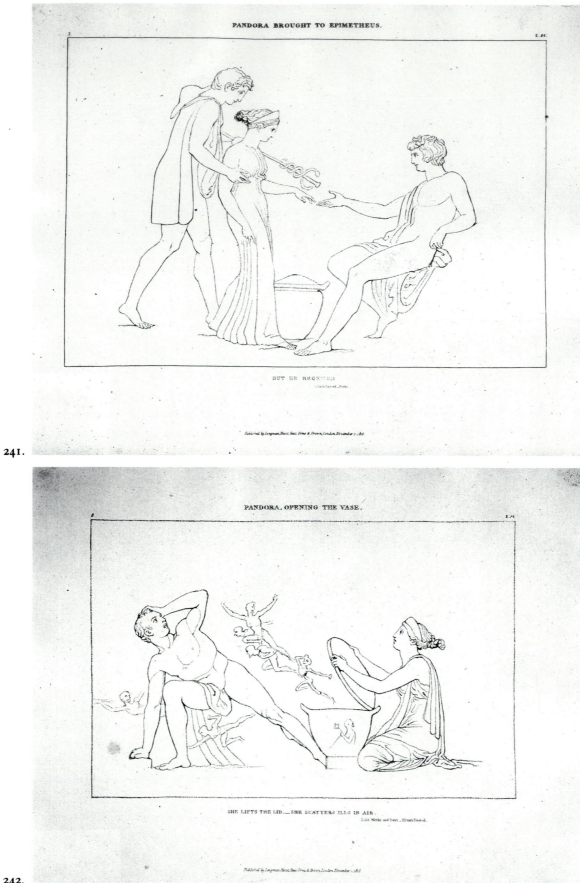

PANDORA BROUGHT TO EPIMETHEUS.

BUT HE REGNIED

241.

PANDORA, OPENING THE VASE.

SHE LIFTS THE LID.—SHE SCATTERS ILLS IN AIR.

242.

GOLDEN AGE.

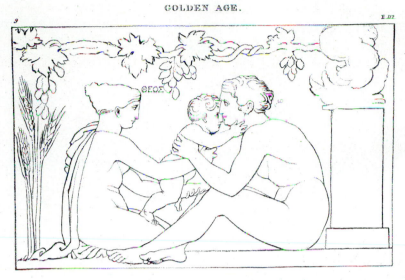

AN AGE OF GOLD

LIKE GODS THEY LIVED WITH CALM UNTROUBLED MIND.

L.151. Works and Days. ... Elton's Hesiod.

Published by Longman, Hurst, Rees, Orme & Brown, London, November 1, 1816.

243.

GOOD DÆMONS.

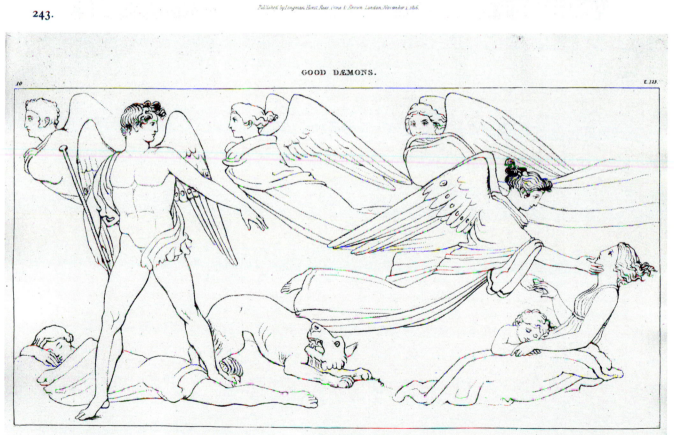

EARTH-WANDERING DÆMONS THEY THEIR CHARGE BEGAN,

THE MINISTERS OF GOOD, AND GUARDS OF MAN;

L.163. Works and Days. ... Elton's Hesiod.

Published by Longman, Hurst, Rees, Orme & Brown, London, November 1, 1816.

245.

246.

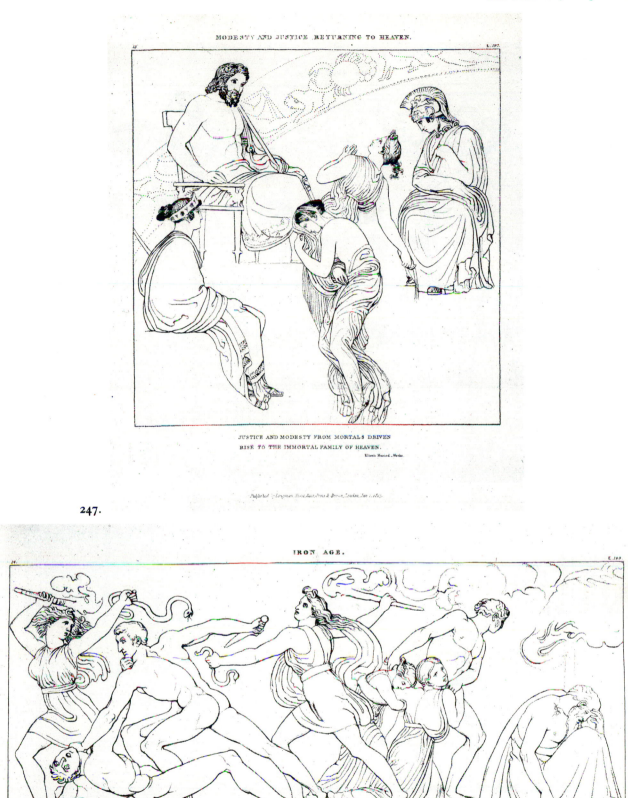

247.

248.

PLEIADES.

AND WHEN THEY SINK BELOW
THE MORN-ILLUMINED WEST, TIS TIME TO PLOUGH

Elton's Hesiod Works.

Published by Longman, Hurst, Rees, Orme & Brown, London Jan 1 1817.

253.

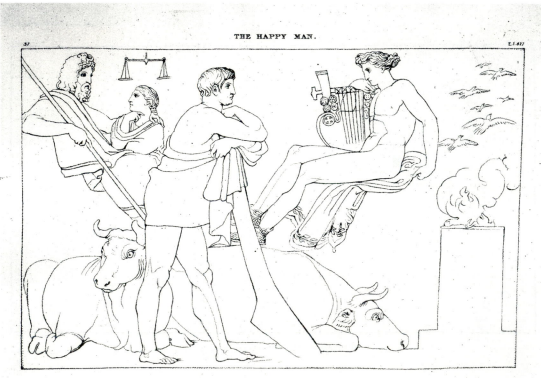

THE HAPPY MAN.

HE TO WHOSE NOTE THE AUGURIES ARE GIVEN
NO RITE TRANSGRESS'D, AND VOID OF BLAME TO HEAVEN.

Days. Elton's Hesiod.

Published by Longman, Hurst, Rees, Orme & Brown, London Jan 1 1817.

254.

THEOGONY

THEY TO HESIOD ERST
HAVE TAUGHT THEIR STATELY SONG:

255.

HESIOD AND THE MUSES.

AND GAVE UNTO MY HAND
A ROD OF MARVELLOUS GROWTH A LAUREL BOUGH

256.

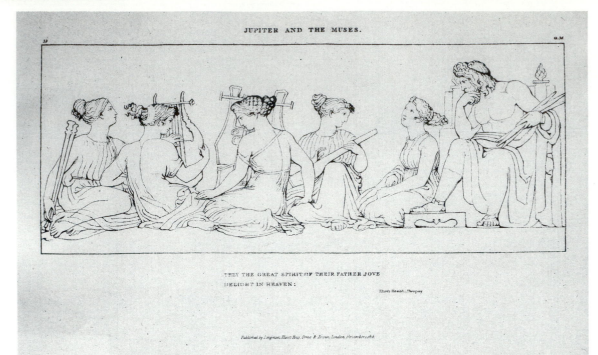

JUPITER AND THE MUSES.

THEY THE GREAT SPIRIT OF THEIR FATHER JOVE
DELIGHT IN HEAVEN;

Elton's Hesiod.—Theogony

Published by Longman, Hurst, Rees, Orme & Brown, London, November 1816.

257.

NIGHT   LOVE   EREBUS   CHAOS

THEN LOVE MOST BEAUTEOUS OF IMMORTALS ROSE

Elton's Hesiod.—Theogony.

Published by Longman, Hurst, Rees, Orme & Brown, London, Jan. 1, 1817.

258.

VENUS.

THE WAFTING WAVES
FIRST BORE HER TO CYTHERA'S HEAVENLY COAST
Theogony. Elton's Hesiod. l. 265.

Published by Longman, Hurst, Rees, Orme & Brown, London, November 1. 1816.

259.

VENUS.

HER APHRODITE GODS AND MORTALS NAME
THE FOAM BORN GODDESS.
Elton. Hesiod.—Theogony.

Published by Longman, Hurst, Rees, Orme & Brown, London, November 1. 1816.

260.

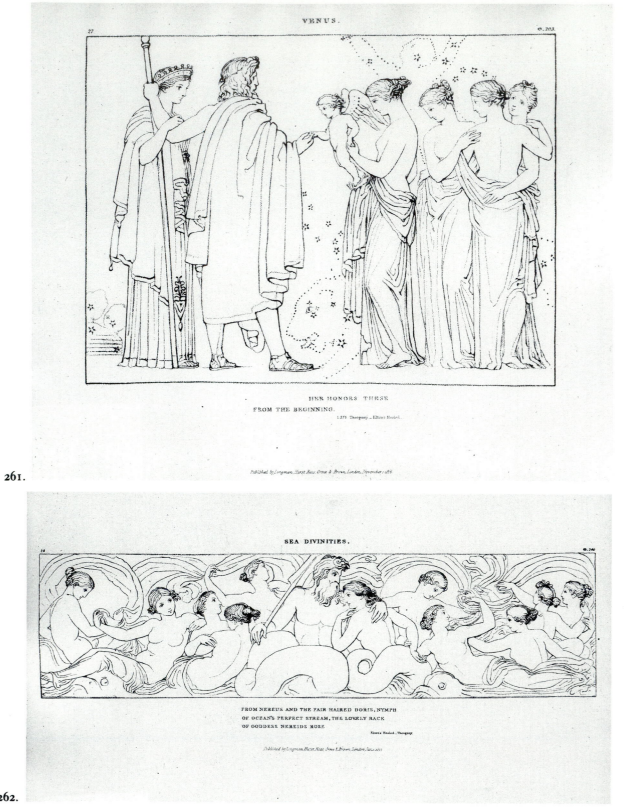

261.

262.

TYPHAON ECHIDNA GERYON.

ECHIDNA THE UNTAMEABLE OF SOUL
ABOVE A NYMPH WITH BEAUTY BLOOMING CHEEKS
Elton's Hesiod.—Theogony.

Published by Longman, Hurst, Rees, Orme & Brown, London, Jan 1, 1817.

263.

ASTRÆUS AND AURORA.

THE MORNING TO ASTRÆUS BARE THE WINDS
OF SPIRIT UNTAMED, WEST SOUTH AND NORTH
Elton's Hesiod.—Theogony.

Published by Longman, Hurst, Rees, Orme & Brown, London, Jan 1, 1817.

264.

SATURN AND HIS CHILDREN.

DID SATURN HUGE

DEVOUR

Elton's Hesiod. Theogony

Published by Longman, Hurst, Rees, Orme & Brown, London, Jan. 1. 1817.

265.

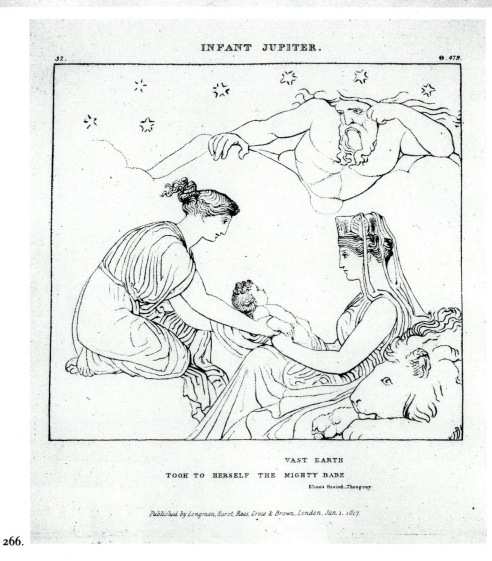

INFANT JUPITER.

VAST EARTH

TOOK TO HERSELF THE MIGHTY BABE

Elton's Hesiod. Theogony

Published by Longman, Hurst, Rees, Orme & Brown, London, Jan. 1. 1817.

266.

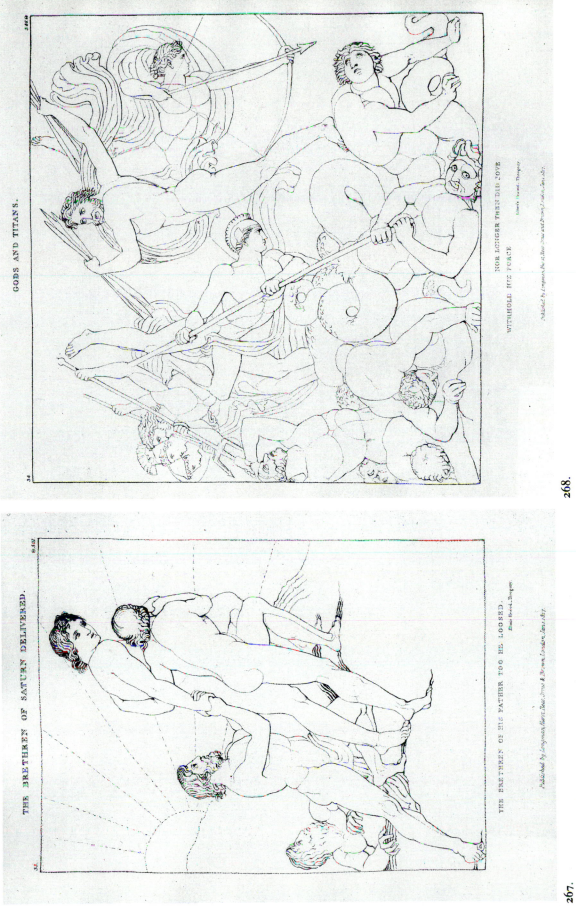

GODS AND TITANS.

NOR LONGER THEN DID JOVE

WITHHOLD HIS FORCE

Hesiod's Theogony

Published by Longman & Co. in New York and Brown, London, June 1817.

268.

THE BRETHREN OF SATURN DELIVERED.

THE BRETHREN OF HIS FATHER TOO HE LOOSED.

Hesiod's Theogony

Published by Longman, Hurst, Rees, Orme & Brown, London, June 1 1817.

267.

GIANTS AND TITANS.

THE WAR UNEATED GYGES, BRIAREUS
AND COTTUS BITTEREST CONFLICT WAGED

Elton's Hesiod. Theogony.

Published by Longman, Hurst, Rees, Orme and Brown, Jan. 1, 1817.

269.

FURIES   CERBERUS   PLUTO   PROSERPINE   HARPIES   DEATH

THE HOLLOW SOUNDING PALACE
OF PLUTO STRONG THE SUBTERRANEAN GOD

Elton's Hesiod. Theogony.

Published by Longman, Hurst, Rees, Orme & Brown, London, June 1, 1817.

270.

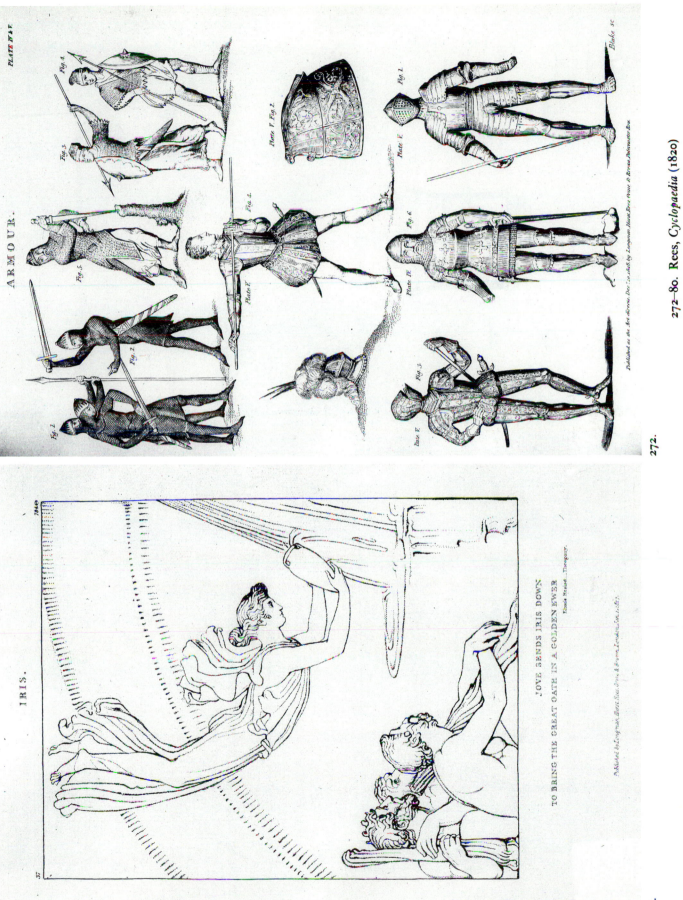

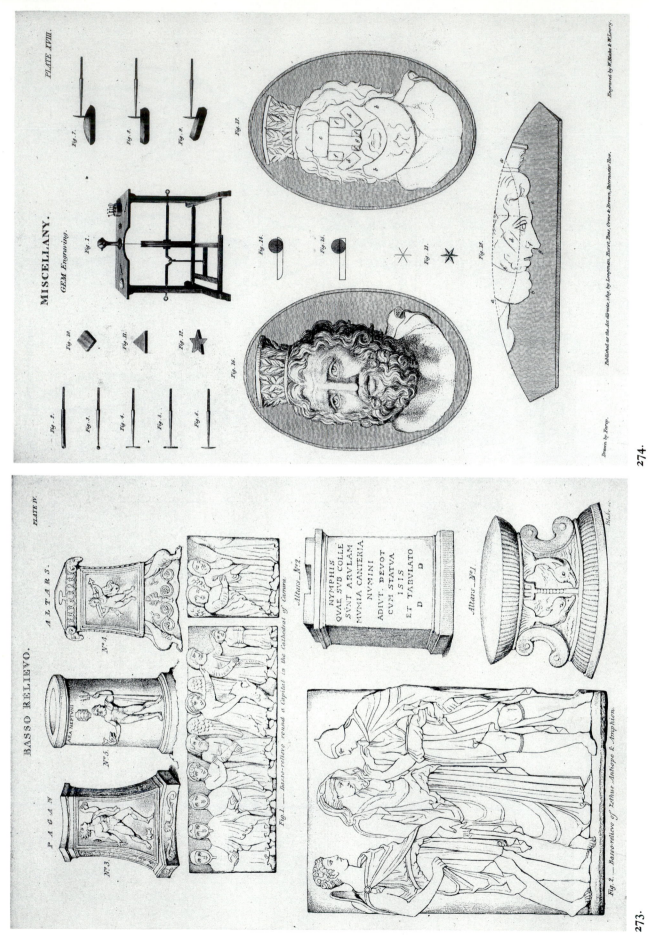

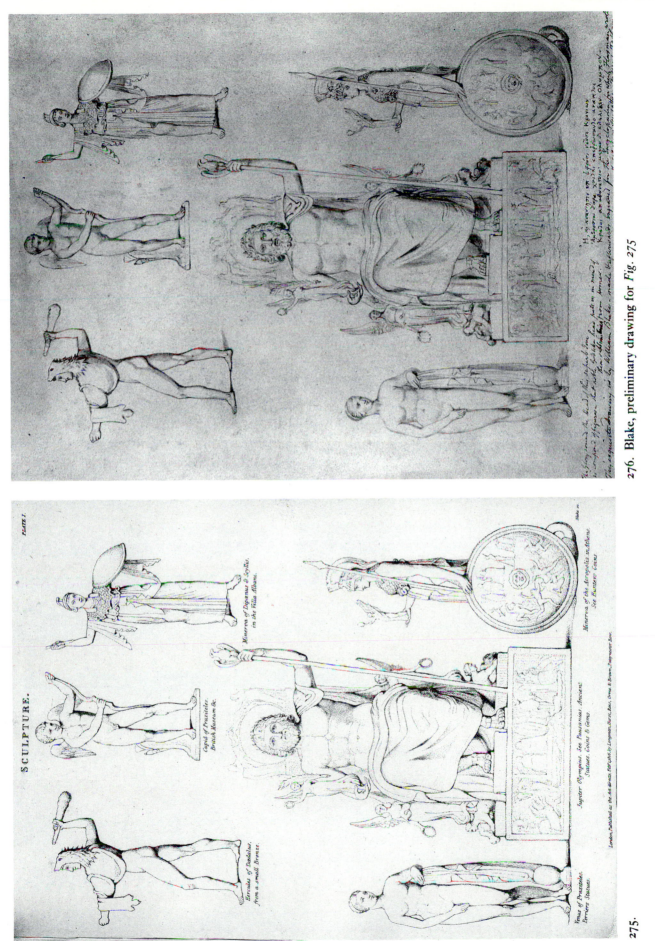

276. Blake, preliminary drawing for *Fig. 275*

275.

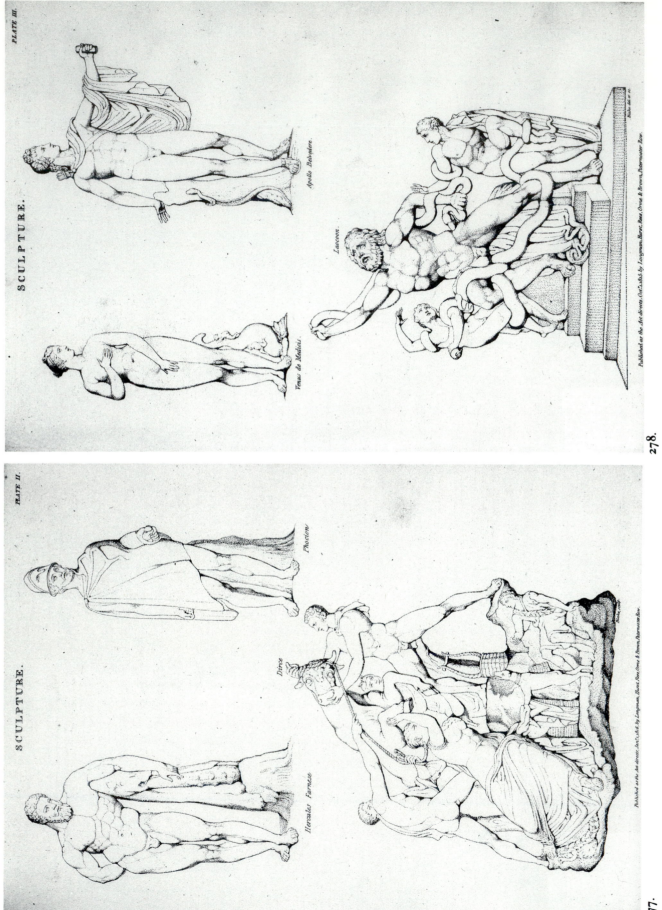

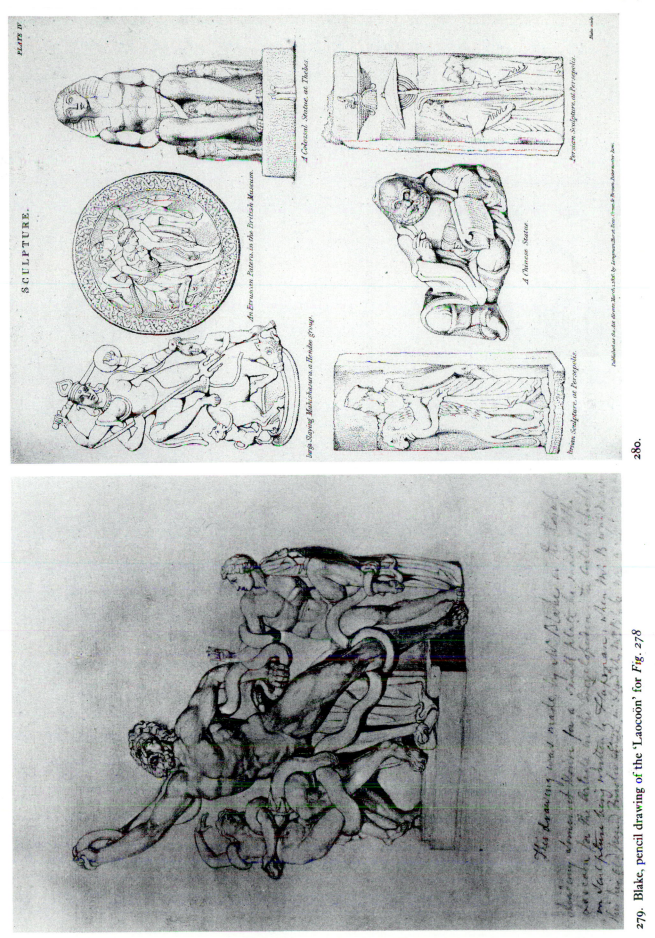

279. Blake, pencil drawing of the 'Laocoön' for *Fig.* 278

Blake, del. et Sculp.

Theocritus,

*A Grecian Poet, of Sicily Flourished 273 years
before the Birth of Christ, and quitting his
native country, governed by Hiero, King of
Syracuse, went over to King Ptolemy in Egypt,
by whom he was greatly patronized.*

Vide Idyllium. 17.

London, Published by D.r Thornton. 1821.

281.

Blake, del. et Sculp.

Publius Virgilius Maro.

Poetarum Latinorum Princeps.

*Born 69 years before the Birth of Christ; was 7 years older
than Augustus; lost his Estate, at 30; recovering it was nearly killed
by Arius, the Centurion; some think he began his Eclogues, at 31;
which took him 3 years. Commenced his Georgics, at 34, which
occupied him 7 years; and at 41 began his Æneid, which employed
him 11 years; at 52, Virgil died, 19 years before the Christian Æra.*

London, Published by D.r Thornton. 1821.

282.

281–6. *Pastorals of Virgil* (1821)

Octavius Augustus Cæsar.

Was Nephew to Julius Cæsar, and 18 years old when Cæsar was assassinated; joins Antony, and Lepidus, and defeats Brutus and Cassius, at the Battle of Phillippi, 41 years B.C. — Antony marries Octavia, Sister to Augustus, whom he deserts for Cleopatra, Queen of Egypt, whom Cæsar defeats in a naval battle at Actium, 31 years before Christ. — Shuts the Temple of Janus, the world having been created 3948 years, when a new Æra commences, the Birth of Christ: — dies, 14 years after that period, at 76, having reigned 44 years.

Blake, del. et Sculp.

London, Published by Dr Thornton, 1821.

From Antique Coins.

POLLIO   GALLUS

AGRIPPA

VARUS   MECÆNAS

Blake del et Sculp.

POLLIO was a Poet, a General, & a great favourite to Augustus, & was twice Consul.
GALLUS was made Prefect of Egypt, a Poet, who slew himself having ruled Tyrannically.
AGRIPPA a famous General to Augustus, commended in all his battles & was married to Julia daughter to Augustus.
VARUS was of noble extraction; Father to Maia, Virgils wife, was also a Poet, & Governor of Cisalpine Gaul.
MECÆNAS was prime Minister to Augustus, & died 7 Years after the birth of Christ.

London Published by Dr Thornton, 1821.

283.   284.

Blake, del. et Sculp.

Caius Julius Cæsar,
Assassinated 44 years before the Christian Æra.
Virgil: æt. 26.

London, Published by D.ʳ Thornton, 1821.

285.

ΕΠΙΚΟΥΡΟΣ

Blake, del. et Sculp.

Epicurus.
A Grecian Philosopher, Flourished 264 years before
Christ. His philosophy was transfused into Latin
by the great Roman Poet Lucretius, who
flourished 105 years before Christ, and wrote
his "De Rerum Natura" on the Nature of
Things. He placed the summum bonum on
Tranquillity of Mind, arising from Virtue, and
the Contemplation of Nature.

He is said to have been born 342 B.C. Died 270 B.C. æ: 72.

London, Published by D.ʳ Thornton, 1821.

286.

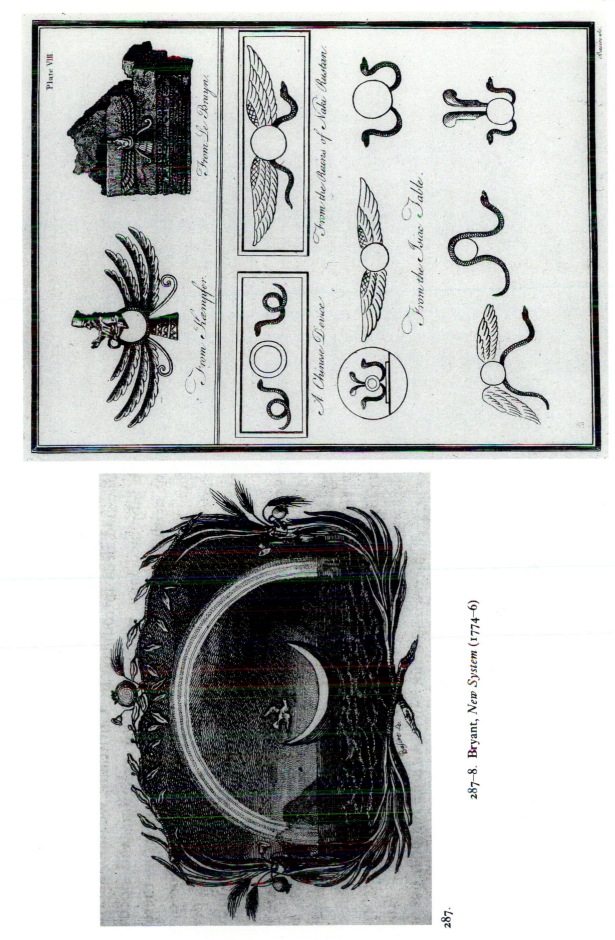

287–8. Bryant, *New System* (1774–6)

Portrait of Henry III from his Monument.

289.

289–94. Gough, *Sepulchral Monuments* (1786)

Portrait of Queen Eleanor from her Monument.

Pl. XLIX. p. 125.

Portrait of Queen Philippa from her Monument.

Pl. LXIII. p. 164.

Portrait of Richard II. from his Monument.

293.

Pl. LV. p. 139.

Portrait of Edward III. from his Monument.

292.

295. Salzmann, *Gymnastics for Youth* (1800)